Meetings: their law and practice

Philip Lawton and Eric R Rigby

Fifth edition

THE M & E HANDBOOK SERIES

Pitman Publishing
128 Long Acre, London WC2E 9AN

A Division of Longman Group UK Limited

First published 1966
Second edition 1977
Third edition 1985
Fourth edition 1987
Fifth edition 1992

© Macdonald & Evans Ltd 1966, 1977
© Longman Group UK 1985, 1987, 1992

British Library Cataloguing in Publication Data
A catalogue entry for this book is available
from the British Library

ISBN 0-7121-1422-X

All rights reserved; no part of this publication may be reproduced, stored in a
retrieval system, or transmitted in any form or by any other means, electronic,
mechanical, photocopying, recording, or otherwise without either the prior written
permission of the Publishers or a licence permitting restricted copying in the United
Kingdom issued by the Copyright Licensing Agency, 90 Tottenham Court Road,
London W1P 9HE. This book may not be lent, resold, hired out or otherwise
disposed of by way of trade in any form of binding or cover other than that in which
it is published, without the prior consent of the Publishers.

Founding Editor: P.W.D. Redmond

Typeset by FDS Ltd, Penarth
Printed and bound in Singapore

Contents

Part two: General legal provisions affecting meetings

Part three: Company meetings

Preface to the fifth edition

When we completed the 4th edition of this Handbook in 1987 we were able to sit back and relax secure in the knowledge that it would be at least five years before we needed to think about revising the book. However, the introduction of new legislation meant that we had to brace ourselves and start the preparations for the 5th edition just three years later. We have taken this opportunity to rearrange the book quite significantly so that an introduction to the general principles relating to meetings appears before any detailed legal provisions are encountered.

The first change which will be evident to those who were familiar with the old edition is the inclusion of a new Part two which deals with general legal provisions affecting meetings. This part deals with the *ultra vires* rule and natural justice, defamation, public order and police powers. We felt that it would be logical to deal with these provisions together as they could affect all types of meetings.

Some of the most significant changes have been brought about by the amendment of the Companies Act 1985 by the 1989 Act, and the relevant provisions of the new sections have been fully accommodated within the text.

Wherever possible the text has been updated by the inclusion of new cases and, in addition, explanation of rules quoted has been clarified by the inclusion of brief details of some of the cases which had previously been cited in the text.

Changes in local authority meetings have been reflected by the inclusion of the main provisions of the Local Government and Housing Act 1989 in relation to the constitution of committees and sub-committees.

The effect of these changes will make the book even more

valuable to students of the Institute of Chartered Secretaries and Administrators and to those on BTEC Higher courses in Business and Finance and Public Administration. In addition it is expected that the book will provide a convenient source of reference to those involved in meetings of local authorities and the separation of the general principles relating to meetings should cause it to be essential reading to committee members of all types of clubs, societies and associations.

The specimen examination questions in Appendix 3 are all past questions of the Institute of Chartered Secretaries and Administrators, and the authors wish to thank the Institute for granting permission to use these.

1992

PL
ERR

Table of cases

Table of statutes

Table A

Part one

Meetings in general

1
Holding a meeting

1. Definitions

In *Sharp* v. *Dawes* (1876) a meeting was defined as 'an assembly of people for a lawful purpose' or 'the coming together of at least two persons for any lawful purpose'. It follows, therefore, that the word 'meeting' covers a wide range of assemblies, from the formal meeting of a board of directors of a registered company to the social meeting of friends.

The behaviour of people at any kind of meeting is governed by the law of the land as it affects each individual. For many types of assembly this is quite sufficient and there is no need for special rules and regulations for such assemblies as theatre and cinema audiences or friends who go out for a meal together. The law relating to meetings is therefore confined to the regulation of assemblies which consider matters of general public concern or the consideration of affairs which are of common concern to members of the assembly.

Furthermore, these meetings are divided into two types:

(a) *public meetings* which consider matters of public concern and to which all members of the public have access, subject to the physical limitations of the place where the meeting is held or conditions imposed under the Public Order Act 1986 (*see* chapter 15), but irrespective of whether persons attending the meeting are required to pay; and

(b) *private meetings* which are attended by people who have a specific right or special capacity to attend, such as the committee of a brass band or golf club or the members of a registered company. (*See* chapter 16 for a consideration of the nature of the constitution of such bodies.)

Legality of meeting

2. Place of meeting

(a) *Meetings in public places:*
  (i) There is no common law right to hold meetings in public places, such as highways, parks, etc.
  (ii) Nevertheless, an individual having a right to be there is presumed to have a right to join with others who happen to be there, i.e. his is not so much a positive right to meet there as a negative right not to be removed, so long as there is no infringement of statutory or local regulations. However, in *Hirst* v. *Chief Constable of the West Yorkshire Police* (1986) the Court said that they 'should not interfere by interlocutory injunction with the right to demonstrate and to protest any more than they interfere with the right of free speech, provided that everything is done peaceably and in good order'.
  (iii) The following cases are important in this connection:

  Aldred v. *Miller* (1924): A meeting held in a *highway* is not necessary unlawful, unless there is interference with the primary function of the highway to afford passage.
  Burden v. *Rigler* (1911): Although there is no right to hold such a meeting, the fact that a public meeting is held upon a highway does not necessarily render the meeting unlawful, unless other circumstances exist to do so, e.g. the causing of an obstruction. There are many statutory rules relating to obstruction of the highway. Section 137 of the Highways Act 1980 is one of the more important of these. It says: 'If a person without lawful authority or excuse, in any way wilfully obstructs the free passage along a highway he shall be guilty of an offence.' See *Hirst's* case above for a consideration of this section. Contrast *Arrowsmith* v. *Jenkins* (1963), *Hubbard* v. *Pitt* (1975) and *Nagy* v. *Weston* (1965).
  De Morgan v. *Metropolitan Board of Works* (1880): In this case, it was held that no right on the part of the public to hold meetings on a *common* is known to the law.
  Slee v. *Meadows* (1911): Local authorities can regulate the holding of public meetings in areas within their

jurisdiction. See also the provisions of the Public Order Act 1986 dealt with in chapter 15.

R v. *Barnet London Borough Council ex parte Johnson and Jacobs* (1991). A local authority owned land acquired as a public park. Byelaws relating to the use of the park were in force and these provided for the local authority to permit activities which would otherwise have been prohibited. A local committee applied to use the park for a festival promoting local artists and community groups. Permission was granted subject to conditions barring the participation of political groups in the festival. The High Court held these conditions to be invalid and unreasonable because the presence of political and quasi-political groups at fairs, fetes, festivals and carnivals is commonplace, and such groups are all part of community life. The Court of Appeal upheld this decision saying that the conditions were unlawful because they were intended to inhibit the manner in which the public made use of the park rather than to regulate public enjoyment of the park.

(b) *Meetings in private places:*
   (*i*) People who meet on private property without the permission of the owner or other lawful occupier are trespassers, and can, of course, be requested to withdraw — but payment of an admission charge, implies permission granted.
   (*ii*) If, after being requested to withdraw, the trespasser persists in his offence, the lawful occupier (or his agent) can remove him.
   (*iii*) Only such force as is reasonably necessary to effect the removal may be used; if unreasonable violence is used, the trespasser will have a right of action for assault: *Collins* v. *Revison* (1754).
   (*iv*) If payment is made for admission, that apparently constitutes a form of licence to attend; therefore a person who has paid for admission cannot be removed from the private premises so long as he behaves himself in an orderly manner and does not infringe any of the rules by which he is bound: *see Hurst* v. *Picture Palaces* (1915).

Whether or not a licence is revocable is entirely a question of the contravention of the contract: *Winter Garden Theatre* v. *Millenium Ltd* (1948). Where there is no contract between the parties and the licence is purely gratuitous it is revocable at the will of the licensor but the licensee must be given a reasonable time, having regard to all the circumstances, to comply with the revocation. The licensor does not have to specify the amount of time in his notice of revocation, *see Minister of Health* v. *Bellotti* (1944), or the right to use reasonable force to eject recalcitrant individuals (*see* chapter 4).

3. Public assemblies and processions

In the context of obstruction of the highway it must be remembered that the highway can be used by members of the public for passing and re-passing and purposes reasonably incidental thereto: *Harrison* v. *Duke of Rutland* (1893). There is therefore a basic distinction between a public meeting on the highway and a public procession on the highway. The public meeting is a civil trespass against the official body or person in whom the highway is vested. A trespass on the highway will only amount to a public nuisance if it interferes in an appreciable way with the public right of passage and an impediment may be too small to be properly called a nuisance: *R* v. *Ward* (1836), *R* v. *Bartholomew* (1908), *Burden* v. *Rigler* (1911). However, it is now a prima facie nuisance for a group of demonstrators to sit down on the highway: *R* v. *Maule* (1964).

The Public Order Act 1986 requires advance notice of public processions and gives senior police officers the power to impose conditions on public processions and assemblies. For further discussion of this topic see chapter 15 on public order.

4. Modern technology and meetings

With the development of modern technology the possibilities for holding meetings and conferences simultaneously in different venues connected by audio-visual or similar links has become possible. Teleconferencing, for example, is a modern day reality where groups of delegates gathered in different parts of the world can take part in the same conference proceedings aided by satellite communications and audio-visual links. The question then arises whether, as a matter of law, such events can amount to a meeting given that a meeting is 'the coming together of at least two persons for any lawful purpose' and that 'meet' means 'to come face to face with or into the company of another person'.

The issue arose in *Byng* v. *London Life Assurance Ltd* (1989) where too large a number of shareholders for the venue turned up at an extraordinary general meeting and had to be accommodated in overflow rooms connected to the main venue by audio-visual links. One of the issues in the case was whether there was a meeting. The following extract from the judgment of Browne-Wilkinson V-C in the Court of Appeal appears to reflect that attitude of the courts:

'The rationale behind the requirement for meetings in the Companies Act is that the members shall be able to attend in person so as to debate and vote on matters affecting the company. Until recently this could only be achieved by everyone being physically present in the same room face to face. Given modern technological advances, the same result can now be achieved without all the members coming face to face: without being physically in the same room they can be electronically in each other's presence so as to hear and be heard and to see and be seen. The fact that such a meeting could not have been foreseen at the time the first statutory requirements for meetings were laid down, does not require us to hold that such a meeting is not within the meaning of the word 'meeting' in the Companies Act. Thus, communication by telephone had been held to be a "telegraph" within the meaning of the Telegraph Acts 1863 and 1869, notwithstanding that the telephone had not been invented or contemplated when those Acts were passed: *Attorney General* v. *Edison Telephone Co. of London Ltd* (1880).

I have no doubt therefore that, in cases where the original venue proves inadequate to accommodate all those wishing to attend, valid general meetings of a company can be properly held using overflow rooms provided, first, that all due steps are taken to direct to the overflow rooms those unable to get into the main meeting, and secondly, that there are adequate audio-visual links to enable those in all the rooms to see and hear what is going on in the other rooms. Were the law otherwise, with the present tendency towards companies with very large numbers of shareholders and corresponding uncertainty as to how many shareholders will attend meetings, the organisation of such meetings might prove to be impossible.'

The requirement is therefore that those present must be able to hear and be heard, and to see and be seen. This principle will presumably also apply to meetings of bodies other than companies. A conference telephone conversation, lacking a visual link, cannot amount to a valid meeting in law: *Re Associated Color Laboratories Ltd* (1970) and *Higgins* v. *Nicol* (1971).

Progress test 1

1. What is the difference between a public and a private meeting? **(1, 2)**

2. Distinguish the essential differences between an assembly and a procession on the highway. **(3)**

3. To what extent and under what condition does the law recognise as valid a meeting held in more than one venue? **(4)**

2
Convention, constitution and conduct of meetings

Number of persons attending

1. Sharp v. Dawes (1876)

In this case a meeting was defined as 'the coming together of at least two persons for any lawful purpose.' Thus, it may be stated that a meeting usually consists of two or more persons. Mellish LJ said: 'It is clear that, according to the ordinary use of the English language, a meeting could no more be constituted by one person than a meeting could have been constituted if no shareholder at all had attended. No business could be done at such a meeting.'

2. In Re Sanitary Carbon Co. (1877)

This case appeared to lend support to the above decision, as it was held that a meeting of a company attended by one shareholder only was not validly constituted — even though that shareholder held the proxies of all the other members. Therefore, as a general rule one individual alone does not constitute a meeting even if he or she represents two or more members, for example by being both a member and a proxy for another member (*see also Re M. J. Shanley Contracting Ltd* (1979)) or by being a member both in his or her own right and as a trustee for another: *James Prain & Sons Ltd, petitioners* (1947). In *Neil McLeod & Sons Ltd, petitioners* (1967) Lord President Clyde reiterated the general rule saying ' . . . a meeting is not properly constituted if only one individual is present, for there is no one for him to meet'.

3. Re London Flats (1969)

The articles of a company required a quorum of two. It was held that a decision made by one shareholder after the other had left the room was a nullity. Plowman J described the powers of the Court and Secretary of State (discussed below) to order a company meeting of one as exceptional and held that they did not displace the general rule that 'a single shareholder cannot constitute a meeting'.

4.   One person can, in exceptional circumstances, constitute a valid meeting
Despite the above decisions, one person can constitute a valid meeting; e.g.

(a)   Where one person held all the shares of a particular class, that person alone was held to constitute a valid meeting of that class of shareholder: *East* v. *Bennett Bros.* (1911).
(b)   Where the rules permit, it is possible to appoint a committee of one, and thus hold a committee 'meeting' of one member.

> NOTE: Several other cases occur in connection with company meetings, where a 'meeting' of one person is valid. *See* chapter 18.

(c)   Section 367 of the Companies Act 1985 states that the Secretary of State may direct a valid meeting to be held on the application of any member of the company. This may include a direction that one member of the company present in person or by proxy shall be deemed to constitute a meeting.
(d)   Section 371 states that the courts may direct a valid meeting to be held even if there is only one person entitled to attend.
(e)   Where the directors have fixed a quorum of one.

Validity of a meeting

5.   The requisites of a valid meeting
The validity of a meeting may be questioned for a number of reasons; therefore, in order to ensure that decisions taken at a meeting are not subsequently nullified, the convenors must conform to certain basic requisites, namely:

(a)   A meeting must be properly *convened*.
(b)   It must be properly *constituted*.

(c) It must be properly *held* in accordance with the rules governing the meeting.

6. Failure properly to convene
This might arise out of:

(a) *Omission to send notice* to every person entitled to attend, but the omission may be excused:

    (*i*) Where the rules governing the meeting provide that *accidental omission* to send notice to, or the non-receipt of notice by, any person entitled to receive notice shall not invalidate the proceedings of the meeting concerned (e.g. Table A, art. 39).

    (*ii*) Where *all* persons entitled to attend are present without notice and all 'expressly assent to that which is being done': *Express Engineering Works* (1920). *See also* Table A, art. 38.

    (*iii*) Where those not summoned were *beyond summoning distance*, e.g. where a member was abroad: *Smyth* v. *Darley* (1849); or where a member was *too ill to attend* in any case: *Young* v. *Ladies' Imperial Club* (1920).

    (*iv*) It is, however, always advisable to send proper notice to all persons entitled to attend a meeting, and not rely upon the apparent disability of a member at the time as an excuse for failing to summon him. Even if the member informs the convenors that he will not be able to attend the meeting, that should not be relied upon as a waiver of notice: *Re Portuguese Consolidated Copper Mines* (1889), *Rex* v. *Langhorne* (1836).

(b) *Inadequate (short) notice*; if, for example, only 7 days' notice is given instead of the 21 days' notice required by the regulations. In this case, too, inadequacy of notice might be excused if all, or a specific proportion of, the members so agree: *Machell* v. *Nevinson* (1809), *In Re Oxted Motor Co.* (1921), Table A, art. 38.

(c) *Ambiguity of the notice*; that is, it must be free from anything calculated to confuse or mislead: *Kaye* v. *Croydon Tramways* (1898), *Henderson* v. *Bank of Australasia* (1890).

(d) *Omission of important contents*; in particular failure to mention that special business is to be transacted. For example in *Smith* v. *Deighton* (1852) a meeting of church wardens passed a resolution authorising them to borrow money on the security of the church rates in order that damage caused by a fire might be repaired. This was held to be invalid because the notice did not state clearly the special business for which the meeting was called.

It is, of course, also essential to state place, date, day and time of the meeting; although it would usually be permissible to dispense with an indication of the actual time, where one meeting is to be held immediately after another; in that case, the notice may indicate that the second meeting will commence 'at the conclusion' of the first meeting.

(e) *Unauthorized issue of notice.* The notice must be given by the person or persons authorized to convene the meeting: *Re State of Wyoming Syndicate* (1901); thus, the issue of notice by the secretary without the authority of the convening body is inadequate and the meeting rendered invalid: *Re Haycraft Gold Reduction Co.* (1900). Nevertheless, if the notice is adopted and ratified by the proper summoning authority *before* the meeting is held, it may become a good notice; in which case the meeting is not invalid: *Hooper* v. *Kerr* (1900).

See chapter 6 for a detailed discussion of notices.

7. Failure to ensure that a meeting is properly constituted

The constitution of a meeting might be questioned and decisions taken might be invalidated on the following grounds.

(a) *Irregularity of chairman's appointment.* It is the first duty of the chairman to ensure that his own appointment is valid. If he has not been validly appointed in accordance with the rules, the meeting is not properly constituted.

(b) *Absence of quorum.* The quorum prescribed by the rules must be present. Absence or inadequacy of the quorum may arise in the following cases:

   (*i*) *Failure to muster a quorum.* If the prescribed quorum is not present when the meeting is due to start, the meeting should be formally adjourned because, legally, there is no meeting.

   (*ii*) *Failure to maintain a quorum.* If a quorum is not maintained it would be open to anyone to draw the chairman's attention to the matter. It is then the chairman's duty to declare a 'count out' and to adjourn the meeting.

However, much may depend on how the organization's regulations on quorum are drafted and whether they require a quorum to be present throughout the meeting: *see Henderson* v. *Louttit* (1894) and *In Re Hartley Baird Ltd* (1955), discussed in chapter 18.

8. Failure to hold the meeting in accordance with the regulations governing the meeting

(a) Chairman's failure to ensure that the sense of the meeting is properly ascertained with regard to any question which is properly placed before it: *National Dwellings Society* v. *Sykes* (1894).
(b) Chairman's refusal to allow the proposal of a legitimate and relevant amendment: *Henderson* v. *Bank of Australasia* (1890). In the latter case the court set aside the resolution on the grounds of the chairman's failure to admit a relevant amendment to it.

9. Natural justice

Even where a meeting has been properly convened, constituted and conducted, and the regulations of the particular body followed to the letter, the validity of the meeting may yet be challenged on the basis of natural justice. This often happens where there has been a lack of 'common fairness' and the legal rights of an individual have been affected. For example, where as a result of a meeting's decision the aggrieved party has been expelled from a professional association or trade union, or has been refused renewal of a licence when he has a legitimate expectation that it shall be renewed. (For further discussion, *see* chapter 13.)

Progress test 2

1. Define a meeting, and cite any cases to support or qualify your definition. **(1–3)**

2. Discuss the rule that one person cannot constitute a meeting. **(3, 4)**

3. Contrast the effects of the following cases as they affect the constitution of a meeting: **(a)** *Sharp* v. *Dawes* (1876); **(b)** *East* v. *Bennett Bros.* (1911).   **(1, 4)**

4.   What are the requisites of a valid meeting? Mention three leading cases on the law of meeting and the points decided. **(1–5)**

5.   In what respects might the validity of a meeting be questioned?   **(5–8)**

3
Regulations governing meetings

The following are matters which ought to be included in the regulations governing meetings.

1. Appointment of officials

(a) Appointment of chairman, deputy chairman, secretary etc.
(b) Duration of appointment.
(c) Filling casual vacancies.

2. Chairman's powers

(a) Power to use a casting vote — which he has no power to use at common law: *Nell* v. *Longbottom* (1894).
(b) Powers of adjournment.
(c) Power to decide points of order etc.

3. Convening meetings
In particular:

(a) Form of notice.
(b) Period of notice, e.g. for 'special' business.

4. Constitution of the quorum
That is:

(a) Minimum number of members necessary to transact business; also, whether proxies may be included in the quorum.
(b) Provision for adjournment if quorum is not present.

5.   Order of business

(a) Listing various routine items which are to constitute 'ordinary' business; all other items to be regarded as 'special' business.
(b) Indicating the order in which 'ordinary' business items will be dealt with.

> NOTE: This would not, however, prevent the meeting from amending the recognized order.

6.   Voting

The method or methods to be adopted, and the rules to be applied in each case:

(a) *Show of hands:* the common law method of voting.
(b) *Poll*, where, for example, the number of votes a person is entitled to use may be dependent upon the number of shares he holds. There is a common law right to demand a poll vote, *see R* v. *D'Oyly* (1840), but the rules may exclude or restrict that right. The time for making the demand is immediately upon the conclusion of taking the vote by a show of hands or whatever method is prescribed by regulation: *R* v. *Vicar of St Asaph* (1883). *See also R* v. *Wimbledon Local Board* (1882), *Campbell* v. *Maund* (1836), *R* v. *Cooper* (1870) and other cases on this topic. (*See* chapters 20 and 21 for further discussion of this area.)
(c) *Voice*, which includes:
   (*i*) *acclamation*, when the voting is unanimous, or nearly so; and
   (*ii*) *oral consent or negation*, i.e. voting 'aye' or 'nay' or 'yes' or 'no'.
(d) *Ballot:* a method which is used when secrecy of the voting is desired, for example, in electing officials, etc.
(e) *Division.* The parliamentary method, the members being counted by tellers as they divide and proceed to their respective lobbies.

7.   Debate

The rules governing the conduct of debate. These ought to include various rules supporting the chairman's authority, as these would enable him to ensure that debate is conducted in an orderly and efficient manner, for example:

(a) *The order of speaking* to be decided by the chairman.

(b) *Seconding of motions:* whether a seconder is required. At common law a seconder is *not* required: *Re Horbury Bridge Coal Co.* (1879).

(c) *Withdrawal of a motion.* When a motion is before the meeting, it cannot be withdrawn except with the consent of the meeting. A motion for withdrawal cannot be put while an amendment is under discussion. The chairman may seek to stop debate on any particular motion after reasonable discussion, and may take a vote of the meeting on the question of cessation, *Wall* v. *L & N Assets Corpn* (1898).

(d) *Time limit* (if any) fixed for speeches, and provision for extension of the time limit in exceptional circumstances.

(e) *Second speech.* Only the mover of the original motion may speak twice on that motion.

(f) *Remedies available* for dealing with disorder and points of order.

(g) *Equality of opportunity.* Although it may not be written into the rules, it is the duty of the chairman to ensure that, so far as it is possible, each member shall have an equal opportunity of speaking.

> NOTE: Other 'rules' are a matter of custom or common courtesy towards the chair, and are rarely set out in written form; for example, a speaker is usually expected to stand while addressing the chairman; when the chairman rises the speaker should resume his seat.

8. Motions

(a) *Form of motion,* e.g. whether it is required to be in writing.

(b) *Disposal:* that is, how a motion may be disposed of, e.g. it may be 'dropped' or 'shelved'.

9. Amendments

(a) *Form of amendment,* e.g. whether it is required to be in writing.

(b) *Order* in which amendments are to be put to the meeting.

(c) *Amendments* to amendments: the method of dealing with amendments to amendments, if permitted by the rules.

10. Resolutions

(a) *Form of resolution* for special purposes, requiring a specified majority, e.g. where a two-thirds or three-fourths majority may be required.

(b) *Resolutions in writing,* permitting the passage of a resolution in writing, e.g. where it is signed by all members of an executive committee such a resolution may be valid as if it had been passed at a duly constituted meeting of that committee. (*See* further chapter 19.)

11. Proxies

(a) *Power to appoint* a proxy (or proxies) bearing in mind that there is *no* power to do so at common law: *Harben* v. *Phillips* (1883), *Clubb* v. *Hong Kong Computer Society* (1990).

(b) *Form(s) of proxy,* if any, permitted, e.g. a two-way proxy may be permitted.

(c) *Rights* of a proxy at meetings.

(d) *Deposit* of proxy forms, e.g. it may be necessary to deposit them not less than (say) 48 hours before the meeting concerned is due to commence.

12. Adjournment
Rules governing adjournment of:

(a) *debate*; and

(b) *meetings,* in so far as they are not dealt with in defining the powers of the chairman.

13. Committees

(a) *Appointment.* Power to appoint committees.

(b) *Constitution* and powers of committees.

14. Alteration of rules governing meetings, e.g.:

(a) *Procedure,* kind of resolution, period of notice required.

(b) *Restrictions* if any, upon the power to alter rules.

15. Suspension of rules governing meetings e.g.:

(a) *Circumstances* in which suspension may be permitted.

(b) *Procedure,* kind of resolution, period of notice required.

16. Rescission of resolutions

(a) *Time limit*; the period which must elapse before a resolution can be rescinded, e.g. a period of six months may be required.
(b) *Procedure*, kind of resolution, period of notice required.

17. Minutes

(a) *The keeping of minutes* — where they are to be kept and by whom.
(b) *Precautions* to be taken to safeguard the minutes.

Progress test 3

1. List some of the usual contents of the regulations, rules or standing orders governing meetings of any association, society or other body with which you are familiar.   **(1–17)**

2. The rules governing the meetings of a society are silent on the following subjects:

(a) Chairman's power to use a casting vote;
(b) Members' right to demand a poll vote;
(c) Seconding of motions.

What is the position in each case at common law?   **(2, 6, 7)**

3. Suggest at least six rules governing the conduct of debate that might usefully be included in the regulations governing meetings of a social club.   **(1–17)**

4
The chairman

Appointment and qualifications

1. Manner of a chairman's appointment

This depends upon the kind of meeting over which he is to preside:

(a) The chairman of a limited company is appointed in accordance with that company's Articles of Association. *See*, for example Table A, art. 42.

(b) The chairman of county council meetings is appointed in accordance with regulations laid down by statute.

(c) The chairman of any meeting for which no specific rules are provided may be appointed for that meeting by the majority vote of those present, before dealing with any of the business for which the meeting is being held.

Normally a ballot will be used for the appointment of a chairman taking the form of either a secret vote or of drawing lots. This avoids the embarrassment of making the electors openly avow their preferences. Where a society's regulations require a ballot to be taken this will be interpreted as a drawing of lots unless the context or custom requires otherwise: *Eyre* v. *Milton Proprietary Co. Ltd.* (1936). Any irregularity in the appointment of a chairman must be challenged forthwith or it will be regarded as regularised by the tacit acquiescence of the meeting: *Cornwall* v. *Woods* (1846). Where an outgoing chairman seeks re-election he may vacate the chair before the election takes place and appoint a deputy to preside pending the result of the election: *R* v. *White* (1867). However, a candidate for the chair cannot preside over the election or act as scrutineer or in any other official capacity in relation to the election. If a candidate does so, his election will be invalid: *Fanagan* v. *Kernan* (1881).

2. Duration

The duration of the chairman's appointment is also dependent upon the regulations (if any) which govern the meeting; thus, he may be appointed for one particular meeting only, for a period of (say) one year, or even for life.

A deputy chairman will preside in the absence of the elected chairman. A regular deputy chairman is often appointed in the manner prescribed in the rules, and for a fixed period; if, however, there is no regular deputy, the meeting must elect one if the elected chairman is absent or is, for any reason, unable or unwilling to act.

3. Qualifications

To enable a chairman to carry out his duties successfully and to exercise his powers for the greatest benefit of the meeting, he must obviously possess an adequate knowledge of meeting procedure. But the successful chairman must also possess certain essential qualities; in particular:

(a) *Personality.* He must have the ability to command respect of the meeting, and this largely depends upon his personality and bearing.

(b) *Impartiality.* He must possess a sense of fairness, and make his decisions with strict impartiality. If he is not the head of the organization he should leave the chair when he wishes to address the meeting himself in formal debate.

(c) *Strength of character.* He must be courteous and yet have the strength of character to be firm when ruling on points of order and in enforcing the rules of the meeting. Strength of character must not, however, be confused with the overbearing, dogmatic and obstinate attitude of the inadequate chairman who may, for a time, force his ideas upon the meeting but certainly loses its respect.

(d) *Resourcefulness.* To enable him to make quick decisions, deal with quarrelsome members and answer awkward questions, he must have an adequate supply of tact, patience and good humour; these are essential in the make-up of the resourceful chairman.

(e) *Ability to maintain discipline.* To possess and exercise this ability he must set a good example by his own punctual and regular attendance at meetings, and by his own sense of orderliness.

(f) *Clarity of speech.* The making of lengthy speeches is not one of the chairman's normal duties; if, therefore, he is able to announce clearly the decisions of the meeting, that is all that is normally required of him. The garrulous chairman is generally regarded as a poor one — a good chairman is often the one who says least.

4.   The status of a president
There is often some confusion over the respective function and status of 'chairman' and 'president'. It is, of course, normal practice in the USA to appoint a 'President' of a corporation rather than a 'Chairman'.

In the UK, however, the status of a president may be explained as follows:

(a) *Where he is appointed as alternative to a chairman,* he exercises the full powers of a chairman within the regulations governing the meetings over which he presides. Where a limited company follows this practice, care must be taken to ensure that the Articles of Association give the necessary authority.

(b) *Where his appointment is additional to that of chairman:*
   (*i*)   His nomination to the presidential chair is often by way of appreciation for long service with the company or other body.
   (*ii*) His office may be merely nominal, in which case he will function in a consultative rather than authoritative capacity, and in no way detract from the authority of the chairman.

Duties and privileges

5.   Duties
Some of the chairman's duties may be set out in the regulations governing meetings, but many more are implicit in his appointment or arise out of common law. Thus, his duties, whether express or implied, may be summarized as follows:

(a) *Notice.* Before the meeting commences he ought to satisfy himself that it has been properly convened. However, in *Arcus* v. *Castle & Wellington Hospital Board* (1954) under the standing orders of a hospital it was provided that the chairman's decision on any point of order should be final. At the beginning of a requisitioned meeting the chairman ruled that the meeting had not been validly called. The court held that the question of whether a meeting was validly called was not a point of order within the standing orders.

(b) *Constitution.* He must also ensure that the meeting is properly constituted, i.e.

    (*i*) that his own appointment is in order; and

    (*ii*) that a quorum is present.

(c) *Conduct.* During the whole course of the meeting, he must ensure that the proceedings are conducted strictly in accordance with the rules which govern the meeting.

(d) *Preservation of order.* He has a duty to preserve order. For this purpose he may have power to order the withdrawal of offenders, but this is a power which depends upon the nature of the meeting and where it is held.

(e) *Order of business.* He must ensure that business is dealt with in the order set out in the agenda paper — unless the meeting consents to a variation of the order. He may decide points of order and other incidental matters, which require decision at the time, *Re Indian Zoedone Co.* (1884). A point of order is raised when, in the opinion of a member, the rules or regulations governing a meeting are being broken or there are genuine doubts about the correctness of the procedure being followed. This might include any informality or irregularity such as the absence of a quorum, the belief that a motion under discussion is not within the scope of the notice, or the use of offensive and abusive language. Points of order should be put to the chairman as directly and briefly as possible and should not be used to spoil or interrupt a speaker's delivery. The chairman's ruling on a point of order is final, though once raised others present should be given the opportunity of speaking upon it if they so desire.

(f) *Discussion.* He has a duty to allow reasonable time for discussion; on the other hand:

    (*i*) he must restrain irrelevant discussion;

    (*ii*) he must allow no discussion unless there is a motion before the meeting;

    (*iii*) he must give equal opportunity to those who wish to speak.

Those in the minority must be allowed to express their views on the subject under discussion; nevertheless, a small, noisy minority must not be permitted to monopolize the proceedings. A good chairman who knows that a motion on the agenda is likely to be contentious will try to ascertain who wishes to speak on the motion before the beginning of the debate and will try to call upon them, alternating various points of view so far as is practicable.

(g) *'Sense of the meeting'.* He must ensure that the sense of the meeting is properly ascertained with regard to any question which is properly before the meeting. *See National Dwellings Society* v. *Sykes* (1894); for example, by putting motions and amendments to the meeting in proper form. Where a proposed amendment so mutilates the wording of the original motion that its sense is altered, the chairman must decide whether it is so far from the intention and meaning of the original motion that it should be disallowed as not being within the scope of the original motion or as being a direct negative of it.

6.   Powers

The chairman derives his powers principally from the rules which govern the meeting over which he presides, but also, to some extent, from common law. His powers from either or both of these sources may be summarized as follows:

(a) *To maintain order:* To this end he must use his decision in dealing with emergencies as they arise.

(b) *To decide points of order* as they arise, and to give and maintain his rulings on any points of procedure.

(c) *To use a casting vote* where there is an equality of votes, and if the rules confer this power. A chairman has *no* casting vote at common law: *Nell* v. *Longbottom* (1894).

(d) *To order the removal of disorderly persons.* Where necessary, reasonable force may be used to effect the removal, if the person concerned has failed to withdraw after being requested to do so by the chairman. At a private meeting the chairman has the power to order the removal of any person who has no right to be present. In both the above categories a trespass is committed. Where a member of a society or organization is disorderly and refuses to leave on being requested to do so the degree of force used to eject him or her must be limited to that level which the occasion reasonably requires: *Collins* v. *Revison* (1754). According to *Hawkins* v. *Muff* (1911) the chairman who has authorized the removal of the member is liable in damages for the tort of assault if excessive violence is used, but this is so only if there was an authorization of the removal of the actual party complaining of the violence used against him or her: *Lucas* v. *Mason* (1875).

A person who is disorderly in such a manner as to amount to a breach of the peace may be charged with that breach and given into the custody of a police officer. Merely to annoy and disturb by constantly saying 'hear, hear', making audible and derogatory comments upon the speaker's statement and putting annoying questions to the speaker do not of themselves amount to a breach of the peace justifying the arrest of the offender, so that the latter may successfully bring an action against those responsible (including the chairman) for false imprisonment: *Wooding* v. *Oxley* (1839). In order to be proper and justifiable the breach must be continuing at the time the offender is given into charge of a police officer or facts must exist which create a reasonable apprehension that the breach of the peace which has ceased will be renewed: *Baynes* v. *Brewster* (1841).

The issue of ejection is more delicate where individuals have a right to attend, as in company meetings. The problem may be resolved by the chairman putting a motion to the meeting that disorderly members be asked to leave and ejected if necessary. In *Barton* v. *Taylor* (1886) Lord Selbourne said that a chairman must have 'The power . . . reasonably necessary for the proper exercise of the functions of any assembly.' Therefore in extreme cases the chairman may properly direct the expulsion of a member from the meeting without the authority of a suspensive resolution. For a recent example in relation to local government meetings, *see R* v. *Brent Authority ex parte Francis* (1985). Alternatively the chairman may adjourn the meeting: *John* v. *Rees* (1970).

(e) *To adjourn the meeting.* Unless the rules give him express power to adjourn in specified cases, the chairman derives his power of adjournment from the meeting. If he were to adjourn without the consent of the meeting, another chairman may be appointed by the meeting and business resumed: *see National Dwellings Society* v. *Sykes* (1894), *Catesby* v. *Burnett* (1916). The cases in which a chairman appears to have the power to adjourn at common law arise when a meeting is adjourned for the express purpose of taking a poll: *R* v. *D'Oyly* (1840); or where a residual common law power to adjourn arises because the circumstances render it impracticable to apply a society's rules or company's articles that the chairman may adjourn with the consent of the meeting, the sense of the meeting being impossible or too difficult to ascertain: *Byng* v. *London Life Association Ltd* (1989). A third case would be where, after earnest and sustained efforts to restore order to a disorderly meeting the chairman finds it impossible to do so: *John* v. *Rees* (1970). *See* chapter 11 for further discussion of adjournment.

7. Addressing the Chair
The following rules apply:

(a) *A male chairman* is usually addressed as 'Mr. Chairman'; alternatively, he may be addressed as 'Sir' — or, for example, where the chairman is a church dignitary, as 'My Lord'.
(b) *When a woman is in the chair*, there are several possibilities:
    (*i*) 'Mr. Chairman', and even 'Sir', are used in some cases, on the ground that it is the chair which is being addressed.
    (*ii*) 'Madame Chairman' (or 'Madame President');
    (*iii*) 'Madame'; or
    (*iv*) By name, e.g. 'Mrs. Carter, Ladies and Gentleman – –'
(c) 'Chairperson' (or even simply 'the chair') is acceptable when either sex occupy the chair.
(d) *When addressing the chair and others collectively:*
    (*i*) *Normally,* the chairman takes precedence; that is, he or she should be addressed first, as in 'Mr. Chairman, Ladies and Gentleman – –'
    (*ii*) *If a distinguished guest is present*, the guest should be given precedence; for example, 'My Lord or My Lady, Mr. Chairman, Ladies and Gentleman', etc.

Removal

8. Removal of chairman
This will normally be controlled by the regulations of the body concerned. However, a chairman who has been elected by the

meeting can be removed by the meeting. This is normally achieved by a member proposing a vote of no confidence in the chair, this being seconded and carried.

Progress test 4

1. What are the qualities a chairman ought to possess to enable him to carry out his duties and exercise his powers for the greatest benefit of the meeting? **(3)**

2. State the main duties of a chairman and the possible effects of his failure to carry out these duties. **(5)**

3. Comment on the following statement: 'The chairman's duty is to carry out the wish of the majority.' **(5)**

4. What is the duty of the chairman as regards the maintenance of orderly behaviour and the adjournment of meetings, and the use of his casting vote? **(5, 6)**

5
The agenda

General

1. Definition

Literally, the word 'agenda' means 'things to be done', but in practice it is more commonly applied to the *agenda paper*, which lists the items of business to be dealt with at a meeting. The agenda is an important document since matters of which appropriate notification have not been given cannot be dealt with at a meeting unless they are of an informal character, and then only under the heading of 'any other business': *Smith* v. *Deighton and Billington* (1852), *Young* v. *Ladies' Imperial club* (1920).

2. Form of agenda

An agenda may take various forms, according to requirements and, in some cases, to the kind of meeting to which it refers, namely:

(a) *A 'skeleton' form of agenda*, i.e. in bare outline or summary form, giving headings only of the items to be dealt with. As a rule, this form is used when it is to be included as part of the notice circulated to those entitled to attend the meeting.

(b) *A detailed form of agenda*, with a complete heading to identify the meeting, and setting out in draft form the resolutions to be submitted to the chairman.

(c) *A 'bell curve' structure* is sometimes recommended for agendas. This usually involves items of a simple nature coming before those items which may be difficult or contentious. It is considered that the most difficult item should appear just past the middle followed by simple items towards the end of the meeting.

The theory is that the agenda maker links the agenda structure to the timing of the meeting in order to take advantage of the psychological, physiological and personal energies and presence of key individuals. However, this may not always be suitable nor workable given the rules of some organizations or the requirements of the law.

(d) *The chairman's copy of the agenda paper* may be supplied with more detail than the copies issued to those attending the meeting, and a wide margin may also be left on his copy for the purpose of note-taking.

> NOTE: The secretary may also provide himself with a more detailed copy of the agenda paper. After the meeting, he can then convert successful resolutions into draft minutes (*see* **7**, below).

Preparation

3.   Contents of an agenda paper
The following points are important in this connection:

(a) *Heading.* The agenda paper should be suitably headed, to indicate the kind of meeting, also where and when it is to be held. (Although it may not always be necessary in practice, for examination purposes it is recommended that the name of the organization holding the meeting should be shown as a bold heading at the top of the agenda paper.)

(b) *Arrangement.* Items must be arranged in the order (if any) indicated in the rules governing the meeting. Whether the rules indicate the order or not, the items ought to be arranged in a logical order. A typical order of business would be as follows:

  (*i*)   Apologies for absence
 (*ii*)   Minutes of the previous meeting
(*iii*)   Correspondence
(*iv*)   Reports of chairman, treasurer, etc.
  (*v*)   Non-routine business of an important nature
 (*vi*)   Date of next meeting.

It is often considered advisable to deal first with the routine items of business, so as to leave more time for special or non-routine business, which may need more time for discussion.

(c) *Items of business included.* No business should be placed on the agenda paper unless it comes within the scope of the notice convening the meeting, and is within the power of the meeting to deal with it.

(d) *Any other business.* Although it is very common to find this item on agendas, its use is not advisable. The main problem posed by its use are:

    (*i*) members may be forced to consider and debate items for which they have not prepared;

    (*ii*) the item is usually at the end of the agenda and members may be prepared to vote in favour of a motion merely because they are ready to go home.

Therefore, if this item is used the chairman must confine its use to the consideration of informal or unimportant matters.

(e) *Ease of reference.* To ensure ease of reference:

    (*i*) The contents ought to be sufficiently clear and explicit to enable members to understand what business is to be dealt with.

    (*ii*) In a lengthy agenda, each item should be numbered, and in the more detailed form of agenda it is often advisable to use headings and even sub-headings to show the subjects to be dealt with.

4. Preparation

The rules of an organization may state what is to be included in an agenda, if not, the head of the organization will be responsible and he will normally delegate the preparation to the secretary. Obviously it is impossible to lay down a standard method of preparing an agenda paper, as so much depends upon the nature and importance of the meeting concerned; however, the following points ought to be borne in mind in most cases:

(a) *Ensure that no relevant item of business is omitted.* This can be achieved in various ways, namely:

    (*i*) *Consult with the chairman* and any other officials who may have business to include.

    (*ii*) *Refer to the minutes* of the last meeting for any business or decisions which were then deferred, and for reminders of the routine annual, half-yearly or quarterly recurring items.

    (*iii*) *Keeping a special file or folder* of documents, such as reports, correspondence, etc, which are likely to be required at the next meeting. Prior to that meeting, sort and arrange these documents.

(b) *Refer to the rules* governing the meeting, particularly if they regulate the order in which items of business are to be dealt with. Care must be taken to arrange the items in a logical order for the following reasons:

(*i*) If it is properly drawn up and well-arranged, an agenda is self-explanatory; furthermore, it prevents confusion, reduces the number of questions put to the chairman, and shortens the meeting.

(*ii*) The chairman is less likely to have to request the meeting to agree to an alteration in the order of business.

(c) *Where motions are to be submitted in writing,* ensure that they are received within any time limit imposed by the rules. In a detailed form of agenda, it may be the practice to include in the agenda, the actual words of the motion, if the rules so provide.

NOTE: In the chairman's copy of the agenda, the names of proposers and seconders of the motions may be stated.

(d) *Obtain approval* of the agenda in its final form, prior to inclusion in the notice or separate circulation. Such approval may be obtained informally from the chairman or, e.g. in the case of a limited company, by formal resolution of the board of directors.

5. Specimen of a 'skeleton' agenda

The Paramount Company Limited

AGENDA

for the Seventh Annual General Meeting
to be held at City Hall, Bishopgate, London EC
on Monday, 12th July, 19-.

1. Auditors' Report.
2. Directors' Report and Accounts.
3. Dividend.
4. Election of Directors.
5. Remuneration of Auditors.

6.   Specimen of a more detailed agenda

This specimen is based on the above 'skeleton' agenda and suitable for the chairman.

The Paramount Company Limited

AGENDA

for the Seventh Annual General Meeting
to be held at City Hall, Bishopgate, London EC
on Monday, 12th July, 19-.

Item No.	*Agenda*	*Chairman's notes*
1	*Notice:* The Secretary to read the notice convening the meeting.	Read.
2	*Auditors' Report* to be read by the Secretary.	Read.
3	*Directors' Report and Accounts:* The Chairman will ask the meeting whether the directors' report and accounts shall be read, or taken as read.	Taken as read.
4	Chairman will address the meeting, and conclude by proposing: 'That the Directors' Report and Accounts for the year ended 31st March, 19–, as audited and reported on by the company's auditors, be and they are hereby approved and adopted.'	
	Chairman will ask Mr F.Carr (probably a director) to second the motion.	Seconded by Mr F.Carr
	Chairman will invite questions, and after dealing with any questions, put the motion to the meeting, and declare the result.	Moved and carried unanimously.
5	*Dividend:* The Chairman will move: 'That a dividend of 15 per cent less income tax, recommended in the directors' report for the	

Item No.	Agenda	Chairman's notes
	year ended 31st March, 19–, be and it is hereby declared payable on 19th July, 19–, to all shareholders whose names appeared on the Register of Members on 30th June, 19–.	
	The Chairman will ask Mr B. Craig (another Director) to second the motion.	Seconded by Mr Craig.
	Chairman to put the motion to the meeting, and declare the result.	Moved and carried.
6	*Election of Director(s):*	
	The Chairman will propose: 'That Mr Frederick Cooper, the Director now due to retire by rotation, be and he is hereby re-elected a Director of the Company.'	
	Chairman will ask Mr A. Cookson (a shareholder) to second the motion.	Seconded by Mr Cookson.
	Chairman will put the above motion to the meeting and declare result.	Moved and carried.
7.	*Appointment of Auditors:*	
	The Chairman will ask Mr W. Scott (a shareholder) to move, and Mr R. Jenkins (a shareholder) to second the following motion:	
	'That Messrs Price and Harris be and they are hereby re-appointed Auditors of the Company, to hold office from the conclusion of this meeting until the conclusion of the next annual general meeting, at a renumeration of 25,000 (twenty-five thousand) pounds.'	Moved by Mr Scott, seconded by Mr Jenkins, and carried.
	Chairman will put the motion to the meeting, and declare result.	
8	*Chairman will declare proceedings at an end,* and (where applicable) reply to vote of thanks.	

Use in preparation of minutes

7. Retention of agenda papers

(a) *Chairman's copy of the agenda paper.* Although the chairman's notes on his copy of the agenda paper may sometimes be of assistance to the secretary when writing up his minutes, it is considered that, the minutes having been approved and signed, the chairman's copy of the agenda paper ought to be destroyed. Failure to do so might cause confusion later, if it is found that the hastily-drafted notes of the chairman do not coincide with the secretary's minutes as finally drafted.

(b) At least one copy of the agenda papers should be retained by the secretary from which to prepare his minutes — particularly if he uses a detailed form of agenda paper with a wide margin for notes, similar to that provided for the chairman.

> NOTE: As a rule, the secretary prefers to prepare notes for the minute book in a small note book, rather than on the agenda paper. (*See also* Chapter 23.)

Progress test 5

1. What are the requisites of an agenda? Draft a specimen agenda for a meeting of one of the following: (a) annual meeting of an association; (b) board meeting of a company or association; (c) committee of a company or association. **(3)**

2. Describe the measures you would adopt in the preparation of an agenda for the council meeting of an association or similar body with which you may be familiar. Do you favour the retention of agenda papers? Give your reasons for retention or otherwise. **(4, 7)**

3. What are the advantages of a carefully prepared agenda to the chairman of a meeting and to the secretary, respectively? Draft an agenda for a board or committee meeting in order to illustrate and emphasize your conclusions. **(4)**

6
Notices

Purpose, content and entitlement

1. The convening of meetings

As indicated in the last chapter, the secretary's first duty in preparing for a meeting is to prepare an agenda. His next important duty is to convene the meeting, that is:

(a) Preparing (or supervising the preparation of) the notice of the meeting.
(b) Despatching notices to all persons entitled to attend the meeting.

2. Definition

(a) The notice of a meeting is any form or method of communication adopted by the convenor(s) to summon to the meeting all persons entitled to attend.
(b) Thus, notice must be served in the form, or by the method, laid down in the rules governing the meeting; or
(c) If the rules make no such provision, then any reasonable form or method may be used, namely:

  (*i*)   verbal notice;
  (*ii*) press notice;
  (*iii*) bill posting;
  (*iv*) handbills distributed from door to door;
  (*v*)   separate handwritten or typewritten notices;
  (*vi*) notice board;
  (*vii*) broadcasting.

Where clubs are concerned if the regulations of the club do not stipulate the method of giving notice it is within the general function of the committee of a club to say how notices are to be given on each particular occasion: *Labouchere* v. *Earl of Wharncliffe* (1879); though in relation to clubs the courts prefer to give more weight to reasonableness and fairness rather than stick to a rigid interpretation of its rules. Where the subject matter of a meeting is more important, such as where a change to its rules or the expulsion of a member is being considered, it is best to send a copy of the notice to each member rather than simply affixing a copy to the club's notice board: *Re GKN Sports & Social Club* (1982). Similarly the result of a trade union meeting should be construed in a 'benign and loose way of reading' rather than as if they were statutes, *per* Harman J in *Hamlet* v. *General Municipal Boilermakers and Allied Trade Unions* (1987).

3. **Contents**

(a) For meetings generally the principal contents are as follows:
   (*i*) Place of the meeting.
   (*ii*) Date, day and time of the meeting.
   (*iii*) Business to be transacted.
   (*iv*) Details of any special business to be transacted.
   (*v*) Kind of meeting, where applicable, e.g. annual general meeting.
   (*vi*) Date of the notice.
   (*vii*) Signature of the person convening (or authorized to convene) the meeting, usually the secretary's.

The special requirements as regards notices convening *company* meetings are dealt with separately. *See* chapter 17.

(b) Failure to state clearly the purpose of a meeting and give all material information to allow it to be fully understood may render the notice defective. The courts look at notices fairly and not with a view to exercising criticism or finding defects. In *Henderson* v. *Bank of Australasia* (1890) Chitty J said:

> 'I think the question may be put in this form: What is the meaning which this notice would fairly carry to ordinary minds? That, I think, is a reasonable test. Another matter of very considerable importance in dealing with this as a practical question, is, how did the meeting itself understand the notice?'

In *Tiessen* v. *Henderson* (1899), Kekewich J said:

> 'A shareholder may properly and prudently leave matters in which he takes no personal interest to the decision of the majority. But in that case he is content to be bound by the vote of the majority; because he knows the matter about which the majority are to vote at the meeting. If he does not know that, he has not a fair chance of determining in his own interest whether he ought to attend the meeting, make further inquiries, or leave others to determine the matter for him.'

In this case the notice of an extraordinary general meeting for the reconstruction of a company did not disclose the pecuniary interest of a director. Non-disclosure of this material fact invalidated the resolution. In *Young* v. *Ladies' Imperial Club* (1920) a committee meeting of a club removed a member's name from their list of members, following an incident. The notice of the committee meeting did not state the fact that there was an intention to expel her. This omission was deemed to be a defect in the notice. *See also Hughes* v. *Union Cold Storage Co.* (1934); *Normandy* v. *Ind Coope & Co.* (1908); and *Pacific Coast Coal Miners Ltd* v. *Arbuthnot* (1917). In the third case cited, Viscount Haldane noted that the uninformative notice had been particularly inappropriate for the members who had appointed as their proxies at the meeting the directors who wanted the resolution adopted and who would benefit from it.

(c) *Special business.* The notice must clearly state the nature of any special business to be dealt with. The regulations of a society, club or company will usually define what is meant by special business. Failing any definition in the regulations, the test for what is special business is the construction which the recipient of a notice would put upon it to enable him 'to decide for himself whether he should do any more' per Kekewich J in *Normandy* v. *Ind Coope & Co.* (1908). *See also Smith* v. *Deighton and Billington* (1852) (discussed in chapter 2, **6(d)**); *Harrington* v. *Sendall* (1903); *Kaye* v. *Croydon Tramways Co.* (1898); *Tiesson* v. *Henderson* (1899) and *Baillie* v. *Oriental Telephone & Electric Co. Ltd* (1915).

It is sufficient to give a general indication of the nature of the special business and there is no obligation to state the precise terms of the resolutions to be proposed: *Betts & Co. Ltd* v. *MacNaughton* (1910). However, it may be desirable to send an explanatory circular with the notice: *see Young* v. *South African and Australian Exploration and Development Syndicate* (1896).

Different rules apply to meetings of company boards, *see La Compagnie de Mayville* v. *Whitley* (1876) and chapter 19.

4.   Entitlement to notice

In general, notice must be given to *all* persons entitled to attend the meeting; failure to do so might affect the validity of the meeting: *R* v. *Shrewsbury* (1735). In *John* v. *Rees* (1970) a considerable amount of noise, disagreement and some minor violence broke out at a Constituency Labour Party meeting. After the Chairman and those who supported him left the meeting, the opposing faction continued with the meeting and ·passed a resolution of disaffiliation from the National Labour Party. A meeting of the local branch was later convened by the national agent who did not send notice of the meeting to the rebel faction. The rebel faction succeeded in having the second meeting declared improperly convened because notice was not sent to them. But the omission to send notice may be *excused*, for example:

(a) The rules often provide for *waiver* of notice, where the omission is accidental.

(b) Where *all* persons entitled to attend are present without notice, and *all* 'expressly assent to that which is being done.': *Re Express Engineering Works* (1920).

(c) Where those not summoned were *beyond summoning distance*, e.g. where a member was abroad: *Smyth* v. *Darley* (1849); or where a member was *too ill to attend* in any case: *Young* v. *Ladies Imperial Club* (1920). *See also*, Table A, art. 88.

(d) It is, however, always advisable to send proper notice to *all* persons entitled to attend a meeting, and not rely upon the apparent disability of a member at the time as an excuse for failing to summon him.

Even if the member informs the convenors that he will not be able to attend the meeting, that should not be relied upon as a waiver of notice: *Re Portuguese Consolidated Copper Mines* (1889); *Rex* v. *Langhorn* (1836).

5.   Authority to convene

Notices must be issued, or communicated by whatever method

the rules demand, by the person or body authorized to do so by the regulations governing the meeting concerned, e.g. by the secretary, or by the secretary on the instructions of a governing body. A meeting summoned without authority is invalid: *Re State of Wyoming Syndicate* (1901). However, where a notice in proper form has been sent out without due authority, the sending of the notice may be subsequently ratified by the persons with authority to convene and the ensuing meeting will be validly held: *Hooper* v. *Kerr, Stuart & Co.* (1900).

6. Period of notice
The following general rules are applicable:

(a) *The length of notice* required is usually provided for in the rules; if not, 'reasonable' notice must be given.

(b) *Longer notice* is usually required for a meeting at which 'special' business is to be transacted, e.g. 21 days' notice may be required, whereas only 14 days' notice may be required for ordinary business.

(c) Unless otherwise provided in the rules, it is implied that the number of days stated are *clear days*, i.e. they are *exclusive* of the day of service of the notice and of the day of meeting: *Re Railway Sleepers Supply Co.* (1885).

(d) *Failure to give adequate notice* may result in the meeting being rendered invalid, if, for example, only 7 days' notice is given instead of the (say) 21 days' notice required by the regulations concerned.

(e) *Inadequacy of notice* may, however, be excused if all, or some specified proportion of the members entitled to attend the meeting so agree: *Re Oxted Motor Co.* (1921); *see* Table A, art. 38.

Method of service

7. Service of notice

(a) As already indicated above, the period of notice required is usually measured in 'clear days', which exclude the day of service of the notice and the day on which the meeting is to be held. But the day of service of the notice may have different interpretations.

(b) In some cases, the rules may indicate when notice is *deemed* to have been served, e.g.

    (*i*) 24 hours after posting; or

    (*ii*) at the time of posting.

(c) If the rules are silent on the subject, reference must be made to the Interpretation Act 1978. This provides that a notice is deemed to be served on the day on which, if posted, it would be delivered in the ordinary course of post. The Act does not apply to service of notice of a public procession under the Public Order Act 1986, s. 11.

8. Specimen of a simple form of notice, embodying a 'skeleton' agenda

THE GUILDHALL ASSOCIATION
75, Main Street,
Leeds, 8.

20 January, 19–.

NOTICE IS HEREBY GIVEN that a meeting of the Management Committee of this Association will be held at the Headquarters of the Association on Wednesday, the 6 February at 2.30 pm for the transaction of the business itemised in the appended agenda.

(*Signed*) . . . .

General Secretary.

Agenda

1. Minutes of last meeting.
2. Consider matters arising.
3. Receive applications for membership.
4. Financial Statement.
5. Correspondence.
6. Receive reports from (*a*) Welfare Sub-Committee (*b*) Building Committee.

Notice and convention of meetings

9. Failure properly to convene a meeting

As already indicated, this is one of the defects in respect of which the validity of a meeting might be questioned. However, a person who is present and who votes at the meeting will not be entitled to challenge an invalidity in the notice: *Re British Sugar Refining Co.* (1857). The question of invalidity might, however, arise in various ways; in particular:

(a) *Omission to send notice* to every person entitled to attend, i.e. where there are no grounds for excusing the omission.

(b) *Inadequate (short) notice*, i.e. where no provision is made for excusing the inadequacy.

(c) *Ambiguity of the notice*. A notice must be free from anything calculated to confuse or mislead. In *Kaye* v. *Croydon Tramways* (1898) a notice, convening an extraordinary general meeting of a company for the purposes of approving the sale of its undertaking to another company, failed to disclose that the members would have to approve the receipt by their directors of a large payment from the purchasing company. Even though the resolution was adopted at the meeting, the Court of Appeal held it was invalid because the 'tricky notice' failed to give 'a fair, candid and reasonable explanation' of the business to be dealt with at the meeting. *See also Henderson* v. *Bank of Australasia* (1890).

(d) *Omission of important contents*, such as the failure to mention that special business is to be transacted. Matters of which appropriate notification has not been given cannot be dealt with at a meeting unless they are of an informal character: *Smith* v. *Deighton and Billington* (1852), *Young* v. *Ladies' Imperial Club* (1920). Although it is normally essential to state place date, day and time of the meeting, it would, no doubt, be permissible to dispense with any mention of the actual time, where one meeting is to be held immediately after another; in that case, the notice may indicate that the second meeting will commence 'at the conclusion' of the first meeting.

(e) *Unauthorized issue of notice*. The issue of notice by the secretary without the authority of the convening body is inadequate and the meeting rendered invalid: *Re Haycraft Gold Reduction Co.* (1900).

Nevertheless, if the notice *is* adopted and ratified by the proper convening body before the meeting is held, it may become a good notice, in which case the meeting is not invalid: *Hooper* v. *Kerr* (1900). *See also Breckland Group Holdings Ltd* v. *London and Suffolk Properties Ltd* (1988).

10. The irregularity principle

The principle in *Re Vale of Neath* (1852) said that members wishing to challenge the validity of a notice must act with promptness. Similarly the lawfulness of a decision taken by a meeting may not be questioned if the only factor alleged to make it unlawful is a mere informality or irregularity and the intention of the members is clear: *Burland* v. *Earle* (1902). This was so in *Browne* v. *La Trinidad* (1887) where inadequate notice of a board meeting to one of the directors did not invalidate a members' meeting summoned by that board meeting to remove him from office. Mr. Browne could have called another directors' meeting but failed to do so and, as the decision of the members to remove him was unanimous, there was no point in going through the procedure again.

In one case a notice summoning a general meeting was issued on the authority of a board meeting at which only two directors were present. It was later discovered that a resolution reducing the quorum from three to two had not been validly passed six years previously. The general meeting, in accordance with the notice, resolved to wind up the company in January 1985. In July an application was made to the court to declare the resolution invalid. The court refused to interfere 'for the purpose of forcing companies to conduct their business according to the strictest rules, where the irregularity complained of can be set right any moment.': *Southern Counties Deposit Bank Ltd* v. *Rider & Kirkwood* (1895).

The court will not grant an injunction restraining other parties from acting on the resolutions passed at a meeting if it is of the view that any irregularity in the notice could have been cured by the issuing of another notice, *see Bentley Stevens* v. *Jones* (1974). For further consideration of the irregularity principle *see* chapter 20:8.

Progress test 6

1.   State what a notice of meeting is, give its essentials; and discuss the legal effect of an imperfect notice. **(2, 3, 9)**

2. List some of the commonly used methods of convening meetings. If there are no regulations affecting the convening of meetings, what is the position as regards **(a)** period of notice, **(b)** place of the meeting?   **(3, 6)**

3. State in brief, numbered paragraphs the essentials of a valid notice of a meeting.   **(2–7)**

4. When will irregularity in a notice not render a meeting invalid?   **(10)**

7
Quorum

1. Definition

A quorum may be defined as the minimum number of persons entitled to be present at a meeting (or their proxies, if permitted) which the regulations require to be present in order that the business of the meeting may be validly transacted.

While the general rule is that the existence of a meeting involves the contemporary presence of at least two persons: *Re Sanitary Carbon Co.* (1877), the rules of an organization may require a quorum of more than two. However, in the absence of particular regulations or special custom, a majority of the members of a body must be present at a duly convened assembly in order that an effective meeting should exist. For example, at common law, in the absence of any specific provision, the acts of a corporation must be done by a majority of the corporation, corporately assembled: *Merchants of the Staple of England* v. *Bank of England* (1887). This majority rule will apply also to meetings of any select body to which specific functions have been delegated, in the absence of specific regulations on the matter: *R* v. *Varlo* (1775).

2. Casual meeting

The casual meeting of sufficient members to constitute a quorum does *not*, however, constitute a valid meeting. It fails because proper notice of the meeting must be given to all persons entitled to attend it (*see* chapter 6). Thus, where there are only two persons on a board of directors' their casual meeting together does not constitute a valid meeting, if either of them objects: *Barron* v. *Potter* (1914). For further discussion, *see* chapter 17.

3. Absence of quorum

Absence or inadequacy of the quorum may arise in the following cases:

(a) *Failure to muster a quorum.* If the prescribed quorum is not present when the meeting is due to start, the meeting should be formally adjourned because, legally, there is no meeting. To save a meeting, some leniency is frequently permitted by the rules, e.g. half-an-hour extensions may be permitted, and if a quorum is not present within half-an-hour from the time originally appointed for the meeting, it must be adjourned to (say) the same day in the following week at the same time and place.

(b) *Failure to maintain a quorum.* Subject to specific rules on quorum, any business transacted at a meeting while a quorum is not present is invalid: *Re Romford Canal Co.* (1883). If a quorum is not maintained, it is open to anyone present at a meeting to draw the chairman's attention to that fact. It is then his duty to declare a 'count out' and adjourn the meeting.

Whether the chairman's declaration of a 'count out' can effectively invalidate business subsequently completed at the meeting may depend, to some extent, upon the wording of the rules. In this connection, compare the cases of *Henderson* v. *Louttit* (1894) and *Re Hartley Baird Ltd* (1954) in chapter 18.

(c) *Effect of absence of quorum.* The general principle is that business transacted is invalid: *Re Romford Canal Co.* (1883). However there are exceptions such as where the irregularity principle applies, *see Southern Counties Deposit Bank Ltd* v. *Rider* (1895). Third parties entering into contracts as a result of such decisions could enforce the contracts as the organization may have implied or ostensible authority to contract in the eyes of the third party.

(d) *Incompetent quorum.* Only persons competent to take part in the business of a meeting constitute a quorum; thus, at common law, a quorum must be a 'disinterested' one: *Yuill* v. *Greymouth Point Elizabeth Railway Co.* (1904). Therefore, unless the rules permit, a person may be denied the right to vote at, and unable to form part of a quorum of, a meeting transacting business in which that person has conflicting interests. *See* Table A, arts. 94 and 95.

The rule of the 'disinterested quorum' is dealt with more fully in chapter 28.

Progress test 7

1. Explain in relation to a quorum: (*i*) failure to muster; (*ii*) its maintenance. What rules usually apply in these cases? **(2)**

2. What is the nature and purpose of a quorum? **(1)**

3. In what respects might a quorum prove incompetent to act? What is a 'count out', and what is the chairman's duty when his attention is drawn to it? **(2)**

4. Explain how the absence or inadequacy of quorum might arise. **(2)**

8
Motions

Form and presentation

1. Definition

A motion is a proposition or proposal put forward for discussion and decision at a meeting.

2. Acceptance of a motion

After a motion has been put to the vote and agreed it becomes a resolution; that is, the resolution is the 'acceptance' of the motion.

3. Form of motion

The following rules govern the form of the motion:

(a) A motion must be in the form required by the rules governing the meeting, e.g. it may be required in writing, signed by the proposer, and handed to the chairman.

(b) It must be within the scope of the notice convening the meeting, and relevant to the business for which the meeting was called.

(c) It must be proposed at the meeting and, if required by the rules, seconded.

> NOTE: A seconder is *not* required unless demanded by the rules governing the meeting: *Re Horbury Bridge Coal Co.* (1879).

(d) It must be set out in definite terms, and free from any ambiguity.

(e) It should *not* be negative in form. In general a motion should be affirmative; there are, however, certain exceptions to this rule, e.g. the 'previous question' (referred to later in this chapter) is a formal or procedural motion which is quite correctly put in the form, 'That the question be *not* now put.'

(f) A motion and, if it is carried, the resulting resolution, would begin with the word 'That—'.

4. Presentation

A motion must be presented:

(a) In form and manner prescribed by the rules.

(b) By any person at the meeting who is qualified to do so, i.e. by the member himself or, if the rules permit, by a proxy appointed by the member.

(c) In the order shown on the agenda paper — unless the order is altered by decision of the meeting.

5. Disposal

A motion may be disposed of in various ways:

(a) In most cases, after adequate time has been allowed for discussing it, it is *put to the vote*, and either carried or rejected by the meeting.

(b) If various amendments have been accepted, it may be put to the meeting as a *substantive motion*, and either carried or rejected.

(c) It may be *shelved* if the 'previous question' is moved and accepted by the meeting, i.e. 'That the question be not now put.'

(d) It may be *dropped:*

> (*i*) by the proposer himself, with the consent of the meeting; or
>
> (*ii*) because of failure to find a seconder, i.e. where the rules require a seconder to a motion.

(e) A motion for *adjournment*, if carried, disposes of a motion, but this may be only a temporary disposal, i.e. until the adjourned meeting is held.

6. A 'dropped motion'

As indicated above, a 'dropped motion' is one which has been disposed of in one of the less customary ways; thus

(a) The term 'dropped motion' is more commonly associated with the case where a person who gave notice of a motion decides to withdraw it.

Strictly, such a motion 'belongs' to the meeting, and it cannot be withdrawn without the meeting's consent; moreover, it cannot be revived without giving fresh notice.

(b) The term is also sometimes applied to a motion which has failed to find a seconder, where one is required by the rules.

Amendments

7. Definition

An amendment may be defined as a proposal to alter a motion submitted to a meeting; e.g.

(a) by adding, inserting or deleting words of the original motion;
(b) by substituting words, phrases or complete sentences for others in the original motion; or
(c) by any combination of the above forms of alteration.

> NOTE: An amendment must not be confused with a 'rider', which adds to a motion, but does not amend it; see later reference in glossary.

8. Rules governing amendments

It may be found that rules do not deal as fully with amendments as they ought to do; consequently, the chairman is often given little assistance from that source, and a great deal is left to his discretion in deciding whether to accept or reject amendments.

He must, however, bear in mind that his failure to admit a relevant amendment might invalidate a resolution, as in *Henderson* v. *Bank of Australasia* (1890).

The following are the principal rules governing amendments which may be expressly stated or merely implied:

(a) *When moved*. An amendment may be moved after a motion has been proposed, but *before* the question is put to the vote.
(b) *Notice*. It can be moved *without* previous notice — unless notice is required by the rules.
(c) *Form:*
    (*i*) If previous notice *is* required, preferably it should be in

writing, signed by the mover, and given or sent to the chairman (or secretary) before the meeting.

(*ii*) If previous notice is *not* required, it should be formally moved and, if the rules so provide, seconded.

(*iii*) It must not be a mere negative of the original motion; the same result can be achieved by the voting against it. Note, however, that a direct negative *is* permissible in Scotland, where it is commonly used to reach a quick decision.

(d) *Proposer*. It may be moved or seconded (if required by the rules) by any member who has not already spoken on the motion; after that all members have a right to speak, i.e. even if they have already spoken on the original motion, unless the rules provide to the contrary.

NOTE: Where proxies are permitted by the rules, the mover (or seconder) of the amendment may not necessarily be a member.

(e) *Relevance:*

(*i*) It must be relevant to the original motion which it purports to amend.

(*ii*) It must not conflict with anything which the meeting has already agreed upon.

(*iii*) It must not go beyond the scope of the notice convening the meeting, nor beyond the power of the meeting, e.g. it must not introduce anything which, if accepted, might commit the meeting to something more onerous than was intended in the original motion or even beyond its power to decide.

(f) *Withdrawal*. It cannot be withdrawn without the consent of the meeting — as is the case with a motion.

(g) *Second speech*. As a rule, the mover of an amendment has no right of reply; this, of course, differs from the case of the mover of the original motion, who automatically has the right of second speech in discussion.

(h) *Only one amendment* should be permitted before the meeting at any one time; that is, the chairman ought to refuse to accept an amendment while another is already being discussed.

(i) *Persons debarred*. The chairman will not usually accept an amendment proposed by:

(*i*) the mover of the original motion; or

(*ii*) one who has already moved an amendment to the original
motion.

NOTE: Subject to the rules, there is nothing to prevent the mover
of the original motion from voting *against* it, either in its original or
amended form.

(j) *Amendment to an amendment.* If permitted by the rules, the
chairman may allow an amendment to an amendment which is
already before the meeting — but it is always liable to cause
confusion.

(k) *Voting on an amendment to an amendment.* If the chairman allows
an amendment to an amendment, the usual practice is to vote
upon the *second* amendment first; if it is adopted it is embodied
into the first amendment, which is then put to the meeting and
voted upon.

(l) *Voting on amendments.* Amendments are usually put to the vote
in the order in which they affect the original motion, i.e. *not* in the
order in which they were moved. But see later reference to the
'popular' method of dealing with amendments (**9 (a)**).

(m) *Special business.* An amendment to a motion for the passing of
a special form of resolution (e.g. a special or extraordinary
resolution in the case of a limited company) should not be
permitted — except to correct an error of grammar or spelling.

(n) *Equality of votes.* If the votes for and against an amendment are
equal (and assuming that the chairman does not exercise a casting
vote), it is deemed to have been *rejected*.

9. Procedures for dealing with amendments

Where several amendments are proposed, the alternative
methods of dealing with them are as follows:

(a) *The 'popular' method.* The procedure is:
 (*i*) After each amendment has been discussed, *all* amendments are put to the vote *in the order in which they affect the
 original motion,* and not in the order in which they were
 moved.
 (*ii*) *Substantive motion.* All amendments adopted by the
 meeting are then incorporated in the original motion,
 which is then put to the vote as a substantive motion.

(iii) *Amendments of the substantive motion* are permissible, unless the rules provide to the contrary — but such amendments must not merely re-introduce the original motion or any of the amendments already rejected by the meeting.

(iv) *If the substantive motion is rejected*, the original motion is not revived.

This procedure is exemplified below.

Example

The original motion was worded:

'That the common seal be and the same is hereby adopted as the common seal of the company, and that one key thereof be retained, when not in use, at the registered office of the company, and that the duplicate key be deposited with the company's bankers for safe custody, to be released only on written request.'

Amendments were proposed in the following order:

Amendment No. 1   *Voting order*

That the words 'in a sealed envelope' be inserted after the words 'when not in use.'

                                                        Accepted   2

Amendment No. 2

That the words 'signed by one or more of the company's authorized signatories' be added at the end of the original motion.'   Accepted   4

Amendment No. 3

That the words 'an impression of which is affixed in the margin hereof' be inserted after the words 'That the common seal.'   Accepted   1

Amendment No. 4

That the words 'the duplicate key' be deleted and the words 'two duplicate keys' be substituted.   Defeated   3

The substantive motion reads as follows:

'That the common seal, *an impression of which is affixed in the margin hereof*, be and same is hereby adopted as the common seal of the company, and that one key thereof be retained, when not in use, *in a sealed envelope* at the registered office of the company, and that the duplicate key be deposited with the company's bankers for safe custody, to be released only on written request, *signed by one or more of the company's authorized signatories.'*

(b) *The 'parliamentary' method.* The procedure is:

(*i*) Each amendment must be in writing, and has to be submitted to the chairman of committees before the debate.

(*ii*) The chairman has power to select only representative and relevant amendments, i.e. in order to expedite the business of the committee the debate may jump from one selected amendment to another, omitting those in between which the chairman regards as repetitive, irrelevant or frivolous. (*See* Appendix 1, reference to the term kangaroo closure.)

(*iii*) At the debate, the selected amendments must each obtain a seconder as they are put to the meeting.

(*iv*) The original motion is then linked with *each* of the amendments in turn, and a limited time is allowed for discussion on each amendment before it is put to the vote; thus there is no need to put a substantive motion to the meeting.

Other forms of motion

10. Substantive motion

(a) The original motion, after discussion, may be altered by subsequent amendments.

(b) The form in which the motion is finally put to the meeting (after any amendments approved by the meeting have been incorporated in it) is known as the *substantive motion*.

11. Formal motions

These are procedural motions, intended to regulate the procedure and conduct of a meeting, with the principal objects of facilitating and expediting the business to be transacted at the meeting. The 'Closure' and 'Previous Question' are examples of formal motions. These and other formal motions are dealt with in chapter 9.

12. 'Dilatory motions

This is the term which is often used to describe the misuse of a formal (or procedural) motion, i.e. where it is being used for a dilatory purpose, with the object of impeding the progress of the meeting, or of preventing discussion on a motion before reasonable time has been given to it.

Progress test 8

1. Distinguish between a motion and a resolution. Explain (a) dropped motion, (b) substantive motion.   **(1, 2, 6, 10)**

2. What are the rules as regards (a) form, (b) presentation, and (c) disposal, of a motion?   **(3, 4, ,5)**

3. Draft a specimen motion for inclusion in the agenda of any organization of which you are a member. In what ways might this method subsequently be dealt with at the meeting for which it is intended?   **(3, 4, 5)**

4. Discuss the effects of the case in *Re Horbury Bridge Coal Co.* (1879) on the subject of motions.   **(3)**

5. What are the essentials of a valid amendment?   **(8)**

6. What is an amendment? How does it differ from a 'rider'? **(1 and Appendix 1.)**

7. Explain how a motion may be amended. Is an amendment to an amendment permissible?   **(7, 8)**

8. In what circumstances, if at all, can a substantive motion be amended?   **(9)**

9
Formal (procedural) motions

Use of formal motions

1. Definition

A formal or procedural motion is one which concerns the form or procedure of the meeting at which it is proposed, and not the actual business for which the meeting was convened.

Consequently, no notice is required of such a motion, nor does it need to be in writing.

2. Purpose

(a) Formal motions are designed to expedite and facilitate the business of a meeting.

(b) When used for their *intended* purpose, they can effectively terminate, defer or prevent discussion of business when it is a waste of time to continue with the business in hand. If, for example, a motion has already been moved, seconded and fully discussed, a formal motion might be used, for the benefit of the meeting, to interrupt discussion and take the sense of the meeting by putting the motion to the vote.

3. Dilatory motions

In practice, some of the formal motions are open to misuse. Where they are used frivolously, or with the object of curtailing discussion on the legitimate business of the meeting, they are usually referred to as 'dilatory' motions.

4. The chairman's duty

(a) The chairman must, obviously, use *discretion* in preventing formal motions from being used for a dilatory purpose.

(b) Thus the chairman may *reject a formal motion* if he considers it has been proposed frivolously or, for example, where it has apparently been proposed with the object of curtailing discussion on a matter which has not been given reasonable time for discussion.

(c) Nevertheless, he must be careful about refusing a motion for *adjournment* of the meeting. Even though it may be moved for a dilatory purpose, he must bear in mind that the right to adjourn is primarily with the meeting. He is then faced with a problem — whether to refuse the motion, or to put the motion to the vote of the meeting, which will waste the time of the meeting and, no doubt, enable the mover of the motion to achieve *his* purpose.

If the rules governing the meeting provide that the chairman 'may' adjourn when so requested by the majority of members present, he is *not* bound to comply with that request if he considers it is not in the interests of the meeting to do so. *See Salisbury Gold Mining Co.* v. *Hathorn and Others* (1897).

5. Amendment

A formal motion cannot be amended; in some cases, however, a formal motion may be overridden by another formal motion, e.g. the 'Previous Question' can be overridden by a motion for adjournment of the meeting.

Types of formal motion

6. The principal formal motions
These are usually worded as follows:

(a) 'That the meeting proceed to the next business.'

(b) 'That the meeting postpone consideration of the subject.'

(c) 'That the question be now put — usually known as the 'Closure'.

(d) 'That the question be *not* now put — usually known as the 'Previous Question.'

(e) 'That the debate be adjourned.'

(f) 'That the meeting be adjourned.'

(g) 'That the recommendation be referred back to the committee.'

These formal motions are dealt with more fully in the following paragraphs.

7. 'That the meeting proceed to the next business'

(a) *Purpose:* to curtail discussion of a motion which is frivolous or time-wasting, and prevent the motion being put to the vote.

(b) *Disposal:*
- (*i*) If *adopted*, the original motion is dropped at once without further discussion and no vote is taken, i.e. the meeting then proceeds to the next business. In this respect it has the same effect as the 'Previous Question' motion.
- (*ii*) If *rejected*, discussion on the original motion continues. In this respect it differs from the 'Previous Question' motion.

(c) If the rules permit, the 'next business' motion may be proposed again, having been rejected in the first instance, but usually only after a specified time limit of (say) half-an-hour.

8. 'That the meeting postpone consideration of the subject'

(a) *Purpose.* If it is considered futile to commence discussion of a motion because of inadequate knowledge, e.g. where there has been delay in receiving reports from a committee, this formal motion may be used to postpone consideration of the original motion until later in the same meeting or, more likely, until a subsequent meeting.

The same motion may, however, be used *during* or *after* discussion of the original motion.

(b) *Disposal:*
- (*i*) If *adopted*, discussion of the original motion is merely postponed, usually to afford time to obtain further information concerning it; that is, the motion is *not* 'shelved'.
- (*ii*) If *rejected*, discussion on the original motion may be commenced or resumed.

(c) Before the 'postponement' motion is put to the vote, the mover of the original motion is usually allowed the right of reply;

that is, he is given the opportunity to state why (if he is still of that opinion) discussion on the original motion should commence or continue.

(d) If the 'postponement' motion is rejected, it is usually permissible to move it again, but only after any time limit specified in the rules has elapsed.

9.   'That the question be now put'
This is known as the 'closure' or 'gag'.

(a) *Purpose.* This is used to curtail prolonged discussion of either the original motion or of an amendment to it.

(b) *Disposal:*

(i) *If adopted,* the original motion (or amendment to it) is at once put to the vote, without further discussion. Moreover, the proposer of the original motion loses his right of reply.

(ii) *If rejected,* discussion on the original motion (or on the amendment to it) is resumed.

(c) The 'closure' may be moved by the chairman or by any member; if moved by a member, the chairman must be careful not to accept it unless reasonable time has been allowed for discussion.

NOTE: The above is the ordinary form of 'closure', but reference will be made later to two additional forms of 'closure' which are rarely used outside of the House of Commons, namely the 'guillotine' and 'kangaroo' forms of 'closure'.

10.   'That the question be *not* now put'
This is known as the 'Previous Question'.

(a) *Purpose.* To get the meeting to decide whether the 'previous question' (i.e. the original motion) shall be put to the vote at all, or whether it shall be 'shelved' without any further discussion.

(b) *When moved.* As a rule, it can be moved only when the original motion is under discussion, usually at the close of a speech on the original motion. Note, however, that it cannot be moved on an *amendment to the original motion*.

(c) *Proposer.* It cannot usually be moved by one who has already spoken on the original motion.

(d) *Disposal:*

(*i*) *If adopted*, the original motion is dropped at once, without further discussion, i.e. it is 'shelved' without being put to the vote, and cannot be moved again at that meeting.

(*ii*) *If rejected*, the original motion must be put to the vote at once, without further discussion.

NOTE: The mover of the original motion usually loses his right of second speech in *either* case.

(e) *How superseded.* Although it is not permissible to move an amendment to the 'Previous Question', it can be superseded by a motion for adjournment of the meeting.

11. 'That the debate be adjourned'

(a) *Purpose.* To adjourn discussion of a motion until later in the same meeting, or until a subsequent meeting, to give members time to consider the subject, or to await further information. Alternatively, it may be used to defer debate on a relatively unimportant motion which has been unduly prolonged, in order to deal with a more important matter on the agenda.

(b) *Disposal:*

(*i*) *If adopted*, the subject under discussion is deferred until later in the same meeting (if time permits) or until the next meeting. Indeed, the motion may, in fact, be worded to include the time or date to which the debate is to be adjourned.

(*ii*) *If rejected*, the debate on the subject in hand may be resumed.

(c) *The mover of the original motion* is usually given the right of reply, i.e. before the 'adjournment' motion is put to the vote.

(d) *When the debate is resumed* at the same, or next, meeting, the person who successfully carried the 'adjournment' motion is generally permitted to re-open the debate.

12. 'That the meeting be adjourned'

(a) *Purpose.* This motion may be moved by the chairman or by any member at the close of any speech, or on concluding any business of the meeting, with the object of closing the meeting by adjourning it to a later date, for any one of the following reasons:

    (*i*) because of unfinished business on the agenda, e.g. where a hall, in which the meeting is being held, was hired for a specified period;

    (*ii*) because the business of the meeting cannot be conducted effectively owing to unruly behaviour of the members, and adjournment is necessary in order to allow tempers to cool;

    (*iii*) because there has been an effective demand for a poll vote and, as this may take some considerable time, that part of the business is to be dealt with at the adjourned meeting.

(b) *Disposal:*

    (*i*) *If adopted*, the unfinished business is resumed at the next ordinary meeting of the kind adjourned, unless the 'adjournment' motion included a date for the adjourned meeting, or the chairman is permitted by the rules to fix the date.

    (*ii*) *If rejected*, it is usually permissible to move the motion again after a reasonable time, or after any specified period set out in the rules.

(c) *The mover of the original motion* usually has the right of reply before the 'adjournment' motion is put to the vote.

(d) As already stated, the 'adjournment' motion may be used to supersede the 'previous question' motion.

> NOTE: Apart from the reasons for adjournment given above, the chairman may adjourn because of failure to muster a quorum or because of failure to keep a quorum (i.e. on a 'count out'), but it might be argued that on each of these occasions there was, technically, 'no meeting' and that the adjournment was merely a formality.

13. 'That the recommendation be referred back to the committee'

(a) *Purpose*. Ostensibly, to refer the committee's recommendation back to it for further consideration, e.g. because part of the committee's recommendations are not acceptable to the appointing body. The motion is, however, sometimes used as a polite way of rejecting the committee's recommendations.

(b) *Disposal:*

    (*i*) *If adopted*, the committee is given an opportunity to give further consideration to its original recommendations, and to submit new or amended recommendations, usually within a time limit imposed by the appointing body.

(*ii*) *If rejected,* it does not signify that the committee's recommendations are necessarily fully, or even partly, acceptable to the appointing body. If, after further discussion, they are to be adopted, a motion to that effect may be moved. It will probably include a vote of thanks for the committee's recommendations, unless a separate motion is moved for that purpose.

NOTE: Although the 'reference back' motion is often included with the formal (or procedural) motions, it may be argued that, strictly, it is neither formal nor procedural as it is not used to interrupt debate.

Progress test 9

1. State the nature and purpose of a formal motion. **(1, 2)**

2. Explain the chairman's duty in respect of formal motions. **(4)**

3. In what forms are the following motions usually put to a meeting: **(a)** the 'closure', **(b)** the 'previous question'? What are the effects in each case of their being (*i*) carried, (*ii*) rejected? **(9, 10)**

4. Briefly describe the procedure following the application of the 'guillotine' closure, and explain its purpose. (*See* Appendix 1.)

5. What is the purpose and effect of the 'kangaroo' closure? (*See* Appendix 1.)

10
Summary of procedure at a meeting

Omitting the preliminaries, such as the chairman's opening address, reading of notice, adoption of minutes, etc, a typical meeting procedure might follow the lines described below.

1. Motion
A member puts forward a motion, either at the beginning or end of his speech. If required by the rules, he has already submitted the motion in writing to the proper person, and within any specified time limit.

2. Seconding the motion
The chairman having asked for a seconder (if required by the rules), the motion is seconded.

3. Discussion
Discussion on the motion may follow, for which the chairman must allow reasonable time and opportunity to all who wish to speak.

4. Formal motion
At this stage, i.e. during discussion, a member may interrupt the proceedings by moving a formal motion, e.g. the 'Previous Question' or the 'Closure'.

In this case, it has been assumed that discussion is resumed; that is, either:

(a) the chairman refuses to accept the 'Previous Question' motion, on the grounds that it has been moved for a dilatory purpose; or
(b) the 'Closure' motion, having been put to the vote, is rejected.

5. Amendments

Arising out of the resumed discussion, one or more amendments may be moved and discussed.

> NOTE: During the discussion of an amendment, it is, of course, possible that a member may move a formal motion, e.g. the 'Closure' or one of the other permissible formal motions, bearing in mind that the 'Previous Question' cannot usually be moved on an amendment.

6. Amendments put to the vote

Assuming that the procedure is not interrupted by the adoption of a formal motion, the amendments are now separately put to the vote — in the order in which they affect the original motion.

7. Substantive motion

All amendments adopted, having been noted by the chairman and/or secretary, are then embodied in the original motion. Finally, the original motion, as amended, is put to the vote as a *substantive* motion.

8. Amendments to substantive motion

If permitted by the rules, one or more amendments may be moved to the substantive motion — so long as they do not merely reserve any of the earlier successful amendments, or introduce something which substantially changes the substantive motion or goes beyond the scope of the meeting.

11
Adjournments

1. Definition

Adjournment is the act of extending or continuing a meeting for a purpose of dealing with unfinished business: *Scadding* v. *Lorant* (1851).

2. Notice of an adjourned meeting

Fresh notice of an adjourned meeting is *not* necessary: *Wills* v. *Murray* (1850), *Kerr* v. *Wilkie* (1860); unless:

(a) specifically required by the rules, e.g. if the meeting is adjourned for (say) thirty days or more; or

(b) fresh business is to be introduced at the adjourned meeting: *R* v. *Grimshaw* (1847); or

(c) the original meeting is adjourned *sine die*, i.e. without fixing a date for the adjourned meeting.

3. How a meeting may be adjourned

(a) *Adoption of a formal motion* for adjournment of the meeting, i.e. passed by a simple majority of those attending and voting — unless there is an effective demand for a poll vote.

If a meeting is invalid in the sense that members have been wrongfully excluded, the meeting itself may not have power to adjourn. In *Harben* v. *Phillips* (1883) four directors were wrongfully excluded from a board meeting. The three directors present at the board meeting purported to adjourn it and the adjourned board meeting purported to make certain decisions. At first instance, Chitty J said that the first meeting was 'an unlawful meeting, that it was not properly constituted and that everything that was done at it is invalid', including the adjournment. Similarly, in the Court of Appeal, Cotton LJ expressed very great doubt whether the first board meeting could be a proper meeting.

The case of *Re Portuguese Consolidation Copper Mines Ltd* (1889) is another example. There was a board meeting of which inadequate notice was given. Only two directors attended. They resolved that two directors should be a quorum, purported to allot certain shares and adjourned the meeting. The adjourned meeting purported to ratify the allotment. The Court of Appeal held that, there having been no proper notice of the first meeting it was 'no valid meeting, and being an invalid meeting, could not adjourn itself'.

Nevertheless there is authority which supports the view that there can be a general meeting even when that meeting is incapable of conducting business: *Fletcher* v. *New Zealand Glue Co. Ltd* (1911): *Byng* v. *London Life Assurance Ltd* (1989). Similarly under Table A, arts. 40, 41, an inquorate meeting is treated as a meeting capable of adjournment. See the rules on postponement below at **5(c)**.

(b) *Action of the chairman.* In the absence of express rules concerning powers of adjournment a chairman has no general right to adjourn a meeting at his own will and pleasure where there are no circumstances preventing the effective continuation of the proceedings: *National Dwellings Society* v. *Sykes* (1894). Although the power of adjournment is strictly with the meeting, nevertheless there are occasions on which the chairman himself has power to adjourn, namely:

(*i*) *Where the rules give him express power* to adjourn, in any case, or for any specific purpose, stated in the rules.

(*ii*) *To take a poll vote.* His right to adjourn a meeting for the purpose of taking a poll vote arises out of common law: *R* v. *D'Oyly* (1840). This was a case in which the meeting was adjourned by the presiding officer against the wishes of the meeting solely with a view to taking a poll which had been demanded. There was no undue or unjustified interruption of business. Lord Denman CJ said: 'it is on him (the chairman) that it devolves both to preserve order in the meeting, and to regulate the proceedings so as to give all persons entitled a reasonable opportunity of voting. He is to do the acts necessary for these purposes on his own responsibility and subject to being called upon

to answer for his own responsibility and subject to being
called upon to answer for his conduct if he has done any
thing improperly.' *See also Jackson* v. *Hamlyn* (1953).

(*iii*) *When it is impossible to maintain order,* in which case he may
adjourn without fixing a date for the adjourned meeting,
or for only a short period to allow tempers to cool. (Even
in these cases, however, he should attempt to get the
consent of the meeting to the adjournment.)

In *John* v. *Rees* (1970) a case concerning, *inter alia*,
disorder at a constituency Labour Party meeting, Megarry
J stated the following guidelines on the use of the
chairman's power to adjourn in situations of disorder:

'The first duty of the chairman of a meeting is to keep order
if he can. If there is disorder, his duty, I think, is to make
earnest and sustained efforts to restore order, and for this
purpose to summon to his aid any officers or others whose
assistance is available. If all his efforts are in vain, he should
endeavour to put into operation whatever provisions for
adjournment there are in the rules, such as by obtaining a
resolution to adjourn. If this proves impossible, he should
exercise his inherent power to adjourn the meeting for a
short while, such as 15 minutes, taking steps to ensure so far
as possible that all persons know of this adjournment. If
instead of mere disorder there is violence, I think that he
should take similar steps, save that the greater the violence
the less prolonged should be his efforts to restore order
before adjourning. In my judgment he has not merely a
power but a duty to adjourn in this way, in the interests of
those who fear for their safety. I am not suggesting that
there is a power and a duty to adjourn if the violence
consists of no more than a few technical assaults and
batteries. Mere pushing and jostling is one thing; it is
another when people are put in fear, where there is heavy
punching, or the knives are out, so that blood may flow, and
there are prospects, or more, of grievous bodily harm. In
the latter case the sooner the chairman adjourns the
meeting the better. At meetings, as elsewhere, the queen's
peace must be kept.

If then, the chairman has this inherent power and duty,

what limitations, if any, are there in its exercise? First, I think that the power and duty must be exercised bona fide and for the purpose of forwarding and facilitating the meeting, and not for the purpose of interruption or procrastination. Second, I think that the adjournment must be for no longer than the necessities appear to dictate. If the adjournment is merely such period as the chairman considers to be reasonably necessary for resolution of order, it would be within his power and his duty; a long adjournment would not. One must remember that to attend a meeting may for some mean travelling far and giving up much leisure. An adjournment to another day when a mere 15 minutes might suffice to restore order may well impose an unjustifiable burden on many; for they must either once more travel far and give up their leisure, or else remain away and lose their chance to speak and vote at the meeting.'

(iv) *Failure to muster a quorum.* Here, although technically there is not a valid 'meeting', the chairman must formally adjourn it to a new date, or proceed in any other way directed by the rules.

(v) *Where there is a 'count out',* i.e. where the quorum is not maintained; here again the chairman must formally adjourn, as there is no longer a valid meeting.

(vi) The chairman may exercise a common law residual power to adjourn when the machinery provided in the regulations of a society or the articles of a company concerning adjournment has broken down and circumstances render it impossible to ascertain the sense of the meeting on the matter of adjournment. This occurred in *Byng* v. *London Life Association Ltd* (1989). The articles provided that 'the chairman may with consent of any meeting at which a quorum is present (and shall if so directed by the meeting) adjourn the meeting . . . '. It was impossible to take a vote on adjournment because of, *inter alia*, a breakdown in audio-visual links between rooms where members attending a meeting were housed. In exercising his decision to adjourn the chairman must, on the facts which he knows or ought to know, take into account *all* the relevant factors and *not* irrelevant ones. He must not reach a conclusion which no reasonable chairman, properly directing himself as to his duties, could have reached. On the facts in *Byng's case* the chairman had improperly exercised his residual powers to adjourn because in adjourning the meeting from the Barbican, London to the afternoon of the same day at the Café Royal, London he had failed to take into consideration several relevant factors. First, that there were over five months in which to pass a resolution approving a merger: second, that there were repeated attempts from members to obtain an adjournment *sine die*; and third, that there were objections from members that they would not be able to attend that afternoon at the Café Royal and that these same members would not therefore be represented at the meeting, since under the articles there was insufficient time to deposit proxies.

4.   Other important Court decisions on the subject of adjournment
The following cases are additional to those already referred to above:

(a) *Salisbury Gold Mining Co* v. *Hathorn and others* (1897). If the rules provide that the chairman *may* adjourn a meeting when so requested by the majority of members present, there is an implication that he can use his discretion, and is *not* bound to carry out the wish of the majority if he does not think it is in the interests of the meeting to do so.

(b) *National Dwelling Society* v. *Sykes* (1894); also *Catesby* v. *Burnett* (1916). A chairman is not entitled to adjourn a meeting before the business of the meeting has been completed; if he does so without sufficient cause, upon his leaving the chair the meeting may appoint another chairman and continue the business for which the meeting has been convened.

(c) *Jackson* v. *Hamlyn and others* (1953) (*Gordon Hotels case*). An adjourned meeting is merely a continuation or extension of the original meeting. This case is perhaps better known in another connection, i.e. it established that proxies deposited between the original meeting and the adjourned meeting are not valid.

5. Postponement

Postponement must be clearly distinguished from adjournment.

(a) *Postponement* is the action of deferring a meeting to a later date, even before the meeting is held; *adjournment* refers to the extension or continuation of a meeting which has actually been held.

(b) If a meeting has been properly convened, it cannot be postponed or cancelled by subsequent notice — unless the rules so provide: *Smith* v. *Paringa Mines* (1906). Thus, unless the rules permit postponement, the meeting must be held and, with the consent of the majority of those present and voting, formally adjourned.

(c) *If the meeting has not been properly convened,* e.g. where the notice is faulty as to date or place of the meeting; or if, for any reason, it is subsequently found to be impossible or impracticable to hold the meeting at the date or in the place originally stated in the notice, the following alternative procedures may be adopted:

   (*i*) Give notice of the postponement to those entitled to attend, by advertisement in the press and/or by post, explain the reason for the postponement, and at the same time (or subsequently) send a fresh notice in correct form, stating the re-arranged date; or

   (*ii*) Notify those entitled to attend by advertisement and/or post, explaining the circumstances and stating that, although the meeting will be held, in order to comply with common law, no business will be transacted; that is, the meeting will be held but adjourned immediately to a time and place to be arranged.

Progress test 11

1. Explain the phrase 'adjournment of a meeting' and the common law rule relating thereto. How is this common law provision sometimes modified by the regulations governing particular meetings? **(1, 2, 3)**

2. In what circumstances is the chairman of a meeting entitled

(a) to refuse to accept an amendment, (b) to adjourn without consent of the meeting?   (2, 3)

3.   What do you understand by adjournment? In what circumstances may a chairman adjourn a meeting on his own responsibility? In what circumstances has he no option but to adjourn? When is notice of the resumed meeting required? Can a meeting once convened properly be postponed?   (1, 2, 3, 5)

4.   List the various ways whereby a meeting may be adjourned. Discuss the effects of any decided cases on the subject of adjournment and of the adjourned meeting.   (3, 4)

5.   Distinguish between adjournment and postponement of a meeting. What is the proper course to be adopted when it is desired to postpone a meeting after it had been properly convened? If the meeting has been properly convened (e.g. if inadequate notice is given), what is the correct procedure? (1, 5)

12
Minutes

The taking of minutes

1. Definition
Minutes may be defined as a written record of the business transacted at a meeting.

2. Contents
Although the contents will vary according to the kind of meeting, the following items are typical.

(a) *Heading.* This usually includes:
  (i) *Name of the body,* e.g. company, which held the meeting.
  (ii) *Kind of meeting,* e.g. annual general meeting.
  (iii) *Place of the meeting.*
  (iv) *Day and date* of the meeting. (The time is not usually stated.)

> NOTE: Obviously, the name of the body concerned need not be shown in the minute book, but examination candidates ought to include it when drafting specimen minutes.

(b) *Names of those present,* including (where applicable) those 'in attendance', i.e. those who are there by invitation, or *ex officio*, and not as members. The recording of names applies more particularly to board meetings and other comparatively small assemblies. In the case of large meetings, only the *number* present needs to be recorded, if at all.

(c) *Minutes of resolution.* These are records of decisions taken and resolutions passed, e.g. *Resolved:* 'That the Official Seal, an impression of which is impressed in the margin hereof, be and the same is hereby adopted as the Official Seal of the company.'

(d) *Minutes of narration*. These are records of items of business which do not require formal resolutions. Thus, the above minute of resolution might have been preceded by the following minute of narration: 'The secretary produced a design for the Official Seal of the Company.'

(e) *Names of proposers and seconders*. Whether to record the names of proposers and (where necessary) seconders in the minutes is usually dependent upon the size or kind of meeting concerned; for example:

(i) *Board meetings and committee meetings*. Names of proposers and seconders are *not* usually recorded.

(ii) *General meetings*. In the case of large meetings, names of proposers and seconders *are* usually minuted.

(f) *Serial numbers*. Each item of the minutes is usually serially numbered. As will be explained later, this is particularly necessary in the case of loose-leaf minute books, where the numbers may run serially right through the whole book. The use of serial numbers, moreover, facilitates reference and, where applicable, the cross-indexing of minutes according to subject matter.

(g) *Chairman's signature*. The chairman usually appends his signature at the next succeeding meeting, after that meeting has verified the accuracy of the minutes and passed a resolution to that effect. The chairman signing need *not* have been in the chair at the original meeting.

3. The essentials of good minute writing

(a) *Authentic*. As the minutes may subsequently be required as evidence in a court of law, they must give a precise account of the proceedings of the meeting, and nothing more. The minutes of a meeting must not read like a report; thus, it is quite unnecessary to record the discussions and debates which preceded the passing of the various resolutions.

(b) *Complete*. The minutes must be complete, and in sufficient detail to enable a person who was not present at the meeting to understand fully what business was transacted.

(c) *Concise*. Minutes must be as concise as possible, but completeness must not be sacrificed for the sake of conciseness.

(d) *Free from ambiguity.* This means in practice that:
  (*i*) Dates, numbers, amounts, quantities, etc., must be clearly stated.
  (*ii*) Documents, such as share certificates, must be clearly identified, e.g. by number.
  (*iii*) Officials and persons concerned in making decisions, giving or receiving instructions, etc, must be named or otherwise described, so as to indicate with certainty who is intended.

(e) *Past tense.* Minutes, being a record of what was *done*, i.e. decided, must be written in the *past* tense.

4. Specimen minutes

CRAFTS PROTECTION SOCIETY

Minutes of the Management Committee Meeting held
at the Society's Head Office on Tuesday,
20 May, 19-.

Present: Mr A. Moat (Chairman)
    Mr R. Cable
    Mr J. Snaith
    Mr G. Todd
    Mr M. Veitch
In attendance: Mr E. Gilbert, General Secretary

1. *Minutes:* The minutes of the Management Committee Meeting held on 16 April, 19-, having been circulated to all members of the Committee, were taken as read, approved, and signed by the Chairman.

2. *Casual vacancy:* The Chairman having expressed the regrets of the committee concerning the death of Mr Martin Welsh, it was
    Resolved: 'That Mr James Laing be and he is hereby appointed a member of the Management Committee, to fill the casual vacancy caused by the death of Mr Martin Welsh.'

3. *Correspondence:* The General Secretary read letters received from the Society's Midlands Branch Office, namely
    Letter No. 1456: Staff bonuses recommended, amounting to £9856 were approved.
    Letter No. 1467: Suggested improvements in office procedure

were noted, but the General Secretary was instructed to write to the secretary of the Midlands Branch for a detailed report of the suggested improvements, together with figures of the cost involved.

4.   *Applications:* The General Secretary read a list of 35 applications for membership of the Society, and it was

Resolved: 'That the 35 applications for membership of this Society, numbered 1031 to 1065 both inclusive, be and they are hereby accepted.'

The General Secretary was instructed to issue letters of acceptance forthwith.

5.   *Resignations:* Letters of resignation from membership of the Society were read from: Ellis & Webb Ltd, Leeds, and Carson & Sons, Burnley, and the General Secretary was instructed to acknowledge and accept their resignations.

6.   *Publicity:* The General Secretary produced a letter from the Society's publicity agent, requesting an increase in the sum budgeted for the financial year ending 31 March, 19–, namely from £30,000 to £36,500.

It was decided to defer consideration of the matter until the next meeting of the Management Committee, and the General Secretary was instructed to write to the publicity agent to that effect.

7.   *Contracts:* The quotations of several suppliers of office furniture were submitted by the General Secretary, and it was

Resolved: 'That the quotation of Atlas Suppliers Ltd dated 12 May, 19–, amounting to £10,565 for office furniture be accepted.'

8.   *The next meeting* of the Management Committee was fixed for 12 noon on Tuesday, 17 June, 19–, at the Head Office of the Society.

(*Signed*) . . . .

Chairman

5.   The minute book

(a) *A bound minute book* is still favoured by many secretaries and has its advantages over the loose-leaf minute book in some respects:

(*i*)   The minutes are less liable to falsification and loss of loose sheets.

(*ii*) Many of the rather elaborate precautions required when using a loose-leaf minute book are unnecessary.

(b) *A loose-leaf minute book,* on the other hand, is perhaps more in keeping with modern methods; that is, the minutes are usually dictated (either to a shorthand typist or into a dictating machine) by the secretary from his notes, typed on loose sheets and, subsequently, put into the loose-leaf binder which constitutes the minute book. Though the loose-leaf minute book is not without its disadvantages, it does have points in its favour.

(c) *Advantages* of the loose-leaf minute book are:

(*i*) The tedious work of writing minutes into the bound book is avoided. Although it is possible to have the minutes typed on a sheet and pasted into the bound book, the book soon becomes bulky and the additional thickness tends to put undue strain on the outside covers.

(*ii*) At suitable intervals, the earlier sheets of minutes can be removed from the loose-leaf binder, and securely filed away in the safe or strong-room. Thus, apart from saving space, there is a saving in cost as one loose-leaf binder replaces any number of bound books.

(d) *Precautions.* The usual precautions taken to prevent falsification of the records and removal of the sheets are as follows:

(*i*) A suitable locking device is incorporated into the spine of the book itself, the keys being kept by, say, the chairman and secretary.

(*ii*) The minute book itself is kept in a safe or strong-room, preferably fire-proofed.

(*iii*) Blank sheets are placed in the charge of the secretary or other responsible official.

(*iv*) Sheets are numbered serially throughout the minute book.

(*v*) Each sheet is initialled by the chairman at the time of signing the minutes of the last preceding meeting.

For the use of computer records *see* chapter 23.

Reading and alteration

6. Reading the minutes

(a) *Not compulsory.* The reading of minutes at the next meeting is not compulsory, unless the rules specifically require it.

(b) *Often 'taken as read'.* In practice, with the consent of the meeting, they are often taken as read, particularly if copies of the minutes have been circulated to members prior to the meeting.

7. Approving the minutes

(a) *After the minutes are read* (or taken as read), a motion is put to the meeting, recommending their adoption as a true record of the proceedings of the preceding meeting to which they refer; if approved, they are signed by the chairman. 'Approval' here is to be regarded merely as *verification* of the accuracy of the minutes. Thus, a member who votes in favour of 'approving' the minutes does *not* thereby indicate that he was necessarily in agreement with resolutions passed at the last meeting; nor does he 'confirm' the minutes, as neither confirmation nor ratification is necessary.

(b) *Minutes as evidence.* Even after signature by the chairman, the minutes are only *prima facie* evidence; that is, they are not the *only* admissible evidence of the proceedings at the meeting to which they refer: *Re Fireproof Doors* (1916). It is, however, possible to include a provision in the regulations that (in the absence of fraud or bad faith) the minutes, having been signed by the chairman, shall be *conclusive* evidence: *Kerr* v. *Mottram* (1940). (*See further* chapter 23)

8. Alteration of the minutes

(a) *No erasures* should be made during preparation of the minutes, i.e. in the minute book itself or in the sheet to be inserted in a loose-leaf minute book. Any errors made should be ruled out and the substituted word or words neatly written or typed above or alongside.

(b) *Errors subsequently discovered,* i.e. at the next meeting, or at a later date, should be dealt with formally. In any case of doubt as to the accuracy of the minutes, an amendment may be put to the motion for their adoption; if the amendment is carried, the necessary alteration(s) must be made.

> NOTE: As a general rule, no alteration can be allowed after the minutes have been signed by the chairman. Nevertheless, as already indicated, evidence may be brought to prove that the minutes are incorrect: *Re Fireproof Doors* (1916), unless the rules provide that the

minutes, having been signed by the chairman, shall be conclusive evidence in the absence of fraud or bad faith: *Kerr* v. *Mottram* (1940).

Progress test 12

1. What are minutes? State what information you would record therein and the safeguards you would introduce where the minute book is of the 'loose-leaf' variety.   **(1, 2, 5)**

2. What are the main contents of the minutes of a meeting? Distinguish between minutes and reports.   **(2, 3(a))**

3. Draft minutes recording the following items of business at a meeting of the management body of trade association:
(a) Minutes; **(b)** Finance; **(c)** Applications for memberships;
(d) Appointment of a public relations officer.   **(2, 3)**

4. To what extent do the minutes of a meeting constitute legal evidence? How, and in what circumstances, can they be altered?   **(7(a), 8)**

Part two

General legal provisions affecting meetings

Introduction

This part of the book covers the provisions of law which are not exclusively concerned with meetings but which have a significant impact on the actions of those involved in meetings of all types. The provisions outlined in this part will therefore be applicable to some extent to all the different types of meeting covered by this text.

The ultra vires rule and the rules of natural justice

1. The constitution of clubs and ultra vires

(a) *The constitution or rules* governing a club or society are regarded as a form of self-made (autonomic) subordinate legislation. These rules are upheld by the courts on the basis of contract. When an individual joins a club he or she, in effect, agrees to be bound by that club's rules. So long as those rules are not repugnant to the law or in breach of the rules of natural justice the courts will, within certain limits, enforce them.

(b) *An organ of a club or society*, such as a disciplinary committee, must act within the ambit of the powers given to it under the club's constitution. If it goes beyond them it will be regarded as acting *ultra vires*. Its decision may then be regarded as null and void. Such decisions by a statutory tribunal give the injured party a remedy by way of *certiorari*, declaration and possibly injunction. In the case of domestic 'tribunals', the remedies of declaration and/or injunction may lie.

(c) *As regards the decisions of public and similar bodies* much depends on the right to judicial review. This is a complicated area beyond the scope of this book. In *The Council of Civil Services Unions* v. *Minister for the Civil Services* (1985) Lord Diplock analysed the cases where judicial review is available to challenge the action of a public body and his judgment is worthy of study. The case of *R* v. *Panel on Takeovers and Mergers, ex parte Datafin plc* (1987) is an example of the courts' increased willingness to subject the decision of such bodies to judicial review. The panel has no statutory prerogative or common law powers and it is not in contractual relationship with the financial market or with those who deal in that market, but nevertheless it was held to be subject to judicial review to determine whether it may have reached its decisions *ultra vires* or in breach of the rules of natural justice.

2. *Lee* v. *Showmen's Guild of Great Britain* (1952)

In this case a travelling showman was found by his Guild's Complaints Committee to have practiced 'unfair competition' to the detriment of another member. He was liable to a fine under its rules and on non-payment of it was automatically expelled. The Court of Appeal held that on the true construction of the rule under which the plaintiff was charged, his conduct could not be said to be 'unfair competition'. Therefore the fine and expulsion were *ultra vires* and void.

NOTE: This case did not involve any question of breach of the principles of natural justice, still less of malice or bad faith. As Lord Somervel was at pains to point out, the plaintiff was heard by the committee which made 'praiseworthy efforts to try to get the trouble resolved'.

3. **The Arbitration Act 1979**

It is illegal to exclude the jurisdiction of the court: *Czarnikov* v. *Roth Schmidt* (1922). However, the case of *Scott* v. *Avery* (1856) allows parties to a dispute to agree to go to arbitration rather than a court. The Arbitration Act 1979 allows parties to a 'domestic' dispute to exclude the possibility of an appeal to the courts on a point of law, *once the dispute has arisen* between the parties. Domestic has a special meaning under the Act. A domestic arbitration agreement is one which does not provide for arbitration in a foreign state and to which neither a foreign individual nor corporation is a party. Also the power to state a case for a decision of the High Court was abolished. Nevertheless, decisions of arbitrators are still subject to judicial review if they act *ultra vires* or in breach of the rules of natural justice.

4. **The extent to which the courts will interfere**

In *Lee* v. *Showmen's Guild of Great Britain* it was said that if a member is expelled by a committee in breach of contract, the court will grant a declaration that their action is *ultra vires*. It will also grant an injunction to prevent his expulsion if that is necessary to protect a proprietary right of his or protect him in his right to earn his livelihood, *see Amalgamated Society of Carpenters* v. *Braithwaite* (1922). However, the court will not grant an injunction to give a member the right to enter a social club unless there are proprietary rights attached to it, *see Baird* v. *Wells* (1890).

5. When will a committee's decision be ultra vires?
In most cases arising before such a domestic tribunal, the task of the committee can be divided into two parts.

(a) *It must construe the rules correctly.* This is a question of law and the committee must construe the rules properly if it is to keep within its jurisdiction.

(b) *It must apply the rules to the facts.* This is essentially a question for the committee.

(c) Sometimes **(a)** and **(b)** are inextricably mixed together. When this happens, the question of whether the committee has acted within its jurisdiction often depends on whether the facts adduced before it were reasonably capable of being held to be a breach of the rules. If the facts were not reasonably capable of being held to be a breach and yet the committee held them to be a breach, then the only inference is that the committee has misconstrued the rules and exceeded its jurisdiction. In such a case the committee has acted *ultra vires*.

6. The rules of natural justice
The concept of 'natural justice' is a difficult and complex one. It often merges or is equated with a duty to act fairly. However, it is implicit that a meeting carrying out a judicial or quasi-judicial function should show fairness and honesty of purpose in so doing.

The application of the rules of natural justice depends very much on the nature of the body hearing a case or application, etc as well as the nature of the subject matter and decision which the body is called upon to make. There appears to be a spectrum ranging from a duty to act fairly in decisions of an administrative type to the full-blooded application of natural justice principles in decisions of a judicial nature. Quasi-judicial decisions will fall in the middle of this spectrum and the relevant case law is often full of ambiguities.

7.   The rules
The main rules of natural justice are:

(a) *Nemo judex in causa sua* — no man should be a judge in his own cause.

(b) *Justice must be seen to be done.* This arises from both of the other rules and, like the requirement that the proper procedural requirements must be followed, is a development which in some senses goes beyond them.

(c) *Audi alteram partem* — basically no person should be judged or disciplined without being afforded an opportunity to be heard.

8.   No man should be a judge in his own cause

(a) *The basis of setting aside a decision of a meeting* exercising a judicial or quasi-judicial jurisdiction is that of bias. The cases distinguish between, on the one hand, a possible, general bias which does not disqualify, as opposed on the other, to the individual prejudice or bias which does. Contrast *Williams* v. *Beesley* (1973), where the plaintiff alleged that any judge would be prejudiced against him because he was a layman suing a solicitor, with *Roebuck* v. *NUM (Yorkshire Area) (No. 2)* (1978), where the chairman of the committee which expelled the plaintiffs from the union was disqualified from acting by bias arising from his personal interest in the case.

   The common law distinguishes two types of bias, that arising from financial interest and that arising from such causes as relationship to a party or status as a witness.

(b) *Any direct pecuniary interest,* however small, is sufficient to disqualify a person from acting as a judge, *see Dimes* v. *Grand Junction Canal* (1852). In this case the Lord Chancellor granted a number of judgments in favour of a canal company of which he was a shareholder. His decrees were set aside because of his pecuniary interest. It was irrelevant that in fact there was no bias. The courts are anxious to prevent the *appearance* of bias. *See also Sergeant* v. *Dale* (1877) and *R* v. *Barnsley Licensing Justices ex Barnsley Victuallers Association* (1960).

(c) *A relationship to a party or witness is described as a challenge to favour.* This may arise in various circumstances involving such matters as personal friendship or relationship and participation by a judge in proceedings leading to the hearing so that he can be regarded as both accuser and judge. In *R* v. *Barnsley MBC ex parte Hook* (1976), a complaint was made against the plaintiff market trader who had sworn at a fellow trader. The plaintiff's licence was withdrawn by the licensing committee on which sat the trader who had made the complaint. It was held that this was a breach of natural justice as the prosecutor was sitting in judgment. In *Cooper* v. *Wilson* (1937) a police sergeant was dismissed by the Chief Constable of Liverpool. He appealed to the watch committee who rejected the appeal. However, the Chief Constable was sitting on the watch committee when they made the decision. This was a breach of natural justice as the Chief Constable was sitting in judgment on an appeal against his own decision. *See also Ward* v. *Bradford Corporation* (1972) and *R* v. *Altrincham Justices ex parte Pennington* (1975). The question is often one of degree, *see Cottle* v. *Cottle* (1939). A challenge to favour may also arise where a person has expressed views on earlier occasions which might be thought to affect that person's ability to give both parties a fair hearing.

(d) *The test for bias.* There is no need to prove actual bias. In the case of a pecuniary interest, disqualification is automatic. Where other grounds of bias are alleged, the party complaining must show 'a real likelihood of bias' or 'a reasonable suspicion of bias', though there is some dispute over which of these is the proper legal test for bias.

In *Hannam* v. *Bradford CC* (1970), a local authority had to decide whether or not to dismiss a teacher. There was a recommendation from the school governors to dismiss her. The local authority decided to dismiss the teacher. However the decision was quashed because three members of the local authority were also governors of the school in question. Even though they had not been present when the governors made their decision to dismiss, they were biased because they would have a built-in tendency to support their colleagues. Similarly in the case of *Metropolitan Properties* v. *Lannon* (1969) a member of a rent assessment committee had to set a fair rent for a flat. The chairman of the committee lived in a flat of which his father was the tenant and whose landlord was a company associated with the landlords in the case which was before the chairman. The Court of Appeal held that this was a case of bias since the chairman was acting against the landlords in different circumstances. The question was not whether there actually was bias but whether there was a reasonable *suspicion* of bias. *See also R* v. *Crown Court ex parte Cooper* (1990), *R* v. *Barnsley Licensing Justices* (1960), *R* v. *Colchester Stipendiary Magistrates ex parte Beck* (1979) and *Anderton* v. *Auckland City Council* (1978).

(e) *Necessity is a defence to the bias rule*. In one case the government of a Canadian province had asked the courts to determine whether judges' salaries were subject to tax. The Privy Council said that the judges were right to decide this issue as it was a necessity. Similarly, in *Jeffs* v. *New Zealand Production and Marketing Board* (1967), the Board had the power to make zoning orders giving milk production in certain areas to certain dairy companies. In this case the dairy company involved had been given a loan by the Board and therefore the Board had an interest in the company's prosperity. The Privy Council held that since the Board had been given power by statute to make loans and zoning orders, although this might give rise to some bias, this was something envisaged by the statute as sometimes necessary in the Board's formulation and implementation of policy. The Board's decision was not set aside on the basis of bias.

9. Justice must be seen to be done

(a) This principle is a fundamental one and relates to both of the basic rules of natural justice. Indeed, 'doing what is right may still result in unfairness if it is done in the wrong way', *Maxwell* v. *Department of Trade* (1974) (per Lawton LJ). The rules of natural justice may even apply to what may be regarded as 'open and shut' cases. For the dangers of regarding any case as open and shut, *see John* v. *Rees* (1970).

(b) The maxim that justice must be seen to be done explains a wide range of cases where courts have invalidated decisions of committees or tribunals because of defects in their composition or serious irregularities in their procedure often described as 'grave irregularity'. In *Ward* v. *Bradford Corporation* (1972), Lord Denning MR disapproved of a person who is not a member of a tribunal retiring with the members because it *might* 'give the impression that he is taking part in their deliberations when he is not entitled to do so, for then justice would not be seen to be done'. In *Re B (Adoption by Parents)* (1975) a social worker involved in adoption proceedings retired with the justices. Their determination was quashed because justice had not been seen to be done. The mere presence of a non-member does not invalidate the decision if he did not participate in the decision: *Lane* v. *Norman* (1891), *Leary* v. *NUVB* (1971).

(c) Sometimes a tribunal's decision is invalid because of the non-participation of some of the members. This can arise in a number of ways. For example, there may have been improper delegation to some members of the power of deciding as opposed to the duty of collecting evidence on which the tribunal will make up its own mind: *Jeffs* v. *NZ Dairy Products and Market Board* (1967).

(d) Once it is established who constitutes a tribunal, it is clear that all the members must participate in its decision: *R* v. *Kensington and Chelsea Rent Tribunal* (1974), *Morris* v. *Gestetner Ltd* (1973). Justice may not be seen to be done unless the members of a tribunal engage in consultation between themselves before reaching their decision: *Parr* v. *Winterington* (1859). In *Ex parte Ladbroke Group* (1969) the complainant had unsuccessfully applied for the renewal of a betting licence. The chairman of the committee sat some distance from his colleagues and appeared to reach his conclusion without consulting them. Justice had not been seen to be done and their decision was quashed.

10. A right to be heard

As with the other rules, the actual opportunity to make representations depends very much on the nature of the body hearing the case and its position on the 'administrative-judicial' spectrum. There are many corollaries of the basic right to be heard. These are often problem areas and are dealt with below. It must be remembered that it is no more settled what the right to be heard involves than where it applies. However, the landmark decision which reasserted the right to be heard is *Ridge* v. *Baldwin* (1964). The case concerned a Chief Constable who was dismissed by the watch committee without a hearing. The House of Lords decided that this was a breach of natural justice and that he should have been heard in his own defence. They overruled many previous authorities which decided to the contrary.

(a) *Does the rule require that notice be given of the proceedings?* Notice is often regarded as important: *Cooper* v. *Wandsworth Board of Works*

(1863). The parties, including witnesses, must be made aware of the possible outcome of a tribunal's hearing: *Sheldon* v. *Bromfield JJ* (1964) and *R* v. *Hendon Justices ex parte Gorcheim* (1973). However, a breach of the rule may sometimes arise from the complete absence of a hearing: *Fleet Mortgage* v. *Lower Maisonette* (1972) and *Hiles* v. *Amalgamated Society of Woodworkers* (1968).

(b) *Should there be a right to legal representation?* In *Enderby Town Football Club* v. *Football Association* (1971) the plaintiff club was fined and appealed to the Football Association claiming a right to be legally represented. This right was rejected under the rules of the FA, and this decision was held valid and not in breach of the rules of natural justice. The court considered whether a domestic tribunal can make an absolute rule not to hear legal representatives. Lord Denning MR said that such a rule would be valid as long as it was construed as directory in nature and not imperative. This would leave it open to the tribunal to permit legal representation in an exceptional case where the justice of the case so requires. *See Pett* v. *Greyhound Racing Association Nos. 1 and 2* (1969) and 1970), *Fraser* v. *Madge* (1975), *R* v. *Secretary of State for the Home Department ex parte Tarrant* (1984). In the latter case it was held that prisoners charged with mutiny should be allowed legal representation because of the complexity of the offence. Contrast *R* v. *Maze Prisoners ex parte Hone* (1988) where the court held that there was no need for legal representation where a prisoner was charged with assault against a prison officer.

(c) *Do the rules of evidence apply?* It must be remembered that a duty to act fairly does not necessarily imply an obligation to observe all the rules of evidence and procedure as in a court of law. However, where more serious disciplinary hearings are concerned, the basic rules of law such as a person being presumed innocent until proven guilty must not be overlooked. In *Tsui Kwok Leung* v. *AG* (1990) a superintendent found a constable guilty of disciplinary offences and as a result the constable was punished. At the hearing the superintendent had stated that the defence had not rebutted the case presented by the prosecution. It was argued by the constable that there was a breach of natural justice. The court agreed with him saying that there had been a serious error in the decision-making process — the superintendent had failed to apply the basic rules of evidence; including the elementary rule that those facing charges had nothing to rebut and no obligation to give evidence. Although the rules of evidence do not have to be the same as those in court they must be *basically fair*.

(d) *To what extent does the rule require an opportunity to know of all the evidence?* This again depends very much on the nature of the tribunal. In *R* v. *Gaming Board ex parte Benaim* (1970) it was held that the Board was bound to observe the rules of natural justice. However, it was held that the Board need not disclose the source of evidence available to it but must give the applicant for a licence the opportunity of satisfying it of relevant matters and that the Board should inform them of its impression so that the applicant has an opportunity to disabuse it of that impression. This was very much a case concerning public policy. In *R* v. *Board of Visitors of Blundeston Prison* (1982) the existence of a witness to a prison disturbance was not disclosed to the plaintiff or Board of Visitors. This was held to be a breach of natural justice. A tribunal must afford 'a real and effective opportunity to the litigant to deal with or meet' the case against him: *R* v. *Architects Registration Tribunal ex parte Jagger* (1945). In *R* v. *Aston University ex parte Roffey* (1969) students who were forced to leave college for failing exams were entitled to comment on evidence about their personal circumstances which was also considered when the decision about them was made. *See also R* v. *Leyland JJ ex parte Hawthorne* (1979), *McInnes* v. *Onslow Fane* (1978), *Cinnamond* v. *BAA* (1980) and other cases on this matter.

(e) *A right to cross-examination.* This often depends on the seriousness of the particular case but it must be remembered that domestic or administrative tribunals, even if acting quasi-judicially, are not bound by the technical rules of evidence. In *R* v. *Hull Prison Board ex parte Germain (No. 2)* (1979) it was held that someone who was charged with a serious disciplinary offence was entitled to cross-examine witnesses on important matters. Similarly in *R* v. *Ngai Wak* (1985) an application was made for judicial review of decisions made at a disciplinary hearing against the applicant under the Customs and Excise disciplinary regulations of Hong Kong. The applicant had been found guilty of prejudicing the good order and discipline of the customs force by improperly obtaining cargo clearance while he was off duty, by requesting another officer to stamp certain forms. The finding of the tribunal was quashed because the applicant was not allowed to cross-examine the officer whom he had allegedly asked to stamp the documents. It was held that there was a breach of natural justice because this was an important matter in the case against the applicant. However, in *Bushel* v. *Secretary of State for the Environment* (1981) objectors at a motorway inquiry were not entitled to cross-examine the Ministry of Transport's witnesses. *See also University of Ceylon* v. *Fernando* (1960), *R* v. *Deputy Governor of Camphill Prison ex parte King* (1985) and other cases on this matter.

(f) *Must reasons be given for a decision?* Once more, much depends on the nature of the tribunal. In *Payne* v. *Lord Harwich of Greenwich* (1981) a parole board did not inform a prisoner of its reasons for refusing parole. The court held that since the constitution of the Board was covered by a comprehensive code not requiring the giving of reasons, the Board did not have to do so and it was not in breach of natural justice. In *McInnes* v. *Onslow Fane* (1978) it was held that a person applying to become a boxing manager need not be given an oral hearing, told of the case against his application or given reasons for the decision. However, in *R* v. *Civil Service Appeal Board, ex parte Cunningham* (1991) the applicant was a prison officer who was seeking review of the Board's decision to award him £6,500 compensation for unfair dismissal from the prison service. The Board refused to give reasons for its decision. The court held that the Board should give reasons for its decision since 'any other conclusion would reduce the Board to the status of a free wheeling palm tree'. Here the Board was not a domestic body, it was a fully judicial body — in no way administrative. Therefore natural justice may require reasons to be given and much depends on the character of the decision-making body: contrast *Padfield* v. *Minister for Agriculture* (1968) with *R* v. *Trade and Industry Secretary ex parte Lonrho plc* (1989).

(g) *Where 'trial at first instance' is not properly conducted, can this be cured by a right of appeal?* In *Leary* v. *NUVB* (1971) a union member was expelled and appealed eventually to his union NEC which confirmed the earlier decision to expel him. The court said that while a complete re-hearing by an original tribunal or some other body competent to decide an issue might satisfy the requirements of natural justice, a plaintiff where there was a right of appeal from an original decision was entitled to natural justice both before the original and the appellate tribunal. Therefore the decision to exclude him from membership was bad.

In *Calvin* v. *Carr* (1979) it was said that there is no general rule as to whether appellate proceedings could cure a defect of natural justice in original proceedings. There is, however, a broad spectrum from where the enquiry stage merges with the appellate stage to where a complainant might be prejudiced unless there is a fair hearing at both stages. The test is whether after both the original and appellate stages the complainant had had a fair deal of the kind he had bargained for when joining the organization.

In *Hamlet* v. *General Municipal Boilermakers and Allied Trade Unions* (1987) it was stated that as a matter of general principle the courts will not generally intervene where a right of appeal exists; the applicant should follow through the procedure to the appropriate body. Where a right of appeal exists it must not be abused. The case of *Miles* v. *Amalgamated Society of Woodworkers* (1968) is a good example of this and other aspects of natural justice. Miles, a member of a trade union, was summoned before a management committee to answer a charge of having acted in a manner contrary to the decisions of the union's governing bodies. On the basis of his defence a majority of the committee found the charge to be not proven. There was a rule which gave a member aggrieved with the decision of a management committee the right to appeal to the executive council. A minority member of the management committee made such an appeal. The executive council reversed the decision of the management committee and expelled Miles, without giving him notice of appeal or the opportunity to be heard. It was held that the right of appeal could be exercised only by the person accused. Since the committee had found the charge not proven the question of appeal could not arise and the appeal was a nullity. The court went on to say that it was contrary to natural justice to hear the appeal without giving the accused an opportunity to be heard, and where natural justice is involved the court will interfere with the decision of a domestic tribunal even where the rules have been complied with.

11. Legitimate expectation: *McInnes* v. *Onslow Fane* (1978)

In this case, Megarry J said that where a court is entitled to intervene it must be considered what type of decision is in question. He suggested a rough classification as follows:

(a) *Forfeiture cases*, where a decision takes away some existing right or position through expulsion from an organization or by the revocation of a licence. The rules of natural justice apply in such cases, e.g. *Ridge* v. *Baldwin* (1964), *Edwards* v. *SOGAT* (1971), *R* v. *Wear Valley DC ex parte Binks* (1985).

(b) *Application cases*. These are usually at the other extreme. They include where a decision merely refuses to grant to the applicant the right or position that he seeks, such as membership of the organization or a licence to do certain acts. Natural justice is much less likely to apply.

(c) *Expectation cases*. This is an intermediary category. They differ from application cases only in that the applicant has some legitimate expectation, from what has already happened, that his application will be granted. e.g. on application for renewal of a licence, *see Weinberger* v. *Inglis* (1919), *Breen* v. *AEU* (1971) and *R* v. *Barnsley MBC* (1976).

Natural justice issues are relevant in this last category because they raise the question of what it is that has happened to make the applicant unsuitable for the membership or licence for which he was previously thought suitable.

12. Membership

As seen from the above, a person cannot complain on the basis of a refusal to allow him to join a club. 'If a man applies to join a social club and is blackballed he has no cause of action.' In *Faramus* v. *Film Artists Association* (1964) emphasis was laid on the distinction between a provision prescribing a qualification for membership and a provision terminating membership. In that case it was said that the rules of natural justice will apply to expulsion but not procedures for admission, even if, as in *Faramus's* case, the breach of admission procedure only comes to light several years later and is in effect the grounds for expulsion.

However, public policy may intervene as in *Nagle* v. *Feilden* (1966). Here the court refused the application of the stewards of the Jockey Club to strike out Nagle's claim for a declaration that the stewards' policy refusing licences to women trainers was contrary to public policy. As Lord Denning said, 'we are not considering a society club. We are considering an association which exercises a virtual monopoly in an important field of human activity.'

13. Conclusion

Natural justice is often of relevance to meetings. However, it is a difficult and ambiguous area of the law. It must also be remembered that a breach of the rules of natural justice may result from an act which is *ultra vires* the rules of a society, club or professional body etc. Often the courts will only interfere when an aggrieved person has exhausted the domestic remedies available to him, e.g. an appeal to a higher committee. *See White* v. *Zuzych* (1951), *Annamunthodo* v. *OWTU* (1961), *Lawlor* v. *Union of Post Office Workers* (1965) and *Leigh* v. *NUR* (1970).

Progress test 13

1. Explain the grounds on which a member of a club, society, trade union or similar body may complain to the court because of a decision of a meeting of such a body being *ultra vires* or contrary to the rules of natural justice. **(1–13)**

2. Explain the relevance of the rules of natural justice and the principles of *ultra vires* to meetings. **(1–13)**

3. Can anyone resort to the courts because they have been refused membership of an organization and, if so, on what basis? **(11, 12)**

4. Explain what is meant by the *audi alteram partem* rule of natural justice in the context of disciplinary meetings. **(10)**

14
Defamation

The action

1. Definition
Various acts concerned with defamation have not even attempted to define it, and those judges and authors who have made an effort to do so have not produced an entirely satisfactory definition. Perhaps the following is one of the best examples:

> 'Defamation shall consist of the publication to a third party of matter which in all the circumstances would be likely to affect a person adversely in the estimation of reasonable people generally'. (Faulks Committee Report.)

2. Defamatory 'statements'
These may be made about any natural person (human being) or artificial legal person (corporate body) and certain unincorporated associations which have the necessary personality recognized by law. This would include a partnership but not a trade union: *EETPU* v. *Times Newspapers Ltd* (1980). However, the officials of such unions could be defamed by innuendo (*see* **18**) when statements are made about the union itself.

> NOTE: It is the law that a statement which is defamatory of a group at large cannot be sued on by the individual members unless the individual member can show that the defamatory statement was understood as referring to him, e.g. a statement that all trade unionists are rascals does not allow any trade union member to bring an action for defamation.

Although a defamatory statement can be made in a variety of

ways (e.g. in writing, verbally, pictorially or by gesture), legal action for defamation may be divided broadly into those for:

(a) Libel

(b) Slander.

3. Libel

Legal action for libel may be taken:

(a) Where the defamatory statement was made in writing, in print, or some other *permanent* form. Since the passing of the Defamation Act 1952, the broadcasting of defamatory words 'by wireless telegraphy' is also to be regarded as publication in permanent form — provided it is broadcast for 'general reception'. It should also be noted that television is within the scope of the 1952 Act.

(b) Whether the plaintiff can prove actual damage or not, i.e. he need *not* have suffered any pecuniary loss.

4. Slander

Legal action for slander may be taken in the following situations.

(a) Where the defamatory statement was made orally, or in some *transient* form of expression, e.g. slander may be expressed merely by gesture.

(b) Where the plaintiff can *prove* that he sustained actual damage. But this does not apply in all cases; thus it is *not* necessary for the plaintiff to prove that he suffered any actual pecuniary damage in the following cases:

   (*i*) Slander imputing a crime for which he could be sentenced to imprisonment.

   (*ii*) Slander imputing certain infectious or contagious diseases to the plaintiff.

   (*iii*) Slander imputing unchastity or immorality of a woman or girl. (The Slander of Women Act 1891, s. 1.)

   (*iv*) Imputations in relation to the plaintiff's office, profession or trade.

   (*v*) Imputations calculated to injure the plaintiff in his calling, even though the defamatory words were spoken of him otherwise than in the way of his office, profession or vocation. This last exception was added by the Defamation Act 1952, s. 2.

5.   Libel and slander may be distinguished in the following respects

(a) *Form*. Libel is defamation in a permanent form. Slander is defamation in some transient form.

(b) *Proof*. In the case of libel, proof of actual damage is *not* necessary, i.e. it is presumed in law that damage must result from the defamation. In the case of slander, actual damage must be proved, although, as stated above, there are exceptions.

(c) *Nature of offence*. Libel can be both a tort and a crime; that is, not only a civil offence but also a criminal offence. Slander, on the other hand, is not itself a crime, though it may constitute a crime in certain circumstances, e.g. where it incites to murder or provokes a breach of the peace.

Defences

6.   Defences

In an action for defamation, certain defences are available to the defendant according to the circumstances and/or occasion. These are dealt with in **7–12** below.

7.   Justification

(a) To succeed with this form of defence, the defendant must prove that the defamatory words complained of were true in substance and in fact.

(b) But the plea of justification must not be considered in a meticulous sense, and so long as the defendant meets the *sting* of the charge, he is not bound to justify anything contained in the charge which does not add to its sting: *Edwards* v. *Bell* (1824).

(c) It is no longer necessary for the defendant to prove the truth of each distinct and several defamatory imputation, so long as he can prove that a substantial portion of the allegations were true, if the remainder, whose truth is not proven, are not such as will materially injure the plaintiff's reputation (Defamation Act 1952, s. 5).

NOTE: Justification is usually an expensive from of defence; moreover, if it fails, the damages awarded are often substantially higher than they might otherwise have been. It is not, therefore, surprising that the plea of justification is rarely used.

8. Fair comment

This is a defence which is available only on matters of *public* concern. It is a defence which protects defamatory criticism or expressions of opinion, and is available not only to newspapers but to every British subject.

But a plea of fair comment cannot succeed unless the following ingredients are present:

(a) *Public interest.* The matter commented upon must be of public interest, e.g. all matters of State and politics, local government, and the conduct of public officials. etc, are properly the subject of fair comment.

(b) *Truth.* The comment must be based on facts admitted or proved to be true, and relevant to the facts; thus, truth is vital, and an honest though mistaken belief that is true is no defence: *Cooper* v. *Lawson* (1938); also *Silkin* v. *Beaverbrook Ltd* (1958). The Defamation Act 1952 (s. 6) renders it unnecessary to prove that *all* the facts were accurately stated, provided that the opinion expressed was 'fair comment' having regard to the remaining allegations which are proved to be true.

(c) *Absence of malice.* The comment must not be made maliciously, i.e. it must not be 'merely a cloak for malice': *Thomas* v. *Bradbury Agnew & Co.* (1906); for example, malice may be inferred if there is undue publication. For a definition of malice and relevant cases, *see* **10**.

(d) *Statement of opinion.* The comment must be an honest expression of the defendant's opinion, i.e. the inference which he draws from facts; if, therefore, he does not indicate that what he says is merely his comment or opinion, and not a statement of facts, he cannot get protection from a defence of fair comment.

9. Absolute privilege

This provides a complete defence, even though the statement complained of was false or malicious. The circumstances or occasions on which a plea of absolute privilege is available may be classified as:

(a) *Parliamentary*. This is privilege in respect of statements made by Members of Parliament in the House of Lords or in the House of Commons.

(b) *Statutory*. This is privilege given by statute in respect of Parliamentary documents, newspaper reports of judicial proceedings and broadcast reports of judicial proceedings.

(c) *Judicial*. This applies to statements made in civil, criminal or military courts and also in certain tribunals exercising judicial functions.

(d) *Legal professional*. This is privilege given in respect of statements made between client and legal adviser.

10. Qualified privilege

If the plaintiff can prove that the defamatory statement complained of was made maliciously, a plea of qualified privilege is of no avail to the defendant.

In *Horrocks* v. *Lowe* (1974) Lord Diplock stated that where the only evidence of malice is the contents of the defamatory speech itself, the test of malice is whether the defendant did not honestly believe what he said was true, i.e. was he either aware that it was not true or indifferent to its truth or falsity? Therefore it could be said that malice occurs where the defendant knows a statement to be false or where he is indifferent to its truth or falsity. Furthermore, where this is the case there is no need to prove whether or not the defendant intended to harm the reputation of the person defamed.

In *Egger* v. *Viscount Chelmsford* (1964) Lord Denning MR stated:

> 'It is a mistake to suppose that in a joint publication, the malice of one defendant infects his co-defendant. Each defendant is answerable severally, as well as jointly, for the joint publication, and each is entitled to his several defence whether he be sued jointly or separately from the others. If the plaintiff seeks to rely on malice to aggravate damages, or to rebut a defence of qualified privilege, or to cause a comment otherwise fair, to become unfair, he must prove malice against each person whom he charges with it. . . .'

If however, malice is not proven, qualified privilege extends to the following:

(a) *Fair and accurate reports of proceedings in Parliament,* appearing in a newspaper or elsewhere.

(b) *Fair and accurate reports of judicial proceedings* to which the public has access.

(c) *Fair and accurate reports of public meetings,* if publication is for the benefit of the public.

(d) *Statements made in discharge of a legal, moral or social duty,* to a person who has an interest in receiving such statements; thus, a former employer's reference concerning the character of the servant is protected by qualified privilege when given to a prospective employer.

> NOTE: In *Blackshaw* v. *Lord* (1983) it was held that for this purpose a report of mere general interest to the public is insufficient. The public at large has to have a legitimate interest in receiving information contained in a report and the publisher has to have a corresponding duty to publish it to the public at large. Whether such legitimate interests exist depends on the particular circumstances. In this case the defendant had no duty to publish what was then mere rumour about the plaintiff even if it were fair and accurate comment.

(e) *Fair and accurate reports of proceedings of certain courts and legislatures* outside Great Britain, etc, contained in newspapers and certain periodicals. This is an extension of the statutory defence of qualified privilege conferred by the Defamation Act 1952 (s. 7) on 'newspapers' within the statutory definition and certain periodicals (*see* **13**).

11. Unintentional defamation

The Defamation Act (s. 4) provides a remedy, which may avoid proceedings for libel or slander, where there has been unintentional defamation by publishers, printers and newspaper proprietors.

(a) It provides that a person alleged to have published defamatory words of another person may avoid proceedings for libel or slander by:

> (*i*) Showing that the words complained of were published *without intent to defame* the person making the complaint;

    (*ii*) Showing that *reasonable care had been exercised* by his servants, agents and himself; and

    (*iii*) *Offering to make amends* — by publishing (or joining in the publication of) a correction and apology.

(b) *If the offer is accepted* by the person aggrieved and performed, it will constitute a bar to further proceedings, thought not against any other person jointly responsible for the publication.

(c) *If the offer is not accepted* by the person aggrieved, the defendant must *prove* in his defence:

    (*i*) That the words complained of were published *innocently* in relation to the plaintiff;

    (*ii*) That the *offer was made as soon as practicable*, i.e. after he had notice that the words were alleged to be defamatory of the plaintiff; and

    (*iii*) That the *offer has not been withdrawn*.

(d) *An offer to publish a correction and apology* (or to join in publication with others) for the purpose of this section , must be accompanied by an affidavit, setting out the facts on which the defendant relies, to show that the words complained of were published without intent to defame, and without negligence.

NOTE: The affidavit must be carefully worded as, according to s. 4(2), no evidence apart from the facts set out in the affidavit is admissible on behalf of the defendant.

(e) *In default of agreement* between plaintiff and defendant as to the form and manner to be adopted of publishing the correction and apology, s. 4(4) provides that this may be decided by the court, whose decision shall be final.

12. Apology and payment into court

The Libel Act 1843 (also known as Lord Campbell's Act) provides a defence in an action for libel in a newspaper, i.e. by providing proof that an apology has been published or offered, and that payment has been made into court by way of amends. This has never been a popular form of defence, and as more recent legislation has provided the newspaper proprietors with more popular alternatives, it has become virtually obsolete.

Special rules as to qualified privilege

13. Protection given to newspapers

As already stated (*see* **10**), the Defamation Act (s. 7) gives a *qualified* privilege in respect of reports published in a 'newspaper' as defined in that Act.

The newspaper statements having qualified privilege are listed in a Schedule to the Act, and divided into two categories as described in **14** and **15**.

14. Schedule: Part I

Statements privileged without explanation or contradiction. These can be summarized as follows.

(a) A fair and accurate report of any proceedings in public of:
   (*i*) *The legislature* of any part of HM dominions outside Great Britain.
   (*ii*) *An international organization* of which the United Kingdom or HM Government in the United Kingdom is a member, or of any international conference to which that government sends a representative.
   (*iii*) *An international court.*
   (*iv*) *A court exercising jurisdiction* throughout any part of HM dominions outside the United Kingdom, or of any proceedings before a court-martial held outside the United Kingdom under the Naval Discipline Act 1957, the Army Act 1955, or the Air Force Act 1955.
   (*v*) *A body or person appointed to hold a public inquiry* by the government or legislature of any part of HM dominions outside the United Kingdom.

(b) A fair and accurate copy of, or extract from, any *register* kept in pursuance of any Act of Parliament which is open to inspection by the public, or any other document which is required by the law of any part of the United Kingdom to be open to inspection by the public.

(c) *A notice or advertisement* published by, or on the authority of, any court within the United Kingdom, or any judge or officer of such a court.

15. Schedule: Part II
— *Statements privileged subject to explanation or contradiction* (i.e. if the defendant has been requested by the plaintiff to publish a reasonable letter or statement by way of explanation or contradiction, and has refused or neglected to do so, or has done so in a manner regarded as inadequate or unreasonable, the provisions of s. 7 cannot be relied upon).

(a) A fair and accurate report of the decisions of any of the following associations:

(*i*) An association formed in the United Kingdom for the purpose of *promoting or encouraging the exercise of or interest in any art, science, religion or learning* . . .

(*ii*) An association formed in the United Kingdom for the purpose of *promoting or safeguarding the interests of any trade, business, industry or profession* . . .

(*iii*) An association formed in the United Kingdom for the purpose of *promoting or safeguarding the interests of any game, sport or pastime* . . .

NOTE: The decisions referred to, and in respect of which a qualified privilege is given, relate to a person who is a *member* of, or subject to by virtue of any contract to the *control* of, the association.

(b) A fair and accurate report of the *proceedings at any public meeting held in the United Kingdom,* for a lawful purpose, on a matter of public concern, whether admission be general or restricted.

(c) A fair and accurate report of the proceedings of any meeting in the United Kingdom of:

(*i*) *Any local authority,* or committee of the same.

(*ii*) *Any justice or justices of the peace,* acting otherwise than as a court exercising judicial authority.

(*iii*) *Any commission, tribunal, committee or person* appointed for the purposes of any inquiry by Act of Parliament, etc.

(*iv*) *Any person appointed by a local authority to hold a local inquiry* in pursuance of any Act of Parliament.

(*v*) *Any other tribunal, board, committee* or body constituted by any Act of Parliament.

NOTE: The meetings referred to above must *not* be meetings to which representatives of newspapers and other members of the public are denied admission.

(d) *A fair and accurate report of the proceedings at a general meeting of any company* or association constituted, registered or certified by or under any Act of Parliament, or incorporated by Royal Charter, not being a private company within the meaning of the Companies Act 1985.

(e) *A copy, or fair and accurate report or summary, of any notice* issued for the information of the public or on behalf of any government department, officer of state, local authority, or chief of police.

16. Loss of qualified privilege
The protection of s. 7 will be lost:

(a) If malice is proved by the plaintiff; or
(b) If the matter published is prohibited by law; or
(c) If the statement published is not of public concern, or not for the public benefit.

17. Interpretation of 'newspaper'
A 'newspaper' is defined in the Act, s. 7(5) as:

> 'Any paper containing public news or observations thereon, or consisting wholly or mainly of advertisements, which is printed for sale and is published in the United Kingdom, either periodically or in parts or numbers, at intervals not exceeding 36 days.'

Inference of defamation

18. Innuendo

(a) *A statement may be defamatory by innuendo*, i.e. even though it may not appear directly to cast aspersion upon a person's private character, competence or professional morals, it may have an indirect, hidden or extended meaning, commonly referred to as innuendo.
(b) The defamatory nature of such a statement need not be understood by everyone, i.e. the implication may be apparent to only a limited number of persons.
(c) The person purporting to have been defamed may not be specifically named in the statement; it is sufficient if there are some

who could reasonably be expected to *infer* that the plaintiff was the person referred to.

(d) Thus, the plaintiff, in order to prove defamation by innuendo, may be required to show:

> (*i*) That, although *prima facie* the statement complained of does not refer to him, it might reasonably, in all the surrounding circumstances, be understood to do so; or
>
> (*ii*) That, although the words used, when taken out of context, were not defamatory, they would be likely to convey a defamatory meaning when published to persons with knowledge of the circumstances. For example, a newspaper advertisement introduced a caricature of a well-known amateur golfer, together with a limerick which included his name. It was held to be defamatory, as there was an inference that he had been paid for the advertisement, and, consequently, was not entitled to retain his amateur status: *Tolley* v. *Fry & Sons Ltd* (1931).

Progress test 14

1. Define defamation, and list the defences available to the defendant in an action for defamation.   **(1)**

2. Explain briefly some of the effects of the Defamation Act 1952.   **(3, 4, 5, 6, 13)**

3. 'The greater the truth, the greater the libel.' Explain.

15
Public order, meetings and police powers

1. Public order and meetings generally

As already indicated in chapter 1, there is no positive right in law to hold a public meeting anywhere. Like many of our civil liberties, meetings, assemblies and processions are at least residual freedoms. Limitations on freedom of assembly involve the state of the law at any given time, and the way in which the law is enforced and changed. Current political thought, and the political and social stability of the country at any time will usually be reflected in the law.

When freedom of assembly is used for innocuous purposes such as expressing support for the relief of famine or poverty in poor countries it is often subject to little interference. However, where the expression of escalating dissatisfaction with government policy is the purpose of an assembly or procession, then official tolerance may wither and enforcement of the law becomes strict. The violent clashes of the 1930s between fascists and communists are an historical example of this which resulted in the provisions of the Public Order Act 1936. Events such as riots in major cities in the UK, violent industrial unrest, football hooliganism and the re-emergence of extremist organizations have, *inter alia*, led to the enactment of the Public Order Act 1986 which attempts to reform and rationalize the law relating to public order and the Football Spectators Act 1989, which controls the admission of spectators at designated football matches in England and Wales. Disorderly conduct by persons attending football matches is further provided for in the Football (Offences) Act 1991.

However, the fact that assemblies may be used as a means of achieving political change is to be expected in a democracy abounding with various interest and pressure groups.

Demonstrations have been described as 'trying to achieve by weight of numbers what cannot immediately be achieved by the ballot box'. The problem is that this sometimes becomes, for whatever reason, violent and disorderly and therefore unacceptable. Lord Scarman's Report on the inquiry into the Red Lion disorders of 1974 states:

'The fact that those who at any one time are concerned to secure the tranquillity of the streets are likely to be the majority must not lead us to deny the protestors their opportunity to march; the fact that the protestors are desperately sincere *and are exercising a fundamental human right* must not lead us to overlook the rights of the majority.'

In *Hirst* v. *Chief Constable of the West Yorkshire Police* (1986) Otton J suggested that on a proper analysis of the law, the freedom of protest on issues of public concern would be given the recognition it deserves. Similarly in *R* v. *Barnet London Borough Council ex parte Johnson and Jacobs* (1991), the court recognized that the presence of political and quasi-political groups at fairs, fetes, festivals and carnivals throughout Britain is commonplace, and that such groups are all part of community life. It was therefore improper for a local authority to impose conditions on a festival held in a public park which excluded such groups.

2. Preservation of order

(a) In most meetings, disorder can be traced to the following principal causes:

(i) *Organized opposition.* This consists of people whose main object is to disturb or even break up a meeting. Usually they prefer to congregate at the back of the meeting. If this is apparent before the meeting starts, the stewards must ensure that such people are kept to the front of the meeting and kept apart as much as possible. This weakens their organization and, if they do attempt a disturbance, it simplifies the work of the 'chuckers-out'.

(ii) *Irrelevant interruption of speeches.* Some of these may be of a violent character, but in most cases they are caused by audible running commentaries or by small groups of members who form themselves into 'whispering sub-committees'. Both of these distract and annoy, but a tactful chairman ought to be able to quell these disturbances without calling upon the stewards.

(*iii*) *Intolerant speakers* may make insulting remarks concerning those who are opposed to them. In such cases, it is the chairman's task to deal tactfully with the situation, otherwise, if the speaker is allowed to continue on the same lines, the subsequent speeches will almost certainly develop into a 'slanging match', and the meeting will end in disorder.

(b) If the chairman is unable to preserve order under his own powers, e.g. by adjournment, (*see John* v. *Rees* (1969)) he may, in certain circumstances, seek the statutory remedies provided by the Acts discussed below.

Legislative provisions

3. Public Meeting Act 1908 and Representation of the People Act 1983

(a) The remaining provision of the 1908 Act is as follows.

(*i*) Any person who at a lawful public meeting acts in a disorderly manner for the purpose of preventing the transaction of the business for which the meeting was called together shall be guilty of an offence: s. 1.

(*ii*) Any person who *incites* others to commit an offence under this section shall be guilty of a like offence.

(b) Thus, the Act makes *deliberate interruption* of a public meeting an offence, and imposes appropriate penalties.

(c) If a police officer reasonably suspects a person of committing an offence under the Public Meeting Act 1908, he may, *at the request of the chairman*, demand immediately the person's name and address. If the person concerned *refuses* such request or gives a false name and address, he commits an offence.

(d) *Disturbance at election meetings.* This is covered by the Representation of the People Act 1983, s. 97. It is an *illegal practice* to act in a disorderly manner or to incite others to do so for the purpose of preventing the transaction of business of:

(*i*) a political meeting held in any constituency between the date of the issue of a writ for the return of a member of

Parliament for the constituency and the date at which a return to the writ is made;

(*ii*) a meeting held with reference to a local government election in the electoral area for that election from the last date on which notice of the election may be published and ending with the day of election.

A constable has powers similar to those discussed under the 1908 Act. That Act does not apply to meetings covered by s. 97 of the 1983 Act.

4. The Public Order Act 1936

(a) The purposes of this Act are clearly stated in its title as 'An Act *to prohibit the wearing of uniforms* in connection with political objects and the maintenance by private persons of associations of military or similar character; and to make further provision for the preservation of public order on the occasion of *public processions* and in public places' (authors' italics).

However the Act is now largely repealed and superseded by the Public Order Act 1986.

(b) The main effect of the Act's remaining provisions is to forbid:

(*i*) The wearing of uniforms in connection with political objects.

(*ii*) Quasi-military organizations.

5. Main provisions of the Public Order Act 1936

The following are the remaining provisions of the Act in greater detail.

(a) *Political uniforms* (s. 1): A person is guilty of an offence who, in any public place or at any public meeting, wears a uniform which signifies his association with any political organization or with the promotion of any political object. As to what constitutes a uniform. *see* the discussion in *O'Moran* v. *DPP* (1975) and in *Whelan* v. *DPP* (1975).

But the chief of police may, with the consent of the Secretary of State, permit the wearing of a uniform at ceremonial, anniversary or other occasions, if he is satisfied that there is no risk of public disorder. Organizations such as the Boy Scouts' Association are non-political and are not concerned with the promotion of political objects.

(b) *Quasi-military organizations* (s. 2): If members or followers of an association (whether incorporated or not) are organized, trained or equipped for employment in usurping the functions of the police, or of the armed forced of the Crown; or are organized and trained or organized and equipped for employment in the use or display of force to promote a political object, or in such manner as to cause a reasonable apprehension of such purpose, then any person who takes part in the control or management of the association or in the organizing or training, is guilty of an offence. This does not prevent the convenors of a public meeting on private premises from employing a reasonable number of stewards to preserve order; nor does it prevent the giving of instructions to them as to their duties, nor the provision of badges or other distinguishing signs, s. 2(6) of the 1936 Act.

6. Definitions in the Public Order Act 1936
The following are defined in the Act.

(a) *Meetings:* 'A meeting held for the purpose of the discussion of matters of public interest, or for the purpose of the expression of views on such matters.'

(b) *Public meetings:* 'Any meeting in a public place and any meeting which the public or a section thereof are permitted to attend, whether on payment or otherwise.'

(c) *Private premises:* 'Premises to which the public have access, whether on payment or otherwise, only by permission of the owner, occupier or lessee of the premises.'

7. The Public Order Act 1986
By s. 9 of this Act the common law offences of riot, rout, unlawful assembly and affray were abolished. They were replaced by the following.

8. Riot and violent disorder.

(a) *Riot.* This offence is committed:
    (*i*) where 12 or more persons are present together, and
    (*ii*) they use or threaten unlawful violence for a common purpose (*see* **(f)**), and
    (*iii*) the conduct of them (taken together) is such as would

cause a person of reasonable firmness present at the scene
(*see* (**f**)) to fear for his personal safety.

Where these circumstances arise, each of the persons using
unlawful violence for the common purpose is guilty of riot: s. 1.

(**b**) *Mental element (mens rea) of riot.* A person is guilty of riot only
if he intends to use violence or is aware that his conduct may be
violent (s. 6). This does not affect the determination for the
purposes of riot of the number of persons who use or threaten
violence (s. 6). Therefore it appears that where 12 or more persons
are involved in the riot and only one or two of those are
apprehended and are proved to have intended to use violence or
are proved to be aware that their conduct may have been violent,
they are guilty of riot even though the others involved have not
been apprehended and proved to have the necessary *mens rea*. In
Kamara v. *DPP* (1974) Lord Hailsham said that riot can take place
in enclosed premises and may be committed in private.

(**c**) *Director of Public Prosecutions.* A prosecution of an offence of
riot or incitement to riot may only be instituted by or with the
consent of the Director of Public Prosecutions.

(**d**) *Violent disorder.* The offence is committed:
  (*i*) where three or more persons are present together, and
  (*ii*) they use or threaten unlawful violence, and
  (*iii*) the conduct of them (taken together) is such as would
       cause a person of reasonable firmness present at the scene
       to fear for his personal safety.

If these conditions hold, then each of the persons using or
threatening unlawful violence is guilty of violent disorder: s. 2.
Where a trial involves three or more defendants and the jury are
unable to decide upon the guilt of more than two of them, a
direction should be made to acquit all of the defendants: *R* v.
Fleming and Robinson (1989).

The important distinction between riot and violent disorder
is that in the latter there is no requirement of a 'common purpose'.

(**e**) *Mental element (mens rea) of violent disorder.* A person is guilty of
violent disorder only if he intends to use or threaten violence or
is aware that his conduct may be violent or threatens violence. As
with riot the determination of the number of persons who use or
threaten violence is not affected by this mental element: s. 6(7).

(**f**) *Common elements of riot and violent disorder.*

(*i*) It is immaterial whether or not those involved use or threaten unlawful violence simultaneously.

(*ii*) It is not necessary that a person of reasonable firmness is, or is likely to be, present at the scene of the offence.

(*iii*) Both riot and violent disorder may be committed in private as well as in public places.

(*iv*) Both riot and violent disorder are arrestable offences (*see* **31(d)**).

9. Affray

(**a**) *The common elements* in **8(f)** (*ii*) and (*iii*) also apply to affray (s. 3). A person is guilty of affray if he uses or threatens unlawful violence towards another and his conduct is such as would cause a person of reasonable firmness present at the scene to fear for his personal safety. The following points should be noted:

(*i*) One person acting on his own is sufficient for affray.

(*ii*) Where two or more persons use or threaten the unlawful violence of all of them together must be considered.

(*iii*) The use of words alone is insufficient to amount to a threat for the purposes of affray.

(**b**) *The mental element (mens rea) of affray.* This is the same as for violent disorder except that s. 6(7) does not apply to affray.

10. Fear or provocation of violence

(**a**) *A person is guilty of an offence* where he either uses towards another person threatening, abusive or insulting words or behaviour, or distributes or displays to another person any writing, sign or other visible representation which is threatening, abusive or insulting, *and he does so:*

(*i*) with intent to cause that person to believe that immediate unlawful violence will be used against him or another by any person or another, or

(*ii*) to provoke the immediate use of unlawful violence by that person or another, or

(*iii*) whereby that person is likely to believe that such violence will be used or it is likely that such violence will be provoked: s. 4.

(b) *Mental element (mens rea) of fear or provocation of violence.* A person is guilty of this offence only if:

    (*i*) he intends his words or behaviour, or the writing, sign or other visible representation to be threatening, abusive or insulting, or

    (*ii*) he is aware that it may be threatening, abusive or insulting: s. 6.

(c) *General.* Fear or provocation of violence may be committed in a public or private place. However, where the words or behaviour or writing, etc are used, distributed or displayed by a person inside a dwelling, there is no offence if the other person is also inside that or another dwelling (s. 4). If on the other hand the persons affected are part of a passing procession, then the fact that, for example an abusive or insulting sign is placed in the front window of a dwelling will not itself be a defence.

The words 'uses towards another person' mean 'uses in the presence of and in the direction of another person directly'. The words must be addressed directly at another who is present and either in earshot or aimed at and being punitively in earshot: *Atkin* v. *DPP* (1989). The words 'such violence' mean 'immediate unlawful violence' and immediate does not mean 'instantaneous': *R v. Horseferry Road Magistrates Court ex parte Siudatan* (1990).

11. Harassment, alarm or distress

(a) *Where a person either:*

    (*i*) uses threatening, abusive or insulting words or behaviour, or

    (*ii*) displays any writing, sign or other visible representation which is threatening, abusive or insulting;

within the hearing or sight of a person likely to be caused harassment, alarm or distress thereby, he is guilty of an offence: s. 5.

(b) *Mental element (mens rea) of harassment, alarm or distress.* A person is guilty of this offence only if:

    (*i*) he intends his words or behaviour, or the writing, sign or visible representation to be threatening, abusive or insulting, or

    (*ii*) he is aware that it may be threatening, abusive or insulting, or (*iii*) he intends his behaviour to be or is aware that it may be disorderly: s. 6.

(c) *General aspects of the offence*. An offence under s. 5 may also be committed where the prohibited activities are carried out by a person inside a dwelling and the person likely to be caused harassment. alarm or distress thereby is also inside that or another dwelling.

(d) *Defence*. It is a defence for the accused to prove:
   (*i*) that he had no reason to believe that there was any person within hearing or sight who was likely to be caused harassment, alarm or distress, or
   (*ii*) that he was inside a dwelling and had no reason to believe that the words or behaviour used, or the writing, sign or visible representation displayed, would be heard or seen by a person outside that or in any other dwelling, or
   (*iii*) that his conduct was reasonable: s. 4.

(e) *Arrest*. A police constable may arrest a person without a warrant if:
   (*i*) he engages in further offensive conduct which the constable warns him to stop, *and*
   (*ii*) he engages in further offensive conduct immediately or shortly after the warning: s. 5.

The further conduct need not be of the same nature as the first offensive conduct. 'Offensive conduct' means that which the constable reasonably suspects to constitute an offence under s. 5. An offence under s. 5 requires an element of alarm to a third party. It is not necessary for that third party to feel alarm for himself, it is enough if he feels it for someone else: *Lodge* v. *DPP* (1988).

Although a police officer can be a 'person likely to be caused harassment alarm or distress' by another's 'threatening insulting or abusive behaviour', if the officer is not caused harassment, alarm or distress by such words or behaviour, it is unlikely that he will be able to arrest a person under s. 5(4), since if there is no one else in the area, the officer cannot be in a position to suspect that an offence under s. 5(1) has been committed: *DPP* v. *Orum* (1988). In *R* v. *Ball* (1990) it was said that there is an important difference between s. 5 and s. 4. Unlike s. 4, conduct under s. 5 does not have to be directed towards another person; it is enough that another person would be likely to be harassed. The test under s. 5 is objective throughout.

The deposit of a letter containing threatening, abusive or insulting words through a letter box does not amount to an offence under s. 5 since the conduct in question takes place inside a dwelling house: *Chappell* v. *DPP* (1989).

12. Intoxication

This means any intoxication whether caused by drink, drugs or other means, or by a combination of means: s. 6.

For the purpose of the mental element of any of the offences under ss. 1–5, a person whose awareness is impaired by intoxication shall be taken to be aware of that of which he would be aware if not intoxicated. However, this will not be the case if the accused shows either:

(a) that the intoxication was not self-induced, or
(b) that it was caused solely by the taking or administration of a substance in the course of medical treatment: s. 6.

13. Violence

(a) *For the purposes of offences under ss. 1–5* violence means any violent conduct, including violent conduct towards property as well as towards persons. This does not apply to affray where the unlawful violence must be towards another person.
(b) *Violence is not restricted to conduct causing or intended to cause injury or damage* but includes any other violent conduct. An example of this is throwing at or towards a person a missile of a kind capable of causing injury, even where it falls short of the target or hits someone else: s. 8.

14. Dwelling

(a) This means any structure or part of a structure occupied as a person's home or as other living accommodation.
(b) This is so whether the occupation is separate or shared with others.
(c) However, any part of a structure which is not occupied as a person's home or as other living accommodation is not a dwelling.
(d) 'Structure' includes a tent, caravan, vehicle, vessel or other temporary or movable structure: s. 8.

15. Breach of the peace
The Public Order Act 1986 does not affect the common law powers in England and Wales to deal with or to prevent a breach of the peace: s. 40.

(a) *Meaning.* 'Breach of the peace' is a traditional legal expression and is a grounds of arrest. It occurs:
  (*i*) whenever harm is actually done or is likely to be done to a person, or in his presence to his property, or
  (*ii*) when a person is in fear of being so harmed through an assault, an affray, a riot or other disturbance (e.g. violent disorder, fear or provocation of violence).

This definition was given by the Court of Criminal Appeal in *R* v. *Howell* (1981).

(b) *Arrest.* 'Every citizen in whose presence a breach of the peace is being, or reasonably appears is about to be, committed has the right to take reasonable steps to make the person who is breaking or threatening to break the peace refrain from doing so; and those reasonable steps in appropriate cases will include detaining him against his will.' Therefore anyone can arrest at common law for a breach of the peace: *Albert* v. *Lavin* (1981). *See also Howell's* case above, *Lansbury* v. *Riley* (1914), *Beatty* v. *Gillbanks* (1882), *Wise* v. *Dunning* (1902), *Marsh* v. *Arscott* (1982), *Grant* v. *Taylor* (1986) and other relevant cases.

Where a police officer genuinely suspects on reasonable grounds that a breach of the peace is likely to occur inside private premises he is entitled to exercise his common law power to arrest for breach of the peace without a warrant: *McConnell* v. *Chief Constable of Greater Manchester police* (1990). *See also Thomas* v. *Sawkins* (1935). Whether a constable's belief that a breach of the peace is likely is reasonable or not must take into account the circumstances in which the constable makes a spur of the moment decision: *G* v. *Chief Superintendent of Police, Stroud* (1986).

(c) *Obstruction of constables.* Any person who assaults, resists or wilfully obstructs a constable in the execution of his duty is guilty of an offence: the Police Act 1964, s. 51. The difficult aspect of this offence is determining when a police constable is acting in the course of his duty. However, the most important application of this provision in the context of meetings is when a constable exercises his duty to prevent breaches of the peace which he reasonably apprehends: *Duncan* v. *Jones* (1936). If it appears:

(*i*) that facts existed from which a constable could reasonably have anticipated a breach, as a real and not merely as a remote possibility, and

(*ii*) that he did so anticipate,

then he is under a duty to take such steps whether by arrest or otherwise as he reasonably thinks necessary. *See King* v. *Hodges* (1974) and *Piddington* v. *Bates* (1960).

A constable may be under a duty to give instructions to members of the public, for example to remove an obstruction from the highway. No breach of the peace may be anticipated but a deliberate refusal to obey such an instruction may amount to an obstruction of the police. *See Stunt* v. *Bolton* (1972), and, in relation to picketing, *Kavanagh* v. *Hiscock* (1974).

In *Newrot and Shaler* v. *DPP* (1988) it was held, *inter alia*, that there was no power of arrest for abusing a constable and, where there is no evidence that the constable believed a breach of the peace had occurred or was likely, attempting to escape should not be unlawful when the arrest was unlawful.

16. Picketing

(a) In *Hubbard* v. *Pitt* (1976) the defendants, a local pressure group, picketed the offices of a firm of estate agents by standing before them in a line along the public footway holding placards and distributing leaflets. There was room on either side of the picket line and between individual members of it for the public to pass along or across the footway. An injunction was granted by Forbes J on the basis that the right to picket was confined to picketing in connection with an industrial dispute. The Court of Appeal disapproved of this basis but the majority upheld the grant of an interlocutory injunction on the grounds that the defendants may be committing a private nuisance. Lord Denning dissenting said that the right to picket is not confined to industrial disputes and is lawful so long as it is done merely to obtain or communicate information or peacefully to persuade. The right to demonstrate and protest were, in his view, rights which it is in the public interest that individuals should possess and exercise without impediment so long as no wrongful act is done. This line of reasoning was followed to some extent in *Hirst* v. *Chief Constable of West Yorkshire Police* where a group of animals' rights supporters picketed a shop and distributed leaflets. Their appeal against conviction for the offence of wilfully obstructing the highway under the Highways Act 1980, s. 137, was successful on the basis that the Crown Court failed to consider whether the obstruction was without lawful authority or excuse (per Glidewell LJ). Otton J said that the right to demonstrate and protest on matters of public concern are rights which it is in the public interest that individuals should possess and exercise without impediment, as long as no wrongful act is done and there is no obstruction to traffic. The correct approach to s. 137 is to ask:

(*i*) whether there was an obstruction of the highway, which included any occupation, unless *de minimis*, of part of the road;

(*ii*) whether the obstruction was wilful in the sense of deliberate; and

(*iii*) whether the obstruction was without lawful authority or excuse, which covered activities otherwise lawful in themselves that might or might not be reasonable depending on all the circumstances.

(b) Regarding industrial disputes, the question whether a picket is in furtherance or contemplation of a trade dispute and therefore protected from civil action against the union is beyond the scope of this book. However, it has always been clear that pickets, like anyone else, are liable for crimes of violence and disorder. The miners' strike and scenes at Wapping in London in relation to the printers' dispute in the early 1980s illustrate the fragile line that divides the 'law of picketing' from 'public order laws'. This narrow line is made more obscure by offences such as fear or provocation of violence and harassment, alarm or distress under the Public Order Act 1986. Picketing peacefully to persuade may easily turn into picketing to obstruct or intimidate in the sense of these offences.

17. Racial hatred

Acts intended or likely to stir up racial hatred are covered by Part III of the Public Order Act 1986. Racial hatred means hatred against a group of persons in Great Britain defined by reference to colour, race, nationality (including citizenship) or ethnic or national origins: s. 17.

Offences under Part III of the Public Order Act most relevant to meetings

18. Use of words or behaviour or display of written material

(a) A person who uses threatening, abusive or insulting words or behaviour or displays any written material which is threatening, abusive or insulting is guilty of an offence if:

> (*i*) he intends thereby to stir up racial hatred, or
>
> (*ii*) having regard to all the circumstances, racial hatred is likely to be stirred up by his behaviour or display: s. 18.

(b) This offence may be committed in a public or a private place. No offence is committed where the words or behaviour are used, or the written material is displayed, by a person inside a dwelling and are not seen except by other persons in that or another dwelling.

(c) *Defences.*

> (*i*) Where the accused proved that he was inside a dwelling and had no reason to believe that the words or material used or the written material displayed would be heard or seen by a person outside that or any other dwelling, he has a defence to an action under s. 18.
>
> (*ii*) A person who is not shown to have intended to stir up racial hatred is not guilty of an offence under this section if he did not intend his words or behaviour or the written material to be threatening, abusive or insulting and was not aware that it might do so: s. 18.

19. Distributing written material

(a) *A person* who publishes or distributes written material which is threatening, abusive or insulting is guilty of an offence if he intends to stir up racial hatred or if racial hatred is likely to be stirred up: s. 19.

(b) *Publication or distribution* of written material means for these purposes its publication or distribution to the public or a section of the public.

(c) *Defence*. It is a defence for the accused who is not shown to have intended to stir up racial hatred to prove that he was not aware of the content of the material and did not suspect, and had no reason to suspect, that it was threatening, abusive or insulting.

20. Possession of racially inflammatory material; s. 23
This section may be used against those who are present at meetings and in possession of racially inflammatory material but are not caught in the act of distributing it.

21. Processions and assemblies
The Public Order Act 1986 gives the police wide powers of control over processions and assemblies and as already indicated much depends on the exercise of discretion by the police.

22. Advance notice of public processions: s. 11
(a) *Advance notice* is required of any proposal to hold a public procession intended:
> (*i*) to demonstrate support for, or opposition to, the views or actions of any person or body of persons, or
> (*ii*) to publicize a cause or campaign, or
> (*iii*) to mark or commemorate an event;

unless it is not reasonably practicable to give any advance notice of the procession: s. 11.

(b) *Exceptions*. Notice is not required by s. 11 where the procession is one which is commonly or customarily held in that area or is a funeral procession organized by a funeral director acting in the normal course of his business: s. 11.

(c) *The notice*.
> (*i*) *Contents*. The notice must specify the date when it is intended to hold the procession, the time when it is intended to start it, its proposed route and the name and address of at least one of the persons proposing to organize it.
> (*ii*) *Service*. The notice must be delivered to a police station in the police area in which it is proposed the procession will start. If delivered not less than six clear days before the date when the procession is intended to be held, the notice may be delivered by post by the recorded delivery service.

However, the Interpretation Act 1978, s. 7 does not apply (*see* chapters 6 and 7). If the notice is not delivered as stated above it *must* be delivered by hand not less than six clear days before the date when the procession is intended to be held or, if that is not reasonably practicable, as soon as delivery is reasonably practicable.

(d) *Offences under s. 11.* Each of the persons organizing a public procession is guilty of an offence if the requirements as to notice have not been satisfied or the date, time of starting or route of the procession differ from those specified in the notice.

(e) *Defences.*

    (*i*) It is a defence for the accused to prove that he neither knew of, suspected nor had reason to suspect, the failure to satisfy the requirements as to notice or the difference of time, date or route.

    (*ii*) To the extent that an alleged offence turns on a difference of date, time or route it is a defence to prove that the difference arose from circumstances beyond his control or from something done with the agreement of a police officer or by his direction.

23. Imposing conditions on public processions

(a) *If the senior police officer* reasonably believes:

    (*i*) that a public procession may result in serious public disorder, serious damage to property or serious disruption to the life of the community, or

    (*ii*) the purpose of those organizing the procession is the intimidation of others with a view to compelling them to refrain from an act they have the right to do, or to do an act they have the right not to do,

he may give directions imposing conditions on the organizers of the procession and those taking part. The conditions may be such as appear to the senior police officer necessary to prevent (*i*) and (*ii*) above. These may include conditions as to the route of the procession or prohibiting it from entering any public place specified in the directions.

The senior police officer must have regard to the time or place at which and the circumstances in which any public procession is being held or is intended to be held, and to its route or proposed route: s. 12.

(b) *Offence.* It is an offence for persons who organize and/or take part in a public procession knowingly to fail to comply with a condition imposed under s. 12.

(c) *Defence.* It is a defence for a person organizing and/or taking part in a public procession to prove that the failure to comply with a condition arose from circumstances beyond his control: s. 12.

(d) *Incitement.* A person who incites another taking part in a procession to fail to comply with a condition is guilty of an offence: s. 12.

(e) *The senior police officer.* This means:

> (*i*) in relation to a procession being held, or intended to be held in a case where persons are assembling with a view to taking part in it, the most senior in rank of the police officers present at the scene;
>
> (*ii*) in relation to a procession intended to be held but not falling within (*i*) above, the chief officer of police. In these circumstances the direction must be given in writing: s. 12.

24. Prohibiting public processions: s. 13.

(a) *Within the provinces.* If the chief officer of police reasonably believes that the powers under s. 12 will not be sufficient to prevent serious public disorder resulting from the holding of a public procession then he shall apply for a prohibition order. The procedure is:

> (*i*) application by the chief officer of police to the council of the district for an order prohibiting the holding of all, or a specified class, of public processions in the district or part concerned. The prohibition may be for such period not exceeding three months as may be specified in the application;
>
> (*ii*) on receiving the application, a council may with the consent of the Secretary of State make an order either in the terms of the application or with such modification as may be approved by the Secretary of State: s. 13.

(b) *Within the City of London or the Metropolitan police district.* Where the Commissioner of Police for the City of London or the

Commissioner of Police for the Metropolis reasonably believes that the powers under s. 12 will not be sufficient to prevent serious public disorder resulting from the holding of a public procession he may with the consent of the Secretary of State make an order similar to the one in (*i*) above.

(c) *Basis of reasonable belief.* The Act simply states 'because of particular circumstances existing in any district or part of a district (or in London "in his police area or part of it"). No further guidance is given on what may amount to particular circumstances. This appears to give considerable discretion to the police, subject of course to any check imposed by the Secretary of State and/or the council.

(d) *Revocation of orders.* Orders may be revoked or varied in the same way that they are made.

(e) *Writing.* Any order made under s. 13 must be recorded in writing as soon as practicable after being made.

(f) *Offences.* A person who organized or takes part in a public procession, the holding of which he knows is prohibited by an order made under s. 13, is guilty of an offence. It is also an offence to incite a person to take part in a public procession which is prohibited: s. 13.

25. Imposing conditions on public assemblies: s. 14.

(a) *If the senior police officer,* having regard to the time or place at which and the circumstances in which any public assembly is being held or intended to be held, reasonably believes the sort of disorder referred to in **23** above will result then he may give directions imposing on the persons organizing or taking part in the assembly such conditions — as to the place at which the assembly may be (or may continue to be) held, the maximum duration of the assembly, the maximum number of people who may constitute it — as appear to the senior police officer necessary to prevent disorder, damage, disruption or intimidation: s. 14.

In imposing conditions there must be relevant evidence on which the senior police officer forms his judgment. In *Police* v. *Reid* (1987), the defendant was charged with knowingly failing to comply with a condition imposed on a public assembly. The senior officer gave evidence that he defined intimidation as putting people in fear of discomfort. The court held that the issue was whether demonstrators acted with a view to compelling visitors not to go into South Africa House or merely with the intention of making them feel uncomfortable. The latter was not intimidation. Since the senior officer did not claim that they acted with a view to compelling, he had no grounds for imposing the condition and the case was dismissed.

(b) *Senior police officer* has the same meaning as in **23(e)** above.

(c) *Writing*. Any direction given by a chief officer of police in relation to an assembly intended to be held must be given in writing.

(d) *Offence*. A person who organizes or who takes part in a public assembly and knowingly fails to comply with a condition imposed under this section is guilty of an offence. It is also an offence to incite a person taking part in a public assembly knowingly to fail to comply with a condition imposed under s. 14.

26. Delegation of powers

The chief officer of police may delegate to such extent, and subject to such condition as he may specify, any of his functions under ss. 12–14 to a deputy or assistant chief constable or in the City of London and the Metropolitan Police District to an Assistant Commissioner of Police: s. 15.

27. Definitions

(a) *Public assembly* means an assembly of 20 or more persons in a public place which is wholly or partly open to the air.

(b) *Public place* means any highway or any place to which at the material time the public or any section of the public has access, on payment or otherwise, as of right or by virtue of express or implied permission.

Cases on the meaning of public place decided on the basis of the definition in the 1936 Act may still be of assistance. These include *Crawley* v. *Frost* (1976) where it was decided that a football ground could be a 'public place', while in *R* v. *Edwards and Roberts* (1978) it was decided that although the public may be able to obtain access to private premises through the private front garden of a house if they have some lawful purpose for so doing, this will *not* make such gardens public places within the definition. Finally, in

Lawrenson v. *Oxford* (1981) it was held that a public house was a public place within the meaning of the Act:

> 'The references to "permission" and "payment or otherwise" do, in my view, indicate that it is not necessary to go so far as to say that once a person becomes an invitee, the place cannot be regarded as a "public place". There will be places where the public can be excluded, but when they are not excluded, they are a "public place" for the purpose of the definition contained in the Act' (Woolf J).

See also Law Commission Working Paper No. 82 (Offences against Public Order), para. 4.27.

(c) *Public procession* means a procession in a public place.

NOTE: For definition of meetings and public meetings under the 1936 Act, *see* **6**.

Police powers

28. Police powers and duties

The powers and duties of the police relating to entry of meeting places, and the arrest or removal of disorderly persons, were not by any means clearly defined, and obviously depended upon where the meeting was held. The position of common law and under various recent statutory provisions is summarized in the following paragraphs.

29. Meetings held in public places

The police may:

(a) *Remove or arrest* individuals or disperse the meetings, where a breach of the peace occurs, or is reasonably anticipated.

(b) *Exercise the necessary authority* to prevent obstruction.

(c) *By the provisions of the Public Order Acts 1936 and 1986* arrest without warrant anyone a constable reasonably suspects is committing the following offences.

    (*i*) 1936 Act: Prohibitions on uniforms: s. 1.

    (*ii*) 1986 Act: Affray: s. 3; fear or provocation of violence: s. 4; breach of conditions imposed on public processions and incitement thereto: s. 12; breach of prohibition imposed on public processions and incitement thereto: s. 13; breach of conditions imposed on public assemblies and incitement thereto: s. 14; use of words or behaviour or display of written material (racial hatred): s. 18.

For the grounds of arrest for an offence under s. 5: harassment, alarm or distress, *see* 11(e) above.

For the purposes of ss. 12, 13 and 14 *the constable must be in uniform.*

(d) *Arrest without warrant for arrestable offences.* The Police and Criminal Evidence Act 1984 (s. 24) states that *any person may arrest without a warrant:*

   (*i*) anyone who is in the act of committing an arrestable offence, and

   (*ii*) anyone he has reasonable grounds for suspecting to be committing such an offence.

Where an arrestable offence has been committed, anyone who is guilty of the offence or whom the person arresting has reasonable grounds for suspecting to be guilty, may also be arrested without a warrant. In addition, a constable may arrest anyone who is about to commit an arrestable offence or anyone whom he has reasonable grounds for suspecting to be about to commit such an offence. A constable may also arrest suspects when he has reasonable grounds for suspecting that an arrestable offence has been committed.

An arrestable offence means an offence for which the sentence is fixed by law, e.g. murder or treason; for which a person of 21 years of age or over (not previously convicted) may be sentenced to imprisonment for a term of 5 years; and certain statutory offences referred to in s. 2, Police and Criminal Evidence Act 1984.

NOTE: Riot and violent disorder are arrestable offences.

30. Meetings held on private property

(a) The powers and duties of the police in relation to meetings held on private property (whether held for public purposes or not) were stated in a Home Office report of 1909, namely:

   (*i*) The police have no power to enter, except by leave of the occupiers of the premises or promoters of the meeting — or where they have reason to believe that a breach of the peace is being committed.

(*ii*) Although it is no part of the police duties to eject trespassers from private premises, they *may* (in their capacity as private citizens) assist in ejecting them, if requested to do so by the occupiers of the premises or promoters of the meeting — but they are not under legal obligation to do so.

(*iii*) Where there is an actual breach of the peace, they may, and indeed have a duty to , intervene. In that event, even if they have not seen any such breach committed, they may arrest without warrant a person charged by another for such a breach, where there are reasonable grounds to anticipate that the breach is likely to be continued or immediately renewed.

Private property would include a *public* building which has been hired by the convenors of the meeting for the occasion.

(b) *The decision in Thomas* v. *Sawkins* (1935) modified the somewhat narrow interpretation of police powers stated above; in this case:

(*i*) The police forced their way into a public meeting held in a hall hired by the promoter for the occasion, having been refused permission by the promoter.

(*ii*) The promoter brought an action for technical assault.

(*iii*) *It was held* that the police are empowered to enter a meeting held on private premises, not only where a breach of the peace has been or is being committed, but also when they have reasonable grounds for believing that a breach of the peace is *likely to be* committed.

(c) Although the position may vary considerably between local authorities, the assistance of the police in controlling meetings on private property can usually be procured, so long as the promoters are prepared to meet the cost of such special service.

(d) Several years ago, however, the Home Office, showing some concern over frequent cases of organized interference at political meetings, suggested that the police should (at the invitation of the promoters), be present at such meetings without charge, when it is anticipated that there will be interference which would be likely to lead to a breach of the peace.

31. The Police and Criminal Evidence Act 1984, s. 17: entry and search without search warrant

This provides that a constable who has reasonable grounds for believing that the person whom he is seeking is on the premises may enter and search the premises, using such reasonable force as is necessary for the purpose:

(a) of executing
  (*i*) a warrant of arrest issued in connection with or arising out of criminal proceedings; or
  (*ii*) a warrant of commitment issued under s. 76 of the Magistrates' Courts Act 1980;
(b) of arresting a person for an arrestable offence, *see* **31(d)**;
(c) of arresting a person for an offence under
  (*i*) s. 1 of the Public Order Act 1936 (prohibition of uniforms in connection with political objects);
  (*ii*) s. 4 of the Public Order Act 1986 (fear or provocation of violence);
  (*iii*) any enactment contained in ss. 6 to 8 or 10 of the Criminal Law Act 1977 (offences relating to entering and remaining on property). Only a constable in uniform may exercise powers of entry and search for this purpose;
(d) of recapturing a person who is unlawfully at large and whom he is pursuing; or
(e) of saving life or limb or preventing serious damage to property (the reasonable belief requirement does not apply to **(e)**). The power to search is only a power to search to the extent that is reasonably required for the purpose for which the power of entry is exercised. For the purposes of **(c)** (*iii*), the right of entry and search are only exercisable by a constable in uniform.
(f) dealing with a breach of the peace. When this section became law all the rules of common law under which a constable had power to enter premises without a warrant were abolished *except* for any power of entry to deal with or prevent a breach of the peace. For revised codes of practice concerning statutory powers of stop and search, searching of premises etc., see P. & C.E. Act 1984 (Codes of Practice) (No. 2) Order 1990 (No. 2580).

Public meetings on private premises

32. Promoter's rights
Where a public meeting is held on *private* premises (including

public premises hired by the promoter for the occasion), the promoter's right of expulsion may be summarized as follows.

(a) *Where no admission charge is made*, any person who attends does so only by leave of the promoter; consequently:

(*i*) *He can be requested to leave the meeting* at any time, whether he has behaved in an orderly manner or not.

(*ii*) *If he refuses to leave*, or fails to do so within a reasonable time, he becomes a *trespasser*, and may be forcibly removed. Only reasonable force may be used, otherwise the person forcibly removed may bring an action for assault, as in *Collins* v. *Revision* (1754); *see also Lucas* v. *Mason* (1875).

(b) *Where a charge for admission has been made* to enter private premises, the person paying the admission charge is obviously in a much stronger position:

(*i*) If he is improperly requested to withdraw, or improperly ejected, he is entitled to sue the promoters for breach of contract, i.e. for the cost of admission: *Wood* v. *Leadbetter* (1845).

(*ii*) If he has conducted himself properly and observed the conditions contained in his contract with the promoters, his licence conferring admission to the premises cannot be revoked before its purpose has been achieved and, if, as in *Hurst* v. *Picture Palaces* (1913), after refusing to withdraw, he is ejected, he may bring an action for assault.

(c) *To summarize* the position:

(*i*) The promoter has a right to request a person to leave a meeting held on private premises; if, however, he has paid for admission, his expulsion from a meeting can be legally justified only on the grounds of his failure to conduct himself in a proper manner.

(*ii*) In either case, i.e. whether he paid an admission charge or not, and whatever the grounds for his expulsion, only reasonable force may be used.

33. Attendance of outsiders and admission of the press
This subject is considered in chapter 38.

Progress test 15

1. What is a public meeting? Is there a right at common law to hold meetings in public places? **(2)**

2. Explain briefly some of the more important provisions of the Public Order Act 1986. **(7)**

3. What do you understand by the term 'public meeting'? Would a meeting of a company or of a registered body be so regarded? Name any circumstances where common law rights (if any) in this connection are affected by statute. **(6)**

4. Is there any general right to assemble in a public place, or a right to meet on the public highway? Does this prevent a meeting being held in either of the two places? Give the reasons supporting your contention. **(8)**

5. What is a 'public assembly' and a 'public procession' and what conditions may be imposed on them? **(21–27)**

6. Does the law recognize the right to demonstrate and protest and, if so, to what extent? **(16)**

Part three

Company meetings

16
Companies and company meetings

NOTE: In this Part, unless otherwise indicated, section numbers refer to the Companies Act 1985, as amended.

Introduction to company law

1. Company law

Company law in the United Kingdom is contained in the Companies Act 1985 as well as in a huge body of case law. This great consolidating Act has already been overtaken by more recent legislation affecting company law. One of the more important of these is the Insolvency Act 1986 which reformed the law relating to company meetings during the course of winding up.

Other relevant legislation includes the Company Directors Disqualification Act 1986 and the Financial Services Act 1986. More recently the Companies Act 1989 introduced some important changes with far reaching effects on the law of company meetings, in particular the introduction of the 'Elective Regime' for private companies.

The provisions of these Acts in so far as they are relevant to meetings are dealt with in this section. Further changes in company law will follow as EC directives are implemented in United Kingdom law. The most far reaching of these from the point of view of meetings is the Fifth EC Directive on Company Structure and Administration.

Types of company

2.   Companies under the Companies Acts

(a) Companies may be registered under the Acts as follows:
- (*i*) Companies limited by shares.
- (*ii*) Companies limited by guarantee which have no share capital.

NOTE: There are also companies limited by guarantee which have a share capital but from 22 December 1980, no company could be formed as or become such a company.

- (*iii*) Unlimited companies which may, or may not, have a share capital.

(b) *Limited liability*. This means that the liability of members is limited:
- (*i*) *By shares*, each member's liability being limited to the amount, if any, which is unpaid (i.e. owing to the company) on his shares. This type of company is the most common and is used as a legal structure or 'person' to carry on business.
- (*ii*) *By guarantee*, each member's liability being limited to the amount he undertakes to pay to the assets of the company if and when it is wound up. This type of company is usually semi-charitable and non-profit making, e.g. a trade association or certain professional and educational bodies. They may, and often do, obtain a certificate from the Department of Trade and Industry allowing them to dispense with the word 'limited' in their name (s. 30).

(c) *Unlimited companies*. These are companies not having any limit on the liability of their members and are consequently very few in number. Such a company may take advantage of s. 254 which exempts an unlimited company from the obligation to file accounts except where it is the subsidiary of one or more limited companies or where it has a limited subsidiary.

3.   Public and private companies

(a) The Companies Act 1985, s. 1(3) states that 'public company' means:

(*i*) a company limited by shares or limited by guarantee; and

(*ii*) having a share capital; and

(*iii*) the memorandum of which states that the company is to be a public company; and

(*iv*) in relation to which the provisions of the Companies Act as to the registration or re-registration of a company as a public company have been complied with.

NOTE: 'Private company' means a company that is not a public company.

(b) *Other requirements of a public company:*

(*i*) that there are at least two subscribers (this was seven prior to 1980);

(*ii*) that the name of the company includes the words 'public limited company' or an acceptable abbreviation such as 'plc', or their Welsh equivalents;

(*iii*) that the company's memorandum is in a prescribed form which is specified by regulations made by the Secretary of State (s. 3).

(c) *Section 117 requires* that the amount of the share capital stated in the memorandum with which the company proposes to be registered must not be less than the authorized minimum (currently £50,000, s. 118).

(d) *Section 117 requires* that the requirements as to share capital are complied with before the company commences business.

NOTE: The registrar when satisfied that these requirements are complied with will issue a certificate under s. 117 which is conclusive evidence that the company is entitled to do business and exercise any borrowing powers.

4. Differences between public and private companies

Some of the more important differences are as follows:

(a) A public company may offer its shares to the public whereas it is an offence for a private company to do so (s. 81), except that in very limited circumstances a private company may issue advertisements offering its securities where they are of a private character under orders of the Secretary of State (FSA 1986, ss. 170, 171).

(b) When a company allots certain shares or securities there are strong pre-emption rights (s. 89). That is, existing shareholders must first be given the right to take up these 'new' shares. These pre-emption rules are stricter in the case of public companies. Private companies may exclude these rules by a provision in their memorandum or articles (s. 91).

> NOTE: Private companies will often have pre-emption clauses in their articles concerning the transfer (as opposed to allotment) of shares. Members are thereby required to offer their shares to other members before selling to an outsider.

(c) The disclosure requirements in relation to accounts etc. are more demanding for public companies.

(d) Additional requirements apply to distributable profits of public companies.

(e) Many of the rules relating to share capital are stricter for public companies.

(f) Private companies may adopt the 'Elective Regime' which simplifies certain of the administrative requirements of companies. (*See* **10(e)** below.)

Legal status

5.   The constitutional documents of registered companies

(a) *The Memorandum of Association* is the more important of these and takes precedence over the *Articles of Association* where their wording conflicts. In law, a company has a personality of its own, separate and distinct from that of its members: *Salomon* v *Salomon & Co. Ltd* (1897). The basic characteristics of the company's particular corporate personality are identified in the memorandum.

Section 2 of the 1985 Act requires the memorandum of every company to state:

    (*i*)   its name;

    (*ii*) the situation of the registered office (i.e. whether in England or Scotland);

    (*iii*) its objects, and

in the case of the company limited by shares or by guarantee to have clauses stating:

    (*iv*) that the liability of its members is limited; and

    (*v*) the amount of the share capital or guarantee.

(b) *The Articles of Association* are primarily concerned with the internal government of the company. They operate as a contract dealing with the relationship as between the company and its members and as between each member (s. 14). This is very important from the point of view of meetings. Companies' Regulations provide a series of specimen sets of articles. The most important of these is Table A which is designed for companies limited by shares. Its provisions as relevant to meetings are dealt with throughout Part Three.

Table A applies to companies if no other articles are adopted. However, companies may adopt different articles and/or exclude the provisions of Table A if they so desire (s. 8). Table A articles will also deal with the powers and duties of directors and the relationship between the company in general meeting and the board of directors. That is, the articles will state the division of powers as between these two important organs of a company (*see* 7).

6. The contractual capacity of companies

(a) *Ultra vires*. Registered companies are artificial legal persons which can only do legally those things which they were incorporated to do as defined in their objects clause. These objects and the powers to fulfil them are contained in the Memorandum. If a company acts or contracts beyond the scope of these objects and powers, including acts and contracts which are not reasonably incidental to the attainment of those objects, it is said to be acting *ultra vires*.

Until recently an act of the board or individual director which was *ultra vires* the company could not be ratified by the members in general meeting: *Ashbury Carriage Co* v. *Riche* (1875), *Precision Dippings* v. *Precision Dippings Marketing* (1985); and *Rolled Steel Products Ltd* v. *British Steel Corp.* (1982). However, the latter case indicates that the exercise by directors of express powers of the company contained in its memorandum for an improper purpose is a question of directors' power to contract on behalf of their company and not a question of corporate capacity and can therefore be ratified by ordinary resolution. Generally any action which is *ultra vires* is null and void and neither the company nor the third party can sue on it, except as provided by s. 35.

This basically provided that an *ultra vires* contract may be:

(*i*) enforced against the company by the third party where the contract was decided upon by the directors and the third party acted in good faith which is presumed;

(*ii*) the company acting *ultra vires* cannot rely on s. 35.

(*iii*) as between the company and the directors the operation of the *ultra vires* doctrine has not been affected.

(b) *Agency.* As artificial or 'fictitious' persons, companies must act through the agency of human beings, normally their directors. The rules of agency are therefore variously adapted to apply as between the company as principal, directors in the role of agent and persons dealing with the company as third party. (Compare *Royal British Bank* v. *Turquand* (1856), *Irvine* v. *Union Bank of Australia* (1877), and *Freeman and Lockyer* v. *Buckhurst Part Properties Ltd* (1964)). These rules may hold the company liable even where the director has acted beyond the scope of his authority (i.e. *ultra vires* his power but not beyond the company's).

Where the requirements of s. 35, above, were satisfied, the power of the direction to bind the company was deemed to be free from any limitation under the memorandum of articles.

(c) *Ultra vires and agency: the new legal regime.* The Companies Act 1989 substitutes new s. 35–35B for the previous s. 35 of the 1985 Act. The revised law states, in effect, that those who deal with a company will not be prejudiced by any limitation in its objects clause. Lack of capacity by reason of anything in the company's memorandum cannot be used to challenge the validity of an act done by the company (s. 35(1)).

Furthermore, in favour of those dealing in good faith, the power of the board of directors to bind the company, or authorize others to do so, shall be deemed free of any limitation under the company's constitution (s. 35A(1)). This includes both the Memorandum and Articles of Association and limitations deriving from:

(*i*)   a resolution of the company in general meeting or a class meeting, or (*ii*) from any agreement between the members of the company or of any class of shareholders.

Dealing and good faith. For the purposes of s. 35A:

 (*i*) a person 'deals with' a company if he is a party to any transaction or other act to which the company is a party;

(*ii*) a person shall not be regarded as acting in bad faith by reason only of his knowing that an act is beyond the powers of the directors under the company's constitution; and

(*iii*) a person shall be presumed to have acted in good faith unless the contrary proved (s. 35A(2)).

Proceedings by members. In the case of a breach of the objects clauses in the memorandum a member may restrain the transgression by injunction before any legal obligation to a third party is entered into, (s. 35(2)). Similarly the power of directors to bind the company under s. 35A does not affect any right of members of the company to seek to restrain directors from doing an act which is beyond their powers by seeking an injunction before any legal obligation, between the company and a third party, is entered into (s. 35A(4)).

Directors' duties are not affected by s. 35 and it remains the duty of directors to observe limitations on their capacity flowing from the company's memorandum (s. 35(3)). Nor does s. 35A(1) affect any liability incurred by directors, or any other person, by reason of the directors exceeding their powers (s. 35A(5)). A new section 332A imposes stricter rules where a company enters into a transaction which is outside the directors' powers, and the parties to the transaction include a director of the company or its holding company, or a person connected with such a director.

Third Parties' duties. A party to a transaction with a company is *not* bound to enquire as to whether:

 (*i*) the transaction is permitted by the company's memorandum; or

(*ii*) as to any limitation on the powers of the board of directors to bind the company or authorize others to do so (s. 35B).

It is also important to note that s. 142 of the Companies Act 1989 inserts s. 711A into the Companies Act 1985. This provision abolishes the doctrine of constructive notice under which third parties were deemed to have knowledge of the contents of the memorandum and articles of a company, and other documents which are required to be registered with the Registrar of Companies.

(d) *Meetings and ratification.* It is important to distinguish between two very different situations;

    (i) *An act ultra vires the company may now be ratified.* Where a company enters into a transaction or does an act which is beyond its capacity, the new statutory provisions allow the action to be ratified by the company by special resolution. Such ratification does not affect any liability incurred by the directors or any other person; relief from any such liability must be agreed to separately by special resolution s. 35(3). Therefore, to ratify an act which is *ultra vires* the company and directors' consequent breach of duty to the company in entering upon such an action requires *two separate* special resolutions.

    (ii) Where directors act beyond their powers under the articles but within the powers of the company their action may be ratified by the company in general meeting by ordinary resolution: *Bamford* v. *Bamford* (1970). In *Irvine* v. *Union Bank of Australia* (1877) there was no limitation on the company's borrowing powers but the directors were limited to borrowing a sum equal to half the company's paid-up capital. The court held that the company in general meeting could ratify borrowing by the directors in excess of their borrowing powers.

        The notice calling such a meeting should make clear that the meeting has as its purpose the sanctioning of the directors' conduct, otherwise the resolution may be invalid because of lack of notice: *Kaye* v. *Croydon Tramways Co.* (1898). The director whose action is the subject of the resolution may use his votes in his own favour subject to the limitations of fraud on the minority: *North West Transportation Co. Ltd* v. *Beatty* (1887).

        The ratifying of a particular contract which has been entered into by the directors without authority, and so making it an act of the company, is quite a different thing from altering the articles. To give the directors power to do things in the future, which the articles do not authorize them to do, requires a special resolution to alter the articles: *Grant* v. *UK Switchback Railways Co.* (1888).

(e) *Ratification of other breaches of duty.* Where the issue concerns the power of shareholders' meetings to ratify a breach of directors' fiduciary duties as opposed to a simple breach of their duties of care and skill, the issues can become quite complex. In *Pavlides* v. *Jensen* (1956) the court held that a negligent act could be ratified by ordinary resolution. However, in *Daniels* v. *Daniels* (1978) gross negligence from which the directors personally profited was not ratifiable as it amounted to a fraud on a minority. Where directors make a profit at the expense of the company and seek to use their votes as members to ratify their actions, much appears to depend on whether they are acting in good faith. If they acted in good faith then they may ratify: *Regal (Hastings) Ltd* v. *Gulliver* (1967), but if they acted in bad faith then they cannot: *Cook* v. *Deeks* (1916). For a more in-depth consideration of these issues *see*: Prentice, 'Jurisdiction of Shareholders' Meetings' (1977) 40 MLR 587; Partridge, 'Ratification and the Release of Directors from Personal Liability' (1987) CLJ 122; Sullivan [1985] CLJ 236; Smart [1987] JBL 464.

> NOTE: The director must have acted bona fide in the interests of the company. Ratification approving a prior performance of the board or director must be distinguished from an exercise of power by general meeting where it validly exercises the relevant power itself. The latter is an issue of division of power between the company in general meeting and the board of directors.

Company meetings

7. The division of power between the general meeting and board of directors

(a) The Articles of a company will state the division of power between these two organs of the company. The former Table A, art. 80, was badly drafted and caused problems of interpretation. It was replaced by Table A, art. 70 which states:

> 'Subject to the provisions of the Act, the memorandum and the articles and to any directions given by special resolution, the business of the company shall be managed by the directors who may exercise all the powers of the company. No alteration of the memorandum or articles and no such direction shall invalidate any prior act of the directors which

would have been valid if that alteration had not been made or that direction had not been given. The powers given by this regulation shall not be limited by any special power given to the directors by the articles and a meeting of directors at which a quorum is present may exercise all powers exercisable by the directors.'

The generally accepted view of the division of powers is aptly stated below:

'A company is an entity distinct alike from its shareholders and its directors. Some of its powers may, according to its articles, be exercised by directors, certain other powers may be reserved for shareholders in general meeting. If powers of management are vested in the directors, they and they alone can exercise these powers. The only way in which the general body of shareholders can control the exercise of the powers vested by the articles in the directors is by altering their articles, or, if opportunity arises under the articles, by refusing to re-elect the directors of whose actions they disapprove. They cannot themselves usurp the powers which by the articles are vested in the directors any more than the directors can usurp the powers vested by the articles in the general body of shareholders': *John Shaw & Sons (Salford) Ltd* v. *Shaw* (1935) (Greer LJ).

In this case legal proceedings were instigated by the board of directors. The articles delegated the power of management, including the right to take such action, to them. The company in general meeting passed a resolution that the legal proceedings should be discontinued. This resolution was held to be of no effect. It was for the directors to determine whether or not legal action should be taken.

Article 70 may still cause problems. In particular, an alteration of the articles must be bona fide for the benefit of the company as a whole: *Allen* v. *Gold Reefs of West Africa Ltd* (1900). *Quare* whether the same test also applies to a direction by special resolution under art. 70.

NOTE: Much depends upon the interpretation of the relevant articles. *See ASCFS Ltd* v. *Cunningham* (1906), *Marshal Valve Gear Co.*

v. *Manning* (1909), *Scott* (1943), *Re Emmadart Ltd* (1979), *Estmanco* v. *GLC* (1982).

Many thousands of companies in the UK probably still have the old Table A, art. 80. The controversy over the interpretation of this article centred on whether the words 'such regulations, being not inconsistent with the aforesaid regulations or provisions, as may be prescribed by the company in general meeting' included an ordinary resolution. The *Marshal Valve* case above held that they did. However, in *Breckland Group Holdings Ltd* v. *London & Suffolk Properties Ltd* (1988) the court held that *Marshal*'s case could not stand against the overwhelming weight of authority to the contrary. Nevertheless the authority to the contrary has been strongly criticized, *see Goldberg* (1970) 33 MLR; *Sullivan* (1977) 93 LQR 569; *Mackenzie* (1983) 4 Co Law 99. In Hong Kong, where art. 80 is still standard, the Court of Appeal in *Tang Kam Yip* v. *Yau Kung School* (1986) stated *obiter*:

> 'What of a special resolution which is inconsistent with the original articles but does not purport to amend these articles? It seems to me that such a special resolution would be binding on the directors if it related to their powers. I go further: provided that an ordinary resolution of the members is not inconsistent with some other article there is no good reason why it should not bind the directors in their management of the business: *see Marshal Valve* case and compare *ASCFS Ltd* v. *Cunningham* (1906) where the action failed because the equivalent article required an extraordinary resolution.'

Per Sir Alan Huggins V.P. *See* comments by Tyler (1987) Vol 17 HKLJ 230.

(b) *Default powers of the general meeting*. The general meeting does have powers to act where:

(*i*) Directors act beyond their powers (but *intra vires* the company) — the company in general meeting may resolve to adopt their action:

> 'The ratifying of a particular contract which had been entered into by the directors without authority, and so making it an act of the company, is quite a different thing

from altering the articles. To give the directors power to do things in future, which the articles did not authorize them to do, would be an alteration of the articles to ratify a contract which has been made without authority' : *Grant* v. *UK Switchback Railways Co.* (1888).

(*ii*)   There is a lack of quorum at board meetings.

(*iii*) There is a conflict with the board's duties to the company.

(*iv*)   There is dissension between members of the board: *Barron* v. *Potter* (1914).

(**c**) *Circumstances in which the directors may only act with the sanction of members*. Subject to the recent introduction of the Elective Regime for private companies, Companies Legislation in recent years has exhibited a trend requiring the directors to gain the authorization of the company in general meeting before acting. Examples of these, which require authorization by ordinary resolution, include:

(*i*)   Making a voluntary payment to a director in connection with his departure from office, other than a bona fide pension, 1985 Act s. 312: *Re Duomatic* (1969).

(*ii*)   Allotting shares, apart from the shares to be taken by the subscribers of the memorandum, and shares allotted to an employees' share scheme, s. 80.

(*iii*) Allotting shares without first offering them to existing members (though the memorandum of a private company may exclude this provision), ss. 89–95.

(*iv*)   Making a fixed-term service contract with a director for a period of more than five years, s. 319.

(*v*)   Selling company property to a director or buying property for the company from a director if its value is above a certain limit which depends on the size of the company, s. 320.

Examples requiring authorization by special resolution include:

(*i*)   The giving of financial assistance by a private company for the purchase of its own shares, ss. 155(4), 157;

(*ii*)   The redemption or purchase of own shares out of capital by a private company, s. 173(2).

For a list of circumstances requiring special resolutions *see* chapter 19.

(**d**) *Shareholders' remedies in the event of a conflict with directors*. Directors do not normally owe fiduciary or other duties to shareholders as such: *Percival* v. *Wright* (1902). Where the directors put themselves into some other fiduciary relationship with shareholders, such as agent for the purpose of selling their shares, then normal fiduciary duties will arise from that other relationship: *Allen* v. *Hyatt* (1914). In a small, closely-held company the relationship of mutual trust and confidence may lead to the finding of a special relationship in equity which will depend on the circumstances, and the nature of the responsibility which in a real and practical sense the director has assumed towards the shareholder: *Coleman* v. *Myers* (1977). Even in takeover situations, the duties of directors to shareholders are minimal: *Gething* v. *Kilner* (1972) and *Heron International Ltd* v. *Lord Grade* (1983).

Directors are, however, in a fiduciary position as regards the company (*see* 28:3). They must exercise their powers for the company's benefit. If an abuse of these powers is threatened the court will intervene. For example, in relation to an issue of shares under the directors' control, in *Clemens* v. *Clemens* (1976) an issue of shares to directors and an employees' share scheme which would have taken away a minority shareholder's negative control (i.e. the voting power to prevent the passing of a special resolution) was restrained. Alternatively the court may order a general meeting. In *Hogg* v. *Cramphorn Ltd* (1967) the board of directors, in order to avoid a hostile takeover bid, issued shares to friendly parties and altered the voting rights attaching to those shares so that the board could rely on the support of a majority of votes. The court held that this conduct was invalid unless ratified by the company in general meeting. Proceedings were stayed to enable such a meeting to be held. However, only the votes on the pre-existing shares could be used to ratify the issue of shares for an improper purpose. To use the votes of those wrongfully issued shares would have amounted to a *fraud on the minority*.

Other more direct remedies include:

(*i*) Directors can be removed from office by ordinary resolution of which special notice is given, s. 303. (*See* 19:13).

(*ii*) The Articles can be changed by passing a special resolution. These alterations may give the general meeting powers which were vested in the directors. The shareholders may then exercise these powers in general meeting. As already stated, in 7(c) above, the directors are often required to gain the approval of the company in general meeting before exercising certain powers.

(*iii*)   The shareholders can apply for relief under the unfair prejudice provisions of the 1985 Act, ss. 459–461. Alternatively the more extreme remedy of winding-up on the just and equitable grounds may be used, but this is less likely: IA 1986 s. 122:

In *McGuiness* v. *Bremner plc* (1988) a group of shareholders deposited a requisition requiring the directors to convene an extraordinary general meeting. The purpose of the meeting was to replace some of the directors who the shareholders considered to be incompetent. On 23 November 1987 the directors gave notice of an extraordinary general meeting to be held in over six months time on 9 June 1988. This did not constitute a breach of s. 368 as it was then worded (*see* 25:**3(b)**). However, in the circumstances the directors' action was unfairly prejudicial to the shareholders, and the court ordered the meeting to be held on 18 January 1988 as requested by the shareholders.

In *Re Zinotty Properties Ltd* (1984) one of the major factors showing a breakdown in mutual trust and confidence was that the administration of the company was inept, in so far as accounts had not been prepared punctually and no annual general meeting had been held — with the result that, technically, the company had no directors. Even a meeting proposing to wind up the company was inquorate and therefore ineffective. Accordingly it was just and equitable that the company be wound up.

8.   The rule in *Foss* v. *Harbottle* (1843)
This is based on the principle of majority rule and relates to procedure and jurisdiction. When a wrong is done to the company it is for the company to determine (in accordance with its articles) whether to bring legal action. If the company in general meeting determines to ratify a wrong or breach of duty it is not for the court to interfere. Similarly where the directors have power under the articles to decide whether to take legal proceedings and decline in good faith to seek redress: *Shaw* v. *Shaw* (1935), *see* **7(a)** above. There are exceptions to the rule:

(**a**)   The rule does not apply where a company is engaged in or proposing to carry on an *ultra vires* or illegal act.

(b) Where a special majority (75 per cent) is required for certain action then it is not enough for directors to obtain ratification by virtue of an ordinary resolution. *See Salmon* v. *Quinn and Axtens* (1909); *Baillie* v. *Oriental Telephone Co. Ltd* (1915); *Grant* v. *UK Switchback Railway Co.* (1888) and s. 25 CA 1985.

(c) Where the act in question has *infringed the so-called personal rights of a shareholder* e.g. the right of a shareholder to have his vote recorded: *Pender* v. *Lushington* (1877); the right to be paid dividends in cash: *Wood* v. *Odessa Waterworks Co.* (1889); and the right to enforce a pre-emption clause in the articles: *Rayfield* v. *Hands* (1960).

(d) *Where the company is committing a fraud on the minority.* This is a complex area which consists of an expropriation of corporate property in its broadest sense, for example taking a business opportunity for oneself in bad faith: *Cook* v. *Deeks* (1916), or paying oneself excessive remuneration: *Millers Ltd* v. *Maddams* (1938). The wrongdoers then seek to use their voting control to ratify their own wrongdoing. The courts will usually set aside a ratification done in such bad faith: *Menier* v. *Hooper's Telegraph Works* (1887). *See also Smith* v. *Croft (No. 2)* (1988) and **6(e)** above.

(e) *Where the interests of justice require it.* This exception is subject to much doubt. *See Prudential Assurance Co. Ltd* v. *Newman Industries (No. 2)* (1982).

> NOTE: The courts have not been consistent in their application of the rules in *Foss* v. *Harbottle*. In some cases relief has been granted and the rule has not been raised in defence, e.g. *Salmon* v. *Quinn and Axtens* (1909). Sometimes the court has refused to intervene even though the rule was not cited in justification for them refusing. *See also* the power of the court to grant relief against a company for members unfairly prejudiced, ss. 459–61.

9. Unfairly prejudicial conduct

(a) The remedy under ss. 459–461 for conduct which is unfairly prejudicial to the interests of the whole or some part of the membership is, so far, proving to be a very fertile one. The courts are applying it to situations which have an obvious overlap with those:

(*i*) amounting to a fraud on the minority (normally giving rise to a derivative action on behalf of the company).

(*ii*) which could amount to grounds for a just and equitable winding-up.

Thus in *Re Cumana* (1986) where a shareholder director diverted company business to his own advantage, carried out a rights issue to dilute the petitioners' shareholding and paid himself an excessive salary, he was held to have conducted the affairs of the company in an unfairly prejudicial manner. In *Re Bird Precision Bellows* (1984) the removal of a shareholder from office as director, in a quasi-partnership situation, also amounted to unfairly prejudicial conduct. Similarly in *Re O C Transport* (1984) the non-payment of dividends and removal from office of a shareholder who acquired shares on the understanding that he would be a director had the same effect. (For the procedures to remove a director before his period of office is complete *see* 19:**13**.)

(b) In terms of providing a remedy to shareholders in such situations ss. 459–461 are more practical and less extreme as is seen below. Where facts arise, such as those in *Re Cumana*, the remedy benefits the shareholder, whereas, in a derivative action under the fraud on the minority exception to *Foss* v. *Harbottle* (1843) it is the company which benefits. Ordering the purchase of the petitioners' shares under s. 461 is less extreme than ordering the company wound up under IA 86, s. 122(1)(g). Section 461 gives the court wide discretionary powers which could prove useful where breaches of company meetings law have or are likely to occur. These include orders of the court which may regulate the conduct of the company's affairs in future, and orders which require the company:

(*i*) to refrain from doing or continuing an act complained of by the petitioner.

(*ii*) to do an act which the petitioner has complained it has omitted to do.

For the relationship between this remedy and the power of the court to order a meeting under s. 371, *see Re Opera Photographic Ltd* (1989) (discussed in chapter 18:**6(e)**).

10. Meetings as the forum and machinery of corporate democracy

(a) *Artificial.* In terms of modern practice and reality the legislation and case law governing meetings is often artificial and dated. It has a certain Victorian 'air' about it. As will be seen the general meeting of members represents the source of ultimate authority within the company structure. It passes, as special resolutions, those matters which most significantly affect the constitution of the company and elects the directors who in reality run the company. However, the meeting is increasingly less used as a forum of corporate democracy.

(b) *Public companies' meetings* are often poorly attended and individuals who do not attend either vote in favour of the board's recommendations by proxy or remain passive. Large institutional shareholders (e.g. pension funds) tend to work behind the scenes rather than via the machinery of meetings. This helps to reinforce what is termed the managerial revolution — the separation of ownership and control. In terms of shareholder democracy within large companies, it may have a detrimental effect. Modern company law recognizes this problem to some extent. Company legislation and the Stock Exchange require an increasing number of matters to be submitted to members in general meeting for approval (*see* **7(c)** above).

(c) *Small private companies* often operate on a much more informal basis. They are often treated as quasi partnerships by the court. In practice they may often forget the formalities of shareholders' and directors' meetings. The law recognizes this and makes provision for it, as in s. 381A Table A (arts. 53 and 93) and the case law on informal agreements. This trend has been accelerated by the deregulation of private companies and the introduction of the 'Elective Regime' by the Companies Act 1989, ss. 113–7.

Nonetheless, the Jenkins Committee (1962) on Company Law Reform commented that members should take the trouble to get together and go through the procedure of holding a formal meeting as part of the legitimate price paid for the benefits of incorporation. Furthermore, while applying the principle on informal agreements in *Cane* v. *Jones* (1981) the judge commented, 'I would also add that one of the most striking features of this case has been the almost total failure of all concerned to observe the simplest requirements of company law'.

NOTE: Perhaps the nub of the issue is whether the limited company is the best form of legal vehicle for the small business. In the Gower proposals for 'A New Form of Incorporation for Small Firms' an incorporated form was suggested which would have simple rules about internal relations. These would enable them to operate internally with the same informality and absence of legal rules as apply to partnerships. But the price would be at least some reduction in the privileges of incorporation, e.g. limited liability. However, the response has been to introduce provisions relating to the deregulation of private companies which will now be discussed.

(d) *The 'Elective Regime'*
Private companies may by means of an Elective Resolution under s. 379A:
  (i) extend the authority of directors to allot shares without the approval of a general meeting, *see* **7(c)**(*ii*);
  (ii) dispense with the holding of an annual general meeting (*see* chapter 24);
  (iii) reduce the existing level of percentage consent required for holding a shareholders' meeting at short notice (*see* chapter 17);
  (iv) dispense with the laying of accounts and reports before a general meeting; and
  (v) avoid the need for the annual appointment of auditors.

The company may revoke an elective resolution by passing an ordinary resolution to that effect s. 379A(3). An elective resolution will cease to have effect if the company is re-registered as a public company s. 379A(4). For the details of elective resolutions *see* chapter 17.

By s. 117 CA 1989 the 'Elective Regime' may be extended to cover other areas by means of regulations made by the Secretary of State.

(e) *Meetings on winding-up*. The Cork Report on Insolvency (1982) stated that the law of insolvency was so unsatisfactory that unless fresh legislation was soon introduced it would fall into even greater decay and be regarded with contempt by society and those whose needs it is supposed to serve. The procedure, including meetings, was described as cumbersome, complex, archaic and over-technical. The report's recommendations included:
  (i) simplified procedures for debtors to make voluntary arrangements with their creditors;
  (ii) that a process of liquidation of assets replace the present procedure for a creditor's voluntary liquidation.

(*iii*) A new unified jurisdiction known as the Insolvency Court.

(*iv*) For ailing companies, a new provision to enable an administrator to be appointed with power to carry on the business concerned in order to avoid companies being forced into liquidation.

Some of these recommendations are now contained in the Insolvency Act 1986. *See* chapters 30–32.

The future

11. Industrial democracy and the EC Fifth Directive

In many European countries (e.g. Germany) employees have some voice in the running of the company which employs them. The EC Fifth Directive on the harmonization of company law contains proposals which would provide employees with a voice in corporate decision-making. Under these proposals company law would provide for both unitary and two-tier board structures. The latter system comprises an executive board concerned with the day-to-day running of the company, which is answerable to a supervisory board. The supervisory board would have members' and workers' representatives. There is also provision for a works council to allow for grass roots participation in decision-making by workers. The directive contains detailed proposals for the law of company meetings to facilitate these structural changes. However, it will probably be several years before they are enacted in United Kingdom law.

12. Legal theory and company meetings

The issue of who owns and controls companies is one of considerable debate. The law's attempt to justify the power vested in corporate managers has arguably failed. Legal scholars have offered other theories and explanations as new ways of legitimating corporate managerial power which are just as unconvincing. For an analysis of these ideas and alternative ways forward *see* Mary Stokes' essay on 'Company Law and Legal Theory' in Twining's *Legal Theory and Common Law* (1986).

Progress test 16

1.   Categorize companies registered under the Companies Acts. (3)

2.   Compare and contrast public and private limited companies. (3, 4)

3.   Discuss meetings as the machinery of corporate democracy. (7)

4.   Explain the rule in *Foss* v. *Harbottle* and its relationship to the division of power between the company in general meeting and the board of directors.   (7, 8)

17

Convening company meetings

Convening of meetings

1.   The secretary's first duty in preparing for a meeting is to draw up a list of items of business to be dealt with at the meeting. These items constitute the agenda.

The agenda paper should set out the items of business in the order in which they are to be dealt with at the meeting. If they are set out in a logical order, it will be of great assistance to the chairman.

2.   Form of agenda

The agenda prepared for company meetings may be in any of the following forms:

(a) *'Skeleton' form*, giving headings only of the items to be dealt with. This form of agenda is often included with, or forms part of, the notice convening the meeting.

(b) *Detailed form*. This gives much more detail of the business to be transacted at the meeting, and may even set out in draft form the resolutions to be submitted to the meeting. This is particularly the case where it is proposed to pass a special resolution.

(c) *The chairman's copy* of the agenda paper usually contains more detail than the copies issued to those entitled to attend the meeting. To enable him to make notes, a wide margin is usually provided on his copy.

NOTE: For more detailed treatment concerning the preparation of an agenda paper, together with specimens of both 'skeleton' and detailed forms, *see* chapter 5.

3. Kinds of meeting

Notices may be required for various kinds of meeting. In the case of a company incorporated under the Companies Act 1985, or any previous Act affecting the class of registered company with which this section is concerned, the secretary may be authorized, at various times and in suitable circumstances, to convene meetings of the following kinds:

(a) *Annual general meetings* (s. 366, Table A, art. 38).

(b) *Extraordinary general meetings*.

(c) *Class meetings*, meetings of members holding a certain class of shares.

(d) *Directors' (or Board) meetings*. See Table A, art. 88.

(e) *Committee meetings*, principally meetings of committees appointed by the board, e.g. transfer committee, allotment committee, sealing committee, etc.

(f) *Meetings of creditors*, or classes of creditors, e.g. in connection with any form of reconstruction, or on winding-up the company.

(g) *Meetings of contributories*, in the event of a winding-up.

NOTE: See generally Table A, arts. 36–39, 88 and 111–116.

Notice

4. Persons entitled to receive notice of meetings

(a) *Members*. Every member is entitled to have notice served upon him, unless the articles provide to the contrary, for example, the Articles may exclude:

   (*i*) the holders of cumulative preference shares, unless their cumulative dividend is in arrears for a specified period, *see Re Bradford Investments plc* (1990); or

   (*ii*) members whose calls are in arrears: *Re Mackenzie & Co.* (1916); or

   (*iii*) holders of non-voting shares.

Where the articles make no specific provision, a notice of the meeting of a company shall be served on every member of the company in the manner in which notices are required to be served by Table A. For this purpose 'Table A' means that Table A as is for the time being in force (s. 370(1)).

(b) *Auditors.* The auditors of a company are entitled to receive notice of general meetings, which they have a right to attend. They also have a right to be heard at any general meeting which they attend on any part of the business of the meeting which concerns them as auditors (s. 390(1)). An auditor retains his rights under s. 390 even if he has resigned (s. 392A(8)).

Where a private company is proposing to agree a written resolution under s. 381A, the auditor is entitled to receive all communications relating to such a resolution as are required to be supplied to a member of the company under Schedule 15A. The auditors may give notice of their opinion that the resolution affects them as auditors and ought to be considered by the company in general meeting or in a class meeting, as the case may be. They may then attend any such meeting and speak on any part of the business which affects them as auditors (s. 390(2)).

NOTE: For a consideration of informal and written resolutions under s. 381A *see* chapter 19:**16**. *See also* Table A, art. 38.

(c) *Legal personal representatives(s)* of a deceased member, or the trustee in bankruptcy of a bankrupt member. Table A, art. 38 says that, subject to the articles and any restriction imposed on any shares, notice of general meetings shall be given, *inter alia*, to all persons entitled to a share in consequence of the death or bankruptcy of a member. These include personal representatives and trustees in bankruptcy or persons nominated by them (art. 29, 30). They are entitled to all the rights of those shares as if they were the holders except that they cannot attend or vote at any meeting of the company before being registered as the holder of the share or shares (art. 31).

NOTE: In the absence of provisions similar to those in Table A, referred to above, the legal personal representatives are *not* entitled to receive notice of meetings unless they have secured registration of the shares concerned in their own names: *Allen* v. *Gold Reefs of West Africa* (1900). They are entitled to be registered as the holder of shares, in the absence of provisions in the articles to the contrary: *Scott* v. *Scott Ltd* (1940); *Safeguard Industrial Investments Ltd* v. *National Westminster Bank* (1980).

(d) *Joint holders.* Unless there is any provision to the contrary, notice of a meeting is effective if given to the joint holder first-named in the register of members (Table A, art. 112).

(e) *Directors.* Notice of general meetings must be given to directors (Table A, art 38). Article 88 states that it shall not be necessary to give notice of a directors' meeting to a director who is absent from the United Kingdom.

(f) *As between the transferor and transferee of shares.* Section 22 of the 1985 Act requires a person's name to be entered in the register of shareholders in order to be a member. If, after notices have been despatched, a person is entered into the register he is not entitled to receive notice of the meeting. However, Table A, art. 114 provides that every person who becomes entitled to a share shall be bound by any notice in respect of that share which, before his name is entered in the register of members, has been duly given to a person from whom he derives his title.

(g) *Frustration of notice.* When a member's registered address is situated in enemy territory and the company is unable to send notice, the company may carry on its business without serving notices on such members: *Re Anglo-International Bank* (1943). A postal strike may have the opposite effect where it delays receipt of the notice and agenda by members. They may obtain an injunction restraining the holding of the meeting: *Bradman* v. *Trinity Estates* (1989).

5. Contents of a notice

Apart form any special requirements of the Articles, the following are the most important contents.

(a) *Place* of the meeting.

(b) *Date, day and time* of the meeting.

(c) *Kind of meeting* to be held, e.g. annual general meeting, etc. The specification of an annual general meeting as such is required by Table A, art. 38.

(d) *Business* of the meeting, indicating the nature of any business to be transacted in sufficient detail. A notice convening a meeting at which any special business is to be transacted must state the nature of that special business otherwise the notice is irregular.

In *Pacific Coast Coal Mines Ltd* v. *Arbuthnot* (1917) a group of shareholders and directors entered into an agreement between themselves and the company under which certain shares were exchanged for debentures, the capital of the company was reduced and legal action against the directors was dismissed. The notice convening the shareholders' meeting did not state the effect of the agreement. Proxies of shareholders who, before the meeting, had no opportunity of knowing the contents of the agreement were used in support of the resolution approving it. The articles provided that in the case of special business the notice should state its general nature. Some four years later, certain shareholders claimed that the issue of debentures was invalid. The House of Lords held the resolution approving the agreement invalid owing to the absence of notice of the contents of the agreement.

(e) *Form of resolution* to be passed (e.g. where a special resolution or an extraordinary resolution is to be passed), with the precise wording of the resolution, in the case of special or extraordinary resolutions. It appears that the special resolution passed at the meeting must be 'the resolution' set out in the notice (s. 378(2)). In *Re Moorgate Mercantile Holdings* (1980) it was confirmed that notice of a special meeting must contain the entire substance of the resolution. Where the company is under some obligation which requires the resolution to be passed, the notice must say so. In *N.C. Securities* v. *Jackson* (1974), an agreement to issue shares and have them listed on the London Stock Exchange was made by a company, with other parties. The fulfilment of these obligations required the company to pass a resolution in general meeting approving the issue of the shares. After a legal dispute the company was ordered by the court to perform the agreement, and the directors were ordered to recommend the shareholders to vote in favour of the resolution. Instead they circulated to the shareholders counsel's opinion that shareholders could vote as they wished, and stated that if the resolution were passed it would cost the company more than if it were not. It was held that the meeting could not proceed since the circulars did not comply with undertakings given by the company to the court. The company was ordered to send notices convening a fresh meeting accompanied by a circular inviting the shareholders to vote in favour of the necessary resolution. The circular must contain all relevant information, including statements to the effect that the company was contractually bound to issue the plaintiffs shares with a Stock Exchange quotation; and that the rules of the Stock

Exchange required the issue of shares to be approved by the shareholders in general meeting.

(f) *Statements, given 'reasonable prominence'*, to draw attention to the following:

> (*i*) That a member is entitled to appoint a proxy (or more than one if permitted by the Articles) to attend and vote instead of him; and
>
> (*ii*) That a proxy need *not* also be a member (s. 372(3)).

NOTE: It is necessary to point out that s. 372(3) refers only to notices calling a meeting of a company *having a share capital*.

(g) *Resolutions proposed or supported by the directors* give directors a right and a duty to advise members concerning them: *Campbell* v. *Australian Mutual Provident Society* (1908). Accordingly the expense of preparing and distributing information is payable from company funds: *Peel* v. *London & North Western Railway Co.* (1907). In this context though, the power to use corporate funds is limited by directors' fiduciary duties to act in what they bona fide believe is in the company's interests and for a proper purpose: *see Advance Bank of Australia* v. *FAI Australia Ltd* (1987), where the bank's board of directors went to extreme lengths, including hiring a marketing company to telephone shareholders, in order to obtain the re-election of five retiring directors. This was held to be electioneering material and not a dispassionate presentation of information on policy questions. The directors had to bear the cost themselves.

Any information contained in or supplied with the notice in such circumstances must not mislead. This is particularly so where takeovers are concerned. In *Gething* v. *Kilner* (1972) it was stated that directors offering advice or recommending a vote in favour of a takeover bid have a duty to be honest and not to mislead. In *Dawson International plc* v. *Coats Patons plc* (1988) Lord Cullen said:

> 'If . . . directors take it upon themselves to give advice to current shareholders, . . . they have a duty to advise in good faith and not fraudulently, and not to mislead whether deliberately or carelessly. If they fail to do so the affected shareholders may have a remedy, including the recovery of what is truly the personal loss sustained by them as a result.'

See further *Morgan Crucible Co. plc* v. *Hill Samuels & Co. Ltd* (1991) and the Ontario case of *Goldex Mines Ltd* v. *Revill* (1974), where it was said that shareholders have a right to expect that the information sent to them is fairly presented, reasonably accurate, and not misleading.

(h) *Additional contents* (which may be embodied in the printed forms of notice), include:

    (*i*) *The company's name*, which forms the heading of the notice.

    (*ii*) *Date of the notice*, which may be assumed to be the date of posting.

    (*iii*) *Signature* — usually the secretary's signature — which may be autographic, but quite often forms part of the printed notice; for example:

By order of the Board,
A. Blank,

Secretary

    (*iv*) *An agenda*, in 'skeleton' form. This may be on a separate sheet or, alternatively, it may form part of the notice.

(i) *Circulars and explanatory memorandum sent with notice.* These may be sent for various reasons, for example:

    (*i*) where a notice and proposed resolution are not self-explanatory. The circular will read together with the notice in order to establish whether sufficient notice of the business to be conducted has been given (*Re Moorgate Mercantile Holdings* (1980)).

    (*ii*) where the proposed business is other than routine, directors may send out a circular with the notice of meeting explaining why the steps to be taken at the meeting are necessary.

    (*iii*) where the Companies Acts require the directors to circulate statements and representations, e.g. the directors are required to circulate a statement of not more than one thousand words prepared by the appropriate number of members who have requisitioned a meeting (s. 374) and a director who is the subject of an intended s. 303 resolution to dismiss him from office may require the company to send a copy of his representations to every member of the company to whom notice of the meeting is sent (s. 304(2)). Other examples include s. 95(5) concerning the disapplication of pre-emption rights in relation to a particular allotment of equity shares; s. 391A(3) and (4) concerning representations of a retiring auditor whom it is not proposed to reappoint or of an auditor sought to be dismissed; s. 394(3) concerning a statement of circumstances connected with an auditor's resignation and s. 426 explaining the effect of a compromise or arrangement.

(iv) A public *listed* company is obliged to send explanatory circulars to members in the case of major transactions (Acquisitions and Realisations Memorandum, para. 5). Such a company must obtain the prior approval of the Stock Exchange (S/E) to the contents of *all* circulars sent to members. Under Rule 30 of the S/E, the company must forward to the Quotations Department for approval proofs of important documents including notices of meetings and proxy forms. These proofs are not required for an annual general meeting where only routine business is transacted. However, under Rule 42(b), the company must state in a note to the notice convening an annual general meeting the place and time at which copies, or, as the case may be, memoranda of all directors' service contracts of more than one year's duration will be available for inspection. If there are no such contracts then the note must say so.

NOTE: In practice the explanatory statement or circular often forms the body of the document sent to members, with the notice of meeting contained in an appendix.

6.   Service of notice

(a) *The method* of serving notice is usually prescribed by the company's Articles and/or in the conditions of issue of its shares and debentures, e.g. notice by newspaper advertisement may be permitted in the case of holders of bearer securities, such as share warrants or bearer debentures.

(b) *The Act* (s. 370) requires that notices shall be served in accordance with the provisions of Table A in so far as the company's articles do not make other provisions in that respect.

(c) *Table A* makes the following provisions:

(*i*) Notice may be given to any member either personally or by sending it to him by post at his registered address; or

(*ii*) If he has no registered address within the United Kingdom, notice may be sent to him at any address within the United Kingdom supplied by him to the company for the purpose otherwise such a member is not entitled to receive any notice from the company (art. 112).

(*iii*) Proof that an envelope containing a notice was properly addressed, prepaid and posted is conclusive evidence that the notice was given (art. 115).

(*iv*) A notice is deemed to be given at the expiration of 48 hours after the envelope containing it was posted (art. 115). In *Bradman* v. *Trinity Estates plc* (1989) a meeting was convened by a notice dated 6 September 1988 to consider a resolution authorizing a corporate acquisition. When the notice and accompanying circular were sent out, strike action was being taken by the Post Office. Circulars addressed to members within the London area were delivered by courier. Those addressed to members outside of London were posted in unsealed letter boxes. Some of the latter members did not receive their circulars until many days later. Under art. 135 of the company's articles a notice sent by post was deemed to be effected 24 hours after posting. Article 139 provided for an alternative method of service, at the company's option, when by reason of the total suspension or curtailment of postal services within the UK, the company was unable effectively to convene a general meeting by notices sent through the post. It was held that art. 135 (cf Table A, art. 115) could not be interpreted too literally and did not apply where there was such a disruption to the postal service that placing the letters in a letter-box could not reasonably be expected to result in delivery to the shareholder within 24 hours. Also art. 139 envisaged that the curtailment of postal services which prevented delivery to *all shareholders* might have the effect of making the company *unable to convene a general meeting*.

(*v*) A notice must be in writing except that a notice calling a meeting of the directors need not be in writing (art. 111).

(*vi*) Persons entitled to a share in consequence of the death or bankruptcy of a member may be sent or delivered notice (addressed to them by name or title) at the address, if any, within the United Kingdom, supplied, by them for that purpose. Until such an address has been supplied, a notice may be given in any manner in which it might have been given if the death or bankruptcy had not occurred (art. 116).

(d) The Interpretation Act 1978, s. 7 will apply where Table A has been excluded and the company's articles do not make other provision. It says that notice will be deemed to be effected at the time when the letter would be expected to be delivered in the ordinary course of post, provided it is properly addressed and pre-paid.

7. Period of notice and clear days' notice

(a) *Length of notice* for calling meetings must conform to the Articles, but any provision in a company's Articles requiring shorter notice than that required by s. 369 is *void*.

(b) *The minimum notice* required by s. 369 for general meetings of a company (other than an adjourned meeting) is as follows.

(*i*) *Annual general meeting*: Not less than 21 days' notice in writing.

(*ii*) *General meeting* held for the purpose of passing a special resolution: not less than 21 days' notice in writing.

(*iii*) *Any other general meeting*:

Not less than 14 days' notice in writing, in the case of a company other than an unlimited company.

Not less than 7 days' notice in writing, in the case of an *unlimited* company.

NOTE: *Adjourned meetings*. At common law, notice is not required for an *adjourned* meeting: *Wills* v. *Murray* (1850). But the Articles usually provide that notice shall be given; in any case, Table A requires that notice shall be given if a meeting is adjourned for 14 days or more. At least 7 clear days' notice must be given specifying the time and place of the adjourned meeting and the general nature of the business to be transacted. Otherwise notice is not necessary (art. 45). As to consent to short notice and waiver of notice *see* **10**.

Reference has already been made to the interpretation of 'clear days' in relation to period of notice (*see* chapter 6:**7**). In the case of a company, however, the position is as follows:

(c) *First reference* should be made to the company's Articles.

(d) *If the Articles are silent,* Table A applies. Article 38 says that at least 21 *clear* days' notice is required for an annual general meeting and an extraordinary general meeting called for the passing of a special resolution or a resolution appointing a person as a director. Therefore these 21 clear days are exclusive of the day when the notice is given (or the day on which it is deemed to be given) and of the day of the meeting (the day for which it is given or on which it is to take effect) (Table A, art. 1). *See also Re Railway Sleepers Supply Co.* (1885).

All other extraordinary general meetings shall be called by *at least* 14 days' notice, subject to agreement on shorter notice in certain circumstances. The general rule of law in the computation of time is that fractions of a day are not reckoned: *Re Railway Sleepers Supply Co.* (1885); *Re Lympne Investments Ltd* (1972). The majority of English cases indicate that phrases such as 'at least *x* days' notice' and 'not less than *x* days' notice' mean clear days: *The King* v. *Turner* (1910); *Re Hector Whaling Ltd* (1936); *Mercantile Investment and General Trust Company* v. *International Company of Mexico* (1893); and *see The Securities and Futures Commission* v. *The Stock Exchange of Hong Kong Ltd* (1992); contrast the position in Scotland: *Neil McLeod & Sons Ltd Petitioners* (1967).

(e) *If the articles are silent and Table A is excluded,* then reference must be made to the Interpretation Act 1978, s. 7 (*see* **6(d)** above).

8. Authority to convene

To ensure that a meeting is properly convened, it is necessary that it should be summoned by the person or persons having the necessary authority to do so.

(a) *The directors,* acting as a board, are usually empowered to authorize the convening of meetings, and the secretary issues the notices on their instruction. Table A (art. 37) states: 'The directors may call general meetings . . . ' By obtaining *individual* consents to convene a meeting from sufficient directors to form a quorum of the board, a secretary *cannot* convene a valid meeting: *Re Haycraft Gold Reduction and Mining Co.* (1900).

If, however, the secretary convenes a meeting without prior authority, the notice may be ratified by the board before the meeting is actually held: *Hooper* v. *Kerr* (1900).

If there are not within the UK sufficient directors to call a general meeting, Table A, art. 37 says that any director or any member of the company may call a general meeting.

(b) *Table A* (art. 88): Where Table A applies, a director may, and the secretary on the requisition of a director shall, at any time summon a meeting of the directors.

(c) *Where the Articles make no provision* as to the convening of meetings (or where, having made provision, there is no one capable of proceeding), two or more members holding not less than one-tenth of the issued share capital or, if the company has not a share capital, not less than five per cent *in number* of the members of the company may call a meeting (s. 370(3)).

(d) *Requisition by members*. The Act (s. 368) makes provision for the requisitioning of an extraordinary general meeting by a specified minority of members, who may themselves convene the meeting if the directors fail to do so. (*See further* chapter 25).

(e) *On the application of any member of the company, the Secretary of State* has power to convene, or to direct the convening of, a general meeting, where a company has failed to hold an annual general meeting (s. 367).

(f) *The court* has the power to call or direct the calling of a general meeting in the following circumstances.

> (i) If for any reason it is impracticable to call or conduct the meeting of the company in manner prescribed by the articles or the Act (s. 371).
>
> This was held to be sufficient to cover a case in which it was impracticable, owing to the terms of the articles and the state of the shareholding in the company, to get a quorum of thirteen members personally present. The court ordered a meeting of the company under s. 371 on terms that the quorum should be five shareholders personally present: *Re Edinburgh Workmen's Houses Improvements Co. Ltd* (1934).
>
> The application may be made to the court under s. 371 by a director or any member of the company who would be entitled to vote at the meeting; alternatively, the court may act on its own motion.

(*ii*) Where a compromise or arrangement is proposed between the company and its members (s. 425). *See* chapter 26.

(*iii*) Where a member of a company complains that the affairs of the company are being or have been conducted in a manner which is unfairly prejudicial. The court may, *inter alia*, regulate the conduct of the company's affairs for the future, require the company to do any act which it has omitted to do or to refrain from doing or continuing an act complained of, and authorize civil proceedings to be brought in the name and on behalf of the company (s. 461).

(*iv*) The court has an inherent jurisdiction to direct the calling of a meeting, e.g. to enable the company to determine whether an action brought in the company's name by a member should be continued: *Pender* v. *Lushington* (1877), cf *Newman Industries* v. *Prudential (No. 2)* (1983).

(g) *A resigning auditor.* Where an auditor deposits his resignation in writing with the company pursuant to s. 392 accompanied by a statement of circumstances which he considers should be brought to the attention of the members or creditors of the company, s. 392A gives him the right to requisition the directors to convene an extraordinary general meeting of the company. The purpose of the meeting is to receive and consider such explanation of the circumstances connected with his resignation as he may wish to place before the meeting. Directors must act on a requisition made by an auditor within 21 days of its deposit and convene the meeting by not more than 28 days' notice (s. 392A(5)). The auditor has the right to have a statement in writing circulated to the members (s. 392A(3), (4)).

(h) *Serious loss of capital.* On becoming aware of a 'serious loss of capital' the directors of a *public* company are required to convene an extraordinary general meeting for the purpose of considering whether any, and if so what, measures should be taken to deal with the situation (s. 142).

> NOTE: A serious loss of capital occurs where the value of net assets are half or less of the amount of the company's called-up share capital. The meeting must be convened not later than 28 days from the earliest day on which a director is aware of the situation and for a date not later than 56 days from that date.

9. Special notice

In certain cases, the passing of a resolution in general meeting requires what s. 379 describes as 'special notice':

(a) Section 379 provides that notice of intention to move the resolution must be given *to the company* not less than 28 days before the meeting at which it is to be moved.

(b) The company must then give members notice of the motion at the same time and in the same manner as it gives notice of the meeting; or

(c) If it is *not* practicable to give members and the required notice (e.g. because of the time taken to get notices printed or to amend notices already printed), notice must be given by advertisement in the press, or in any other mode permitted by the Articles, not less than 21 days before the meeting. Where, after notice has been given to the company, a meeting is called for a date 28 days or less after it has been given, notice shall be deemed to have been properly given (s. 379(3)).

(d) When special notice is required:

   (*i*) *To remove a director*, by ordinary resolution, before the expiration of his period of office (s. 303).

   (*ii*) *To appoint an 'over-age' director*, i.e. one who would otherwise have been ineligible, having attained the age of seventy (s. 293(5)). In such a case the notice given to the company and by the company to its members must state the age of the person to whom it relates.

   (*iii*) In relation to auditors, resolutions:
   (1) filling a casual vacancy in the office of auditor; or
   (2) reappointing as auditor a retiring auditor who was appointed by the directors to fill a casual vacancy (s. 388(3)); or
   (3) removing an auditor before the expiration of his term of office; or
   (4) appointing as auditor a person other than a retiring auditor (s. 391A(1)).

10. Waiver of notice

(a) *Table A*, art. 39, and the articles of most companies, provide that *accidental* omission to give notice, or non-receipt of notice by any person entitled to notice, shall *not* invalidate the proceedings at the meeting concerned. It is thought that this Article will not apply to auditors, since their right to receive notice is prescribed by statute (*see* **4(b)** above).

In Re West Canadian Collieries Ltd (1962), because some addressograph plates were accidentally mislaid, the company registrar failed to give notice of a meeting to nine shareholders who held 101 shares out of a total issued capital of 692,718 shares. This omission was excused by the court and the meeting was held to be valid. By implication, Article 39 would cover a situation where the whereabouts of a shareholder are unknown to the company, as where communications are returned from his old address and he does not notify the company of his new address.

'Accidental omission' will not cover the situation where notice is not sent because of a mistaken belief that a member is not entitled to attend: *Musselwhite* v. *Musselwhite & Son Ltd* (1962).

(b) *Table A* (art. 88) provides that it is *not* necessary to give notice of a meeting of directors to any director for the time being absent from the United Kingdom.

(c) *Consent to short notice.* Exceptions to the general rule that if inadequate notice is given, the meeting will be void include unanimous consent. In *Re Express Engineering works* (1920) it was stated that 'if you have all the shareholders present, then all the requirements in connection with a meeting of the company are observed'. Another case, *Re Bailey Hay & Co Ltd* (1971), extended this principle to a situation of short notice where all five members were present at a meeting to pass a winding-up resolution but some members abstained. The resolution was passed by the majority votes of two members, the remaining three abstained. Shortly afterwards the abstainers found out about the short notice and then, three years later, challenged the validity of the winding-up. They failed because the court held that the true quality of their acts was to be judged not exclusively by reference to what they did at the meeting, but also in the light of their inaction thereafter.

The Act (s. 369(3)) provides that a meeting called at *shorter* notice than that specified earlier in the same section or in the company's articles, shall not be invalidated on that account if the shorter notice is excused by *all* members entitled to attend and vote (in the case of an annual general meeting), and by a specified majority in the case of any other general meeting. The requisite majority is a majority in number of the members having a right to attend and vote who together hold not less than 95 per cent in nominal value of the shares giving the right to attend and vote at the meeting; or holding not less than 95 per cent of the total voting rights if the company has no share capital. A private company may, by *elective resolution* (s. 379A), reduce the 95 per cent requirement to 90 per cent (s. 369(4)). Table A, art. 38 incorporates these s. 364 provisions on consent to short notice.

A *special resolution* may be validly passed without the usual 21 day period of notice where a majority in number (95 per cent as stated above) assent (s. 378(3)). In giving their consent, the members must have knowledge of the special resolution which it is proposed to pass on a shorter period of notice. Similarly, s. 369(4) will only be satisfied where the fact that a meeting is held on short notice is made known to those attending, *Re Pearce, Duff & Co.* (1960).

The provisions relating to shorter notice by consent are widely used. Consent can be given by various means including:

 (*i*) orally by a resolution passed on a show of hands, though this is probably the least satisfactory method; or

 (*ii*) by a resolution passed at the meeting that the relevant provisions of s. 369 or of the articles shall apply to the meeting; or

 (*iii*) by a separate document to the same effect signed by an appropriate number of shareholders; or

 (*iv*) by the signature of a sufficient number of shareholders of a form of consent endorsed on the notice of meeting.

Progress test 17

1. Describe the measures you would adopt in the preparation of an agenda for the annual general meeting of a public company, of which it may be assumed you are the secretary. **(2)**

2. Draft a specimen agenda in sufficient detail to be of assistance to your chairman at the forthcoming annual general meeting of your company. **(2, 3)**

3. List the kinds of meetings that the secretary of a company may be required to convene. **(3)**

4. In preparing and issuing notices of a general meeting of a company: **(a)** who, apart from members, are entitled to receive such notices; **(b)** what statements, concerning proxies must be given 'reasonable prominence'? **(4, 5)**

5. Who, apart from the directors, may convene, or order the convening of, a general meeting of a company? Explain the circumstances. **(8)**

6. Explain 'special notice', and state when it is required. **(9)**

7. Draft the notice of an annual general meeting of a company at which the following business is to be transacted: **(a)** Presentation of accounts; **(b)** Re-election of a director aged 78 years; **(c)** Fixing of auditors' remuneration; **(d)** Increase of authorized share capital. **(3–9)**

Quorum

1. Definition

A quorum was defined, and the effects of absence or inadequacy of a quorum explained, in chapter 7. It is now necessary to consider the quorum specifically in relation to company meetings.

2. The Articles

The articles of a company usually specify the number of members required to constitute a quorum.

3. Table A

The provisions of Table A will apply if the Articles do not make any other provision, namely:

(a) Two members present in *person or by proxy* are required as the quorum for any general meeting of a public or private company (art. 40). This article requires the quorum to be present for the valid transaction of business at a general meeting. Contrast the situation under previous articles discussed below, *see* **8**. In this connection, Table A (art. 41) also provides the remedy where a quorum is not present, namely:

> 'If such a quorum is not present within half an hour from the time appointed for the meeting, or if during a meeting such a quorum ceases to be present, the meeting shall stand adjourned to the same day in the next week at the same time and place or to such time and place as the directors may determine.'

(b) *Board meetings:* 'The quorum necessary for the transaction of the business of the directors may be fixed by the directors, and unless so fixed shall be two', Table A (art. 89).

> NOTE: If the Articles are silent and Table A excluded, a *majority* of directors must be present to constitute a valid quorum: *York Tramways* v. *Willows* (1882), or where there is an established practice, the number who usually act at meetings: *Re Regents Canal Iron Co.* (1867). It had been held that power in the articles authorizing the directors to determine the number which will form a quorum enables them to fix the number at one: *Re Fireproof Doors Ltd* (1916).
>
> However, if there are vacancies on the board of directors the continuing directors or a sole director may nevertheless continue to act; but if the number of directors is less than the number fixed as the quorum, the continuing directors or director may act only for the purpose of filling vacancies or of calling a general meeting, Table A (art. 90).

4. The Act
The Act (s. 370) makes the following provisions for the unlikely occurrence that the Articles fail to fix a quorum and exclude Table A, namely 'two members personally present shall be a quorum'.

> NOTE: It will be observed that Table A and the Act agree in respect of minimum numbers required. They are not, however, in agreement where proxies are concerned, as the Act requires two members *personally* present (s. 370(3)), whereas Table A art. 40 permits proxies to be counted in the quorum.

5. Committee meetings
In most cases, the constitution of a committee is fixed by the Articles, or by the board of directors at the time of appointing the committee (*see* Table A, Arts 88–98). If, however, no provision is made for the fixing of a quorum, then *all* members of a committee must be present to constitute a valid quorum: *Re Liverpool Housing Stores Ltd* (1890).

6. One person may constitute a valid quorum
Reference was made (in chapter 2) to the cases of *Sharp* v.

Dawes (1876) and *Re Sanitary Carbon Co.* (1877), in which it was decided that two persons at least are required to constitute a valid meeting. In the latter case a meeting was convened to consider a resolution to wind up the company voluntarily. One shareholder attended with proxies for three other shareholders. He proposed the resolution, declared it carried and appointed a liquidator. The court, following *Sharp* v. *Dawes*, declared the meeting invalid. In some jurisdictions, however, and to a much lesser extent in the UK, the rule has been honoured more in the breach than in the observance. For example, in *R* v. *Cogdon, ex parte Hasker* (1877) a meeting of creditors had been convened. One creditor attended holding proxies for two other creditors. He passed a resolution appointing a liquidator. The Supreme Court of Victoria held that the resolution was valid. This was followed in *R* v. *Leech, ex parte Tolstrup* (1879) where it was held that one person, holding proxies for two creditors, may constitute a meeting of creditors (so long as it was duly convened) and may pass valid resolutions. Stawell CJ said (at p. 502):

> 'It is true that it was held in *Sharp* v. *Dawes*, that one shareholder cannot constitute a meeting; but this Court has already decided that one person holding proxies for two creditors, can constitute a meeting, and even vote in a different way in respect of each proxy, as his instructions may direct him: *R* v. *Gogdon, ex parte Hasker* (1877). As the Act allows proxies, we must take it that two creditors were present at the meeting at which the appointment in question was made.'

He added (at p. 503):

> ' . . . I do not feel at liberty to depart from the previous decision of the Court, in *R* v. *Cogdon, ex parte Hasker* (1877). The proxy might be, at different moments, the mouthpiece of different creditors. There is, then, nothing to justify the holding that there was no appointment whatever.'

Sharp v. *Dawes* was a meeting of members of a company whereas the two Victorian cases concerned meetings of creditors. The Insolvency Rules 1986, Rule 12, 4A now state that a quorum for creditors' meetings is at least one creditor entitled to vote, who may be represented by proxy by any person (including the chairman). In *Sharp* v. *Dawes*, Lord Coleridge had qualified his statements by saying 'It is, of course, possible to show that the word 'meeting' has a different meaning from the ordinary meaning . . . '. This was used by Warrington J in cases like *East* v. *Bennett Bros* (1911), discussed in the exceptions to the general rules, *see* **6(a)** below.

If the articles provide for a quorum of persons 'present in person or by proxy', persons present by proxy *can be included* in the quorum. Where the articles state that the quorum is to consist of persons present 'in person' there must be a *physical presence* of the individual shareholder or corporate representative appointed under s. 375. In *Re Harris Ltd* (1956) the company's articles required two people to be present *in person* for a quorum. One of them was abroad and was consequently represented by her attorney. It was held that 'present' meant 'personally present' and that consequently there was no quorum at the meeting. *Clubb* v. *Hong Kong Computer Society* (1990) followed the same approach, the court holding that only those members physically present could count towards the quorum. In *Prain & Sons Ltd* (1947) a company's articles provided that two or more members present *in person or by proxy* should form a quorum. One member was personally present, in addition he was the first named trustee of two trusts which held shares in the company and acted for them at the meeting. He also held a proxy for another shareholder. He formally moved the resolution and thereafter, as proxy for another member, seconded the motion. The court held there was no quorum. The meeting was probably invalid because in effect it was a meeting of one person (contrast the two State of Victoria cases above — the *Cogdon, ex parte Hasker* and the *Leech, ex parte Tolstrup* cases).

A case which took a slightly different approach is *Re McLeod (Neil) & Sons* (1967). Here the articles required three members to be personally present as a quorum. Two persons attended the meeting, one as an individual member and also as a trustee. It was held that, as this latter person attended in a dual capacity, a quorum was present. Both of these cases, although difficult to reconcile as regards attending a meeting in the dual capacity of member and trustee, may be rationalized in a way which is supportive of the principle in *Sharp* v. *Dawes*. In the first case only one person was present and the quorum was invalid whereas in the *McLeod* case at least two members were in attendance at the meeting and Lord President Clyde said that 'a meeting is not properly constituted if only one individual is present, for there is none for him to meet'. The McLeod case does, however, give a different view of the meaning of 'present' to that taken in the *Harris Ltd* case. In *Prain's* case the court expressed the view that 'a meeting at which only one member is present to play multiple parts may be thought to be nothing other than a pantomime.'

Finally, the principle in *Sharp* v. *Dawes* is shown to still have vigour by the decision in *Re Queensland Petroleum Management Ltd* (1989) where it was held that under an article similar to Table A, art. 40 two persons who are both proxies for the same member (in respect of different parts of his shareholding) do not constitute a quorum. Plowman J, in *Re London Flats Ltd* (1969) described what are now ss. 367(2) and 371(2) (which allow the Secretary of State or the court to order meetings of 1 person) as exceptional and held that they did not displace the general rule that 'a single shareholder cannot constitute a meeting.' The case concerned a meeting which was called to appoint a named liquidator. Two members attended, one of whom stated that he intended to propose an amendment that he be appointed liquidator. The other member objected and left the meeting before the amendment was put. The remaining member put the amendment, voted in favour of it and declared the amendment carried. This was held invalid since only one person was present, although the meeting was quorate when it commenced. The decision reflects the situation under the current Table A art. 40 (contrast *Re Hartley Baird* (1955) at 8 below).

Despite these decisions, however, there are several cases connected with company meetings in which *one* person may constitute a valid quorum, namely:

(a) *Class meeting*. Where one member holds *all* the shares of a particular class, e.g. preference shares, that one person alone would constitute a quorum for a 'meeting' of shareholders of that particular class: *East* v. *Bennett Bros.* (1911). Warrington J said (at p. 168):

> 'I think I may very fairly say that where one person only is the holder of all the shares of a particular class, and as that person cannot meet himself, or form a meeting with himself in the ordinary sense, the persons who framed this

memorandum having such a position in contemplation must be taken to have used the word "meeting", not in the strict sense in which it is usually used, but as including the case of one single shareholder. There is, of course, no difficulty in treating the formally expressed assent of the sole shareholder as a resolution. The only question is the purely technical difficulty arising from the use of the word "meeting" in the memorandum.

I think on the whole that I may give effect to obvious common sense by holding that in this particular case, where there is only one shareholder of the class, on the true construction of the memorandum, the expression "meeting" may be held to include that case.'

(b) *Board or Committee meeting.* Where, as in Table A (arts. 88–89) the directors have power to fix a quorum for board meetings, and to appoint and fix a quorum for committee meetings, they may decide that *one* director shall be a quorum for board or committee meetings: *Re Fireproof Doors Ltd* (1916).

Per Astbury J (at p. 936): '[I]t is said a quorum of one is impossible, and it is quite true that one shareholder cannot form a meeting of shareholders, but it is not clear that one director cannot form a quorum.' In that case the seal of the company was required to be affixed by the authority of a resolution of the board of directors and in the presence of at least two directors and the secretary. Lord Parmoor in *Daimler Co. Ltd* v. *Continental Tyre & Rubber Co (GB) Ltd* (1916) had no objection as such to articles providing for a quorum of one at a meeting of directors.

(c) *A sole continuing director* may act but only for the purpose of filling vacancies or of calling a general meeting, even though the number fixed as the quorum is two or more (Table A, art. 90).

(d) *Meeting convened by the Secretary of State.* If the Secretary of State, on the application of a member, convenes or directs the convening of a general meeting under s. 367 (i.e. because the company has failed to hold its annual general meeting), *one* member of the company present in person or by proxy shall be deemed to constitute a quorum at that meeting.

(e) *Meeting convened by the court.* Where the court convenes or orders a meeting to be called under s. 371 (i.e. because the company has found it impracticable for any reason to call a meeting of the company), *one* member of the company present in person or by proxy shall be deemed to constitute a quorum at that meeting. 'Impracticable' means whether in the particular circumstances of the case the desired meeting of the company could, as a practical matter, be conducted: *Re El Sombrero Ltd* (1958). The facts in this case were that the applicant held 90 per cent of the issued shares; the two respondents held the remaining 10 per cent and were the only directors. By seeking to absent themselves from any meetings that were convened, they effectively prevented the majority shareholder from exercising the rights attached to his shares. The court therefore ordered a meeting of one.

Re H.R. Paul & Son Ltd (1973) concerned a takeover, the consequence of which was that directors ceased to be qualified and amendments were proposed to the articles of association so that directors could be properly appointed. There had been a dissentient minority who did not like the takeover or merger and who, by absenting themselves from the meeting convened for these and other purposes, effectively frustrated anything being done because of a lack of quorum. Brightman J said:

> 'The jurisdiction conferred by the section was discretionary and his lordship was therefore not bound to make an order. But to refuse B Ltd's application would deprive a majority shareholder of the right to alter the articles of association and confer on a minority a right of veto not commensurate with their shareholding. His lordship did not accept that the quorum provisions should be regarded as a right vested in the minority to frustrate the wishes of the majority, and he would therefore grant the relief sought.'

A recent case which highlights the relationship of s. 371 to the minority remedies of just and equitable winding-up and unfairly prejudicial conduct is *Re Opera Photographic Ltd* (1989). There were two shareholders one holding 51 per cent, the other 49 per cent. The majority shareholder wished to call a meeting and remove the minority shareholder from office using the s. 303 procedure. Attempts to carry this out were frustrated by the non-attendance of the minority shareholder who argued that, since this was a quasi-partnership, the majority shareholder's right to remove him from directorship was overlaid by equitable considerations. The court held that the quorum provisions could not be regarded as conferring some form of veto on the minority shareholder. Deadlock existed which had to be resolved one way or another. The court ordered a meeting with a quorum of one for the purpose of removing the minority shareholder from office. Whether either party had behaved wrongfully or otherwise would have to be determined in other proceedings for unfair prejudice or just and equitable winding-up. Meanwhile, meetings needed to be conducted to manage or procure the management of the company. If such meetings did not go ahead such a state of affairs would anyway result in either or both members presenting petition on the above mentioned grounds to remedy the continuing deadlock. The majority shareholder could not, in the circumstances, be deprived of his statutory right to remove a director under the s. 303 procedure. Contrast *Kouris* v. *Kouris* (1987); *Re Sticky Fingers Restaurant Ltd* (1991).

For the consideration of the courts' power in the context of share pre-emption rights and one surviving shareholder, *see Jarvis Motors* v. *Carabott* (1964). *See also Re Downs Wine Bar Ltd* (1990) for a consideration of the court's power under s. 371 in relation to the rule in *Foss* v. *Harbottle*.

(f) *Unanimous assent.* In *Baroness Wenlock* v. *River Dee Co.* (1883) Cotton LJ said 'The court would never allow it to be said there is an absence of resolution when all the shareholders, and not only a majority, have expressly assented to that which is being done.' This topic is further discussed in chapter 19:**15**, but for present purposes it may be stated that if the number of members has fallen below that required for a quorum at a members' meeting, then decisions may be taken by unanimous assent. So if, for some reason, a company only has one member then decisions may be taken by that member alone: *see Re Johnston, Dunster & Co.* (1891).

(g) In insolvency proceedings a quorum for the purpose of any meeting of creditors is at least one creditor entitled to vote present in person or by proxy.

7. Disinterested quorum

Directors must not, as part of their fiduciary duties to the company, put themselves into a position of conflict of interest: *Regal (Hastings) Ltd* v. *Gulliver* (1967). That is, they must avoid situations where their interest and that of the company are opposed or may conflict. This would cover situations such as their own service contract, to being interested in, or a party to, some other contract with the company, e.g. buying from or selling to the company. As a result at board meetings the quorum must be a disinterested one: *Re North Eastern Insurance Co.* (1919). Therefore, unless the company's articles permit, a director may not form part of the quorum at a board meeting held for the purpose of dealing with any contract in which he has a conflict of interest; nor is he entitled to vote as a director on such a contract or business. This area is quite complex and is dealt with in more detail in chapter 28.

8.   Re Hartley Baird Ltd (1955)

This case merits special mention, as the decision of Wynn-Parry J appeared to contradict the decision in earlier cases:

(a) *In Henderson* v. *Louttit* (1894) and other cases, which had hitherto been regarded as accepted authorities, it had been held that 'where there is a quorum at the beginning of a meeting, such meeting cannot transact business after the members present have ceased to constitute a quorum'; in other words, that the quorum must be present for the *whole* meeting, and any business completed after the quorum ceased to exist is invalid.

(b) *In Re Hartley Baird Ltd* (1955) the above decision was not followed, where:

(i) The company's articles stated that 'No business shall be transacted at any meeting unless a quorum is present *when the meeting proceeds to business*', i.e. following a former Table A (art. 53) (contrast the present Table A, art. 40).

(ii) One member left before the vote was taken (on a motion for reduction of capital), so that the number present was less than that required for a quorum.

(iii) It was held that the resolution passed was *valid*.

NOTE: Wynn-Parry J contended that the article as worded was 'clearly designed to save, by adjournment, a meeting properly convened but at which no quorum turned up . . . but it did not meet the case where a quorum was present at the commencement of the meeting but ceased to be present when the meeting proceeded to vote.'

Table A, art. 40 provides that 'no business shall be transacted at any [general] meeting unless a quorum is present'. *See also* article 41 at 3 above.

Progress test 18

1. (a) Define a quorum. (1) (b) What rules apply to the quorum for board meetings? (6)

2. What constitutes a quorum for a general meeting of (a) a public company, (b) a private company, which has adopted Table A? (3)

3. Mention some circumstances in which *one* person may constitute a valid quorum of a meeting. (6)

19
Motions and resolutions

General

1. Definitions

Although the words 'motion' and 'resolution' are often used indiscriminately — even in the Companies Act 1985 — strictly speaking, they merit separate definitions:

(a) *A motion* is a proposition or proposal put forward for discussion and decision at a meeting, i.e. *before* it has been put to the vote.

(b) *A resolution* is the 'acceptance' of the motion, i.e. *after* it has been put to the vote and agreed to by the necessary majority.

NOTE: It must be borne in mind, however, that the resolution in its final form may be different from the motion as it appeared in its original form as various amendments may subsequently have been put to the meeting and accepted. (*See* chapter 8:**10** substantive motion.) But as to special and extraordinary resolutions, *see* **2** below.

Notice

2. Notice and amendment of resolutions

An amendment may be validly put where it is within the scope of the notice calling the meeting. The freedom to amend resolutions will vary according to:

(a) *Whether the original resolution forms part of the ordinary business.* As specific notice of ordinary business need not be given where the articles distinguish between ordinary and special business, any amendment may be made to a resolution which is part of ordinary business, provided that it does not take the resolution outside the category of ordinary business.

(b) *Ordinary resolution.* There appears to be greater freedom in the amendment of an ordinary resolution.

(c) *Special or extraordinary resolutions.* No amendments of substance may be made to such resolutions. *See Re Moorgate Mercantile Holdings Ltd* (1980) discussed in **8** below.

As regards *ordinary resolutions* and *special business* the test of sufficiency of notice is that it should enable a member to decide whether or not to attend to protect his interests. Accordingly an amendment should not be allowed where it would affect a member's decision not to attend (*Betts & Co. Ltd* v. *MacNaughton* (1910)). In the latter case one of several resolutions proposed in the notice was that three named persons should be appointed directors. The notice stated that the purpose of the meeting was to consider and if thought fit pass these resolutions 'with such amendments as shall be determined upon at such meeting'. The resolution on appointment of directors was proposed at the meeting, but an amendment was carried that, in addition to the three persons originally nominated, two additional named directors should be appointed. It was held that the appointment of the additional directors was within the scope of the special business indicated in the notice. Contrast *Clinch* v. *Financial Corporation* (1868).

As regards meetings of boards of directors it has been held that they may transact business of an ordinary or special nature without notice of special business (*La Compagnie de Mayville* v. *Whitley* [1896]). This is a sensible rule in view of the urgency of a lot of business with which directors have to deal. *See also Cotter* v. *National Union of Seamen* (1929).

3. Form, presentation and disposal of a motion

These were dealt with in chapter 8 and the rules stated there need not be repeated here, as they apply to company meetings.

Types of resolution

4. Kinds of resolution

(a) There are three kinds of resolution referred to in the Act:
  (*i*) Ordinary resolutions.

(*ii*) Extraordinary resolutions.

(*iii*) Special resolutions.

(b) The kind of resolution required for any particular purpose is determined either by statute or by the Articles of the company concerned, but an *ordinary resolution* requiring a simple majority of votes cast is adequate unless otherwise provided in the Act or in the Articles. Such a resolution is the basic way of ascertaining the sense of a company general meeting by giving it specific and formal shape.

(c) The law also provides for an informal, unanimous resolution which does not have to be passed at a meeting to be valid, *see* **15** below.

5. Ordinary resolution

(a) *When used*. This, the commonest form of resolution, is used for all routine business at *general* meetings, and for all business at board meetings.

(b) *Majority required*. It is passed by a *simple majority* of members entitled to vote, and actually voting, at a meeting of which proper notice has been given in accordance with the Articles. Abstainers do not count, e.g. if an ordinary resolution is put to the vote and four vote in favour and three against, with eight abstaining, the resolution is carried.

> NOTE: The rule in *Foss* v. *Harbottle* (1843) has established a general principle that, where the majority passes an ordinary resolution which is within its powers to pass, the court will not normally intervene, i.e. the minority cannot normally object. For a brief discussion of the exception to this principle, *see* chapter 16:8.

6. Extraordinary resolution (s. 378(1))

(a) *Definition*. An extraordinary resolution is one 'passed by a majority of not less than *three-fourths* of such members as, being entitled to do so, vote in person or, where proxies are allowed, by proxy, at a general meeting of which notice specifying the intention to propose the resolution as an extraordinary resolution has been duly given'.

> NOTE: A three-fourths majority means that at least three-fourths of

those actually voting must vote *in favour* of the resolution before it is deemed to be passed. If, for example, there are at least 15 votes in favour out of a total of 20 votes cast, that would amount to a three-fourths majority. Abstentions and disallowed votes are not counted (s. 378 (5)).

(b) *When required.* Such a resolution is required only where either the Act or the Articles of a company so provide. The Act requires an extraordinary resolution in the following cases:

Section 125: To vary class rights at a separate meeting of that class where the rights are attached otherwise than by the memorandum and there is no variation procedure in the Articles of Association.

Table A, art. 117, specifies an extraordinary resolution for giving sanction to a liquidator to distribute surplus assets in kind instead of realising them for cash.

Under the Insolvency Act 1986:

Section 84: To wind up voluntarily, because the company cannot, by reason of its liabilities, continue its business.

Section 165: To sanction the liquidator to compromise with creditors, debtors or contributors in a members' winding up.

(c) *The period of notice required* for a meeting at which an extraordinary resolution is to be passed is *not* specifically stated in the Act; therefore, it will vary according to the kind of meeting at which the resolution is to be passed, i.e.:

(*i*) *21 days' notice* at least, if it is to be passed at the annual general meeting;

(*ii*) *14 days' notice* at least, if it is to be passed at an extraordinary general meeting;

(*iii*) *7 days' notice* at least, if it is to be passed at an extraordinary general meeting of an *unlimited* company.

NOTE: As stated, in 17:**10**, the Act provides that inadequate notice may be excused if, in the case of an annual general meeting, all members entitled to attend and vote agree, and in the case of any other meeting, a specified majority agree (s. 369). A private company's members may agree to an extraordinary resolution in writing (s. 381A(6)). *See* informal resolutions below.

(d) *Contents of notice.* It appears that the principles in *Re Moorgate Mercantile Holdings* (1980) (discussed below at **8**) apply to extraordinary resolutions, since the notice requirements as to specifying the nature of the resolution in s. 378(1) for such resolutions is the same as that in s. 378(2) for special resolutions.

(e) *Registration*. A copy of every extraordinary resolution must be filed with the Registrar within 15 days after it has been passed (s. 380).

(f) *A copy of every extraordinary resolution* must be annexed to, or embodied in, every copy of the Articles issued after the passing of the resolution (s. 380(2)). However, if Articles have *not* been registered, a copy of every extraordinary resolution must be forwarded to any member at his request on payment of 5p, or less if the company so directs (s. 380(3)).

(g) *Stock Exchange regulations*. In the case of a company whose shares are listed on the Stock Exchange, *four* copies of any extraordinary resolution must be delivered to the share and loan department of the Stock Exchange concerned.

7.   Special resolution (s. 378(2))

(a) *Definition*. A special resolution is defined in the Act as 'a resolution passed by the same majority as required for an extraordinary resolution at a general meeting of which *not less than 21 days' notice* specifying the intention to propose the resolution as a special resolution has been given'. It will be observed that a special resolution differs from an extraordinary resolution only as regards the notice required, i.e. a special resolution requires at least 21 days' notice in *all* cases.

(b) *Inadequate notice* may be excused, i.e. if less than 21 days' notice is given, subject to compliance with the provisions of s. 369(3) in the case of the annual general meeting or s. 378(3) in the case of other meetings (95 per cent holding rule).

(c) *When required*. A special resolution is required only where prescribed by the Act, and in any additional cases where the company's Articles so provide; that is, the Articles may demand a special (or extraordinary) resolution where an ordinary resolution would suffice for the purposes of the Act.

(d) *The Act requires a special resolution* for almost any alteration of the company's constitution or capital structure. These include the following purposes:

Section 2: To provide a registered office in Wales.

Section 4: To alter the 'objects' clause of the Memorandum of Association.

Section 9: To alter the Articles of Association.

Section 17: To alter conditions in the Memorandum of Association.

Section 28: To change the company's name.

Section 35: To relieve any liability of directors or any other person incurred because the directors have acted outside the company's objects.

Section 43: To re-register a private company as public.

Section 51: To re-register an unlimited company as limited.

Section 53: To re-register a public company as private.

Section 95: To display pre-emption rights on the allotment of shares.

Section 120: To create reserve liability by rendering share capital incapable of being called up except in the event of winding up.

Section 135: To reduce the company's share capital.

Section 157: To enable a private company to give financial assistance for the purchase of its own shares.

Section 164: To authorize an off-market purchase of the company's own shares.

Section 165: To authorize contingent purchase contracts of the company's own shares.

Section 167: To release the company's rights to contracts under ss. 164 and 165.

Section 173: To authorize a private company to redeem or purchase its own shares out of capital.

Section 250: To make a dormant private company exempt from auditing.

Section 307: To alter the memorandum to make the liability of directors unlimited.

Section 308: To approve the assigning of office by a director.

Insolvency Act 1986

Section 84: To resolve that the company be wound up voluntarily.

Section 110: To accept shares, etc as consideration for the sale of company property.

Section 122: That the company be wound up by the court.

(e) *Registration.* A copy of every special resolution must be filed with the Registrar within 15 days after it has been passed (s. 380).

(f) *A copy of every special resolution* must be annexed to, or embodied in, every copy of the Articles issued after the passing of the resolution (s. 380(2)).

> NOTE: If Articles have *not* been registered, a copy of every special resolution must be forwarded to any member, at his request, on payment of 5p, or less if the company so directs (s. 380(3)).

(g) *Stock Exchange regulations.* In the case of a company whose shares are listed on the Stock Exchange *four* copies of any special resolution must be delivered to the share and loan department of the Stock Exchange concerned.

8.   The requirement that the special resolution as passed is substantially the same as that proposed

In *Re Moorgate Mercantile Holdings Ltd* (1980) Slade J summarized the principles relating to notices of, and the subsequent amendment of, special resolutions. He said that:

(a) If a notice of the intention to propose a special resolution is to be a valid notice for the purpose of s. 378(2), it must identify the intended resolution by specifying either the text or the entire substance of the resolution which it is intended to propose. In the case of a notice of intention to propose a special resolution, nothing is achieved by the addition of such words as 'with such amendments and alterations as shall be determined on at such meeting'.

(b) If a special resolution is to be validly passed in accordance with s. 378(2), the resolution as passed must be the same resolution as that identified in the preceding notice. The phrase 'the resolution' in s. 378(2) means 'the aforesaid resolution'.

(c) A resolution as passed can properly be regarded as 'the resolution' identified in a preceding notice, even though

  (*i*) it departs in some respects from the text of a resolution set out in such notice (for example by correcting those grammatical or clerical errors which can be corrected as a matter of construction, or by reducing the words to more formal language) or

  (*ii*) it is reduced into the form of a new text, which was not included in the notice, provided only that in either case there is no departure whatever from the substance.

(d) In deciding whether there is complete identity between the substance of a resolution as passed and the substance of an intended resolution as notified, there is no room for the court to apply the *de minimis* principle or a 'limit of tolerance.' The substance must be identical. Otherwise the condition precedent to the validity of a special resolution as passed, which is imposed by s. 378(2), namely, that notice has been given 'specifying the intention to propose the resolution as a special resolution', is not satisfied.

(e) It necessarily follows from the above propositions that an amendment to the previously circulated text of a special resolution can properly be put to and voted at a meeting if, *but only if*, the amendment involves no departure from the substance of the circulated text, in the sense indicated in propositions **(c)** and **(d)** above.

(f) References to notices in the above propositions are intended to include references to circulars accompanying notices. Notices and circulars should ordinarily be treated as one document.

(g) All the above propositions may be subject to modification where all the members, or a class of members, unanimously agree to waive their rights to notice under s. 378(2) (cf. s. 380(4)(d)).

> NOTE: In the case itself the notice stated the proposed resolution as 'the share premium account of the company amounting to £1,356,900.48p be cancelled' whereas the resolution presented at the meeting stated 'that the share premium account of the company amounting to £1,356,900.48p be reduced to £321.97p'. It was voted for unanimously by those present at the meeting. Nevertheless, on the principles stated above it was held not to have been validly passed in accordance with s. 378(2).

9. Elective resolutions

As part of the de-regulation of private companies the Companies Act 1989 introduced into the 1985 Act new provisions dealing with the elective regime (*see* 16:**10(d)**). Under this regime an *elective resolution* is required in order for a *private company* to make an election under any one of the following provisions:

Section 80A: Duration of directors' authority to allot shares

Section 252: Dispensing with laying of accounts and reports before general meeting

Section 366A: Dispensing with holding of annual general meeting

Section 369 or 378: Majority required to authorize short notice of meeting

Section 386: Dispensing with annual appointment of auditors.

An elective resolution is effective if:

(*i*) at least 21 days' notice in writing is given of the meeting stating that an elective resolution is to be proposed and stating the terms of the resolution; and

(*ii*) the resolution is agreed to at the meeting, in person or by proxy, by all the members entitled to attend and vote at the meeting (s. 379A(2)). An elective resolution may be agreed to informally in writing in accordance with s. 381A.

Members may revoke an elective resolution by adopting an *ordinary resolution* to that effect (s. 379(3)). Since only a private company may make any of these elections, an elective resolution of a private company is automatically revoked on re-registration of the company as a public company (s. 379A(4)).

Registration and circulation

10. Registration of copies of certain resolutions

The provisions of s. 380 as to the filing with the Registrar of Companies, and members' entitlement to, copies of resolutions applies not only to special, extraordinary and elective resolutions (referred to above), but also to the following:

(a) *Resolutions that have been agreed to by all members of a company* which would otherwise have required the passing of an extraordinary or special resolution.

(b) *Resolutions or agreements which have been agreed to by all members of a particular class* of shareholder, which would otherwise have required a particular majority.

(c) *Resolutions or agreements which bind all members of a particular class* of shareholder, though not agreed to by all of them.

(d) *Resolutions for the winding-up of a company* voluntarily under s. 84(1)(a) of the Insolvency Act 1986.

(e) *Resolutions passed by the directors* of a company in compliance with a direction under s. 31(2) (change of name on Secretary of State's direction).

(f) *Resolutions to give, vary, revoke or renew an authority* to the directors for the purpose of s. 80 (allotment of relevant securities).

(g) *Resolutions of the directors* passed under s. 147(2) (alteration of memorandum on company ceasing to be a public company, following acquisition of its own shares).

(h) *Resolutions conferring, varying, revoking or renewing authority* under s. 166 (market purchase of company's own shares).

11. Chairman's declaration

(a) The chairman's declaration that an *extraordinary* or *special* resolution is carried is *conclusive* evidence of the fact, unless a poll is demanded; that is, without any need to prove the number or proportion of votes recorded for or against the resolution (s. 378(4)). However, the chairman's declaration of the result on a show of hands may be challenged at the time by a proper demand for a poll.

(b) *Table A* (art. 47) makes a similar provision in respect of *all* resolutions. Thus:

> 'Unless a poll is duly demanded a declaration by the chairman that a resolution has been carried or carried unanimously, or by a particular majority, or lost, or not carried by a particular majority and an entry to that effect in the minutes of the meeting shall be conclusive evidence of the fact without proof of the number or proportion of the votes recorded in favour of or against the resolution.'

Therefore in *Graham's Morocco Co. Ltd, Petitioners* (1932) a company petitioned for confirmation of reduction of capital and for approval of a special resolution. On a show of hands, seven of the nine shareholders attending the meeting voted in favour of the resolution. The remaining two voted against. No poll was demanded and therefore the chairman declared the resolution carried. On being satisfied that the conduct of the meeting was regular and the proceedings were not fraudulent, the court decided that the declaration was legally made. The court was bound to accept the chairman's declaration as valid without further inquiry. The court held that the word 'conclusive' meant that the resolution should be so regarded unless a poll was demanded. It was argued that because two of the members attending the meeting lacked the necessary qualification the resolution was not duly carried. The court did not agree.

Similarly in *Arnot* v. *United African Lands* (1901) it was claimed that at a very confused meeting an adjournment was carried and a special resolution was not passed. The minutes recorded that the resolution had been carried by the requisite majority and that no poll had been demanded. It was held that the declaration by the chairman to that effect precluded any inquiry into the number of shareholders who voted for or against the resolution, and in the absence of fraud was *absolutely* conclusive and not merely *prima facie* conclusive.

(c) *Exceptions*. Nevertheless, the chairman's declaration may be set aside, e.g.

    (i) Where the chairman's declaration is, on the face of it, incorrect; *Re Caratal New Mines* (1902). Here the chairman put a resolution and declared the result saying that there were six votes in favour and twenty-three against but that, since there were two hundred voting by proxy, the resolution was carried. The court held that the declaration was *not* conclusive because the chairman could not take into account the proxies when no poll had been demanded.

    (ii) Where, because there was no apparent opposition, the chairman neglected to put the motion to the vote: *Citizens' Theatre Ltd* (1946).

12. Circulation of resolutions and statements

(a) *Shareholder' rights*. Section 376 gives shareholders the following important rights:

    (i) *To introduce resolutions* for consideration at the company's *annual* general meeting; or

    (ii) *To circulate statements* of not more than 1,000 words concerning any resolution to be proposed at *any* general meeting of the company.

(b) *The requisition of the company* must be made in writing by:

    (i) *Any number of members*, representing not less than

one-twentieth of the total voting rights of all members having a right, at the date of the requisition, to vote at the meeting to which the requisition relates; or

(*ii*) *Not less than 100 members* holding shares in the company on which there has been paid up an average sum per member of not less than £100.

(**c**) *Time and place for deposit of the requisition.* Section 377 provides that a company is not bound by s. 376 unless a copy of the requisition, signed by the requisitionists (or two or more documents which among them contain the signatures of all the requisitionists) is deposited at the registered office of the company;

(*i*) *Not less than six weeks* before the meeting, in the case of a requisition requiring notice of a resolution; and

(*ii*) *Not less than one week* before the meeting, in the case of any other requisition, i.e. one requiring circulation of a statement.

(*iii*) The requisitionists tender, with their requisition, a sum reasonably sufficient to meet the company's expenses in giving effect thereto.

(**d**) *Otherwise the company must comply with the requisition*; that is, by giving notice of any resolution to those entitled to receive notice of the next annual general meeting, or by circulating any statement submitted by the requisitionists.

If, after a copy of a requisition notice of a resolution has been deposited at the company's registered office, an annual general meeting is called for a date six weeks or less after the copy has been deposited, the copy is nevertheless deemed properly deposited, (s. 377)(2)).

(**e**) The company is not bound to circulate a statement if, on application by the company or any aggrieved person, the court is satisfied that the rights conferred by s. 376 are being abused to secure needless publicity for defamatory purposes.

NOTE: There is *no* right of appeal to the court against giving notice of a resolution submitted by the requisitionists. The business which may be dealt with at an annual general meeting includes any resolution of which notice is given in accordance with s. 376. Also, notwithstanding anything in the company's articles, notice is deemed to have been given for the purposes of s. 376 despite the accidental omission, in giving it, of one or more members.

13. Resolution to remove a director

(a) A company may remove a director before his period of office has expired notwithstanding any agreement between the company and the director, e.g. a contract of service, or anything in its articles, by passing an *ordinary resolution* to that effect (s. 303). The following are also required:

    (*i*) A resolution to remove a director under s. 303 requires *special notice*, as does a resolution to appoint somebody in his place at the meeting at which he is removed.

    (*ii*) On receiving notice of an intended resolution to remove a director under s. 303, the company must forthwith send a copy of the notice to the director concerned. The director is entitled to speak on the resolution at the meeting, whether or not he is a member (s. 304(1)).

    (*iii*) The director may make representations to the company of a reasonable length in writing and request their notification to members. Unless the representations are received by the company too late for it to do so, the company must, in any notice of the resolution to members, state the fact that the representations have been made. A copy of the representations must also be sent to every member of the company to whom notice of the meeting is sent (s. 304(2)).

    (*iv*) However, copies of the representations need *not* be sent out or the representations read out at the meeting if, on the application either of the company or of any person who claims to be aggrieved, the court is satisfied that the rights conferred by s. 304 are being *abused* to secure needless publicity for defamatory matter.

(b) *Compensation.* Section 303 does not deprive a director who is removed from office under it of any compensation or damages payable to him in respect of the termination of his appointment as director or any other appointment, e.g. managing director, solicitor, auditor, surveyor etc which is also terminated as a result. Nor does s. 303 derogate from any power to remove a director which may exist apart from this section, e.g. by alteration of articles: *Southern Foundries Ltd* v. *Shirlaw* (1940), or which exists in the company's articles.

(c) *Weighted votes.* It is possible for the articles of the company to provide that a director's shares shall carry weighted votes on a resolution to remove him under s. 303: *Bushel* v. *Faith* (1969). Depending on the company's shareholding and voting structure, this may all too often mean that a director can only be removed by first passing a special resolution to remove the article giving him weighted votes (which may also require class consents if it can be regarded as a class right, *see Cumbrian Newspapers Group Ltd* v. *C.W.H. Newspaper and Printing Co. Ltd* (1986)), followed by the ordinary resolution removing him from office.

(d) *Filling the vacancy.* A vacancy created by the removal of a director under s. 303, if not filled at the meeting at which he is removed, may be filled as a casual vacancy. *See* Table A, arts. 78 and 79.

(e) *The person appointed in place of the director removed under s. 303* is treated as if he had become a director on the day on which the person whose place he is appointed was last appointed director. The time at which he is to retire is determined accordingly (s. 303(4)).

NOTE: A private company's power to pass an informal written resolution under s. 381A does not apply to a resolution under s. 303. (Companies Act 1985, Schedule 15A, para. 1). For a consideration of limits on the rights to use the s. 303 procedure *see Re Opera Photographic Ltd* (1989) and contrast *Kouris* v. *Kouris* (1987); *Re Sticky Fingers Restaurant Ltd* (1991).

14. Public companies: appointment of directors to be voted on individually

By s. 292 a motion for the appointment of two or more persons as directors of a public company *cannot be made by a single resolution unless* there is first passed a resolution that it shall be so made without any vote being given against that first resolution.

If a resolution appointing two or more persons as directors is passed without following the above-mentioned procedure, it is *void* and no provision for the automatic re-appointment of retiring directors in default of another appointment applies.

The simplest procedure therefore, where it cannot be guaranteed that there will be no votes against a first resolution proposing that a single resolution be used to appoint two or more persons as directors, is to *vote on each individually.*

Resolution without meeting

15. Valid resolutions without holding a meeting

(a) *In relation to decisions of members,* Table A, article 53 states that:

'A resolution in writing executed by or on behalf of each member who would have been entitled to vote upon it if it had been proposed at a general meeting at which he was present shall be as effectual as if it had been passed at a general meeting duly convened and held and may consist of several instruments in the like for each executed by or on behalf of one or more members.'

And in relation to directors, article 93 provides:

'A resolution in writing signed by all the directors entitled to receive notice of a meeting of directors or of a committee of directors shall be as valid and effectual as if it had been passed at a meeting of directors or (as the case may be) a committee of directors duly convened and held and may consist of several documents in the like form each signed by one or more directors; but a resolution signed by an alternative director need not also be signed by his appointor and, if it is signed by a director who has appointed an alternate director, it need not be signed by the alternate director in that capacity.'

(b) *A line of cases has also developed the doctrine that* ' . . . where a transaction is *intra vires* the company and honest the sanction of all members of the company, however expressed, is sufficient to validate it, especially if it is a transaction entered into for the benefit of the company.' (Astbury J in *Parker & Cooper Ltd* v. *Reading* (1926).)

This principle applies even if the members do not meet together in one room or place, but all of them merely discuss and agree to it one with another separately. Hence it does not matter whether that assent (which may be oral only) is given at different times or simultaneously.

It follows from this that where all the members of a company are directors of it then directors' meetings are *de facto* members' meetings. In *Re Express Engineering works* (1920) a company was formed with five shareholders, each of whom was a director. The company's articles prevented any director from voting on a contract in which he might be interested. At what was ostensibly a directors' meeting, they unanimously approved a contract for the sale of their property to the company in return for debentures. It was held that the company was bound by the unanimous consent of the shareholders. Warrington LJ said:

> 'It happened that these five directors were the only shareholders of the company, and it is admitted that the five, acting together as shareholders, could have issued these debentures. As directors they could not but as shareholders acting together they could have made the agreement in question. It was competent to them to waive all formalities as regards notice of meetings, etc, and to resolve themselves into a meeting of shareholders and unanimously pass the resolution in question. Inasmuch as they could not in one capacity effectually do what was required but could do it in another, it is to be assumed that as businessmen they would act in the capacity in which they had power to act. In my judgment they must be held to have acted as shareholders and not as directors, and the transaction must be treated as good as if every formality had been carried out.'

This principle was applied in *Multinational Gas & Petrochemical* v. *Multinational Gas & Petrochemical Services Ltd* (1983) where the corporate members of the company were treated as having ratified the negligence of the service company through their nominee directors.

(c) *The principle has been extended* to cover acts requiring special or extraordinary resolutions. In *Cane* v. *Jones* (1981) it was said that s. 9 (special resolution to alter articles) is merely laying down a procedure whereby *some* only of the shareholders can validly alter the articles. The principle was applied to an agreement between all the shareholders of the company which had the effect of removing the chairman's casting vote under the articles, even though there had been no meeting and no special resolution. In *Re Shankey Contracting Ltd* (1980) it was held that with such unanimous consent an extraordinary resolution can be passed without any meeting being held. The principle is best stated by Buckley J in *Re Duomatic Ltd* (1969): 'Where it can be shown that all shareholders *who have a right to attend and vote at a general meeting* of the company assent to some matter which a general meeting of the company could carry into effect, that assent is as binding as a resolution in general meeting would be.'

(d) *Limits to the principle*. In *Re Duomatic*, Buckley J doubted that the principle would apply to approval of the company under s. 312 for payments to directors for loss of office unless all persons who are entitled to assent are given the opportunity to do so. Nor would the principle of Table A (art. 53) be appropriate for an ordinary resolution to alter the capital of the company under s. 121 since that section 'must be exercised by the company in general meeting'. Presumably the principle might apply to a 'class' decision where shareholders of a class unanimously but orally assent to a variation of their class rights (*see* chapter 26). In *Re Barry Artist Ltd* (1985) all the members of a company assented in writing to a reduction of capital. They did not pass a special resolution (cf s. 135). The court held that the unanimous written consent of the members was effective to reduce the company's capital subject to court confirmation. However, the court said that since settled practice was to require a special resolution to reduce a company's capital it would not be prepared to confirm an informal unanimous consent in such cases in future. It is probable that the assent of all joint holders of shares is not required since one joint holder can assent on behalf of the other or others: *Re Gee & Co. (Woolwich) Ltd* (1975).

(e) *Acquiescence*. The cases considered so far proceed on the basis of assent being actively and positively given. The question which may be raised is whether consent to a resolution can be given by acquiescence, such as by abstaining, or even given negatively. In *Re Bailey Hay & Co. Ltd* (1971), the facts of which have been discussed in consent to short notice, chapter 17, Brightman J held that the acquiescence of those shareholders who abstained from voting on a resolution to wind up the company voluntarily must be taken as an *assent* to the resolution, so that it should be deemed to have been passed with the unanimous assent of all the shareholders. His Lordship said:

'The conclusion is that they outwardly accepted the

resolution to wind up as decisively as if they had positively voted in favour of it. If corporators attend a meeting without protest, stand by without protest while their fellow-members purport to pass a resolution, permit all persons concerned to act for years on the basis that that resolution was duly passed and rule their own conduct on the basis that the resolution is an established fact, I think it is idle for them to contend that they did not assent to the purported resolution.'

The case of *Phosphate of Lime Co. Ltd* v. *Green* (1871) appears to indicate that it is sufficient to show circumstances which are reasonably calculated to satisfy the court that the matter to be approved came to the knowledge of all who chose to enquire, all having full opportunity and means of enquiry, in order to show assent by acquiescence. However, acquiescence may only be treated as tacit assent as a result of *attendance at a meeting* at which no objection was raised, and where there was a *failure to challenge the resolution within a reasonable time* after the meeting.

16. Statutory provisions for written resolutions of private companies

(a) Also under the heading of 'De-regulation of private companies' the 1989 Companies Act ss. 113 and 114 introduced into the Companies Act 1985 new ss. 381A, 381B, 381C, 382A and Schedule 15A. These sections provide that anything which in the case of a private company may be done:

(*i*) by resolution of the company in general meeting; or
(*ii*) by resolution of a meeting of any class of members of the company

may be done, *without a meeting and without any previous notice being required*, by resolution in writing signed by or on behalf of all the members of the company, who at the date of the resolution would be entitled to attend and vote at such meeting (s. 381A(1)).

The *date* of the resolution means when the resolution is signed by or on behalf of the *last member* to sign, and members' signatures need not be on a single document provided each signature is on a document which accurately states the terms of the resolution. The new provisions cover a resolution which would otherwise require to be passed as a special, extraordinary or elective resolution (s. 381A(6)).

They also have effect notwithstanding any provisions of the company's memorandum or articles. However, nothing in ss. 381A or 381B affects any enactment or rule of law as to:

(*i*) things done otherwise than by passing a resolution, or

(*ii*) cases in which a resolution is treated as having been passed, or a person is precluded from alleging that a resolution has not been duly passed (s. 381C). Therefore the common law, as discussed in **15** above is not affected.

(b) *Exceptions*. Schedule 15A, para. 1 provides that the procedure for written resolutions of private company's does not apply to:

(*i*) a resolution under s. 303 of the 1985 Act removing a director before the expiration of his period of office; or

(*ii*) a resolution under s. 391 of the 1985 Act removing an auditor before the expiration of his term of office.

It must also be noted that s. 381A applies to anything which in the case of a private company *may* be done by resolution in a general or class meeting. Therefore the procedure will not apply to those things which the Acts say *must* be exercised by the company in general meeting, such as an alteration of share capital under s. 121. *See* s. 121(4); *Mercer* (1991) 12 Co Law 220.

(c) *The rights of auditors in relation to a written resolution.* Section 381B requires that a copy of any resolution proposed to be agreed to under s. 381A is to be sent to the company's auditors. If the resolution concerns the auditors as auditors they may, within seven days from receipt of the copy resolution, give notice to the company stating their opinion that the resolution should be considered by the company in general meeting or by a class meeting. The resolution will not have effect unless:

(*i*) the auditors notify the company that in their opinion the resolution either does not concern them as auditors, or does so concern them but does not need to be considered in a general or class meeting; or

(*ii*) the above mentioned period of seven days has expired without the auditors having given notice to the company.

(d) *The recording of written resolutions.* The company must keep a record of resolutions agreed to, in accordance with s. 381A, and of the signatures. They must be entered into a book in the same way as are minutes of proceedings of a general meeting of the company. Such a record, if signed by a director of the company or by the company secretary, is evidence of the proceedings in agreeing to the resolution. When such a record is made, s. 382A(2) deems the requirements of the act in relation to written resolutions of private companies to be complied with until the contrary is proved.

(e) *Adaptations.* Schedule 15A, Part II adapts certain procedural requirements of the 1985 Act to resolutions under s. 381A. The requirements adapted relate to:

Section 95: Disapplication of pre-emption rights

Section 155: Financial assistance for purchase of own shares

Section 164, 165 and 167: Authority for off-market purchase of own shares etc

Section 173: Approval for payment out of capital

Section 319: Approval of director's service contract

Section 337: Funding of director's expenses.

The adaptations relate to documents which must normally be circulated with notice, or be available for inspection at the meeting or the company's registered office. Schedule 15A generally disapplies these requirements for the purpose of a written resolution under s. 381A. Instead, it requires such documents to be supplied to each relevant member at or before the time at which the resolution is supplied to him for signature.

Furthermore, in relation to purchase of the company's own shares, off-market or contingently, (ss. 164, 165, 167) and purchase out of capital for a private company (s. 173); schedule 15A states that a member holding shares to which the resolution relates shall not be regarded as a member who would be entitled to attend and vote. Therefore their signature to a copy of the relevant resolution is not required.

Progress test 19

1. Distinguish between a motion, a resolution, and a substantive motion. What are the main rules to be followed in drafting a resolution? **(1)**

2. Give one example in each case of business which may be transacted by the passing of the following types of resolution: **(a)** ordinary resolution; **(b)** ordinary resolution of which special notice has been given; **(c)** special resolution; and **(d)** extra-ordinary resolution.

Draft the resolution for the business you have selected in **(b)**. **(4, 5, 6)**

3. Define 'special resolution', and describe the procedure necessary for its passing. List some of the purposes for which a special resolution may be passed.   **(7)**

4. Distinguish between ordinary, extraordinary and special resolutions.   **(5, 6, 7)**

5. When may a 'resolution' be validly passed without a meeting being held for that purpose?   **(15)**

6. What is the procedure to be followed to remove a director? **(13)**

20
Voting

1. Voting in the context of company law

(a) *The exercise of voting rights* is often central to many issues arising in company law. A distinction must first be made between voting in a board of directors' meeting and voting as a shareholder in a general meeting or a meeting of a class of shareholders. At board meetings directors are acting as officers of the company and owe fiduciary duties to it. At meetings of shareholders the general rule is that a member may exercise his property rights in his shares in his own selfish interests: *East Pant Du Mining Co.* v. *Merryweather* (1864). Generally the company has little or no influence over how its members vote and is not entitled to look behind the bare fact of legal ownership, as recorded in its register, where by s. 360 no notice of any trust, express, implied or constructive shall be entered. This distinction between the two types of meeting was highlighted in *N.C. Securities Ltd* v. *Jackson & Steeple Ltd* (1974) which has already been discussed in relation to notices. In that case the plaintiff, *inter alia*, sought an order restraining directors, *as shareholders*, from voting against the resolution approving an issue of shares. Walton J said:

> 'I think that, in a nutshell, the distinction is this: when a director votes as a director for or against any particular resolution in a director's meeting, he is voting as a person under a fiduciary duty to the company for the proposition that the company should take a certain course of action. When a shareholder is voting for or against a particular resolution, he is voting as a person owing no fiduciary duty to the company and who is exercising his own right of property, to vote as he thinks fit. The fact that the result of

the voting at the meeting (or at a subsequent poll) will bind the company cannot affect the position that, in voting, he is voting simply in exercise of his own property rights.

Perhaps another (and simpler) way of putting the matter is that a director is an agent, who casts his vote to decide in what manner his principal shall act through the collective agency of the board of directors; a shareholder who casts his vote in general meeting is not casting it as an agent of the company in any shape or form. His act therefore, in voting as he pleases, cannot in any way be regarded as an act of the company . . . I think that a director who has fulfilled his duty as a director of a company, by causing it to comply with an undertaking binding upon it is nevertheless free, as an individual shareholder, to enjoy the same unfettered and unrestricted right of voting at general meetings of the members of the company as he would have if he were not also a director . . .'

Therefore, the freedom of a shareholder to vote in his own interest extends even to a shareholder who is also a director. It follows that a member who is also a director is not subject to the rule against conflict of interest and duty when voting as a member. In *Northwest Transportation Co. Ltd* v. *Beatty* (1887) a director was held to be entitled to vote as a shareholder, even though his interest in the subject matter was opposed to the interests of the company. Sir Richard Baggallay said:

'Unless some provision to the contrary is to be found in the charter or other instrument by which the company is incorporated, the resolution of a majority of the shareholders duly convened, upon any question with which the company is legally competent to deal, is binding upon the minority, and consequently upon the company, and every shareholder has a perfect right to vote upon any such question, although he may have a personal interest in the subject-matter opposed to, or different from the general or particular interests of the company.'

(b) *Exceptions to the general rule*

   (i) *Statutory*. There are two statutory restrictions on self-interested voting. First, when counting votes in favour of a special resolution of a private company to make a payment out of capital to redeem shares, votes attaching to the shares to be redeemed must be ignored (s. 174(2)). Secondly, when counting votes in favour of a special resolution to confer, vary, revoke or renew authority to make an off-market purchase of its own shares, or to make a contingent purchase contract for its own shares, votes attaching to the shares to be purchased must be ignored (ss. 164(5), 165(2)).

(ii) *Bona fide for the benefit of the company as a whole*. The courts have sometimes said that a resolution of the company would be invalid if members voting for it did not vote bona fide in the interests of the company. An example is when voting to alter the company's articles: *Allen* v. *Gold reefs of West Africa Ltd* (1900). Directors when exercising their powers are subject to the same test to prevent an abuse of their fiduciary duties. In those cases where it is applied to members it is imposed to prevent the misuse of the power of the majority to bind a minority. The same test has been applied to voting in class meetings where the power of the majority is for the purpose of benefitting the class as a whole, and not merely individual members: *British America Nickel Corporation Ltd* v. *M. J. O'Brian Ltd* (1927); *Re Holders Investment Trust Ltd* (1972). It has also been judicially stated that an appointment of a director must be made for the benefit of the company as a whole and not for any ulterior purpose: *Re H.R. Harmer Ltd* (1959).

(iii) *Fraud on the minority*. Where the majority seek to ratify their own oppressive act or expropriation of corporate property, the courts will not accept the resolution to ratify as valid. In *Cook* v. *Deeks* (1917) three out of four directors of a company obtained an offer of a further construction contract for themselves. At a general meeting, by their votes as holders of three quarters of the issued shares, they passed a resolution declaring that the company had no interest in the contract. The resolution was declared invalid because the contract belonged in equity to the company and the action of the directors amounted to a breach of trust. An earlier example is *Menier* v. *Hooper's Telegraph Works* (1874) in which the major shareholder in a company had contracted to make and lay a submarine telegraph cable for the company. They caused the company to abandon the contract because it was more advantageous to do work for another person. James LJ said:

'The minority of the shareholders say in effect that the majority has divided the assets of the company, more or less, between themselves, to the exclusion of the minority. I think it would be a shocking thing if that could be done, because if so the majority might divide the whole assets of the company, and pass a resolution that everything must be given to them, and that the minority should have nothing to do with it. Assuming the case to be as alleged by the bill, then the majority have put something into their pockets at the expense of the minority. If so, it appears to me that the minority have a right to have their share of the benefits ascertained for them in the best way in which the court can do it, and given to them.'

(iv) *Other equitable considerations* may make it unjust for a member of a company to exercise a vote in a particular way. In *Clemens* v. *Clemens Bros Ltd* (1976) the two shareholders, both of whom inherited their shares, were Miss Clemens who held 55 per cent of the votes and her niece who had 45 per cent. The plaintiff niece had resigned her directorship after disagreement with her aunt. The latter passed a resolution authorizing the issue of new shares to directors and an employee trust scheme. This had the effect of reducing the plaintiff's pre-emptive rights to purchase other members' shares and destroyed her negative control (i.e. the power to prevent the passing of special and extraordinary resolutions). The resolution was set aside; Foster J said:

'a court of equity will in my judgment regard these considerations as sufficient to prevent the consequences arising from Miss Clemens using her legal right to vote in the way she has and it would be right for a court of equity to prevent such consequences taking effect.'

Similarly in *Estmanco (Kilner House) Ltd* v. *GLC* (1982) the company had been formed to carry into effect an agreement with the council. The directors began an action in the company's name for specific performance of the agreement but at a shareholders' meeting, where the council was the only shareholder entitled to vote, the directors were instructed to discontinue the action. However, a flat owner in Kilner House began an action as a voteless shareholder in her own name. The court allowed her to continue the action as a derivative action; Megarry V-C said:

'No right of a shareholder to vote in his own selfish interests or to ignore the interests of the company entitles him with impunity to injure his voteless fellow shareholders by depriving the company of a cause of action and stultifying the purpose for which the company was formed.'

(v) *Votes on improperly issued shares.* Where votes were cast in respect of shares issued by the directors themselves or their friends for the purpose of securing the passing of certain resolutions, this was held to be in conflict with the principle that the powers entrusted to the board must be exercised bona fide and for the interest of the company: *Punt* v. *Symons & Co. Ltd* (1903). *See also Piercy* v. *Mills & Co. Ltd* (1920) where it was held improper for directors to use their power to issue shares in order to rob the existing majority shareholders of their voting control. This principle was applied in *Howard Smith Ltd* v. *Amphol Ltd* (1974). It appears that the wrongful issue of shares may be ratified so long as the votes on those shares are not used to do so: *Hogg* v. *Cramphorn* (1967) and *Bamford* v. *Bamford* (1969). After a lawful ratification, the votes on the improperly issued shares may be used as normal.

NOTE: The issue of how voting rights may be used is a controversial one. For further discussion readers are referred to: D.D. Prentice 'Restraints on the exercise of majority shareholder power' (1976) 92 LQR 502 and V. Joffe 'Majority rule undermined?' (1977) 40 MLR 71. For a comprehensive survey, *see* P.G. Xuereb, 'The limitation on the exercise of majority power' (1985) 6 Co Law 199; 'Remedies for abuse of majority power' (1986) 7 Co Law 53 and ' "Voting rights":

a comparative review' (1987) 8 Co Law 16. For a vigorous attack on some developments, *see* L.S. Sealy, 'Equitable and other Fetters on the shareholders' freedom to vote' in *The Cambridge Lectures 1981* (Toronto, Butterworths, 1982), Edited by N.E. Eastham and B. Krivy.

2.   Voting agreements

(a) *By separate contract.* Shareholders may enter into agreements restricting or determining the way in which they exercise their voting rights. Such agreements are valid and may be enforced by mandatory injunction. The case of *Puddephatt* v. *Leith* (1916) is an example. Here the plaintiff had mortgaged fully paid shares to the defendant, the shares being transferred from her name to his. By letter, the mortgagee agreed to vote only after consulting the mortgagor and in accordance with her wishes. It was held that there was a collateral agreement as to the manner in which the voting rights were to be exercised and that a mandatory injunction would be granted to enforce such an agreement.

In *Greenwell* v. *Porter* (1902), the defendants bound themselves by agreement to do all things within their power to secure the election of two named persons as directors of a company and thereafter to vote for their re-election. When the defendants subsequently tried to oppose the re-election of one of the two as director, a prohibitory injunction was granted restraining them from voting in any way inconsistent with the agreement. The fact that the defendants also happened to be directors did not preclude them as shareholders from entering into and being bound by their voting agreement. Another case, *Wise* v. *Lansdell* (1921), held that where the owner of fully paid shares charged them in favour of another person, and gave a blank transfer in respect of the charge, he was entitled to vote so long as his name remained on the register, though having subsequently become bankrupt he could only vote as the mortgagees dictated. However, there are limits on the extent to which the courts will enforce agreements. For example, in *Wilton Group plc* v. *Abrams* (1990) Mr Justice Stott held that a court of equity would not assist parties to enforce any agreement for the sale of shares in a public limited company which purported to confer a service contract on the vendor or a seat on the board to the purchaser, because such agreements were commercially disreputable.

Shareholder agreements of this nature bind only the parties to the agreement, there can be no question of a continuing obligation which runs with the shares: *Greenhalgh* v. *Mallard* (1943). **(b)** *Agreements in the articles.* Voting agreements may also arise out of the s. 13 contract in the articles, so that, for example, a director may be given a right of veto in relation to certain transactions: *Salmon* v. *Quin & Axtens* (1909). Similarly, different voting rights may attach to certain shares on specified matters as in *Bushel* v. *Faith* (1970) where the right of directors to have weighted votes on a resolution to dismiss them was upheld. However, such rights are subject to the difficulties of enforcement and alteration. In *Rights and Issues Investment Trusts* v. *Stylo Shoes* (1964) management shares had a right to eight votes per share and this was validly increased to sixteen votes per share. *See also Cumbrian Newspapers Group Ltd* v. *C.W.H. Newspaper & Printing Co. Ltd* (1986). *See also Lee Panavision Ltd* v. *Lee Lighting Ltd* (1991) where it was held that current directors, facing imminent removal by the members and replacement by a new board, are not at liberty to organize matters so as to bind the incoming directors in respect of the future management of the company.

3. Methods of voting

The methods most commonly used at company meetings are:

(a) *Show of hands,* i.e. one person one vote. This is the 'common law method' of voting: *Re Horbury Bridge Coal Co.* (1879), where Jessel M.R. said that at common law:

> ' . . . votes at all meetings are taken by show of hands. Of course it may not always be a satisfactory mode — persons attending in large numbers may be small shareholders, and persons attending in small numbers may be large shareholders, and therefore in companies provision is made for taking a poll, and when a poll is taken the votes are to be counted according to the number of shares.'

(b) *Poll.* This is a method of voting which gives the right to record votes proportionately to, say, shares or stock held.

> NOTE: The other methods of voting, namely ballot, division and acclamation are seldom used at company meetings.

4.   Table A

Table A makes the following provisions as to method of voting and members' voting rights:

(a) *At general meetings,* a motion put to the vote shall be decided *on a show of hands* in the first place (art. 46).

(b) *But a poll may be demanded,* on or before declaration of the result of the show of hands, by:

- (*i*)   the chairman;
- (*ii*)   at least *two* members present in person or by proxy having the right to vote at the meeting;
- (*iii*)   any member, or members, present in person or by proxy and representing *not less than one-tenth of the total voting rights* of all members having the right to vote at the meeting; or
- (*iv*)   a member, or members, holding shares on which an aggregate sum has been paid up equal to *not less than one-tenth of the total sum paid up* on all shares conferring the right to vote at the meeting (art. 46).

(c) *On a show of hands,* every member present *in person* or (being a corporation) is present by a duly authorized representative, is entitled to one vote, i.e. a proxy has *no* power to vote on a show of hands (art. 54).

(d) *On a poll:*

- (*i*)   Every member is entitled to *one vote for each share* of which he is the holder (art. 54).
- (*ii*)   Votes may be given *either* personally *or* by proxy (art. 59).

5.   The Act

Section 370 makes the following general provisions, to be applied where a company makes no provisions on the subject of voting in its Articles:

(a) In the case of a company originally having a share capital, every member is entitled to *one vote for each share held,* or for each £10 of stock held.

(b) In any other case, every member is entitled to *one* vote.

NOTE: It will be observed that the method of assessing voting power referred to in **(a)** above can only be applied *when a poll is taken,* since on a show of hands each member is, of course, entitled to only *one* vote.

6. Persons entitled to vote

(a) *Corporate shareholders* must be represented by a human agent. One solution would be for the corporate shareholder to appoint a proxy to vote on its behalf. However, s. 375 confers on a corporate shareholder the power to authorize by resolution of its directors, or other governing body, such person as it thinks fit to act as its representative at any general meeting or class meeting of the company. A person so authorized may exercise the same powers on behalf of the corporate shareholder as that company could exercise if it were an individual shareholder, creditor or debenture holder. This includes the power to speak at the meeting and to vote on a show of hands: *Re Kelantan Coconut Estates Ltd and Reduced* (1920), and on a poll. If a corporate representative also acts in his own capacity as a member, he is entitled to only *one* vote on a show of hands (Table A, art. 54). It has been held that 'other governing body' can include a liquidator: *Hillman* v. *Crystal Bowl Amusements and Others* (1973). A corporate representative is to be counted in the quorum. One major advantage of appointing a corporate representative rather than submitting a proxy is that the corporate member may wait until the meeting before deciding which way to vote since the representative only has to produce a certified board resolution as evidence of his appointment.

(b) *Trustees in bankruptcy and personal representative.* A bankrupt who is still registered as a member in respect of his shares remains entitled to attend and vote at company meetings, though he is obliged to vote in accordance with the directions of his trustee in bankruptcy because the trustee has the beneficial interest in the shares: *Morgan* v. *Gray* (1953). Although a trustee in bankruptcy or a personal representative is entitled under Table A to notice of meetings they are not generally entitled to vote or exercise any other right conferred by membership in relation to company meetings unless they are registered as members in respect of a share.

(c) *Joint shareholders.* Table A, art. 55 says that in the case of joint holders, the vote of the senior who tenders a vote, whether in person or by proxy, shall be accepted to the exclusion of the votes of the other joint holders; seniority shall be determined by the order in which the names of the holders stand in the register of members. Where articles like this one vest in the first joint holder the power to vote, the remaining joint holders could attend the meeting, but they would not be allowed to vote. In *Burns* v. *Siemens Brothers Dynamo Works Ltd* (1919) it was held that joint holders can have their holdings split into two or more joint holdings with their names in different orders. Joint holders therefore have a right to instruct the company on the order in which their names are to appear in the register: *Re T.H. Saunders & Co. Ltd* (1908).

(d) *Trustees.* By s. 360 a company is not affected by notice that any of its shares are held in trust. Under Table A, art. 5 the only interest in one of its shares that a company will recognize is an absolute right of the registered shareholder to the whole share, except as is otherwise provided by the articles or by law. If a share of a company is held on trust, a beneficiary of the trust cannot insist that the company accepts its vote instead of the vote of the trustee who is the registered holder of the share. Nevertheless, the court may make an order preventing the company acting on a resolution adopted by means of votes cast in breach of trust: *Mc Grattan* v. *Mc Grattan* (1985).

(e) *The unpaid seller of shares.* If a shareholder has sold his shares to another, but has not at the date of the meeting transferred those shares to the purchaser because he has not yet received payment for them, the unpaid vendor *retains the right to vote* in respect of the shares. However, if the transfer has been registered, but the vendor has not been paid, then the buyer must vote in accordance with the unpaid vendor's instructions: *Musselwhite* v. *C.H. Musselwhite & Sons Ltd* (1962).

(f) *Unpaid shares or dividends in arrears.* By Table A, art. 57, no member shall be entitled to vote at any general meeting or at any separate meeting of the holders of any class of shares in the company, either in person or by proxy, in respect of any share held by him unless all monies presently payable by him in respect of that share have been paid. Sometimes a company's articles give preference shareholders the right to vote in general meeting when their cumulative dividend is in arrears: *Re Bradford Investments plc* (1990) is an example. The ordinary shareholders argued that the preference shareholders could not vote because their preferential dividend was not in arrears since, in the absence of distributable profits, it could not be paid and so could not be in arrears. The preference shareholders argued that the ordinary shareholders could not vote because certain of their shares had been allotted in contravention of the statutory provisions governing the allotment of shares in a public company for a non-cash consideration. The articles contained a provision similar to art. 57 above. The court held the preference shareholders *were* entitled to vote because the articles deemed their dividend payable whether there were distributable profits or not. The ordinary shareholders, however, were not entitled to vote. Due to the improper allotment, there was an immediate liability outstanding in respect of their shares. The article therefore disenfranchised them. Resolutions to appoint new directors passed at the meeting by the preference shareholders were accordingly valid.

(g) *Mental disorder*. By Table A, art. 56, a member in respect of whom an order has been made by any court having jurisdiction in matters concerning mental disorder may vote by his receiver, *curator bonis*, or other authorized person.

(h) *Objections*. In order that difficulties and objections are dealt with promptly, Table A, art. 58 provides:

> 'No objection shall be raised to the qualification of any voter except at the meeting or adjourned meeting at which the vote objected to is tendered, and every vote not disallowed at the meeting shall be valid. Any objection made in due time allowed shall be referred to the chairman whose decision shall be final and conclusive.'

(i) *Freezing orders*. While investigations are in progress about the true ownership of shares in a company, those shares may be subjected to restrictions, imposed by the court or the Secretary of State. These may prevent the votes attached to those shares being exercised (ss. 212, 216, 442, 444, 454 to 457 inclusive).

7. Voting at board meetings

(a) *The conduct of board meetings*. Reference has already been made in 1. above to the fiduciary duties of directors to vote in what they bona fide believe is in the best interests of the company when voting as directors at board meetings. Board meetings are usually informal in character; nevertheless, the Articles may regulate the proceedings.

(b) *In practice*, however, the directors are often allowed to regulate their own meetings.

(c) *Table A* (art. 88) on the subject of board meetings provides that:

    (*i*) 'The directors may regulate their meetings as they think fit.'

    (*ii*) 'Questions arising at any meeting shall be decided by a majority of votes.'

    (*iii*) 'In case of an equality of votes, the chairman shall have a second or casting vote.'

(d) *Table A* (art. 94) which prevents a director from voting on any matter in which he has a material interest conflicting with that of the company is dealt with in chapter 28 (*see* 28:**3(c)**). However, the following points must also be noted:

    (*i*) Article 92 says that all acts done by a meeting of directors, notwithstanding that it is afterwards discovered that they were *inter alia* not entitled to vote, shall be as valid as if they had been entitled to vote. This may still raise problems in relation to Article 95 which states that a director shall not be counted in the quorum present at a meeting in relation to a resolution in which he is not entitled to vote. However, Article 92 only validates 'acts done by a meeting of directors' which assumes a valid quorum is present. Therefore if the meeting is inquorate in relation to a resolution because a director is not entitled to count towards the quorum and to vote on it (art. 95) that resolution will not be validated by Article 92. However, it is possible to argue to the contrary. Even so, if, as in a case of conflict of interest, a director votes knowing that he is disqualified from doing so under Article 94 and his vote is crucial to the passing of a resolution it is arguable that he ought not to be able to take advantage of his wrongdoing, despite Article 92.

    (*ii*) Article 96 provides that the company may by *ordinary resolution* suspend or relax to any extent, either generally or in respect of any particular matter, any provision of the Articles prohibiting a director from voting at a meeting of directors or of a committee of directors.

    (*iii*) Article 97 says that where proposals are under consideration concerning the appointment of *two* or more directors to offices or employments with the company the proposals may be divided and considered in relation to each director separately. Each of the directors concerned shall be entitled to vote and be counted in the quorum in respect of each resolution except that concerning his own appointment.

NOTE: In relation to the appointment of directors of public companies, *see* s. 292, discussed in chapter 27.

(*iv*) If a question arises at a meeting of directors as to the right of a director to vote, the question may, before the conclusion of the meeting, be referred to the chairman. The chairman's ruling in relation to any director, other than himself, shall be final and conclusive (art. 98).

8. The irregularity principle and voting

(a) *The principle*. In *Burland* v. *Earle* (1902) Lord Davey said that a member of a company may not bring an action questioning the lawfulness of a decision taken by a meeting of members or directors of a company if the only factor alleged to make it unlawful is a *mere informality or irregularity* and the intention of the meeting is clear. The concept of ratification is relevant here in that, if it is clear that, on going through the correct procedure the decision would be ratified, a member cannot bring an action questioning the validity of the decision on the basis of the *mere informality or irregularity*.

This is particularly so if there is no evidence that the decision of the meeting would have been different if the correct procedure had been observed. In *Browne* v. *La Trinidad* (1887), Cotton LJ said: ' . . . a court of equity refuses to interfere where an irregularity has been committed if it is within the power of the persons who have committed it at once to correct it by calling a fresh meeting and dealing with the matter with all due formalities'.

In *Pappaioannoy* v. *The Greek Othodox Community of Melbourne* (1978), King J said that the irregularity principle means 'that where it is clear that if the proper procedure had been followed the result would have been the same the court will not interfere merely to ensure regularity of procedure' and that it does not apply if it is not clear that the correct procedure would produce the same result. Some Australian courts have adopted the rule that the onus is on the defendant to show that it is unnecessary to go through

the procedure again, *see* for example *Rivers* v. *Bondi Junction —
Waverley RSL Sub Branch Ltd* (1986).

(b) *Examples of the irregularity principle:*

(i) In *The Southern Counties Deposit Bank Ltd* v. *Rider* (1895) two
directors had acted as a quorum at the board meeting,
though the directors' decision that their quorum should
be two was in fact invalid; the quorum should have been
three. The decision of the directors' meeting to summon
a general meeting of members was challenged. The Court
held that the irregularity as to quorum did not affect the
decision taken at the members' meeting because the
directors had previously acted with two as a quorum for
six years without challenge.

(ii) In *Boschoek Proprietary Co. Ltd* v. *Fuke* (1906) three
individuals acting as the company's directors had not been
properly appointed, for various reasons. They held a
board meeting and instructed the secretary to summon a
general meeting for the purpose of ratifying their acts as
directors. At the general meeting the ratification
resolution was passed unanimously. The court held that,
in the circumstances, the directors' lack of authority to
summon the meeting should be treated as a mere
irregularity which was not sufficient to invalidate any
resolution adopted at the meeting. For other examples of
the application of the principle *see Bentley-Stevens* v. *Jones*
(1974); *Brown* v. *La Trinidad* (1887) and, questionably, *Mac
Dougall* v. *Gardiner* (1875).

(c) *When the principle does not apply.*

(i) The principle of irregularity will *not* be applied if the
irregularity changes the outcome of a vote. Examples
include *Pender* v. *Lushington* (1887); *Shaw* v. *Tati Concessions
Ltd*; and *Burns* v. *Siemens Brothers & Co. Ltd* (1919) (the
latter two cases are discussed in chapter 21 on polls). In
such cases the courts will intervene. *Marks* v. *Financial
News Ltd* (1919) is another example. The plaintiff was the
executor of a shareholder in the defendant company who
had pledged a large number of his shares by way of
equitable security. After the plaintiff had proved the will
the company, not knowing of the pledge and in
accordance with its articles, admitted his right to vote. At

a meeting of the company the chairman disallowed the plaintiff's votes having learned of the pledge. If the plaintiff's votes had been allowed a special resolution altering the articles would not have been passed. The court held that the effect of the articles was that, in the circumstances, the plaintiff was entitled to vote and therefore the resolution was invalid.

(ii) *Where the procedural defect is more than a mere irregularity.* In two cases, *Re Haycraft Gold Reduction & Mining Co.* (1900) and *Re State of Wyoming Syndicate* (1901), the notice convening a meeting of members had been issued by the secretary of the company without the authority of the directors. This was not permitted by the articles of association. In both cases the members had, at the meeting, adopted a resolution for voluntary winding-up, and the court held that it would be going too far to hold that this was a mere irregularity and so the resolutions for voluntary winding-up were declared to be invalid. Similarly, it is more than a mere irregularity to attempt to do by ordinary resolution that which requires a special resolution: *Grant* v. *UK Switchback Railway Co.* (1888); *Salmon* v. *Quinn & Axtens Ltd* (1909).

Progress test 20

1. Explain the difference between a show of hands and a poll, when voting takes place at a company meeting. **(3, 4)**

2. Consider the rules on voting at meetings of directors and relate these rules to the validity of a quorum at directors' meetings. **(7)**

21
Polls

1. A common law right

(a) Although voting must be by show of hands in the first place, there *is* a common law right to demand a poll: *R* v. *Wimbledon Local Board* (1882). In practice this right is often either excluded or restricted by the relevant regulations. Special custom may have the same effect, but the mere fact that at meetings of a certain body no poll has ever been demanded, does not establish a special usage *excluding* a poll at such meetings: *Campbell* v. *Maund* (1836).

A poll is equivalent to an appeal by a party dissatisfied with the decision of the chairman upon the show of hands. In a corporate context the value of a poll lies in the fact that the weighted voting strengths of members may be more accurately assessed. At common law the result of a demand for a poll is that the previous proceedings are abandoned and a nullity, *so far as voting is concerned*, so that effective voting begins with the poll: *Anthony* v. *Seger* (1789).

It is essential, in order to ascertain the sense of a meeting, that on a demand for a poll being properly made the poll should be *actually taken*. In one case the defendant was elected to the office of waywarden on a show of hands. A poll was demanded by supporters of the only other candidate, but before it was taken the defendant announced that he declined to stand as waywarden. As a result the poll was not held, and subsequently the chairman declared that the defendant's election stood. It was held that there had been no election: *R* v. *Cooper* (1870) (contrast Table A, art. 48, considered in **4(a)** below). If a poll is duly demanded and is refused, the resolution or election in respect of which the poll was sought is rendered imperfect: *Ex parte Grossmith* (1841). However, in *MacDougall* v. *Gardiner* (1870) a proper demand for a poll was made and the chairman refused, his action being ratified by a simple majority on a show of hands. The court held that the shareholders who had demanded the poll could not sue to have the chairman's decision declared invalid because of the rule in *Foss* v. *Harbottle* (1843). The crux of the issue here is the *extent* of the personal rights exception to *Foss* v. *Harbottle*. If a shareholder has a personal right to have his vote recorded, as in *Pender* v. *Lushington* (1877), why isn't the right to enforce a properly demanded poll also a right affecting a member in his personal capacity as such? For a consideration of this issue, *see* C. Baxter, 'Irregular Company Meetings' [1976] J.B.L. 323 and by the same author, 'The Role of the Judge in Enforcing Shareholder Rights', [1983] CLJ 96.

(b) *The timing of a poll at common law.* A poll may be taken, in the absence of regulation to the contrary, immediately upon demand being made: *Re Chillington Iron Co.* (1885). In *Re British Flax Producers Co. Ltd* (1889) the articles of the company provided that all questions were to be decided on a show of hands at general meetings unless a poll was demanded, in which case the poll was to be held at a time and place fixed by the directors, within seven days of the meeting. Creditors of the company objected to the taking of the poll immediately upon its being demanded and the court held that, since this was not in accordance with the articles, it was therefore improper. In contrast, where a poll was irregularly demanded but was in fact taken without objection, the irregularity was waived so far as those entitled to vote were concerned, and the poll was held to be valid: *Campbell* v. *Maund* (1836).

Where there are no provisions fixing the duration of a poll, it must continue for a reasonable period having regard to the number and situation of the voters and other relevant factors: *R* v. *Bishop's Consistency Court of Winchester* (1806).

(c) *Differences* between a poll and a vote upon a show of hands. These include:

   (i) On a poll in a company meeting, the number of votes per share held by a member are counted (but *see* s. 374 discussed in 2 below);

   (ii) At common law, persons not present at the voting upon which the poll is sought may participate in the voting on the poll itself. This follows from the principle that the poll is merely an enlargement of the meeting at which it was demanded, so that all persons who were entitled to attend that meeting may take part in the poll when held: *R* v. *Wimbledon Local Board* (1882). Contrast the position of proxies: *Shaw* v. *Tati Concessions Ltd* (1913) discussed at **4(b)** below.

(*iii*) Where persons are entitled to cast more than one vote, as, for example, where proxies are held from other voters, all the votes are counted upon the poll. However, in *Ernest* v. *Loma Gold Mines Ltd* (1897) it was held that, on a show of hands, no person can exercise more than one vote even though he is entitled to vote both in his own right and in a representative capacity.

2. The Act

Section 373 makes it quite clear that, so far as companies are concerned, there *is* a right to demand a poll. It provides:

(a) That any provision in a company's Articles is *void* which would exclude the right to demand a poll, *except*:
  (*i*) on a motion to elect a chairman; or
  (*ii*) on a motion for adjournment of the meeting.

(b) That any article is rendered void which seeks to make ineffective a demand for a poll made:
  (*i*) by not less than five members entitled to vote at the meeting; or
  (*ii*) by a member or members representing not less than one-tenth of the total voting rights of all members entitled to vote at the meeting; or
  (*iii*) by a member or members holding shares conferring a right to vote at the meeting, being shares on which an aggregate sum has been paid up equal to not less than one-tenth of the total sum paid up on all the shares conferring that right.

(c) That a proxy is entitled to demand, or join in the demand for, a poll.

(d) *Other statutory rights to demand a poll*. These include:
  (*i*) On a variation of class rights any holder of shares of the class in question who is present at a class meeting, in person or by proxy, may demand a poll (s. 125(6) (b)); and
  (*ii*) On a special resolution to confer, revoke or renew authority for an off-market purchase of its own shares or

a contingent purchase contract relating to any of the company's own shares, then notwithstanding anything in the company's articles any member of the company may, in person or by proxy, demand a poll (ss. 164(5) and 165(2)); and

(*iii*) On a special resolution approving a payment out of the company's capital for the redemption or purchase of any of its own shares (s. 74(3) and (5)).

(e) *Voting on a poll.* Section 374 facilitates voting by nominee shareholders. It provides that on a poll taken at a meeting of a company of any class of members of a company, a member entitled to more than one vote need not, if he votes, use all his votes or cast all the votes he uses *in the same way*. In *Pender* v. *Lushington* (1877) Pender had split his shareholding among nominees in order to defeat a provision in the articles which fixed a maximum number of votes to which any one shareholder was entitled. The chairman refused to accept the nominees' votes and accordingly declared lost a resolution proposed by Pender, which otherwise would have been carried. Pender was granted an injunction restraining the directors from acting on the basis that the nominees' votes had been bad. The court held that he had a right to sue in his own name to have his vote recorded; this was an *individual* right. Furthermore, the court held that he had a right to sue in the *company's name*, at least until a general meeting decided otherwise.

3. Table A

(a) *General points.* The provisions of Table A (art. 46) on the subject of demanding a poll were stated in chapter 20: **4** and should be compared with those of s. 373 of the Act, stated above. In particular, art. 46 is more generous in that it allows a poll to be demanded by two members rather than five, and also allows a poll to be demanded by the chairman of the meeting. The latter power is given to the chairman in order that he can ascertain the sense of the meeting upon a matter before them. It would seem, therefore, that the chairman must exercise the power whenever he is aware that a poll would reverse a decision obtained by a show of hands.

In *Second Consolidated Trust Ltd* v. *Ceylon Amalgamated Tea & Rubber Estates Ltd* (1943) a resolution had to be passed at a meeting of debenture stock holders by a three-quarters majority. The proxy situation was such that if a poll were demanded and the proxies used for the purpose of the vote, the necessary majority could not be obtained. After a vote on a show of hands had passed the resolution with the necessary majority, the chairman decided not to demand a poll. It was held that the chairman should have demanded a poll and then voted the proxies in accordance with the instructions they contained, so as to ascertain the true sense of the meeting.

(b) *Private companies* usually modify Table A to provide that any one member present, in person or by proxy, may demand a poll. Such a modification is necessary because private companies usually have a small membership. In *Burns* v. *Siemens Brothers & Co. Ltd* (1919), the company had been registered at a time when every company had to have at least seven members. Of its 20,000 shares, seven were held by seven individuals holding one share each. The remaining 19,993 were held in joint names. Mr Burns was the first name on the register for these shares and thus under the company's articles was the only person entitled to vote in respect of the shares. A meeting was held at which it was proposed to pass a special resolution to alter the company's articles. On a show of hands the alteration was adopted by seven votes (of the individuals holding one share each) to one (that of Burns with 19,993 shares); Burns demanded a poll but the chairman ruled that he lacked entitlement under the articles to demand a poll. The court held that for the purposes of the article relating to a demand for a poll, Burns and his co-holder were 'members holding . . . together at least 300 shares' and so could demand a poll. The general irregularity principle (*see* chapter 20) did not apply because this case concerned a procedural error that affected the outcome of a very important decision of the meeting.

> NOTE: Under Table A, art. 46 a poll may be demanded either before or on the declaration of the result of a show of hands. If a poll is demanded before any vote is taken on a show of hands, the chairman should proceed to take a poll without calling for a show of hands at all: *Holmes* v. *Keyes* (1959).

4. Timing of a poll

After an effective demand for a poll the following procedures are undertaken:

(a) *Time, place and method to be adopted.* Usually, the chairman has the power to decide when, where and how the poll is to be taken. *Table A* (art. 49) gives him this power: 'A poll shall be taken as the chairman directs and he may appoint scrutineers (who need not be members) and fix a time and place for declaring the result of the poll. The result of the poll shall be deemed to be the resolution of the meeting at which the poll was demanded'. (*See also Shaw* v. *Tati Concessions Ltd* (1913).)

However, there are two exceptions contained in art. 51 which must be taken forthwith, namely:

    (*i*) on a motion for election of a chairman;

    (*ii*) on a motion for adjournment of the meeting.

> NOTE: To enable members who are not present in the room where the meeting is being held to vote on a poll, s. 372(2)(c) requires that a proxy must be entitled to vote on a poll. Table A, art. 59 provides that votes may be given personally or by proxy on a poll. The power in art. 49 to take the poll in such manner as the chairman directs does not, in view of art. 59, give him power to direct the poll to be taken otherwise than by voting in person or by proxy: *McMillan* v. *Le Roi Mining Co. Ltd* (1906).

A poll demanded on any other question may be taken forthwith or at such time and place as the chairman directs not being more than 30 days after the poll is demanded. The demand for a poll shall not prevent the continuance of a meeting for the transactions of business other than the question on which the poll was demanded (art. 51).

The demand for a poll may be withdrawn before a poll is taken. However, this can be done only with the consent of the chairman. A demand so withdrawn shall not be taken to have invalidated the result of a show of hands declared before the demand was made (art. 48). This is the opposite of the common law position, *see R* v. *Cooper* (1870).

If a poll is demanded before the declaration of the result of a show of hands and the demand is duly withdrawn, the meeting shall continue as if the demand had not been made (art. 51). For a case where a proper demand for a poll was made and the chairman refused, his action being ratified by a simple majority on a show of hands, *see MacDougall* v. *Gardiner* (1876), discussed in 1 above.

(b) *Polls at a later date.* Where a poll on a question before a meeting is conducted some time after the meeting has dispersed, it does not constitute an 'adjourned meeting'. Such a poll is part of the meeting at which the poll was demanded. Therefore, in the interval between the demand for and the holding of the poll, new proxy appointments cannot be made unless the articles provide otherwise: *Shaw* v. *Tati Concessions Ltd* (1913). In this case the chairman of a meeting directed that a poll demanded at the meeting was to be held about six weeks' later. Shaw had proxies for about 58,000 shares and would win the poll unless his opponents were permitted to use proxies they held for over 99,000 shares. On the day before the poll was to be taken, the court ruled that the documents appointing proxies for the 99,000 shares had not been delivered within the time limit set by the company's articles and so had to be disallowed. This ensured that the vote would go in Shaw's favour and not against him. Contrast *McMillan* v. *Le Roi Mining Co.* (1906).

Table A, art. 62 permits new proxy appointments in such circumstances if the poll is to be taken more than 48 hours after it is demanded. The proxy appointments must be deposited with the company at least 24 hours before the time appointed for taking the poll. Table A, art. 63 also provides for proxy appointments to be revoked in the interval between the demand for and the holding of a poll, if the poll is not held on the day on which it was demanded.

(c) *Groups of associated resolutions.* Where groups of associated resolutions are to be voted on and a poll is demanded, it is proper for each resolution to be submitted to a vote separately. This is sometimes required by statute as in the case of appointing two or more persons as directors in a public company, s. 292. In *Patentwood Key Syndicate* v. *Pearse* (1906) the resolutions, having been passed on a show of hands, were submitted to a poll vote *en bloc*. The court ruled that the resolutions were not properly carried. However, the later case of *Re R.E. Jones Ltd* (1933) confirmed resolutions where this same procedure was followed and no objection was registered at the time. It may be surmised, therefore, that in such cases a group of resolutions *may* be taken *en bloc* for voting on a poll, but only if the meeting so agrees. This is similar to the position under s. 292 which requires a first resolution to that effect with no votes against.

5. Further procedures on a poll

(a) *Chairman's announcement.* The chairman, having made his decision, announces the time and place for taking the poll, and explains the method to be adopted.

(b) *If the demand for a poll had been anticipated*, so that voting slips and/or polling lists are already available, he may decide (or be compelled by the Articles) to take the vote at once.

(c) *If, on the other hand, the poll will entail much preparatory work* (or if he considers other business of the meeting to be more pressing), he will probably decide that the poll shall be taken at a later date, and make an announcement to that effect.

(d) *Appointment of scrutineers.* When the poll is taken, the chairman usually appoints scrutineers. Where opposition parties are known to exist and are easily identifiable, he may select one or more scrutineers from each party, or permit each party to appoint its own scrutineers.

(e) *Voting slips are issued* to all members and (where applicable) proxies present, on which they will record:

    (*i*) Vote *for* or *against*.

    (*ii*) Number of votes to which they are entitled.

    (*iii*) Signature.

(f) *Voting slips are collected*, entered on polling lists (either by polling clerks or the scrutineers themselves) and checked by the scrutineers.

(g) *As an alternative* to the issue of voting slips, the members may proceed to tables suitably arranged and lettered (within the hall or in an adjoining room), and themselves sign a polling list, after indicating in a separate column the number of shares and/or amount of stock held. In that case, separate polling lists are provided for votes cast 'for' and 'against' the motion as in the following specimen:

Polling List
BLANK COMPANY LIMITED

In Favour

    At a poll taken at an Extraordinary General Meeting of Blank Company Limited held at the Registered Office of the Company, London Wall, London E.C.2, on.................... 19..... at .....am/pm, the undersigned voted *In Favour* of the following Special Resolution.

> 'That the capital of the company be reduced from £10,000,000 divided into 10,000,000 Ordinary Shares of £1 each fully paid up, to £5,000,000 divided into 10,000,000 Ordinary Shares of 50p each fully paid up, by repaying to the Ordinary Shareholders the sum of 50p per share.'

No. of Shares (or Stock held)	Signature	No. of Shares (or Stock held)	Signature

(h) *After checking and counting the votes* cast 'for' and 'against' the motion, the scrutineers will report the result to the chairman. If the meeting is a large one, the scrutineers usually present their report in writing, stating the number of votes cast 'for' and 'against' the motion. Such a report is illustrated below:

BLANK COMPANY LIMITED

We, the undersigned, having been appointed scrutineers at a poll taken upon the undermentioned Special Resolution at an Extraordinary General Meeting of Blank Company Limited, held at the company's Registered Office, London Wall, London E.C.2, on .... 19... at ....am/pm, hereby report the result of the poll.

Resolution

'That the capital of the company be reduced from £10,000,000 divided into 10,000,000 Ordinary Shares of £1 each fully paid up, to £5,000,000 divided into 10,000,000 Ordinary Shares of 50p each fully paid up, by repaying the Ordinary Shareholders the sum of 50p per share.'

Votes IN FAVOUR of the Resolution _____

Votes AGAINST the Resolution _____

_____

Dated this .... day of .... 19...

_____ Scrutineers

(i) *The chairman announces the result* of the poll, and may or may not state the number of votes cast 'for' and 'against' in accordance with the usual practice of the company concerned.

> NOTE: It should be borne in mind that on taking a poll, *proxies* must be included, but on a show of hands (unless otherwise stated in the Articles) they must be excluded from the reckoning: *Ernest* v. *Loma Gold Mines* (1897). Also, the date of the resolution is the date on which the result of the poll is ascertained: *Holmes* v. *Keyes* (1959).

Progress test 21

1. What are the rights of members of a company to demand a poll? **(1, 2)**

2. Is there a right at common law to demand a poll? The Articles of a company may exclude the right to demand a poll in two exceptional cases. What are the permitted exceptions? **(1)**

22
Proxies

1. Definition

The word 'proxy' is often used indiscriminately to refer to either:

(a) *A document* in writing by which one person authorizes another to attend a meeting (or meetings) and to vote on his behalf; or
(b) *A person* authorized in such a document to act for the appointor, i.e. in the present context, to attend a meeting (or meetings) and to vote on behalf of the appointor.

Appointment of person as proxy

2. At common law

At common law, there is *no* right to appoint a proxy: *Harben* v. *Phillips* (1883). This was applied in *Clubb* v. *Computer Society of Hong Kong* (1990) where Mr Clubb challenged the use of proxies on the election of officers at an annual general meeting when no specific provision was made for them in the society's constitution. The defendant society argued that article 17(d) of its constitution, which provided that the council of the society should have power to use its discretion in the event of any question or matter arising out of any point which was not expressly provided for in the constitution, empowered the council to permit proxies. The court held that it did not despite the fact that other articles, concerned with the dissolution of the society and the disposal of its assets, allowed for a proxy and a postal vote respectively. Article 35, dealing with general meetings, referred to members *present* and this meant present *in person*. The case stands as a warning to societies with badly drafted constitutions.

3. The Act

Section 372 overrides common law, i.e. it empowers any member entitled to attend and vote at a meeting of a company *having share capital:*

(a) To appoint any other person (whether a member or not) as his proxy, to attend and vote instead of him; and
(b) in the case of a proxy appointed to attend and vote on behalf of a member of a *private company*, the proxy is also given the right to speak at the meeting(s) concerned.

4. However, unless the Articles otherwise provide:

(a) The power to appoint a proxy is *not* given to a member of a company *having no share capital.*
(b) A member of a *private* company can appoint only *one* proxy to attend on the same occasion unless the articles provide otherwise s. 372(2)(b) — whereas it is implied (s. 372(3)) that a member of a public company having share capital can appoint *one or more* proxies.
(c) A proxy is not entitled to vote *except on a poll* (s. 372(2)).

> NOTE: Table A, art. 59 *does provide otherwise.* It states that a member may appoint more than one proxy to attend on the same occasion.

The proxy document

5. Deposit of proxies

Section 372(5) provides that articles may not require a proxy, or other document for the purpose, to be deposited more than 48 hours before a meeting or adjourned meeting. (This provision ensures that the convenors of the meeting are given at least 48 hours in which to check proxy forms before the meeting is due to start.)

Table A (art. 62) accordingly provides that the instrument appointing a proxy must be deposited with the company:
  (*i*) not less than 48 hours before the time for holding the meeting or adjourned meeting, or
  (*ii*) in the case of a poll, not less than 24 hours before the time appointed for the taking of the poll.
  (*iii*) where the poll is not taken forthwith but is taken not more

than 48 hours after it was demanded, be delivered at the meeting at which the poll was demanded to the chairman or to the secretary or to any director; and an instrument of proxy which is not deposited or delivered in a manner so permitted shall be invalid.

NOTE: See *Shaw* v. *Tati Concessions Ltd* (1913) where the court held that proxies could not be used on a poll held six weeks after the meeting at which it was demanded because those proxies had not been delivered within the time limit set by the company's articles. Reference to the deposit of proxies usually appears as a footnote in the notice of the meeting, and may be worded as follows: 'Proxies must be lodged at the Company's Registered Office not less than forty-eight hours before the time of the meeting'. Additionally, where applicable, the footnote will give 'reasonable prominence' to the fact that a member is entitled to appoint a proxy, and that the proxy need not be a member (s. 372(3)).

6.　Issue of proxy forms

An invitation issued at the *company's* expense to some only of its members, requesting them to appoint as proxy a person (or persons) specified in the invitation is *prohibited*, unless:

(a) the proxy form was made available to *every* member on written request; or
(b) where it had been sent to a member at his written request and the proxy form, or list of persons willing to act as proxy, is available to every member entitled to vote at the meeting by proxy on their written request (s. 372(6)).

NOTE: Although it is common practice to send proxy forms along with notices of meetings, this section is designed to prevent directors from sending proxy forms, at the company's expense, only to members from whom they might expect support. Any director who does so becomes liable to a fine.

In *Peel* v. *London and North Western Railway* (1907) a circular explaining the directors' policies and proxy forms, made out in the directors' names, were printed and posted (with stamp addressed envelopes) to shareholders. All expenses incurred were paid by the company. An action by shareholders to restrain directors from using company funds was unsuccessful. The court held that it was the duty of directors to put forward reasons which they think justify their policy. In as much as it was the duty of directors to inform and advise shareholders on the facts, it was fairly incidental to and consequential upon their duties to incur the expense subject to any limitation which may exist in the articles.

7. Form of proxy

(a) *Form.* The Articles usually set out the form of proxy to be used, and may or may not require attestation of the appointor's signature.

(b) *Table A* (art. 60) provides that a proxy must be in writing, executed by or on behalf of the executor.

This article provides a specimen of an ordinary proxy form, which is to be followed as closely as circumstances allow (or in any other form which is usual or which the directors may approve). This is worded as follows:

PLC/Limited

I/We,   , of
                                                  , being a
member/members of the above-named company, hereby
appoint   of
                       , or failing him,
of   , as my/our proxy to vote in my/our
name[s] and on my/our behalf at the annual/extraordinary
general meeting of the company to be held on
               19   , and at any adjournment thereof.
Signed on   19

(c) *Where it is desired to afford members an opportunity of instructing the proxy how he shall act* the instrument appointing a proxy shall be in the following form (or in a form as near thereto as circumstances allow or in any other form which is usual or which the directors may approve) (art. 61):

PLC/Limited

I/We, , of
, being a
member/members of the above-named company, hereby
appoint of
, or failing him,
of , as my/our proxy
to vote in my/our name[s] and on my/our behalf at the
annual/extraordinary general meeting of the company to
be held on
19 , and at any adjournment thereof.
This form is to be used in respect of the resolutions
mentioned below as follows:
Resolution No 1 *for *against
Resolution No 2 *for *against
*Strike out whichever is not desired.
Unless otherwise instructed, the proxy may vote as he
thinks fit or abstain from voting.

Signed this day of 19

(d) *A special proxy* is one which is valid for *one* meeting only and at
any adjournment thereof. It is free of stamp duty.
(e) *A general proxy* is valid for more than one meeting.

Revocation and rejection

8. Revocation of proxy
Subject to the provision of the Articles, a proxy may be revoked
by:

(a) *Determination of the authority of the proxy* and receipt by the
company of notice to that effect *before* the meeting to which the
proxy relates or, in the case of a poll taken otherwise than on the

same day as the meeting or adjourned meeting, the time appointed for taking the poll (Table A, art. 63).

(b) *The appointor himself attending* and exercising his vote at the meeting, in which case any vote tendered by the proxy must be rejected: *Cousins v. International Brick Co.* (1931). In this case Romer LJ said: 'When a shareholder, having given a proxy, appears at the meeting and says he prefers to vote in person, he is not revoking the proxy previously given, but doing an act which obviates the necessity of the proxy ever being used at all.'

In the Australian case of *Ansett v. Butler Air Transport Ltd (No. 2)* (1958) members who had appointed proxies attended personally and voted on a show of hands for a poll to be taken for the election of directors. The poll was fixed for a later date. On the taking of the poll, votes were cast by proxies on behalf of shareholders who had been present at the original meeting. The chairman rejected the votes. Myers J said:

> 'If a shareholder attends a meeting at which two resolutions are proposed and he votes on the first, the right of his proxy to vote on the second remains, as it seems to me, unimpaired, because since he has not revoked his proxy it must remain in force in respect of any other act to which it relates. Further, since the option to vote personally or by proxy may be exercised right up to the moment when the vote is taken, it must be an option which is exercisable on each occasion a vote is taken. The defendants have contended strongly that if a shareholder votes personally on one resolution he has thereby irrevocably exercised his option to vote personally on all. I can find, however, nothing in the articles which requires or entitled me to hold that they should be so construed. Indeed, (Counsel for the defendants) conceded that if the proxy voted on the first resolution the principal could vote personally on the second, a concession which, in my opinion, is completely destructive of any notion that the option is one and indivisible.'

(c) *Deposit of a notice of revocation* within any specified time limit.

(d) *Deposit of a new proxy form* in favour of another person, within any specified time limit.

(e) *Transfer of the share(s)* in respect of which the proxy is given, and receipt by the company of notice to that effect before the meeting.

(f) *Verbal intimation to the chairman* prior to the commencement of the meeting.

9. Rejection of proxies

(a) On receipt of proxy forms deposited before a meeting, it will be the secretary's duty (or that of some other responsible person appointed for the purpose) to examine them carefully, and to reject any received *after* the specified time for deposit.

(b) He must also reject any which do not conform to requirements for any of the following reasons:

- (*i*) *Form unsigned or (where required by the Articles, in the case of a corporation) unsealed.*
- (*ii*) *Signature not attested*, i.e. where attestation is required by the Articles.
- (*iii*) *Alterations* of a major character have not been initialled.
- (*iv*) *Incomplete,* deficient, or in any way contrary to the form and content required by the Articles. However, the courts have been loath to endorse the rejection of proxies containing a mistake which is inoffensive in nature and which is unlikely to mislead shareholders. Proxies should therefore be construed with benevolence to avoid frustrating the intention of the givers of the proxy: *Dominion Mining NL* v. *Hill (No. 1)* (1971). In *Isaacs* v. *Chapman* (1915) a proxy to vote 'at any ordinary or extraordinary meeting of the company' instead of at the particular meeting at which the proxy was tendered was held to be valid. In one case the proxy described the meeting as an annual general meeting instead of an extraordinary general meeting: *Oliver* v. *Dalgleish* (1963). Buckley J said 'a mere misprint or some quite palpable mistake on the face of the document does not, in my judgment, entitle the company to refuse to accept the proxy'. Contrast *Davey* v. *Inyaminga Petroleum* (1954) where the form of proxy in the company's articles provided for the insertion of the number of votes which a proxy was entitled to use. Proxies were sent out which did

not contain such information and were held to be invalid. A chairman is not entitled to reject properly executed proxy forms because he believes them to have been obtained by misrepresentation: *Holmes* v. *Jackson* (1957).

A proxy form which has been signed by a member, and has blanks for the date of execution and date of the meeting is valid if the form is completed by some person authorized by him: *Sadgrove* v. *Bryden* (1907). If it is returned to the company, signed by the member but without inserting the name of a proxy, the board has an implied authority to complete it: *Ernest* v. *Loma Gold Mines* (1897). Table A, art. 62 requires a copy of the instrument appointing a proxy and any authority under which it is executed or a copy of such authority certified notorially or in some other way approved by the directors to be deposited with the company as stated in 5 above.

(c) *Methods of dealing with rejected proxies.* Practice appears to differ between companies at this point; if time permits, it is only reasonable to return proxies for amendment. If, however, this is not possible, or if amended proxy forms are not received within the specified time limit, those finally rejected are the subject of an announcement by the chairman, who may also explain the reasons for rejection.

Validity of proxy

10. Dealing with valid proxies

In order to expedite work at the coming meeting, and in anticipation of an effective demand for a poll, it is usual to number serially the valid proxies after they have been checked and passed, and to list them alphabetically.

11. Validity of proxies at 'adjourned' meetings

(a) Proxies deposited prior to the original meeting may be used at the adjournment, for in the absence of any provisions to the contrary, an adjourned meeting is a continuation of the original meeting: *Scadding* v. *Lorant* (1851).

(b) As already stated in 5, s. 372(5) refers to the lodgement of proxies 'forty-eight hours before a meeting or *adjourned* meeting

. . .' from which it can be assumed that, in general, a proxy deposited after the original meeting but before the adjourned meeting is valid — provided that it is lodged in the form and within the time prescribed by the Articles.

(c) Nevertheless, an 'adjournment' to take a poll is *not* an adjournment such as would permit the deposit of *fresh* proxies during the interval between the original meeting and its 'adjournment', as the latter is merely an extension or enlargement of the original meeting: *Jackson* v. *Hamlyn and others (Gordon Hotels Case)* (1953); *see also Shaw* v. *Tati Concessions Ltd* (1913).

12. Corporate representatives

These have been dealt with in chapter 20:6. A corporate representative has certain advantages over a proxy holder. These stem from the fact that a corporate representative has the same rights at a meeting as if he were registered with the shares held by his appointing corporation. Therefore he may:

    (*i*) be counted in the quorum;

    (*ii*) speak at the meeting;

    (*iii*) vote on a show of hands;

and there is no need to notify the company of the appointment of a representative before the meeting (*see* Table A, art. 54). Proof of appointment may, however, be required subsequently by the company.

The appointing corporation may appoint a proxy rather than a representative. Such a proxy is in the same position as if he had been appointed by an individual member.

NOTE: The term corporation means any corporate body whether or not a company within the meaning of the Companies Acts.

Because of the advantages of a corporate representative the practice of selling company-held shares in a takeover bid situation has become quite common in recent years. An aggressive bidder can buy company held shares only a few hours before the meeting on terms requiring the seller to produce a certified board resolution in favour of the purchaser. The purchaser has plenty of time to present evidence of his appointment as corporate representative. Such shares are often, therefore, bought on special terms and at special prices. Individual shareholders cannot obtain similar last-minute terms, since the purchaser cannot lodge any proxies in time.

13. Stock Exchange requirements

Rule 36 of the S/E Rules states that the company must send proxy forms, with provision for two-way voting on all resolutions entitled to be proposed, with the notice convening a meeting of holders of listed securities to all persons entitled to vote at the meeting.

The notes to Rule 36 provide, *inter alia*, that the purpose of this requirement is to ensure that shareholders have adequate opportunity to express their views on all resolutions intended to be proposed, such as the adoption of the annual accounts and re-election of directors. Resolutions which are merely procedural do not require two-way proxy forms. So long as two-way proxy forms are made available, the printing and postal arrangements are matters entirely at the discretion of the company. However, the proxy form must state that if it is returned without an indication as to *how* the proxy shall vote on any particular matter, the proxy will exercise his discretion as to whether he votes and, if so, how. The form must state that a shareholder is entitled to appoint a proxy of his *own choice* and must provide a space for the name of such proxy.

Progress test 22

1. What do you understand by the term 'proxy', and what are the usual rules relating thereto? **(1–9)**

2. On what grounds are proxies deposited before a meeting liable to be rejected? What is the procedure for dealing with (*a*) proxies which have been rejected, (*b*) proxies which have passed inspection? **(9, 10)**

3. The Act requires that every notice calling a meeting of a company must give 'reasonable prominence' to certain information relating to proxies. Draft a footnote to a notice to meet this requirement. **(5)**

23
Minutes

1. Minutes and minute writing

These areas generally were covered, and specimen minutes illustrated, in chapter 12. Everything stated there can be applied to the minutes of company meetings.

2. The minute book

(a) *A statutory requirement*. Section 382 requires every company to keep minutes of all proceedings at *general* meetings, also of board meetings and (where applicable) of meetings of managers, in books kept for that purpose.

(b) *Location*. The minutes of *general* meetings must be kept at the company's registered office (s. 383).

(c) *Inspection and copies* (s. 383):

(*i*) The minutes of *general* meetings must be open to the inspection of any member, without charge, for not less than two hours each day during the period between 9am and 5pm on each business day.

(*ii*) Any member is entitled to be furnished with a copy of the minutes within seven days after making a request on payment of such fee as may be prescribed.

(*iii*) The court has power to compel immediate inspection and to direct that copies be provided, in the case of refusal. The Act also imposes penalties on the company and every officer in default. For the detailed rules of inspection and fees payable for copies, *see* The Companies (Inspection and Copying of Registers, Indices and Documents) Regulations 1991 (S.I. 1991 No. 1998).

NOTE: It will be observed that members are not entitled under s.

383 to inspect the minutes of board meetings; hence the usual practice of keeping *separate* minute books for general meetings and board meetings.

(d) *Loose-leaf minute books.* Companies are permitted to use loose-leaf minute books, s. 722 stating, 'Any register, index, minute book or accounting records required by this Act to be kept by a company may be kept either by making entries in a bound book or by recording the matters in question *in any other manner.*' But penalties are imposed for failure to take adequate precautions against falsification.

In *Heart of Oak Assurance Co. Ltd* v. *James Flower & Sons* (1936), Bennett J rejected a loose-leaf system under the then existing legislation on the basis that: 'anyone wishing to do so... can take a number of leaves out and substitute any number of other leaves. It is a thing with which anyone disposed to be dishonest can easily tamper'. A similar approach was taken in the Australian case of *A Solicitor; ex parte The Prothonotary* (1939), though in *Kirwan* v. *Long* (1936) and *Wilson* v. *Parry* (1937) it was held that loose-leaf systems may constitute minutes. Even though s. 722 now allows them, safeguards against falsification would probably include precautions such as locks and signatures or other identification marks upon *each sheet.* For the usual precautions, see chapter 12.

(e) *Section 723, use of computer for company records,* states that minutes and other records may now be kept 'otherwise than in legible form' as long as the recording is capable of being reproduced in legible form. With the increasing use of computers and word processors this is likely to become more important as a method of keeping minutes. Security systems as safeguards against falsification of minutes are equally important for minutes held on computer.

3. Minutes as evidence of proceedings

(a) Section 382(2) states that minutes kept in accordance with s. 382(1), if purporting to be signed by the chairman of the meeting at which the proceedings were conducted, or by the chairman of the next succeeding meeting, shall be evidence of the proceedings.

(b) *The usual practice* is for the secretary to make notes at the meeting and for the minutes to be subsequently written up in the book. They are then normally signed by the chairman at the beginning of the next general meeting.

(c) *The minutes are evidence only* and therefore may be contradicted by conflicting evidence. Thus the absence of any reference to a resolution in the minutes is evidence that it was not brought before the meeting, but contrary evidence may be adduced to prove that it was passed at the meeting: *Re Fireproof Doors* (1916) (*see* Table A, art. 100). Other examples include:

(*i*)   In the case of *In Re Indian Zoedone Co.* (1884), the chairman disallowed certain votes against the confirmation of a resolution appointing a liquidator, and made an entry in the minute book that the resolution had been confirmed. In the absence of evidence that the votes were improperly disallowed the court declined to question the decision of the chairman. Selbourne LC said:

'As the chairman who presides at such meetings, and has to receive the poll and declare its result, has *prima facie* authority to decide all emergent questions which necessarily require decision at the time, his decision of those questions will naturally govern, and properly govern the entry of the minute in the books; and, though in no sense conclusive, it throws the burden of proof upon the other side, who may say, contrary to the entry in the minute-book, following the decision of the chairman, that the result of the poll was different from that there recorded.'

(*ii*)   In *Betts & Co. Ltd* v. *MacNaughten* (1910) it was held that the entry in the minute book of proceedings at a meeting was not conclusive that the proceedings were regular and the court could enquire into the validity of the notice convening the meeting.

(*iii*)   In *Re Llanharry Hematite Iron Co. (Tothill's Case)* (1866), a director applied for the shares which were necessary to qualify him as director under the articles. A resolution was passed at a meeting of the directors, reciting a list of shareholders, in which the director was put down for the necessary 50 shares. As the director was not present he was subsequently able to show that no allotment of the shares was in fact made.

(d) *The Articles may provide that the minutes shall constitute conclusive evidence of the proceedings.* An example is Table A, art. 47. Where this is the case, their accuracy can only be questioned where bad faith or fraud is alleged: *Kerr* v. *Mottram* (1940); or where there is an error on the face of the minutes: *Re Caratal New Mines* (1902). Even where the articles provide that the minutes are to be conclusive evidence, if there is an ambiguity on the face of the minute or an ambiguity is disclosed on ascertaining the surrounding circumstances, then evidence is admissible for the purpose of showing what the resolution means: *Westralis Pty. Gold Mining Co. (N.L.)* v. *Long* (1897).

(e) *Presumption of validity.* Section 382(4) contains a statutory presumption of validity. It says that where minutes have been made in accordance with s. 382 of the proceedings at any general meeting of the company or meeting of directors or managers, then the meeting is deemed duly held and convened, and all proceedings had at the meeting to have been duly had; and all appointments of directors, managers or liquidators are deemed valid, *until the contrary is proved.*

It has been held that this presumption should be construed liberally between the company and its members, as well as between the company and outsiders: *In Re Portuguese Consolidated Copper Mines Ltd* (1890). The case of *Channel Collieries Trust Ltd* v. *Dover, St Margarets and Martin Mill Light Railway Co.* (1914) also suggests that a beneficial construction should be put on the section. The court had to apply ss. 89 and 99 of the Companies Clauses Consolidation Act 1845 which correspond to Table A articles 90 and 92 respectively. The latter provision validates acts of directors despite defects in their appointment or qualification. The facts were that a sole continuing director, although not constituting a quorum, appointed two new directors (cf art. 90) at a board meeting which he chaired as the only person present. There was a minute to the effect that he, as the sole remaining director, appointed two new directors in place of others who had retired. Neither of these two directors at the date of their appointment held the necessary qualification shares, though they obtained them immediately after their appointment. The court held that the continuing director, though not a quorum, could appoint the new directors by virtue of s. 89 of the 1845 Act. Furthermore, the acts of the *de facto* directors who were not qualified to be appointed were validated by s. 99 of the 1845 Act as they acted *in good faith*. Swinfen Eady LJ said:

> 'It is now settled that this section protects acts both with regard to insiders and outsiders. ... I think that it is a beneficial construction to put upon the section.
>
> Common sense really requires that there shall be some provision giving legal effect to the acts in respect of which there is a technical informality because some slip has been made, where the acts have been done in good faith and where the slip has occurred because the parties have not had present to their minds the legal difficulties in the way of doing what they honestly think they are entitled to do. In most of the cases that arise I think that the directors or persons living know the facts of the case and of course are presumed to know the articles of the company. But it is not present to their minds that they are not doing the matter in a properly formal way. In the case in question it does not appear to have been present to the minds of the two new directors that it was necessary for them to have had their qualification shares at the moment of their appointment and did not validate their appointment if they acquired them a moment afterwards. Of course these matters are done at one and the same board meeting.'

(f) *Forged minutes*. In *Morriss* v. *Kansen* (1946) the appointment of directors and the issue of shares were held to be a nullity where there had in fact been no meeting and the minutes of the purported meeting were therefore a forgery.

(g) *Amendments* may be made by the chairman before he signs the minutes. Such amendments must be initialled by him. Nothing should be erased as this may give rise to a suspicion of falsification. The minutes should not be altered once they have been signed, any further amendment being made by an entry in the minutes of a subsequent meeting. Alteration should be by a resolution which is then minuted. In one case the company secretary altered the minutes of a meeting of the directors. Esher MR (in *Re Cawley & Co.* (1889)) said:

> 'Minutes of board-meetings . . . are kept in order that the shareholders of the company may know exactly what their

directors have been doing, why it is done, and when it was done; ... I trust I shall never again see or hear of the secretary of a company, whether under superior directions or otherwise, altering minutes of meetings, either by striking out anything or adding anything. The proper mode . . . would have been by resolution, and then entering that resolution [on] the minutes.'

For the approval of minutes on a reduction of capital *see Re Anglo-American Insurance Co. Ltd* (1991).

4. Proof of matters not in the minutes

(a) *Any admissible evidence* may be used to prove the proceedings of the company if no relevant entries have been made in its minute book. In *McLean Bros & Rigg Ltd* v. *Grice* (1906) a special resolution was recorded in writing, signed by the chairman and a copy sent for registration with the Registrar-General. A copy was also published in the *Government Gazette*. The court held that this was *prima facie* evidence that all that took place at the meeting was done lawfully.

(b) *Independent evidence*. In *Re Fireproof Doors Ltd* (1916) Astbury J said:

'[I]t was argued that all minutes of resolutions must be entered, and that the minutes alone are exclusive evidence of what is done or decided by a board of directors. From the decisions in *Re Rotherham Alum and Chemical Co.* (1883), and *Knight's Case* (1867), it is clear that a decision of directors need not necessarily appear in the minute book if the court is satisfied that the resolution was passed.'

Therefore independent evidence may be given to establish proceedings which have occurred at a meeting of a board of directors even though there is no entry concerning them in the minutes. However, in *Re Rotherham Alum & Chemical Co.* (1883) a solicitor who was present at a directors' meeting attempted to rely upon an agreement which was not recorded in the minutes and because it concerned payment for pre-incorporation expenses was unable to enforce it. This was despite a resolution to similar effect being passed at a later meeting of the company.

(c) *Presumption of validity of proceedings*. It is often presumed that a resolution has been passed if entries are made in a company's books which would be irregular unless based on a resolution, there being no minute of such resolution. An extreme example of this is in *Re North Hallenbeagle Mining Co.; Knight's Case* (1867) where a shareholder made default in payment of his calls, and notice was sent to him in due form that unless he paid them by a specified date they would be forfeited. When this date passed without payment, the secretary made entries in the books that the shares were forfeited and had been transferred to the company. Despite there being no entry in the minutes of any resolution having been passed by the directors, nor any evidence of any notice of the forfeiture having been sent to the shareholder, the court held that since the entry of forfeiture on the books could not have been properly made without a resolution of the directors, it was bound to assume that such resolution had been passed.

In *Re British Provident Life and Fire Insurance Society, Lane's Case* (1863) it was stated that when the minutes of general meetings are not forthcoming it will be assumed against the company that whatever the directors ought for example, to have submitted to the shareholders was actually so submitted. The presumption was applied to a letter written by a company secretary as to the date when a call was payable. It was presumed *prima facie* evidence to have been written with the authority of a meeting of the directors: *Johnson* v. *Lyttle's Iron Agency* (1877). However, where the secretary acts beyond the scope of his instructions and duties, the presumption is not applied: *George Whitechurch Ltd* v. *Cavanagh* (1902).

5.   Recording of written resolutions

By s. 382A where a written resolution is agreed to in accordance with s. 381A, which has effect as if agreed by the company in general meeting, the company must cause a record of the resolution (and of the signatures) to be entered in a book in the same way as minutes. Such a record, if purporting to be signed by a director of the company or by the company secretary, is evidence of the proceedings in agreeing to the resolution. The requirements of the act with respect to those proceedings is also deemed complied with until the contrary is proved.

Progress test 23

1. What are the provisions of the Act as to **(a)** location, **(b)** inspection, and the taking of copies, of minutes of a company's meetings? **(1)**

2. What are the advantages and disadvantages of loose-leaf minute books? **(2)**

3. Is a company permitted to use a loose-leaf minute book or computer records? If so, what precautions are necessary to safeguard its contents? **(2)**

4. Discuss minutes as evidence of proceedings. **(3–5)**

24
The annual general meeting

1. The purpose of the annual general meeting

The purpose and importance of general meetings is discussed in chapter 16:10. However, it is now proposed to make some specific comments about the annual general meeting.

(a) *It is a form of last resort,* in that it enables directors to give an account of their stewardship of the company, especially in relation to the latest profit and loss account and the dividend proposed. They must also submit themselves to re-election and answer questions. The annual general meeting is wisely treated with respect by most boards of directors who normally prepare for it with care and who ought to be ready for the unexpected or difficult question.

(b) *In the case of public companies,* particularly those listed on the Stock Exchange, wide press coverage is given to the preliminary announcement of the year's figures. Such publicity is required by the Stock Exchange Listing Regulations as soon as possible after the draft accounts have reached final audit stage (para. 4(*a*)). This often precedes the annual general meeting by two months. At the meeting shareholders are therefore more interested in hearing the latest trading position of the company rather than reviewing the accounts of the previous period. Other points follow from this:

    (*i*) *Institutional shareholders* do not often take any active part in the proceedings of the annual meeting, preferring to apply pressure behind the scenes where a company is ailing or the board proposes a course of action with which the institutional shareholder disagrees. *See Prudential Assurance Co.* v. *Newman Industries (No. 2) (1982)* where such a policy failed resulting in long and very expensive litigation.

(*ii*) *The meeting often becomes a social event* for small shareholders who may be more interested in the security of their investment than the welfare of the company. It is easier for such shareholders to realize their investment by sales than to mount an *effective* challenge to the board at the meeting.

(c) *In the case of private companies,* the annual general meeting is one of the minimum requirements for the privileges of incorporation and limited liability. It ought therefore to be adhered to in principle and practice. It can profitably be used to assess the performance of the company and shareholder directors. (*See* the comments in *Cane* v. *Jones* 19:**12**). However, as discussed below, private companies may now dispense with the holding of annual general meetings and the laying of accounts and reports before the company at such meetings.

2. When held

Section 366(1) provides that *every* company must hold an annual general meeting:

(a) in each year, in addition to other meetings held in that year; and

(b) in any case, not more than 15 months after the previous annual general meeting.

The holding of the meeting in the calendar year and within the period of 15 months after the preceding general meeting gives rise to a dual responsibility. In *Smedley* v. *Registrar of Joint Stock Companies* (1919) the company did not hold a meeting in 1917. The previous general meeting was held on March 21, 1916. The court held that two offences had been committed, namely:

(*i*) not holding the meeting within the calendar year and
(*ii*) not holding the meeting within 15 months of the preceding one.

Each default was liable to be dealt with separately.

The calendar year is not calculated from the date of registration of the company but from 1 January ending on 31 December: *Gibson* v. *Barton* (1875). Under the Interpretation Act 1978, s. 5, Schedule 1 'month' means 'calendar month'. A calendar month is the period expiring on the corresponding day in the following month.

3. The first annual general meeting

The AGM need not, however, be held in the year of a company's incorporation, nor in the following calendar year, so long as it is held *within 18 months of incorporation* (s. 366(2)).

4. Notice

The notice convening the annual general meeting must expressly state that the meeting is to be an 'annual general meeting ' (s. 366(1)).

> NOTE: The minimum period of notice required is 21 days (s. 369). If the directors of a company deliberately convene an annual general meeting on a date designed to prevent shareholders from exercising their voting powers the court may restrain them from doing so: *Cannon* v. *Trask* (1875). As to the directors choosing an inconvenient venue, *see Martin* v. *Walker and Others* (1918).

5. Business of the meeting

The main purpose of the annual general meeting is to transact *ordinary* business, which may be specified in the articles as, for example:

(a) To consider (and approve) the directors' and auditors' reports, the accounts and balance sheet.
(b) To sanction the dividend (if any) recommended by the directors.
(c) To appoint (or re-appoint) directors.
(d) To appoint and fix remuneration of the auditors.

This list is taken from Table A, art. 52 of the 1948 Companies Act. The new Table A does not contain a similar article. The 1985 regulations, that is the current Table A, art. 38 merely provides that the notice of the annual general meeting or the extraordinary general meeting shall specify 'the general nature of the business to be transacted'. This offers the opportunity for innovation in the agenda of annual general meetings but in effect requires that no business should be transacted thereat without previous notice in general terms having first being given.

> NOTE: Other business may, however, be transacted at the annual general meeting provided its nature is clearly stated in the notice. In *Boschoek Proprietary Co. Ltd* v. *Fuke* (1906) the directors' report, which was sent with the notice, mentioned certain special business not

referred to in the notice of the general meeting. The notice stated simply that the meeting would be held for the purpose of receiving the directors' report and electing auditors and directors. The notice and report taken together were held to be sufficient notice of the special business.

6. Default

The Secretary of State may call (or direct the calling of) a general meeting of the company, on the application of any member, if default is made in holding an annual general meeting in accordance with the Act (s. 367(1)).

NOTE: A general meeting so held is deemed to be (or it may be resolved at the meeting to be) treated as the annual general meeting in respect of which there had been default (s. 367(4)). Provided appropriate notice has been given, the meeting may be treated as the annual general meeting for both years.

7. Private company: election to dispense with annual general meeting

(a) *The election.* Section 366A provides that a private company may, by elective resolution, dispense with the holding of an annual general meeting. The election has effect for the year in which it is made and subsequent years. It does *not*, however, affect any liability *already incurred* by reason of default in holding an annual general meeting.

(b) *Power of member to require a meeting.* Any member of the company may, by notice to the company not later than three months before the end of the year, require the holding of an annual general meeting *in that year*. This applies in any year in which an annual general meeting would be required to be held but for the elective resolution, and in which no such meeting has been held. If such a notice is given by a member, the provisions of s. 366(1) (annual general meeting each year) and s. 366(3) (penalty on default) apply with respect to the calling of the meeting and the consequences of default.

(c) *Election ceasing to have effect.* If the election ceases to have effect, the company is not obliged to hold an annual general meeting under s. 366 in that year if less than three months of that year then remain. This does not affect any obligation of the company to hold an annual general meeting in that year in pursuance to a notice given by a member, requiring the holding of an annual general meeting.

8.   Laying of accounts

(a) *Accounts and reports to be laid before the company in general meeting.* In respect of each financial year of a company the directors must lay before the company in general meeting copies of the company's annual accounts, the directors' report and the auditors' report on those accounts, s. 241. By s. 244 the accounts must be laid before the company within *ten months* of the end of the relevant accounting reference period for a private company and within *seven for a public company.* These periods may be reduced if the first accounting reference period is more than twelve months, or extended where the company carries on business or has interests overseas.

(b) *Approval and signing of accounts.* A company's annual accounts must be approved by the board of directors and signed, on behalf of the board, by a director of the company. The signature must be on the balance sheet and each copy which is laid before the company in general meeting, or which is otherwise circulated, published or issued, shall state the *name of the person who signed* the balance sheet on behalf of the board.

(c) *Annual general meeting and laying of accounts.* As a matter of practice annual general meetings are timed to accord with the laying before shareholders of periodic accounts, as described above, and the declaration of dividends.

(d) *Private company, elective resolution.*

   (i)   By such a resolution passed in accordance with s. 379A a private company may dispense with the laying of accounts and reports before the company in general meeting (s. 252). An election has effect in relation to the accounts and reports in respect of the financial year in which the election is made and subsequent financial years.

   (ii) Nevertheless under s. 253 the accounts still have to be sent to members, and this has to be done not less than 28 days before the end of the period allowed for laying and delivering them (*see* (b) above). The copy of the accounts etc must be accompanied by a notice informing each member of his right to require the laying of the accounts and reports before a general meeting.

(*iii*) Before the end of 28 days beginning with the day on which the accounts and reports are sent out, any member or auditor may, by notice in writing deposited at the registered office, require that a general meeting be held for the purpose of laying the accounts and reports before the company, (s. 253(2)).

(*iv*) If the directors do not, within 21 days from the date of the deposit of such notice, proceed duly to convene a meeting, the person who deposited the notice may do so himself. The directors shall be deemed not to have duly convened a meeting if they convene a meeting for a date more than 28 days after the date of the notice convening it.

(*v*) A meeting convened by a member shall not be held more than three months from the date of deposit of his notice and shall be convened in the same manner, as nearly as possible, as that in which meetings are to be convened by directors. The member may recoup his reasonable expenses from the company, which in turn shall recoup them from the directors in default.

9. Preparation for an annual general meeting
This is dealt with in chapter 40.

Progress test 24

1. What is the usual business of a company's annual general meeting? **(4)**

2. When must a company hold its first and subsequent annual general meetings? **(1, 2, 3)**

3. In what circumstances has the Secretary of State power to call (or direct the calling of) a company's general meeting? **(6)**

4. Under what circumstances may a private company dispense with the Annual General Meeting and laying of accounts? **(7, 8)**

25
Extraordinary general meetings

1. Power to call an extraordinary general meeting

(a) *The directors* may call an extraordinary general meeting at any time to transact business which cannot conveniently be held over until the next annual general meeting, subject to their giving adequate notice. *See* Table A, art. 37 and *Pergamon Press* v. *Maxwell* (1970).

(b) *Where the company's Articles do not make other provisions.* Two or more members holding not less than one-tenth of the issued share capital (or not less than 5 per cent in number of the members of the company, if it has not a share capital), may call a meeting (s. 370(3)).

(c) *Requisitionists* may themselves convene an extraordinary general meeting under s. 368(4) if the directors fail to comply with their requisition. (*See* 3 below.)

(d) *The court* has power under s. 371 to order the calling of a general meeting, if the company has found it impracticable to do so; this it may do either of its own motion or on the application of a director or of any member who would be entitled to vote at the meeting.

(e) *Table A* (art. 37) provides:

  (i) *The directors* may, whenever they think fit, convene a general meeting.

  (ii) *The members* shall have power to requisition an extraordinary general meeting in accordance with the provisions of s. 368.

  (iii) *Any director or any member* may convene a general meeting, if at any time there are not sufficient directors within the

UK capable of acting to form a quorum; the meeting to be convened as nearly as possible in the same manner as that in which meetings may be convened by the directors.

2. Notice required

Ordinarily an extraordinary general meeting requires not less than 14 days' notice in writing (s. 369), but exception must be made in the following cases:

(a) *21 days' notice* at least is required if it is intended to pass a *special* resolution (s. 378(2));

(b) *7 days' notice* at least is required, in the case of an *unlimited* company.

NOTE: For the passing of a *special* resolution, 21 days' notice is the minimum requirement in *all* cases, i.e. it applies to both limited and unlimited companies.

3. Members' power to requisition under s. 368

(a) *Despite anything in the Articles* to the contrary, members are entitled to requisition the convening of an extraordinary general meeting if:

(*i*) The requisition is made by members holding at the date of the deposit of the requisition *not less than one-tenth of the paid-up capital* carrying voting rights at the company's general meetings; or, if the company has no share capital, not less than one-tenth of the total voting rights of the members at general meetings (s. 368(2)). Shareholders who only have a right to vote in certain events can only join in a requisition if those events have occurred by 'the date of the deposit'. Examples include preference shares carrying votes only when dividends are in arrears, or certain shareholders who can vote only in the event of a winding-up. Similarly, the right to vote may be lost under a company's articles if calls on shares are unpaid, however the right to requisition requires *paid-up* share capital, *see* generally *Re Bradford Investments plc* (1990).

(*ii*) *The requisition sets out the objects of the meeting*, and is deposited at the company's registered office (s. 368(3)).

NOTE: The requisition may consist of several documents in like form, signed by one or more of the requisitionists.

In the case of joint holders, the requisition should be signed by all the joint holders: *Patentwood Key Syndicate* v. *Pearse* (1906). One member holding sufficient paid-up capital may requisition a meeting.

(b) *If the directors fail to comply*; that is, if they do not, within 21 days from deposit of the requisition, convene an extraordinary general meeting, the requisitionists (or a majority of them as regards voting rights) may themselves convene a meeting as nearly as possible in the same manner as required by the Articles. In that event:

  (i)   The meeting must be held *within three months* from the date of deposit of the requisition.

  (ii) *The requisitionists may claim* from the company any reasonable expenses incurred through the directors' default.

  (iii) *The company may retain the expenses* out of fees or other remuneration for services due to the directors in default (s. 368(4)–(6)).

  (iv) *Subsection (8) of s. 368* was added by the Companies Act 1989. It says that the directors are deemed not to have duly convened a meeting if they convene a meeting for a date more than 28 days after the date of the notice convening the meeting. This was added to prevent the potential abuse arising from the decision in *Re Windward Island Enterprises (UK) Ltd* (1982), which allowed directors to convene the meeting for much more than three months from the date of deposit of the requisition, so long as they convened it within 21 days thereof. This effectively prevented the requisitionists from convening a meeting themselves under the procedure outlined above. However, if the directors do so their action could amount to unfairly prejudicial conduct: *McGuinness* v. *Bremner plc* (1988).

  (v)   *Table A, art. 37* requires the meeting to be called for a date not later than eight weeks after the requisition is deposited, but this has now been superseded by the statutory requirement that the meeting must be held not later than seven weeks and two days after the date of deposition (i.e. 21 days to convene, within 28 days plus 2 clear days).

(vi) *Application to the court.* It is nevertheless arguable that an application can be made to the court to call the meeting if the directors do not fulfil their statutory duty to call the meeting 'forthwith', even though the 21 days allowed have not elapsed since the requisition was deposited. The appropriateness of such an application will depend on the urgency of the business to be dealt with and the date, if any, for which the directors have convened the meeting: *see Re Paris Skating Rink Co.* (1877); *McGuinness* v. *Bremner* (1988).

(vii) *Special resolution.* By s. 368(7) the directors are deemed *not* to have duly convened the meeting at which a special resolution is to be proposed unless they give the notice required for special resolutions under s. 378(2).

(viii) *Construing requisitions.* The courts will be pragmatic and not pedantic in construing requisitions by shareholders in order to give them effect, and if the directors respond by convening a meeting to consider only some of the matters contained in a requisition, the requisitionists may ignore it and convene their own meeting: *Isle of Wight Railway Co.* v. *Tahourdin* (1883). Where requisitionists do convene their own meeting they may not consider any matter not covered by the terms of the requisition: *Ball* v. *Metal Industries Ltd* (1957). The company secretary has no power to call a meeting upon requisition. Such power is vested in the directors: *Re State of Wyoming Syndicate* (1901).

4. Right to requisition resolutions and right to requisition meetings compared

(a) The right of members by requisition to bring forward resolutions and have statements circulated at general meetings under s. 376 has been dealt with in chapter 19 on Resolutions. However, it is worth comparing the rights given by s. 376 and s. 368 as follows:

(i) *Voting rights required.* Under s. 376, the total voting rights required to support a requisition are only half those required under s. 368. Also under s. 376(2)(b) not less than

100 members holding shares in the company on which there has been paid-up an average sum, per member, of not less than £100 can requisition a resolution. This is a low requirement for many public companies.

(*ii*) *Obstruction*. The company may try to obstruct the requisitionists in a s. 376 situation by alleging defamation. There is no equivalent provision under s. 368.

(*iii*) *Alternatives*. In relation to the circulation of statements under s. 376 if there is a failure on the part of the company s. 356 gives the dissenting members the right to obtain a copy of the company's register of members and circulate their statement themselves. There is no simple alternative to s. 368.

(*iv*) *Expenses*. In the case of s. 376 the requisitionists pay expenses whereas under s. 368 the company pays. However, since the s. 376 procedure usually consists of additional material which is added to the notice of the meeting, the expense is not excessive. More expense would be incurred where a statement is circulated after the issue of notice convening an AGM or EGM but before the meeting is held. The latter is possible under s. 376, provided the requisition is deposited at the company's registered office not less than one week before the meeting. One way around the problem of expense under s. 376 is for the requisitioned resolution to contain a statement that the expense incurred in giving effect to the requisition shall be defrayed by the company.

5. Auditor's right to requisition under s. 392A

Where an auditor's notice of resignation contains a statement that there are circumstances connected with his resignation which he considers should be explained to the company, he may requisition the directors to convene an extraordinary general meeting to enable him to do so.

The directors must call a meeting forthwith, and at the latest, within 21 days of receiving the requisition. The meeting must be held not later than 28 days after the notice convening it is sent out. The auditor has a right to have a statement circulated or read out at the meeting as well as the right to be heard orally. The company or any aggrieved person may challenge the requisition on the basis of defamation. If the directors do not call the meeting in fulfilment of their statutory obligation, a member (though not the auditor who resigned) may apply to the court under s. 371 for an order that a general meeting be held.

6. Public company's serious loss of capital

Where the net assets of a public company are half or less of its called-up share capital, the directors must, not later than 28 days from the earliest day on which the fact is known to a director of the company, convene an extraordinary general meeting. The meeting must be held on a date not later than 56 days from that earliest day on which the fact about capital became known to a director. The purpose of the meeting is to consider whether any, and if so what, steps should be taken to deal with the situation (s. 142).

Progress test 25

1. What is an extraordinary general meeting, and who has a statutory right **(a)** to convene, **(b)** to requisition, such a meeting? **(1, 3)**

2. What is the prescribed minimum notice required for the convening of an extraordinary general meeting of **(a)** a limited company, **(b)** an unlimited company? How is this affected, if at all, if the meeting is to be held for the purpose of passing a special resolution? **(2)**

26
Class meetings

Purpose of meeting

1. When held

Class meetings are held whenever the Acts or the articles so provide and principally in connection with the variation of rights and privileges attached to different classes of shares, usually by holders of a class of shares likely to be adversely affected.

2. Variation of class rights

(a) The power to vary class rights is usually given in the articles or (more rarely) memorandum, and in the conditions of issue. In that case, the holders of the shares affected must be given an opportunity to meet as a class to consider the effects of the alterations.

(b) Thus, the company's articles may also provide for the holding of meetings of particular classes of shareholders, and for the majority required at such meetings to bind members of the class concerned.

(c) In *Rights and Issues Investment Trust Ltd* v. *Stylo Shoes Ltd* (1964) the defendant company passed special resolutions increasing the issued share capital and doubling the voting rights of the management shares. The latter was done in order to preserve the relative voting strength of the existing management shares. The resolutions were carried by a large majority at a meeting of the company and approved by a class meeting of the ordinary shareholders. Holders of the management shares did not vote on either occasion. It was held by the court that the resolution altering the voting rights was valid. Pennycuik J said:

'So far as I am aware there is no principle under which the members of a company acting in accordance with the Companies Act and the constitution of the particular company and subject to any necessary consent on the part of a class affected, cannot, if they are so minded, alter the relative voting powers attached to various classes of shares. Of course, any resolution for the alteration of voting rights must be passed in good faith for the benefit of the company as a whole, but, where it is so, I know of no ground on which such an alteration would be objectionable and no authority has been cited to that effect. So here this alteration in voting powers has been resolved upon by a great majority of those members of the company who have themselves nothing to gain by it so far as their personal interest is concerned and who, so far as one knows, are actuated only by consideration of what is for the benefit of the company as a whole. I cannot see any ground on which that can be said to be oppressive . . .'

NOTE: There was no legal obligation on the part of the holders of management shares to abstain from voting: *North West Transportation Co. Ltd* v. *Beatty* (1887); *N.C. Securities Ltd* v. *Jackson* (1974).

Methods of variation

3. Variation of rights attached to special classes of shares
Section 125 of the Companies Act 1985 has effect with respect to the variation (including abrogation) of the rights attached to any class of shares where a company's share capital is divided into different classes. It lays down the following procedures:

(a) *Where class rights are attached in documents other than the memorandum* (e.g. the articles or terms of issue), and no variation procedure is contained in the memorandum or articles, those rights may be varied only if:

(*i*) the holders of three-quarters in nominal value of the issued shares of the class in question consent in writing to the variation; *or*

(*ii*) an extraordinary resolution passed at a separate general meeting of the holders of that class sanctions the variation, and

(*iii*) any additional requirement (howsoever imposed) is complied with (s. 125(2)).

NOTE: The procedure in (**a**)(*i*) and (*ii*) above is the *statutory variation* procedure.

(**b**) *Where class rights are attached in documents other than the memorandum* (as in (**a**) above), and a variation procedure is contained in the articles at the time of the company's original incorporation or is later added (i.e. whenever first so included), those rights may be varied as follows:

(*i*) If the variation is connected with the giving, variation or renewal of an authority for the purposes of allotment of certain securities by directors (s. 80) or with a reduction of share capital (s. 135) then the variation can be effected if the *statutory variation procedure* is followed (*see* (**a**)(*i*) and (*ii*)); and

(*ii*) any additional requirements of the memorandum or articles are complied with (s. 125(3)).

If the variation is not so connected:

(*iii*) it may only be effected by means of the procedure set out in the articles (s. 125(4)).

(**c**) Where class rights are attached by the *memorandum,* and no variation procedure is contained in the memorandum or articles, class rights may be varied either:

(*i*) by means of a scheme of arrangement (s. 425); or

(*ii*) if all the members of the company (not just the members of the class) agree to the variation (s. 125(5)).

NOTE: This requirement cannot be overridden by an alteration of the articles because s. 125(7) says that an alteration of a provision in the company's articles relating to variation of class rights or the insertion of any such provision into the articles shall itself be treated as an alteration of class rights.

(**d**) Where class rights are attached by the *memorandum,* and a variation procedure is contained in the *memorandum,* those rights may be varied as follows:

(*i*) If the variation is connected with the giving, variation or renewal of an authority for the purposes of allotment of

certain securities by directors (s. 80) or with a reduction
of share capital (s. 135) then the variation can be effected
if the statutory variation procedure is followed (*see* (**a**)(*i*)
and (*ii*)), and

(*ii*) any additional requirements of the memorandum are
complied with.

If the variations are not so connected:

(*iii*) they may only be effected by means of the procedure set
out in the memorandum (s. 17(2)).

(**e**) Where class rights are attached by the *memorandum*, and there
is *express prohibition on variation in the memorandum then* no variation
can be effected except by means of a scheme of arrangements (ss.
17, 425).

NOTE: Section 125 makes no provision for this situation and
therefore s. 17(2) applies. This prevents alteration of the
memorandum where the memorandum itself prohibits the
alteration of class rights. The only way to vary the rights would be
by a Scheme of Arrangement under s. 425, which requires court
sanction. The only alternative to a scheme is a reconstruction under
s. 110 of the Insolvency Act 1986, but this would involve the
winding-up of the company.

(**f**) Where class rights are attached by the memorandum, and a
variation procedure is contained in the articles which dates from
the time of original incorporation, and variation is not connected
with allotment of securities or reduction of capital, then variation
of those rights may only be effected by means of the procedure set
out in the articles (s. 125(4)).

Conduct of meeting

4. Provision as to meetings

Section 125(6) provides that the following sections of the Act:
Section 369 (length of notice for calling meetings);
Section 370 (general provisions as to meetings and votes);
Section 376 and 377 (circulation of members' resolutions);
and the provision of the articles applying to general meetings;
shall, where relevant, apply to shareholders' meetings concerned
with the variation of class rights, except that:

(a) *The necessary quorum* shall be two persons holding or representing by proxy at least one-third in nominal value of the issued shares of the class in question; and

(b) *At an adjourned meeting* the necessary quorum shall be one person holding shares of the class in question or his proxy; and

(c) *A poll* may be demanded by any holder of shares of the class in question present in person or by proxy.

> NOTE: In *East* v. *Bennett Bros Ltd* (1911) it was held that where there was only one holder of shares of a particular class and he signified his assent to an increase of the shares of that class in a document signed in the minute book; the term 'meeting' could not be interpreted in the ordinary sense and thus the expressed assent of the one shareholder of that class was sufficient to treat the resolution as a valid resolution.

5.   Methods of conducting the proceedings of class meetings

In *Carruth* v. *ICI Ltd* (1937) Lord Maugham observed that in his opinion 'the better and wiser course is to make provision for the holding of truly separate meetings in the ordinary way even at the risk of inconvenience'. The facts were that in reorganizing its share capital ICI convened an AGM, EGM, a class meeting of ordinary shareholders and a class meeting of deferred shareholders in the same venue and at fifteen minute intervals. No attempt was made to clear the room of shareholders who were not entitled to attend any particular meeting. At the last three meetings the proposals were the subject of a poll. The House of Lords held that, since the conduct of the meeting lay in the hands of the chairman, the presence, at a separate meeting of one class of shareholders, of shareholders of a different class did not invalidate the meeting. The decision was based partly on matters of convenience.

This type of procedure has been followed in other cases where no objection has been raised. If there is any likelihood of controversy, separate meetings ought to be held. Where the ICI procedure is adopted then the chairman must be painstaking in his explanation of each stage of the proceedings. Shareholders of each class could be given a different coloured card and their proxies yet another colour to help avoid confusion on a vote by a show of hands; the cards being used to indicate that a shareholder is entitled to vote on a particular motion.

6. Voting in good faith

In *Re Holders Investment Trust* (1971) the resolution for class consent to a variation of rights was of no effect because the majority (who held more than one class of share) had voted with their interests in another class in mind and not with a view to the interests of the class whose rights were being varied. There is a general rule that those voting at a class meeting must vote bona fide (in good faith) for the interests of that class as a whole. Similarly, those voting at any members' meeting for an alteration of articles must vote bona fide for the interests of the company as a whole. *See* generally chapter 20 on voting.

7. What is a class right?

In *Cumbrian Newspapers Group Ltd* v. *Cumberland Printing Co. Ltd* (1986) the court identified three categories of shareholders' rights, two of which amounted to class rights. These were:

(*i*) Rights attached or annexed to particular shares such as voting rights, dividend rights and rights to participate in surplus assets on a winding-up. If articles provide that particular shares carry particular rights not enjoyed by the holders of other shares, it is easy to conclude that the rights are attached to a *class of share*. Such rights are *class rights*.

(*ii*) The second category of rights or benefits which may be contained in articles are conferred on *individuals*, not in the capacity of members but for ulterior reasons connected with the administration of the company's affairs or the conduct of its business. Examples include the right to be the company's solicitor: *Eley* v. *Positive Government Security Life Assurance Co. Ltd* (1875), or the right to be the company's president: *Re Blue Arrow plc* (1987). These are *not* class rights.

(*iii*) The third category covers rights or benefits, that although not attached to any particular shares, are none the less conferred on the beneficiary in *the capacity of member of the company*. This includes the right under the articles for a director's shares to carry weighted votes on a resolution to remove him: *Bushell* v. *Faith* (1969); the right under the articles entitling every member to sell his shares to the directors of the company at a fair valuation: *Rayfield* v. *Hands* (1958); and the right under the articles to appoint a director so long as the member holds 10 per cent of the company's issued share capital: *Cumbrian Newspapers Groups Ltd* v. *Cumberland Printing Co. Ltd* (1986). These *are* class rights.

Though this remains an area of much controversy the above categorization gives some useful guidance on *what is* and *what is not* a class right and therefore on what meetings or consents may be necessary to alter them.

8. What amounts to a variation of class rights

This is a matter of company law and as such outside the scope of this book. Briefly, however, the general rule is that the class rights must literally be varied. It does *not* amount to a variation of rights for a class where other shares are altered to join that class, even though the voting strength of existing class shareholders is weakened. Anything that merely affects the enjoyment of class rights, e.g. relative voting power, without actually varying them will not amount to a variation: *Greenhalgh* v. *Arderne Cinemas* (1946); *White* v. *Bristol Aeroplanes Ltd* (1953); and *Cumbrian Newspapers Group Ltd* v. *Cumberland Printing Co. Ltd* (1986).

For what amounts to a variation of class rights on a reduction of capital, *see Re Old Silkstone Collieries* (1954), in *Re Saltdean Estate Co. Ltd* (1968) and *House of Frazer plc* v. *ACGE* (1987). In the latter case the company passed a special resolution at an EGM attended by ordinary shareholders only, which reduced its share capital by paying off the whole preference capital. The preference shares had a priority to a return of capital on winding-up. The court held that repaying such capital on a reduction of capital was the fulfilment of that right, which thereafter ceased to exist. It did not amount to a variation of class rights requiring separate class consent.

9. Shareholders' right to object to variation (s. 127)

This section applies in the case of a company whose share capital is divided into different classes of shares:

(a) (*i*) If the memorandum or articles authorize the variation of class rights, subject to the consent of any specified proportion of the holders of the issued shares of that class, or the sanction of a resolution at a separate meeting of the holders of those shares; and (*ii*) If (*a*) the rights of that class *are* varied in the manner prescribed, *or* (*b*) the rights attached to any class of shares in the company are varied under s. 125(2), *see* **3(a)**, then application can be made to the court within 21 days to have the variation cancelled, by the holders of not less in the aggregate than 15 per cent of the issue shares of that class, being persons who did not consent to, or vote in favour of, the variation.

NOTE: The application must be made within 21 days after the date on which the consent was given or the resolution was passed, as the case may be.

(b) The application can be made by one or more of the shareholders entitled to apply; they may be appointed in writing to apply on behalf of the others.

(c) If application *is* made to the court within 21 days by the specified minority, the variation of the class rights does not become effective unless and until it receives the confirmation of the court; the court may, however, decide to cancel the proposed variation on the basis that the variation would unfairly prejudice the shareholders of the class represented by the applicant.

(d) In all cases the court's decision to confirm or cancel the variation shall be final.

NOTE: Apparently the court cannot take a middle course, except with the consent of both parties.

(e) A copy of the court order, setting out its decision, must be filed with the Registrar within 15 days after the making of the order. The company and every officer of the company are liable to a fine in case of default.

(f) In s. 127, 'variation' includes abrogation.

10. Meetings under s. 425 (companies and arrangements)

(a) *The scope of s. 425.* The procedure allows a company to reorganize its capital structure or enter into an arrangement with its creditors, or both. It can be used where difficulties exist in changing the rights attaching to a class of shares by the variation of class rights procedure used above. The section uses the terms 'compromise' or 'arrangement' and in *Re Guardian Assurance Co.* (1917) it was held that 'arrangement' is wider than compromise and can cover a situation where there is no pre-existing dispute or difficulty to be resolved. By subsection (5) 'arrangement' includes a re-organization of the company's share capital by the consolidation of shares of different classes, or by the division of shares of different classes, or by both of those methods. Section 425(1) says that where a compromise or arrangement is proposed the court may, on the application of the company or of any creditor or member of it or, in the case of a company being wound up, of the liquidator, order a meeting of the creditors or class of creditors, or of the members or class of members of the company (as the case may be) to be summoned in such manner as the court directs. The following will not be sanctioned by the court:

(i) *An act which would be ultra vires.* If the proposed arrangement, such as a scheme under which the company would sell its undertaking for the benefit of its creditors, is in excess of the powers and objects defined by the company's memorandum of association the court will not sanction it: *Re Ocean Steam Navigation Co. Ltd* (1938).

(ii) *The company must show its support for the scheme.* A requirement of s. 425 is that the company concerned shall show its support for the scheme since schemes of arrangement or compromise are between a company and its members or creditors. Hence a member cannot obtain a court order for calling meetings if the company itself is opposed to the scheme. In *Re Savoy Hotel* (1981) the board of the company, which held 32 per cent of the total voting rights, opposed the scheme. The court held that in the absence of the board's consent or of a provision in the scheme for obtaining the approval of the company by a simple majority in a general meeting, the court had no jurisdiction to sanction the proposed scheme.

(iii) *Expropriation.* In *Re NFU Development Trust Ltd* (1973) the court refused to sanction a scheme which amounted to the expropriation of members' rights without any compensating advantage. This being so it could not be said that they were entering into any compromise or arrangement with the company.

(b) *Procedures*

(i) *Only those involved in or whose interests are affected require meetings.* Therefore, if a proposed arrangement is one between the company and its members, meetings of creditors are not necessary: *Clydesdale Bank, Petitioners* (1950). However, a class is very broadly defined for the purposes of the section which requires a separate meeting or assent of each class or group. Class rights can arise by reason of a difference in interests and careful consideration must be given to this in framing a proposed arrangement. In *Re Hellenic and General Trust Ltd* (1975) it was held that if within a single class of shareholders there are groups whose interests in the scheme are clearly different and opposed, e.g. some of them have their interests with certain intended purchasers, they form a separate class from the other shareholders and approval must be obtained from separate meetings of each group. Similarly, where an arrangement affected policy holders of an assurance company, the holders of policies which had matured formed a different class from those whose policies had not matured, because their interests differed: *Sovereign Life Assurance* v. *Dodd* (1982). To the extent that the assets of the company are insufficient to meet the claims of the other creditors, the subordinated creditors have no interest in the assets of the company. In such circumstances the trustee representing holders of the company's subordinated, unsecured loan stock is not entitled to be given notice of, or to vote at, the meeting: *Re British & Commonwealth Holdings plc* (No. 3) (1992).

(ii) *An application is made to the court* by means of an originating summons for leave to convene the meeting or separate meetings. Even though informal consents may be used there must be at least one meeting to fall within s. 425. If the court approves the application, it will direct the company to convene the meeting by giving notice thereof within the specified number of days and for the meeting to be advertised. Where an order directs that the notice be served on each shareholder then, even if the articles provide that notice may be given to joint holders by service on the first named, *each* joint holder *must* be served.

(iii) *Notice.* Section 426 provides that a statement explaining the arrangement and any material interests of the directors (in whatever capacity) must be sent with the notice. If an explanatory statement is misleading, in failing to disclose directors' interests, the disclosure is insufficient: *Coltness Iron Co. Petitioners* (1951). Where notice was directed to be given by post and advertisement, failure of the advertisement to refer to the explanatory statement meant that the meetings had not been properly convened: *City Property Investment Trust Corp. Petitioners* (1951). All material changes or circumstances which become known to the board between a circular and the holding of a scheme meeting ought to be disclosed to the persons entitled to vote: *Re M. B. Group plc* (1989). The notice must be in a special form used for the purpose and copies of the scheme of arrangement and proxy form will normally also accompany notice of the meeting.

(iv) *Proxies.* These are allowed by s. 425(2). A special form of two-way proxy is normally used. In *Re Dorman Long & Co. Ltd* (1934) it was held that the predecessors of ss. 425 and 426 gave a general right to vote by proxy using any proper form thereof and that the proxies need not be sent to the company's offices before the meeting. It was also held that where directors receive proxies for or against the scheme, pursuant to the court's order, they must use them. The case of *Re Waxed Papers Ltd* (1937) held that the power of voting conferred on the holder of a proxy is wide enough to enable him to vote on a resolution to defer the consideration of the scheme to a future occasion. Because the value of the votes cast is relevant in determining the size of the majority, voting at the meeting will be *by poll* and not by show of hands.

(v) *The majority required.* Section 425(2) requires a duality in the majority in favour of the scheme namely: a majority in *number* representing *three-fourths in value* of the creditors or class of creditors, or members or class of members, as the case may be, present and voting either in person or by proxy at the meeting. Therefore, the majority requires:

(1)   a simple majority of those voting; and

(2)   the simple majority must represent three-fourths in value.

Example _____

All 100 members of a class holding 1,000 shares vote. X holds 260 shares and he votes against. The remaining 740 shares are spread among the other 99 members. Even if they all vote in favour they will not constitute the necessary majority because they cannot muster three-fourths in value. If X held 760 shares and voted in favour and the remaining 99 shareholders voted against, the necessary majority is not constituted because X is not a majority in number of those voting even if he holds three-quarters in value of the shares of that class.

_____

(c) *Sanction by the court.* After the meetings have been held the chairman prepares a report supported by affidavit which is presented to the court. The court then decides whether or not to sanction the scheme. In doing so it will check whether the meetings have complied with ss. 425 and 426 and also whether each class has been fairly represented at the meetings so that if a small number of votes are cast in total the scheme may not be sanctioned. The court is also vigilant to ensure that no part of any majority is tainted by bias or conflict of interest: *Re Hellenic* (1975); *Re Wedgwood Coal & Iron Co.* (1877); *British America Nickel Corporation* v. *O'Brien* (1927); *Re Holders Investment Trust* (1972). The proposal must also be reasonable in an objective sense and, even if the size of the majorities at meetings is more than sufficient, the court will not sanction an inequitable scheme or one which does not accord with other principles set out in the Companies Acts. The court must be satisfied that 'the proposal is such as intelligent and honest members of the classes concerned, acting in respect of their own interests, would approve': *Re Dorman Long & Co. Ltd* (1934).

Once sanctioned by the court the compromise or arrangement is binding on all creditors or the class of creditors, or on the members or class of members, as the case may be, and also on the company. Where the company is in the course of being wound-up it also binds the liquidator and contributories of the company.

An order of the court sanctioning a scheme will have no effect until an office copy of the order has been delivered to the registrar and a copy annexed to every copy of the company's memorandum issued after the order has been made, s. 425(3).

Section 427 makes provision for facilitating company reconstructions and amalgamations and a new section, s. 427A applies ss 425–7 to mergers and divisions of public companies.

Progress test 26

1. What is a 'class' meeting, and what protection does the Act give to a minority of shareholders of a particular class if their rights have been varied?   **(1, 3, 9)**

2. A company's articles provide for the alteration of class rights by resolution of a three-fourths majority, passed at a meeting of the class of shareholders concerned. Such a resolution is passed at a meeting of the company's preference shareholders, permanently reducing the preference dividend from 7½ per cent to 6 per cent. What remedy does the Act provide for the protection of the minority in such a case?   **(9)**

27
Board meetings

1. Purpose

(a) An incorporated body, such as a limited company, must act through properly appointed agents, i.e. the directors, 'by whatever name called' (s. 741).

(b) The directors are responsible for managing the company's affairs and deciding matters of policy (*see* Table A, art. 70 discussed in chapter 16). However, the articles of the company may give rise to a threefold division of power. In *John Shaw & Sons (Salford) Ltd* v. *Shaw* (1935) there were eight directors, three of whom were 'permanent' directors. The ordinary directors had no right at directors' meetings to vote in respect of, or exercise control over, the financial affairs of the company. As regards the management of the company's business the ordinary directors only had such powers of control and voting as might be conferred upon them by the permanent directors from time to time. Similarly, in *Salmon* v. *Quin & Axtens Ltd* (1909), a power of veto over board decisions on certain matters granted in the articles to two managing directors was effective and could not be challenged. In certain circumstances the decisions and actions of one director may be regarded as the decisions and actions of the board where there is an effective *de facto* or implied delegation by the board to that one director: *International Sales & Agencies Ltd* v. *Marcus* (1982). However, there must be a power to delegate in the articles, *see* chapter 29 on committees.

(c) Their decisions are made and their will expressed at board meetings; nevertheless, there are matters which are required (by the Act and/or the articles) to be decided by the company in *general* meeting (*see* 19:**15(d)**).

Business at board meetings

2. The first board meeting

Some or all of the following items of business are likely to be included in the agenda of the first board meeting, which should be held as soon as possible after appointment of the first directors and receipt of the company's Certificate of Incorporation.

(a) *Certificate of Incorporation.* The secretary will produce the Certificate of Incorporation, and its receipt will be recorded.

(b) Appointment of the first directors. Record the appointment of the first directors.

> NOTE: The first directors have already been adequately appointed, having been named as such in a statement in prescribed form, signed by the subscribers to the memorandum, and containing a consent signed by each person named (s. 10).

(c) *Appointment of chairman.* The person appointed will usually also take the chair at general meetings of the company.

(d) *Appointment of secretary.* Record the appointment of the first secretary (or joint secretaries) and fix the terms of his (or their) appointment(s).

> NOTE: The first secretary (or joint secretaries) have already been adequately appointed, having been named as such in a statement in prescribed form, signed by the subscribers to the memorandum, and containing a consent signed by each person named (s. 10).

(e) *Appointment of the company's solicitors.*

(f) *Appointment of the company's brokers.* In the case of a public company, this appointment would be necessary if it was the company's intention to apply to the stock exchange for permission to deal.

(g) *Appointment of the company's bankers.* The resolution passed for this purpose will usually be in the form required by the bank concerned.

(h) *Appointment of the company's auditors.* A public company intending to offer its shares in a prospectus may make such an appointment at this early stage, as they will wish to include the names of the auditors in the prospectus.

(i) *Common seal.* Submit and adopt a design for the company's common seal, and lay down rules for its use and custody, unless already included in the articles.

(j) *Raising capital.* Determination of the method (or methods) to be adopted for obtaining capital. If the company is offering its shares to the public, the principal methods are by prospectus, offer for sale and stock exchange 'placing'.

> NOTE: A company registered as a public company on its original incorporation must have allotted share capital, the nominal value of which is not less than the authorized minimum (currently £50,000): ss. 117 and 118.

(k) *Prospectus or equivalent document.* If the previous item **(j)** is applicable, prepare and/or consider draft prospectus or equivalent document, submitted by the secretary or solicitor.

(l) *Underwriting contract.* If it is intended to underwrite the share issue, consider the terms of the draft underwriting contract, submitted by the secretary or solicitor.

(m) *Purchase agreement.* Where applicable, i.e. if the company has been formed to acquire another business, execute the purchase agreement.

> NOTE: It must, however, be borne in mind that any contract made by a public company at this stage is provisional only, i.e. until it obtains its 'trading certificate' entitling it to commence business (s. 117(2)).

(n) *Instructions to the secretary.* Formal instructions will be given to the secretary at this stage, e.g. to deal further with the appointment of the company's bankers, and to submit application to the stock exchange for permission to deal.

3. Business at subsequent board meetings

Such further business may be divided into those concerned with:

(a) *Policy making,* i.e. considering and making decisions affecting the broad policy of the company. These are principally matters which are likely to be handled by the *full* board, and not delegated to committees, e.g.:

  (*i*) *Development of the company's business,* consideration of the additional capital required, and how it is to be acquired.

  (*ii*) *Acquisition of another company* or of a controlling interest in it; preliminary discussion will begin at board level. For an example of the problems arising where such action was under the control of a committee, *see Guinness plc* v. *Saunders* (1990).

(*iii*) *Receiving reports* of various committees, and making decisions based on recommendations submitted, or on information provided, by committees.

(b) *Routine business.* In the case of a large public company, much of the routine business is delegated to separate standing committees, which will attend to the following:

(*i*) *Transfers.* Approval (or rejection) of transfers submitted for registration.

(*ii*) *Sealing of documents*, such as share certificates.

(*iii*) *Finance.* Routine financial matters rather than high finance.

(*iv*) *Budgetary control*, and other controls given over to committees within certain limits.

(*v*) *Personnel.* Appointments (up to certain levels), resignations, salary increases, welfare, etc.

For a more detailed appraisal of the committee system *see* chapter 29.

Conduct of board meetings

4. Conduct

Regulations affecting the conduct of board meetings are usually set out in a company's articles and (as in Table A) they frequently give the directors the power to regulate their own meetings in most respects.

Table A makes the following provisions on the subject of board meetings (arts. 88–98).

(a) *The directors* may regulate their proceedings as they think fit (art. 88).

(b) *Chairman:*

(*i*) The directors may appoint one of their number to be chairman of the board of directors and may at any time remove him from that office. If the chairman is unwilling to preside or is not present within five minutes after the time appointed for the meeting, the directors present may appoint one of their number to be chairman of the meeting (art. 91).

(*ii*) In case of an equality of votes, the chairman shall have a second or *casting vote* (art. 88).

(c) *Quorum:*

(*i*) The quorum of a board meeting may be fixed by the directors, and unless so fixed the quorum shall be two (article 89).

(*ii*) If there is a vacancy in the body of directors, the continuing directors may act. Where the vacancy reduces the number of directors below that required for a quorum, the continuing directors or director may act only for the purpose of filling vacancies or of calling a general meeting (art. 90).

(*iii*) A director shall not vote in respect of any contract in which he is 'interested' and if he does vote his vote shall not be counted; nor shall he be counted in the quorum present at the meeting (arts. 94 and 95). These prohibitions are, however, subject to various exceptions which are dealt with in the next chapter.

(d) *Convening meetings:*

(*i*) A director may summon a board meeting at any time, and the secretary must do so on the requisition of a director.

(*ii*) It is not necessary to give notice of a board meeting to any director for the time being absent from the United Kingdom (art. 88).

(e) *Voting.* All decisions at board meetings are to be made by a majority of votes (art. 88).

(f) *A resolution in writing,* signed by *all* the directors for the time being entitled to receive notice of a meeting of the directors, shall be as valid and effectual as if it had been passed at a meeting of the directors duly convened and held (art. 93). This article also applies to a committee of directors. Even if the articles do not contain such a clause, the decision in *Re Bonelli's Telegraph Co.* (1871) held that at common law an informal but unanimous agreement of all the directors, without holding a board meeting, is as valid as a resolution passed by them at an actual meeting of the board. Such a resolution should, nevertheless, be recorded in the minutes. Although the Act does not give members the right to inspect the minutes of board meetings, the auditors may wish to do so as part of their normal duties. At common law a director has the right to inspect the minutes of board meetings and may be accompanied by his professional adviser, *see McCasker* v. *McRae* (1966); *Conway & Ors* v. *Petronius Clothing Co. Ltd & Ors* (1978).

(g) *Committees*. The directors have power to delegate any of their powers to committees (art. 72). This topic is dealt with in more detail in chapter 29.

(h) *Attendance at board meetings*. Every director present at any meeting of directors or committee of directors must sign his name in a book to be kept for that purpose (art. 100). In *Re Copal Varnish Co. Ltd* (1917) it was held that a director cannot wilfully refuse to attend a board meeting with the object of preventing a quorum and therefore preventing a particular transaction from being determined. A quorum at board meetings was two and there were two directors. The articles also provided that no share could be transferred to a non-member without the consent of the directors. One of the directors, Percy, refused to attend board meetings in order to prevent a quorum and thus prevent registration of certain share transfers. The other director, Ernest, had a casting vote as chairman. The court held that Percy could not wilfully refuse to attend board meetings and therefore it directed registration of the transfers.

(i) *Validity of acts*. Where it is *afterwards* discovered that there is a defect in the appointment of directors or of any person acting as such, then any acts done by them at meetings are as valid as if they had been duly appointed or were qualified (art. 92). *See* s. 285 and *Morris* v. *Kanssen*, below at **5(b)**(*iii*). In relation to voting, *see* **20:7(d)**.

(j) *Appointment and departure from office*. This is dealt with in Table A, arts. 73–80 and requires *careful* consideration. Some companies' articles require that a director have a share qualification, i.e. a minimum number of shares in the company, and that a person failing to have such a qualification shall vacate office. Most companies' articles contain disqualification provisions, as does Table A, art. 81. Disqualification orders may also be made under the Company Directors Disqualification Act 1988. Section 293 of the 1985 Act lays down an age limit of 70 for directors, and it applies to public companies and private companies which are subsidiaries of public companies. Section 303 also lays down procedures for the removal of a director before his period of office is complete. This is dealt with in chapter 19 on resolutions.

5. If no corresponding provision is made by the articles

In this situation (and assuming Table A is excluded), the decision arrived at in the following cases will apply:

(a) *Chairman.*

   (i) The appointment of a chairman without specifying the duration of such appointment does not entitle him to hold office until he ceases to be a director, as the remaining members of the board may remove him at any time, and appoint another of their number as chairman: *Foster* v. *Foster* (1916).

  (ii) The chairman has *no* casting vote: *Nell* v. *Longbottom* (1894).

(b) *Quorum.*

   (i) A board meeting need not necessarily be held in a boardroom; it can be held under informal circumstances, but the casual meeting of the only two directors of a company cannot be treated as a valid board meeting, if either of them objects: *Barron* v. *Potter* (1914).

  (ii) A disinterested quorum is essential for a board meeting: *Yuill* v. *Greymouth Point Elizabeth Railway Co.* (1904). This is dealt with in more detail in the next chapter.

 (iii) The board must be properly constituted; if, therefore, acts are done as directors by persons who have not been validly elected, they do *not* bind the company: *Garden Gully Quartz Mining Co.* v. *McLister* (1875). If, however, the defect in the appointment or qualification of the director(s) is only discovered *afterwards*, s. 285 provides that their acts shall be valid. Table A, art. 92 mirrors s. 285 and extends it to cover acts done by a *meeting* of directors. In *British Asbestos Co.* v. *Boyd* (1903) the articles contained a clause similar to art. 92. After being appointed secretary of the company, Mr Boyd continued to act as a director whereas under the articles he ought to have vacated office as director. At a meeting of directors Mr Boyd and the only other director passed a resolution, electing a third party, Mr Methuen, as a director under a power in the articles to fill casual vacancies. The three directors continued to act as such *in good faith*. The court held that the irregularities were validated by the articles and what is now s. 285. The appointment of Mr Methuen was confirmed. For other examples *see Briton Medical and General Life Assurance* v. *Jones* (1889); *Dawson* v. *African Consolidated Land and Trading Co. Ltd* (1898); *Boschoek Proprietary Co. Ltd* v. *Fuke* (1906), and *Channel Collieries Trust, Ltd* v. *Dover, St Margaret's and Martin Mill Light Railway Co.* (1914).

However, in *Morris* v. *Kanssen* (1946) s. 285 and Table A, art. 92 were interpreted as applying to a defective appointment and not to a situation where there had been no appointment at all. Therefore a mere slip or procedural defect in the appointment of a director is covered by s. 285. In this case it was held that s. 285 did not cover an originally valid appointment which had been vacated by reason of a statutory provision (s. 291(3)) requiring qualification shares to be taken up within two months.

(*iv*) A majority of directors will constitute a valid quorum for a board meeting: *York Tramways* v. *Willows* (1882).

(c) *Convening meetings*.

(*i*) Reasonable notice of board meetings is necessary, unless they are held on regular dates at a fixed time and place: *Compagnie de Mayville* v. *Whitley* (1896); nevertheless, it is, of course, advisable to send reminders to the directors, even if meetings are held on regular dates. In *Re Homer District Consolidated Gold Mines* (1887) a meeting of two directors (which constituted a quorum) was held at a few hours' notice. Two other directors were unable to attend. The first two directors present at the meeting knew of the objections of those not present. The court held that notice of the meeting was, in the circumstances, unreasonable and inadequate and the resolution of no effect. *See also Broadview Commodities Pte Ltd* v. *Broadview Finance Ltd* (1983).

(*ii*) However, the irregularity principle (*see* 20:8) has been applied to notices of directors' meetings. In *Browne* v. *La Trinidad Ltd* (1887) at a purported meeting of directors of the company it was resolved to summon an EGM of the members. The court at first instance found that the directors' meeting had been improperly convened because Mr Browne, a director, had received *inadequate notice*. Mr Browne was removed from office at the EGM. The court of appeal refused to rule that the proceedings of the members' meeting had been invalidated by the irregularity. Mr Browne had had plenty of time to call another directors' meeting and argue his point of view, but had not done so. The decision of members to remove him at the EGM had been unanimous. There was no point in going through the procedure again.

According to the latter case if the notice is improper then any resolutions passed at the board meeting are not void. Instead, the aggrieved director becomes entitled to requisition another meeting within a reasonable time of becoming aware of the first meeting. This second meeting gives him the opportunity to query and challenge any resolution passed in his absence at the previous meeting. Contrast *Re East Norfolk Tramways Co.* (1877) where Jessel MR suggested that if no notice at all is given to a minority of directors the meeting is invalid, even though the majority's decision would be decisive, because in his view the minority of directors should have *the opportunity* at least to persuade the others to their way of thinking. *Re Homer's* case above supports this view.

(iii) A director with a share qualification may bring a personal action against his fellow directors to restrain them from wrongfully excluding him from board meetings: *Pulbrook* v. *Richmond Consolidated Mining Co.* (1878). Indeed, no director can be excluded from a board meeting unless that has been resolved by the members: *Hayes* v. *Bristol Plant Hire Ltd* v. *Ors* (1957). However, if a director is personally interested in the matter under discussion he may be asked to withdraw: In *Yuill* v. *Greymouth Point Elizabeth Railway & Coal Co. Ltd* (1904). Where a director has been appointed as a managing director, the board may be able to limit his activities to one subsidiary: *Holdsworth (Harold) & Co. (Wakefield) Ltd* v. *Caddies* (1955); although delegating business to a committee in an effort to exclude a particular director may be restrained by an injunction: *Kyshe* v. *Alturas Gold Ltd* (1888).

(*iv*) A director cannot waive his right to notice; failure to give notice to a director may render proceedings at a board meeting void, even though he indicates that he will not be able to attend and does not require notice: *Re Portuguese Consolidated Copper Mines* (1889); *also Rex* v. *Langhorne* (1836).

6. Directors' attendance book

(a) Although it is often the practice at board meetings to pass around an attendance sheet for signatures of directors present, it is perhaps preferable to follow Table A provision (art. 100), i.e. by providing a *book* for the purpose.

(b) In this way, the secretary can produce signed evidence in a convenient form, to establish which of the directors were actually present at any particular board meeting.

(*i*) It should be borne in mind that a director does not make himself responsible for the business transacted at a meeting merely by voting at a subsequent meeting for approval of the minutes: *Burton* v. *Bevan* (1908).

(*ii*) Similarly the presence of a director at a meeting at which the minutes of the previous meeting were confirmed is not sufficient to make him liable for an *ultra vires* investment when he knows nothing of the irregularity agreed upon at the former meeting. However, a fellow director who had taken an active part in and had assented to the illegal investment *is* liable for such: *Re Lands Allotment Co.* (1894).

7. Small private companies

Sometimes the number of directors of such companies may fall to one. Table A (art. 89) for example fixes the quorum for a board meeting at two. As a result, there may be a problem in passing a board resolution. This may be solved in one of the following ways:

(a) *The remaining director* may act for the purpose of increasing the number of directors to that required for a quorum, or to summon a general meeting of the company, but for no other purpose: Table A (art. 90).

(b) *A resolution in writing,* signed by all directors for the time being entitled to receive notice of a meeting of the directors, shall have the same effect as a resolution passed at a meeting of the directors (art. 93).

(c) *The articles* may provide for a quorum of one or alternatively not state the number for a quorum and give directors power to fix a quorum for board meetings. This is a debatable solution because of the majority view that it is impossible to have a meeting of one. (*See* chapters 2 and 18.)

8. Casual meetings of directors and similar circumstances

(a) Directors may meet in a casual manner for the transaction of business, but in order for their meeting to be of any effect they must intend that the meeting be a board meeting. In *Barron* v. *Potter* (1914) at a casual meeting of two directors at a railway station, which had not been properly convened, the chairman proposed the appointment of further directors and the other objected. Warrington J said:

> 'It is not enough that one of two directors should say "This is a directors' meeting" while the other says it is not. Of course if directors are willing to hold a meeting they may do so under any circumstances, but one of them cannot be made to attend the board or convert a casual meeting into a board meeting, and in the present case I do not see how the meeting in question can be treated as a board meeting.'

Contrast with this case that of *Smith* v. *Paringa Mines Ltd* (1906). A meeting of the company's two directors had been properly convened. They met in a passage outside the office of the company but did not enter. The chairman of directors proposed the appointment of a third director. The second director objected, whereupon the chairman exercised his casting vote and declared the third director elected. The court held that there had been a valid meeting, and that the third director had been properly elected.

(b) *Casual meetings and problems of quorum.* Problems of complying with the quorum requirements may arise. In *Bullfinch Supplies Gold Mining Co. N.L.* v. *Butler* (1913) the articles provided for a quorum of three. Two directors met casually in the street and decided to

bring legal action over a certain matter. They then instructed their
solicitor to issue a writ. Once the writ was issued they informed the
other director and asked his consent. It was held that the action
was instituted without the authority of the company. Similarly, in
another case the prescribed quorum of directors was three. After
obtaining the written authority of two directors at a private
interview and the verbal promise of a third director to sign the
authority at another private interview, the secretary affixed the
company's seal to a bond. It was held that the seal was affixed
without lawful authority and that the company was not liable on
the bond: *D'Arcy* v. *Tamar Kit Hill & Carrington Railway Co.* (1867).
Informal consents and resolution *must be unanimous.*

(c) *Informal resolutions and agreements.* Reference has already been
made to Table A, art. 93 in **4(f)**. In *H.L. Bolton (Engineering) Co. Ltd.*
v. *T.J. Graham & Sons* (1954) the three directors of the company
caused contracts to be entered into, plans to be prepared for work
to be done, and notice to quit to be given to two tenants of the
company. The directors often met informally but did not hold
meetings or pass resolutions or record decisions in any minutes.
The full board met normally once a year and the conduct of the
company's business was left to the directors individually. It was
held that having regard to the standing of the directors in control
of the company's business, the intention of the directors was the
intention of the company. This approach is the same 'controlling
mind' approach as used in cases on corporate criminal and tort
liability such as *Tesco Supermarkets* v. *Nattrass* (1972), *R* v. *I.C.R.
Haulage Ltd* (1944) and *Lennard's Carrying Co. Ltd* v. *Asiatic Petroleum
Co. Ltd* (1915). Its applicability to informal meetings is acceptable
in *Bolton's Case* because all three of the company's directors were
involved. However, the informed unanimous resolution approach
is submitted to be the better one. In, *In Re Bonelli's Telegraph Co,
Collies Claim* (1871) a written agreement was signed firstly by two
directors in the company's office and later by the other two
directors elsewhere. The agreement was held to be binding on the
company. Bacon V-C said:

'I quite agree that the "combined wisdom" is required in
this sense, that they must all be of one mind. But I do not
know that it is necessary they shall all meet in one place. I
can conceive a great many circumstances, . . . where the

actual presence of the three directors cannot be procured, but where their combination can be most effectually secured by correspondence, by transmission of messages, or by other means which may be resorted to. If you are satisfied that the persons whose concurrence is necessary to give validity to the act did so concur, with full knowledge of all that they were doing, in my opinion the terms of the law are fully satisfied, and it is not necessary that whatever is done by directors should be done under some roof, in some place, where they are all three assembled.'

This is an application of the informed resolution principles discussed in chapter 19 on resolutions. Contrast, however, *D'Arcy's Case* (1867) above. The latter part of Bacon V-C's statement gives rise to some interesting and practical issues raised by modern circumstances, such as meetings by telephone.

(d) *Directors' meetings by telephone.* As already discussed, it is usually unnecessary to give notice of board meetings to directors who are outside of the jurisdiction. Even so in today's world of international business and finance it may be necessary to consult a director who is overseas and take a board decision urgently. Some companies' articles attempt to provide for meetings by telephone. The courts have explicitly accepted that a meeting can be held simultaneously in different rooms connected by adequate audio-visual links, enabling those in all the rooms to *see and hear* what is going on in the other rooms: *Byng* v. *London Life Association Ltd* (1989). However, in the Canadian case of *Re Associated Color Laboratories Ltd* (1970) it was held that a telephone conversation between directors in Vancouver and California was incapable of constituting a meeting. A similar view was expressed in the Australian case of *Higgins* v. *Nicol* (1971). Therefore, as UK law appears to stand currently, a conversation by conference telephone without visual links cannot amount to a meeting at which binding majority decisions can be taken. An article to that effect would probably be invalid. Some jurisdictions provide for directors' meetings by conference telephone in their Corporate Law statutes. Delaware Corporation Law, s. 141 and Massachusetts Business Corporation Law, s. 59 do so provide. The latter states:

'Unless the organization or the by-laws otherwise provides,

members of the board of directors of any corporation or any committee designated thereby may participate in a meeting of such board or committee by means of a conference telephone or similar communications equipment by means of which all persons participating in the meeting can hear each other at the same time and participation by such means shall constitute presence in person at a meeting.'

In the absence of a UK equivalent to this provision conference telephone 'meetings' would appear to require *unanimous consent* (preferably expressed in writing for reasons of evidence).

Since standard articles state that it shall not be necessary to give notice of a meeting to a director who is absent from the United Kingdom (Table A, art. 88), a problem will only arise where there are insufficient directors within the jurisdiction to form a quorum.

Progress test 27

1. What are the regulations affecting the conduct of board meetings as provided in Table A, in respect of: **(a)** quorum; **(b)** voting; **(c)** resolutions in writing?   **(4)**

2. In relation to board meetings, explain the decisions arrived at in any *three* of the following cases: **(a)** *Foster* v. *Foster* (1916); **(b)** *Nell* v. *Longbottom* (1894); **(c)** *Barron* v. *Potter* (1914); **(d)** *York Tramways* v. *Willows* (1882); **(e)** *Yuill* v. *Greymouth Point Elizabeth Railway Co.* (1904).   **(5)**

Directors' meetings and disinterested quorum

Directors' duties and the rule

1. Directors are in a fiduciary position

(a) As was forcibly pointed out in the decision of *N.C. Securities Ltd* v. *Jackson* (1974) directors when acting as such, particularly at board meetings, are the agents of the company through whom it acts. When voting at such meetings they must vote bona fide for what they consider is in the best interest of the company. The fiduciary duties which they owe to the company are as follows:

   (*i*) They must act and exercise their discretion bona fide in what they consider to be the best interests of the company: *Re Smith & Fawcett Ltd* (1942).

   (*ii*) A director must not allow his duty to the company and personal interest to conflict, that is, he must not be in a position of conflict of interest. Secret profits or otherwise unauthorized profits are not allowed: *see Aberdeen Railway Co.* v. *Blaikie Bros* (1854); *Transvaal Land Co.* v. *New Belgium (Transvaal) Land and Development Co.* (1914) and *Regal (Hastings) Ltd* v. *Gulliver* (1967).

   (*iii*) A director must exercise powers entrusted to him for their *proper purpose*. He and the board as a whole must not take into account irrelevant factors: *Punt* v. *Symons & Co. Ltd* (1903); *Piercy* v. *Mills & Co. Ltd* (1920); *Hogg* v. *Cramphorn* (1967) and *Howard Smith Ltd* v. *Ampol Petroleum Ltd* (1974).

   (*iv*) Directors are not to fetter the exercise of their discretion unless they bona fide believe it to be in the best interests of the company: *Kreger* v. *Hollins* (1913); *Selangor* v.

Craddock (No. 3) (1968); Thornby v. Goldberg (1964) and see also Lee Panavision Ltd v. Lee Lighting Ltd (1991).

2.   Consequences of these duties and directors' meetings

(a) *Contract voidable.* Because a director must not put himself in a position of conflict, a contract made by a company with one of its directors or with a company or firm in which he is interested is voidable at the insistence of the company: *Aberdeen Railway Co.* v. *Blaikie Bros* (1854). In this case, in relation to the rule against conflict of interest, Lord Cranworth said, 'So strictly is this principle adhered to that no question is allowed to be raised as to the fairness or unfairness of a contract so entered into'. Nevertheless, such a voidable contract may be ratified by the company in general meeting and the director concerned is not debarred from voting as a shareholder at such a meeting: *North West Transportation Co. Ltd* v. *Beatty* (1887). Consequently, both as a general rule of equity and company law, prior disclosure by the director of his interest to the *company in general meeting* and their approval of it validates the contract.

(b) *The director is accountable to the company for any secret profit* which he has made by reason of his fiduciary position. In *Boston Deep Sea Fishing Co.* v. *Ansell* (1888), Ansell was the managing director of the company. He entered, on behalf of the company, into two transactions. First he arranged with a firm of shipbuilders to have a ship built for the company's fleet of fishing vessels. Ansell failed to disclose a commission paid to him by the shipbuilder. He also arranged for the company's shipping fleet to be supplied with ice from an ice company in which he was a shareholder. The ice company paid him a bonus as a member introducing business to it. Ansell did not disclose the latter payment. The BDSF company brought legal action against Ansell and successfully forced him to account for both the commission and the bonus. *See also Parker* v. *McKenna* (1874); *Cook* v. *Deeks* (1917); and *IDC* v. *Cooley* (1972).

3.   Waiver clauses in the articles

(a) Because of the inconvenience of directors having to disclose any interests to the company in general meeting, the articles usually relax the general rule by requiring disclosure to the board of directors. As Foster LJ said in *Guinness plc* v. *Saunders* (1988):

'A director is in a fiduciary position. A person in a fiduciary position is not permitted to obtain a profit from his position except with the consent of his beneficiaries or other persons to whom he owes the duty. In the case of a director the consent required is that of the members in general meeting. That is inconvenient in relation to the day-to-day running of a business. It has, therefore, become the practice to relax the general rule by special provisions in the articles. The purpose of s. 317(1) is not to destroy the power to relax the general rule by the articles, but to impose a binding safeguard on that power.'

Articles may also waive or relax the rules relating to the voidability of such contracts and the requirement to account, but they normally require full disclosure as a prerequisite. The extent to which such clauses might be void as provisions exempting officers and auditors from liability under s. 310 was discussed by Vinelott, J in *Movitex Ltd* v. *Bulfield* (1988) where he said:

'Looked at in the light of this analysis of the self-dealing rule, the explanation of the apparent conflict between s. 310 and arts. 78 and 84 [of this company] becomes clear. The true principle is that if a director places himself in a position in which his duty to the company conflicts with his personal interest or his duty to another, the court will intervene to set aside the transaction without inquiring whether there was any breach of the director's duty to the company. That is an over-riding principle of equity. The shareholders of the company, in formulating the articles, can exclude or modify the application of this principle. In doing so they do not exempt the director from the consequences of a breach of a duty owed to the company.'

For a consideration of this issue in relation to the old Table A provisions *see* Baker [1978] JBL 181; and Birds (1976) 39 MLR 394.

The statutory requirement of disclosure, s. 317 and its relationship with the articles is discussed below at **5**.

(b) Table A, art. 85 says that subject to the provision of the Act, and *provided that he has disclosed to the directors the nature and extent of any material interest of his*, a director notwithstanding his office:

(i)   may be a party to, or otherwise interested in, any transaction or arrangement with the company or in which the company is otherwise interested;

(ii) may be a director or other officer of, or employed by, or a party to any transaction or arrangement with, or otherwise interested in, any body corporate promoted by the company or in which the company is otherwise interested; and

(iii) shall not, by reason of his office: (1) be accountable to the company for any benefit which he derives from any such office or employment or from any such transaction or arrangement or from any interest in any such body corporate, and (2) no such transaction or arrangement shall be liable to be avoided on the ground of any such interest or benefit.

For the purposes of the disclosure under art. 85, a general notice given to the directors is deemed to be a disclosure that the director has an interest in any relevant transaction of the nature and extent specified in the notice. Furthermore, an interest of which a director has no knowledge and of which it is unreasonable to expect him to have knowledge shall not be treated as an interest of his (art. 86).

NOTE: The consequences of a breach of the equitable principle are therefore avoided by disclosure under article 85.

(c) *Voting and the quorum.* Table A, art. 94 states that a director shall not vote at a meeting of directors or of a committee of directors on a resolution concerning a matter in which he has a material interest or duty. The material interest or duty may be direct or indirect and must be one which conflicts or may conflict with the interests of the company. Article 95 goes on to say that a director shall not be counted in the quorum present at a meeting in relation to a resolution on which he is not entitled to vote. However, article 94 allows a director to vote where his interest or duty arises only because:

(i)   the resolution relates to the giving of him of a guarantee, security, or indemnity in respect of money lent to, or an obligation incurred by him for the benefit of, the company or any of its subsidiaries;

(*ii*) The resolution relates to the giving to a third party of a guarantee, security, or indemnity in respect of an obligation of the company or any of its subsidiaries for which the director has assumed responsibility in whole or part and whether alone or jointly with others under a guarantee or indemnity or by the giving of security;

(*iii*) his interest arises by virtue of his subscribing or agreeing to subscribe for any shares, debentures or other securities of the company or any of its subsidiaries, or by virtue of his being, or intending to become, a participant in the underwriting or sub-underwriting of an offer of any such shares, debentures, or other securities by the company or any of its subsidiaries for subscription, .purchase or exchange;

(*iv*) the resolution relates in any way to a retirement benefits scheme which has been approved, or is conditional upon approval, by the Board of Inland Revenue for taxation purposes.

NOTE: Other aspects of voting by directors are considered in chapter 20:**7**.

4. The requirement of the disinterested quorum

(a) *Table A*. The combined effect of arts. 94 and 95 are that a director cannot vote on matters in which he has a material interest (subject to the listed exceptions) nor can he count in the quorum for those matters on which he is not entitled to vote. There is therefore under the articles a requirement for a *disinterested quorum*.

(b) *At common law*. In *Yuill* v. *Greymouth Point Elizabeth Railway and Coal Company Ltd* (1904) the company's articles provided that two directors should be a quorum for the transaction of board business and that any director might enter into a contract or be interested in any business with the company, but that no director so interested should vote on the matter. The company went into financial difficulties and two of the directors advanced it a sum of money. At a later board meeting it was resolved that debentures should be sealed and issued to those two directors as part security for their advances of money. Only three directors were present at the meeting including the two interested directors who were advancing money. The debentures were not issued and the directors sought to rely on the resolution. The court held that a quorum of directors meant a quorum competent to transact and vote on the business before the board. Therefore a resolution passed at a meeting of three directors, two of whom were interested in the subject matter of the resolution, was invalid; there was no quorum. Farwell J said:

> 'If there had otherwise been a quorum, I think the other directors would have been justified in asking them [the two interested directors] to retire while the question of giving them security was discussed, because they were interested against the company. Certainly it is a case in which the company is entitled to have the benefit of all the protection it can get from the independent directors.'

Table A. art. 95 therefore reflects the common law position that a quorum must be a disinterested quorum.

(c) *Splitting business.* In *Re North Eastern Insurance Co. Ltd* (1919) it was held that a meeting could not split-up a transaction under consideration in order to defeat provisions in the articles concerning voting and quorum where directors were interested in that transaction. Since arts. 94 and 95 may exclude a director both from voting and being counted in the quorum, the latter needs to be looked at separately for each item of business.

(d) The cases of *Wilson* v. *L.M.S. Railway* (1940) and *Lapish* v. *Braithwaite* (1926) suggest that a director who is also a director of another company which remunerates him by salary only is not deemed to be 'interested' in a contract with that other company.

5.   The statutory requirement of disclosure

(a) *Disclosure of interest*

   (i) The Act (s. 317) requires a director to disclose his interest in any contract or proposed contract of the company, i.e. he must declare the nature of his interest at a board meeting. In the case of a proposed contract, he must disclose his interest:

(1) at the meeting of directors at which the contract is first considered; or

(2) at the next meeting of directors held after he became interested.

Subsection (5) extends the meaning of contract to include any transaction or arrangement, whether or not constituting a contract. Transactions within s. 330 of the Act, namely loans, quasi-loans, guarantees and credit transactions to directors and certain connected persons are likewise included (s. 317(6)).

Failure to make such a disclosure makes a director liable to a fine.

(*ii*) *Disclosure to the full board.* In *Guinness plc* v. *Saunders* (1988) Fox LJ said that s. 317 required disclosure to the full board of directors. The section could *not* be satisfied by a disclosure to a committee of directors.

(b) *General notice.* To avoid the necessity of giving separate notice in respect of each individual contract in which he becomes interested, a director is permitted, under s. 317(3), to give a *general* notice to the effect that:

(*i*) he is a member of a specified company or firm, and that he is to be regarded as interested in any contract which may, after the date of the notice, be made with that company or firm.

(*ii*) he is to be regarded as interested in any contract which may, after the date of the notice, be made with a specified person who is connected with him (within the meaning of s. 346).

This general notice is deemed to be sufficient declaration of the interest in relation to any contract so made, but it will be of no effect unless either it is given at a meeting of the directors, or the director takes reasonable steps to secure that it is brought up and read at the next meeting of the directors after it is given.

(c) *Relationship between s. 317, article 85 and the general principle.* Section 317 does not 'prejudice the operation of any rule of law restricting directors of a company from having any interest in contracts with the company', therefore:

(*i*)   compliance with s. 317 does not, of itself, validate the contract, and

(*ii*)   the director must make disclosure to the general meeting unless the articles provide otherwise, and

(*iii*)   Table A (art. 85) does provide otherwise by requiring disclosure to the directors.

(*iv*)   In *Hely-Hutchinson* v. *Brayhead Ltd* (1967) it was held that non-compliance by a director with the statutory obligation to disclose his interest in a contract under s. 317 does not render the contract void, but the contract remains *voidable* under the principles of equity. This approach was approved by Lord Goff in *Guinness plc* v. *Saunders* (1990) in the House of Lords. However, Fox LJ in the Court of Appeal said that non-compliance with s. 317 had implications in 'civil law in addition to the penalty of a fine'. The articles of the company in *Hely's* case required disclosure to be 'as required and subject to the provisions of [s. 317] of the Act'. In this way the articles often incorporate the requirements of disclosure under s. 317.

Another recent example of this is *Guinness plc* v. *Saunders* (1988) Court of Appeal, (1990) House of Lords. Mr Ward was a director of Guinness plc in 1986 when it took over the Distillers Company plc. The Guinness' bid for distillers was conducted by a committee of three directors including the chief executive, Saunders, and Ward. The chief executive agreed to pay Ward a large sum of money if the bid was successful. After the takeover was successful, a Jersey company controlled by Ward submitted an invoice to Guinness for £5.2 million for services rendered in connection with the bid. Payment of the invoice was approved by the third director on the bid committee, Mr Roux. Guinness sought recovery of the money. The Court of Appeal held that the agreement for the payment was voidable because of non-disclosure. The articles and s. 317 required disclosure to the full board in the proper manner and not just to a committee. Nor was it sufficient disclosure to show that all the members of the board knew about the payment; nothing short of disclosure at a duly convened meeting of the full board would suffice. Also Mr Ward was liable as constructive trustee because, in breach of his fiduciary duty owed to the company, he received property (money) belonging to the person (the company) to whom the duty was owed.

The House of Lords, however, said that on a proper interpretation of the articles there was no contract between Ward and the company as to the special payment because, *inter alia*, Saunders did not have authority to enter such an agreement, only the full board did. Therefore, s. 317 did not apply directly to the case because there was no contract between Guinness plc and Mr Ward. Mr Ward was liable as constructive trustee.

This case is an example of the complexity which can arise in relation to this area and the debate over the true effect of s. 317, *see* for example the judgment of Lord Goff in the House of Lords and McCormack 'The Guinness Saga: In Tom We Trust' (1991) 12 Co Law 90.

(*v*) If a matter before the board is one in which the *whole* of the directors are personally interested, it must be referred to a meeting of the members — unless there are no members other than the directors, in which event the latter may vote, and are deemed to vote as members: *Re Express Engineering Works* (1920).

(g) *Specimen minute.* A declaration by way of a general notice under s. 317, made by a director concerning his interests, may be minuted as follows:

'The secretary reported receipt of a letter from Mr A. Charter (newly appointed director), in which, pursuant to s. 317, he declared his interest in the following companies: Northern Quarries Ltd (Chairman), British Steel Trust Ltd (Director), London Carrying Co. Ltd (Shareholder), New Plastics Ltd (Shareholder). The contents of the letter were duly noted.'

6. Substantial property transactions and disclosure of interest

(a) Generally by ss. 320–322 a company cannot enter into an arrangement whereby:

(*i*) a director of the company or its holding company, or a person connected with such a director, acquires or is to acquire one or more non-cash assets of the requisite value from the company; or

(*ii*) the company acquires or is to acquire one or more non-cash assets of the requisite value from such a director or person so connected, unless the arrangement is first approved *by a resolution of the company in general meeting* and if the director or connected person is a director of its holding company or a person so connected with such a director, *by a resolution in general meeting of the holding company*.

A non-cash asset is of the requisite value if, at the time the arrangement in question is entered into, its value is not less than £2,000 but (subject to that) exceeds £100,000 or ten per cent of the company's asset value: s. 320.

(b) *Exceptions*. These include:

(*i*) the acquisition of non-cash assets between a holding company and its wholly-owned subsidiary or between two such wholly-owned subsidiaries of the same holding company;

(*ii*) if the arrangement is entered into by a company which is being wound up (unless the winding-up is a members' voluntary winding-up);

(*iii*) where the arrangement is made with a person in his character as a member and a transaction on a recognized investment exchange through the agency of a person acting as an independent broker: s. 321.

(c) *Consequences of contravention of s. 320*. By s. 322 if the necessary approving resolutions are not obtained the arrangement is voidable at the instance of the company, subject to certain conditions being satisfied, and the directors are liable to account to, or indemnify, the company.

Progress test 28

1. Explain the principles underlying the requirement of disinterested quorum at board meetings and how this affects the conduct of such meetings.

29
Committee meetings

Appointment and purpose

1. Appointment

(a) *At common law* directors have no powers of delegation other than those contained in the articles: *Howard's Case* (1866); *Cartmell's Case* (1874). In the absence of an express power a board cannot delegate to one of the directors (*Kerr* v. *Marine Products* (1928)), but if expressly authorized a committee may consist of one member: *Re Fireproof Doors Ltd* (1916); *Re Taurine Co.* (1884). Therefore, if permitted by the articles, directors may delegate their powers and duties to committees, and such committees may then have power to bind the company by their decisions, so long as they act *intra vires*. It may be questioned whether the authority of the Articles *is* necessary if a committee is appointed merely to consider or investigate a particular problem, and then to report back to the board, usually with their recommendations. Obviously, it is advisable, and safer, not to put the matter to the test, and to ensure that the articles give the necessary power before making such an appointment.

(b) In *Guinness plc* v. *Saunders* (1990), Lord Goff said:

> 'I have reached the conclusion that art. 91 [of Guinness plc's articles] does not empower a committee of the board of Guinness to authorize special remuneration for services rendered by directors of the company. It is true that the articles of Guinness are conspicuous neither for their clarity nor for their consistency. In particular there is no sensible basis upon which it is possible to reconcile art. 91 with art. 110 without doing violence to the language of one or other

article. But I am satisfied that I should accept Guinness' argument on this point.'

The House of Lords went on to hold that there was no enforceable agreement between Mr Ward and Guinness, it being void for want of authority. This case emphasizes the point made in **(a)** above that the delegation of powers and duties to committees must be clear, both in the articles of the company and the actual resolution of the board which does the delegating. It also underlines the reality that major strategic decisions, such as takeovers, ought to be dealt with by the full board resolving to do certain acts, rather than by a committee of the board. The latter could investigate, report back and make certain recommendations, but the decisions should be taken by the *full board to protect everyone concerned*, not least of whom are the directors on the committee itself.

(c) By Table A, art. 72 the directors have power to delegate any of their powers to committee. Any such delegation may be subject to any conditions the directors may impose. The conditions may be revoked or altered. The delegation may be made collaterally with or to the exclusion of the board's own powers. Subject to any such conditions, the proceedings of a committee with two or more members are governed by the articles (88–98) regulating the proceedings of the directors so far as they are capable of applying. However broad the power in the articles to delegate to a committee, it must not be used in a way designed to exclude a particular director from taking part in managing the company's affairs: *Kyshe* v. *Alturar Gold Ltd* (1888).

2.   Quorum

If there is no quorum fixed, either by the articles or by the directors, *all* members of a committee will constitute a valid quorum of that committee's meetings: *Re Liverpool Housing Stores* (1890).

3.   Powers

When delegating work to a committee, it is essential that the powers of the committee should be clearly defined in writing, i.e. either in the Articles or in the separate resolution by which the committee is appointed. So long as the committee acts within the scope of its authority, the board and the company will be bound by its actions. A committee cannot delegate powers to a sub-committee unless specifically authorized to do so: *Cook* v. *Ward* (1877).

4. Advantages of the committee system

(a) *Specialized knowledge can be applied* to the business for which the committee is appointed; thus the work can be done more thoroughly and more quickly.

(b) *The duties of the directors* can be more evenly distributed, i.e. amongst various committees to which routine work is delegated.

(c) *Business delegated to a committee* can be considered in greater detail than would be possible at a full board meeting.

(d) *Fewer full board meetings* are required, and these are conducted more expeditiously and yet more effectively.

(e) *More time is allowed*, at those board meetings which are necessary, for deciding questions of policy, i.e. without prolonging the meetings on routine matters which are being handled by appropriate standing committees.

5. Disadvantages of the committee system

As with any 'system', it must be properly applied, and unless due care is taken the committee system may be found to have the following disadvantages:

(a) *The authority of the board* (or of any other appointing body) may be weakened, i.e. by delegating too much of its power to committees and the consequent loss of control. To avoid this state of affairs, the chairman of the board is usually also an *ex officio* member of all committees. Moreover, it is also necessary to ensure that the powers of all committees are clearly defined.

(b) *Delays may occur*, e.g. where a dilatory committee fails to report back to the board by a specified date. This, too, is a fault which arises out of loss of control, and is not a valid criticism of the system. Here again, the remedy may lie in the chairman of the parent body acting as *ex officio* member of all committees.

(c) *Weak management may 'hide behind' a committee*, e.g. when making a decision which is likely to be unpalatable. This is primarily a criticism of the management concerned rather than of the committee system, although it does, no doubt, provide a weak management with the necessary opportunity.

(d) *A committee often tends to be dominated* by an overbearing member; therefore, the committee's decisions or recommendations are, in fact, those of that one person alone. Although this may, undoubtedly, be true in a few cases, it is not a valid criticism of the system but of those members of a committee who are weak enough to allow it to happen.

Types of committee

6.   Classification

Committees may be classified according to their power and their function and/or duration.

(a) *The power they exercise:*
 (*i*) Those *having* power to bind the parent body.
 (*ii*) Those *without* any power to bind the parent body; or
(b) *The function and/or duration* of the committee:
 (*i*) *Executive committees*, possessing wide powers of authority.
 (*ii*) *Standing committees*, which are relatively permanent and appointed to do a routine task.
 (*iii*) *Ad hoc committees*, appointed for a particular task only.

7.   Descriptions of the principal forms of committee

(a) *Executive committee.* In a general way this describes any committee having the power to act, generally or specifically. It is, however, more commonly used to describe a body with power to govern or administer; in that sense, therefore, it might be applied to, say, a management committee, or any such committee having plenary power, i.e. full power of authority.

> NOTE: It may be argued that the board of directors is itself a 'committee' (appointed by the shareholders), to the extent that it governs or administers.

(b) *Standing committee.* Such a committee is formed for a specified purpose (or purposes) and, being permanent, its role is to deal with routine business delegated to it at, say, weekly or monthly meetings. Transfer committees, sealing committees, finance committees and allotment committees are typical.

(c) *Ad hoc committee.* This is formed for a particular task only, i.e.

not for the purpose of dealing with routine business (*ad hoc* = 'for this'). Thus, an *ad hoc* committee might be appointed to investigate the possibility, and to advise on the inauguration, of a superannuation scheme. It might equally be described as a 'fact-finding' or 'special' committee. Such a committee is relatively short-lived; that is, having achieved its purpose and reported back to the parent body, it then ceases to exist.

(d) *Sub-committee*. A committee may, if it has the necessary power, appoint one or more of its members to a sub-committee, which may be either a form of standing committee, e.g. where it is to relieve the parent committee of some of its routine work; or an *ad hoc* committee, formed to make a specific investigation.

(e) *Joint committee*. Such a committee may be formed for the purpose of coordinating the activities of two (or more) committees, e.g. a committee consisting of representatives from both employers' and employees' committees. It may be a permanent committee or a special committee, formed to consider one particular problem.

Progress test 29

1. What do you understand by (a) standing committees, (b) *ad hoc* committees? Describe the advantages of the committee system. Have you any criticisms of the system to offer? **(4, 5, 7)**

2. Describe the committee system of carrying out the work of a society or association, dealing (*inter alia*) with (a) purposes and powers, (b) chairman, (c) notice of meetings. **(1, 3)**

3. Classify the various kinds of committee. In what respects can committees be used to assist the board of directors of a large public company? **(6, 7)**

4. The committee system is said to have many weaknesses. Enumerate some of the criticisms which are often levelled at it, and state your arguments for or against their validity. **(5)**

30
Meetings in a winding-up by the court

How a winding-up is effected

NOTE: Unless otherwise indicated, references in this chapter are to the Insolvency Act 1986.

1. **Methods of winding-up**
   According to s. 73, a company may be wound up:

(a) by the court — which may be called a compulsory winding-up;
(b) voluntarily — either as:
   (i) a *members'* voluntary winding-up; or
   (ii) a *creditors'* voluntary winding-up.

2. **The secretary as liquidator**
   Although this section is concerned with the meetings held in a winding-up by the court, it is not suggested that the company secretary is ever likely to be appointed liquidator in this form of winding-up, nor in a winding-up subject to court supervision. He may, however, be appointed liquidator in a *members'* voluntary winding-up and (though very rarely) in a *creditors'* winding-up.

Procedure

3. **Brief outline of procedure in a winding-up by the court**
   In addition to giving some information concerning the purpose, procedure and regulations affecting the various meetings required to be held in a winding-up by the court, it may be helpful also to outline the winding-up procedure in order to indicate the points at which the meetings are held (*see* **4–11** below).

4. Winding-up petition

(a) *The petition is presented* to the appropriate court, i.e. by the company itself, the directors of the company, any creditor or creditors, any contributory or contributories, the supervisor of a voluntary arrangement, the Department of Trade, or the official receiver.

> NOTE: Section 79 defines a 'contributory' as 'every person liable to contribute to the assets of a company in the event of its being wound up', and for the purpose of determining a final list, the term may also include persons *alleged* to be contributories.

(b) *The Registrar fixes time and place* for the hearing of the petition.
(c) *The hearing is advertised* in the *London Gazette* and in a newspaper circulating in the district in which the company's registered office is situated.
(d) *The petitioner (or his solicitor) attends before the Registrar,* merely to satisfy him that all requirements of the winding-up rules have been satisfied.
(e) *The court may appoint the official receiver* (or any other person) to be provisional liquidator — usually where the assets are in jeopardy (s. 135).
(f) The court may, on application of the company or any creditor or contributory, *stay or restrain any legal proceedings* against the company (s. 126).

5. Hearing of the petition

(a) *This may be attended by the company,* any creditor and any contributory.
(b) *The court may make a compulsory winding-up order,* dismiss the petition, adjourn the hearing, or make an interim order, etc, as it thinks fit (s. 125).

6. If the petition is successful
Where the court supports the petition and makes a compulsory order for winding-up:

(a) A copy of the winding-up order must be filed forthwith with the Registrar of Companies (s. 130).
(b) Any transfer of shares or any disposition of the company's

property made after commencement of the winding up are void, unless the court orders otherwise (s. 127).

(c) No actions can be commenced or proceeded with against the company, without leave of the court (s. 130).

(d) The official receiver becomes provisional liquidator, and continues to act until another liquidator is appointed.

(e) The court may appoint a special manager, e.g. if the business of the company is to be carried on (s. 177).

> NOTE: The commencement of the winding-up (referred to above) dates back to the time of *presentation* of the petition for winding-up. If, however, the winding-up began as a voluntary winding-up, the commencement of the winding-up dates back to the passing of the *resolution* for voluntary winding-up.

7.   The official receiver

As provisional liquidator, the official receiver:

(a) *Takes control* of all books and papers of the company immediately the winding-up order is made.

(b) *Serves notice* on the directors and secretary, ordering them to submit to him a statement of affairs, containing particulars of the company's assets, debts and liabilities, and particulars of the company's creditors (s. 131).

(c) *Investigates the company* to ascertain, where appropriate, the causes of the company's failure and in all cases the promotion, formation, business, dealings and affairs of the company. Where he thinks fit he should report his findings to the court (s. 132).

> NOTE: The statement of affairs must normally be submitted to the official receiver within 21 days of the day after notice is given by the official receiver (s. 131).

(d) *Convenes the first meeting of creditors and contributories*, which will now be considered in some detail.

8.   First meeting of creditors and contributories

Although the Act provides for the convening of these meetings, they are governed by the Insolvency Rules 1986 as regards procedure. The combined requirements of the Act and rules are summarized below.

(a) *If it appears to the official receiver* that the realizable assets of the company are insufficient to cover the costs of the liquidation and that the affairs of the company do not require further investigation, then he may give 28 days' notice to the creditors and contributories that he intends to dissolve the company (s. 202).

(b) *Where no such notice is given* one quarter in value of the company's creditors may request the official receiver to summon separate meetings of creditors and contributories for the purpose of choosing someone else as liquidator in his place (s. 136). He must fix the venue for these meetings for not more than 3 months from his receipt of the creditors' request (Rule 4.50(6)).

(c) *Where the official receiver is the liquidator of the company* it is his duty (if he has not given notice of dissolution) to decide whether or not to hold first meetings as soon as practicable within 12 weeks of the making of the winding-up order (s. 136). He must fix a venue for each meeting in neither case more than 4 months from the date of the winding-up order (Rule 4.50(1)).

(d) *When the venue for each meeting has been fixed notice must be given* to the court forthwith and to creditors and contributories at least 21 days before the date of their respective meetings (Rule 4.50(2, 3)). The notices must specify a time and date not more than 4 days before the meeting for lodging of proxies and, in the case of creditors, for lodging of proofs (Rule 4.50(4)).

(e) *Notice of the meetings* shall also be given by public advertisement (Rule 4.50(5)).

(f) *Where he decides not to hold the meetings* he must notify his decision to the court and to the creditors and contributories within the 12-week period. The notice to the creditors must contain a statement of their right to request him to summon a first meeting (s. 136). This notice must be withdrawn where the creditors request a meeting to be held (Rule 4.50(6)).

(g) *Quorum.* In the case of a creditors' meeting a quorum is at least one creditor entitled to vote, whereas in the case of a meeting of contributories a quorum is at least two contributories so entitled, or all the contributories, if their number does not exceed two. Both creditors and contributories may be present in person or represented by proxy by any person (including the chairman) for the purposes of the quorum. A meeting of creditors or contributories shall not commence until at least the expiry of 15 minutes after the time appointed for its commencement where quorum requirements are satisfied by the attendance of either the chairman alone or one other person in addition to the chairman, and the chairman is aware, by virtue of proofs and proxies received or otherwise, that one or more additional persons would, if attending, be entitled to vote.

(h) *Proxies.* With every notice summoning a meeting of creditors or contributories there shall be sent out forms of proxy (Rule 4.60(3)). The time for lodging of proxies must be stated in the notice (*see* **(d)** above) and any proxy which is lodged in this manner will be entitled to vote (Rule 4.67(1)).

At adjourned meetings proxies may be lodged at any time up to midday on the business day immediately before the adjourned meeting (Rule 4.65(7)). Where the chairman holds a proxy which requires him to vote for a particular resolution, and no other person proposes that resolution, he shall himself propose it unless he considers that there is good reason for not doing. If he does not propose it he shall, forthwith after the meeting, notify his principal of the reason why he did not (Rule 4.64).

(i) *Attendance of company's personnel.* When a meeting of creditors or contributories is convened, at least 21 days' notice should be given by the convener to such of the company's personnel as he thinks should be told of or be present at the meeting. Other persons may attend at the discretion of the chairman who may also decide what part they may take in asking and answering questions during the meeting (Rule 4.58).

(j) *Venue.* In fixing the venue for a meeting of creditors or contributories the convener shall have regard to the convenience of the persons (other than whoever is to be chairman) who are invited to attend (Rule 4.60(1)). Meetings shall in all cases be summoned for commencement between the hours of 10.00 and 16.00 hours on a business day, unless the court otherwise directs (Rule 4.60(2)).

(k) *Resolutions.* At a meeting of creditors or contributories, a resolution is passed when a majority (in value) of those present and voting, in person or by proxy, have voted in favour of the resolution. The value of contributories is determined by reference to the number of votes conferred on each contributory by the company's articles (Rule 4.63(1)).

(l) *Suspension and adjournment.*

(*i*) Once only in the course of any meeting the chairman may, at his discretion and without an adjournment, declare the meeting suspended for any period up to one hour.

(*ii*) The chairman may in his discretion, and shall if the meeting so resolves, adjourn the meeting to such time and place as seems to him appropriate. However, special rules may apply if there has been a proposal for the liquidator's removal (*see* Rules 4.113(3) and 4.114(3)).

(*iii*) If within a period of 30 minutes from the time appointed for the commencement of the meeting a quorum is not present, then the meeting stands adjourned to such time and place as may be appointed by the chairman.

(*iv*) The above adjournments shall not be for a period of more than 21 days (Rule 4.65).

(**m**) *Minutes and other records.*

(*i*) The chairman shall cause minutes of the proceedings at meetings to be kept. These must be signed by him and retained as part of the records of liquidation; they should also include a record of every resolution passed.

(*ii*) It is the duty of the chairman to ensure that particulars of all such resolutions are filed in court not more than 21 days after the date of the meeting.

(*iii*) The chairman shall also cause to be made up and kept a list of all creditors or, as the case may be, contributories who attended the meeting (Rule 4.71).

(**n**) *At the first meetings no resolutions other than the following shall be taken:*

(*i*) to appoint a named insolvency practitioner to be liquidator or two or more as joint liquidators,

(*ii*) to establish a liquidation committee,

(*iii*) where joint liquidators are appointed to specify whether acts are to be done by all or only one of them,

(*iv*) to adjourn meetings for not more than 3 weeks,

(*v*) those which the chairman thinks it right to allow for special reasons.

At the creditors' meeting, the following resolutions may also be taken:

(*vi*) to fix terms on which the liquidator is to be remunerated, or to defer consideration of the matter (unless a liquidation committee is to be formed),

(*vii*) at a requisitioned meeting to authorize the payment, as

an expense of liquidation, of the cost of summoning and
holding the meetings (Rule 4.52(1, 2)).
Neither meeting shall pass a resolution which has for its object the
appointment of the official receiver as liquidator.

9.   Appointment of liquidator

(a) *Where meetings of creditors and contributories are held* each meeting
may nominate a person to be liquidator (s. 139).

(b) *Where a different person is nominated* the nominee of the creditors
becomes the liquidator but where the creditors do not make a
nomination the nominee of the contributories takes up the
appointment (s. 139).

(c) *Where the creditors' nominee is entitled to take office* any
contributory or creditor may, within 7 days of nomination, apply
to the court to have the contributories' nominee appointed instead
or jointly with the creditors' nominee (s. 139).

(d) *At either meeting a resolution for the appointment of a liquidator shall
be disposed of as follows:*

(*i*)   if on any vote there are two nominees for appointment,
the person obtaining the most support is appointed (such
support must represent a majority in value of those
present, in person or by proxy, at the meeting and entitled
to vote);

(*ii*) if there are three or more nominees, and one of them has
a clear majority over both or all of the others together,
that one is appointed; and

(*iii*) in any other case, the chairman of the meeting shall
continue to take votes (disregarding at each vote any
nominee who has withdrawn and, if no nominee has
withdrawn, the nominee who obtained the least support
last time), until a clear majority is obtained for any one
nominee (Rule 4.63(2)).

(*iv*) The chairman may at any time put to a meeting a
resolution for the joint appointment of any two or more
nominees (Rule 4.63(3)).

10. Liquidation committee

These are provided for in s. 141 which can be summarized as
follows:

(a) *Where separate meetings of creditors and contributories* have been held for the purpose of choosing a liquidator, those meetings may establish a *liquidation committee*.

(b) *The liquidator (not being the official receiver)* may at any time, if he thinks fit, summon separate meetings of creditors and contributories for the purpose of deciding whether to establish a liquidation committee and, if necessary, doing so.

(c) *The decision of either meeting* will be sufficient to establish a committee.

(d) *Where the official receiver is the liquidator or where no committee has been appointed* the functions of the committee are vested in the Secretary of State.

(e) *The functions of the liquidation committee* are to assist and supervise the work of the liquidator, to sanction the making of a call by the liquidator (s. 160) and to approve any proposal by the liquidator:

    (*i*) to bring or defend any action or other legal proceedings in the name and on behalf of the company,

    (*ii*) to carry on the business of the company,

    (*iii*) to pay any class of creditors in full,

    (*iv*) to make any compromise or arrangement with creditors,

    (*v*) to compromise any claim the company has against others (s. 167).

(f) *The committee normally consists of* at least three and not more than five creditors whose debts are not fully secured (contributories may establish the committee where the creditors choose not to) (Rule 4.152).

(g) *Meetings of the committee.* The liquidator shall call a first meeting to be held within 3 months of his appointment or of the committee's establishment, whichever is the later. The liquidator must call further meetings if requested by a creditor member of the committee within 21 days of receipt of the request; he must also hold meetings on dates specified by resolution of the committee (Rule 4.156).

(h) *Notice.* The liquidator shall give 7 days' written notice of the venue of a meeting to every member of the committee unless this is waived by the member (Rule 4.156).

(i) *Quorum.* A meeting of the committee is duly constituted if due notice of it has been given and at least two creditor members are present or represented (Rule 4.158).

(j) *Voting rights and resolutions*. Each member or his representative has one vote and a resolution is passed when a majority of the members vote in favour of it (Rule 4.165).

(k) *Resolutions by post*. The liquidator may send a copy of proposed resolutions to all committee members by post and if within 7 business days of dispatch no member has required him to summon a meeting to discuss the matters raised by the resolution, the resolution will be deemed to have been passed if and when the liquidator is notified in writing by the majority of members that they concur with it (Rule 4.167).

11. Subsequent procedure

(a) *Duties of the liquidator*. Following his appointment, the principal duties of the liquidator are to collect and realize the company's assets, pay its debts, and distribute any balance among the contributories.

(b) *Powers*. To enable him to carry out his duties, the liquidator is given wide powers under the Act, although some of them can be exercised only with the sanction of the court or of the committee of inspection.

(c) *Meetings*. He also has the power, subject to the provisions of the Act and the control of the court, to summon, hold and conduct meetings of the creditors and contributories, for the purpose of ascertaining their wishes in all matters relating to the winding-up (s. 168). These meetings are referred to in the winding-up rules as liquidator's meetings of creditors and contributories. Other meetings may, however, be convened, namely:

(*i*) Meetings of creditors and contributories to ascertain their wishes, directed to be held by the court, under s. 195, and

(*ii*) Meetings summoned by the liquidator at such times as the creditors or contributories *by resolution* may direct, or when requested *in writing* to do so by one-tenth in value of the creditors or contributories, as the case may be (s. 168).

The liquidator shall, if he considers the request to be properly made in accordance with the Act, fix a venue for the meeting, not more than 35 days from his receipt of the request (Rule 4.57).

NOTE: The relevant winding-up rules affecting notices, venue of meetings, chairman, quorum, resolutions, proxies, adjournment and minutes, have already been stated earlier in this chapter (*see* **8** 'First meetings of creditors and contributories') and are not repeated here.

Progress test 30

1. What rules apply to the convening of separate meetings of creditors and contributories held after the making of a winding-up order? **(8)**

2. How, and by whom, is a liquidation committee appointed in a compulsory winding-up? Describe the committee's constitution, powers and duties. **(8)**

3. When, and for what purposes, are the first meetings of creditors and contributories held in a winding-up by the court? **(8)**

4. In connection with a compulsory winding-up, explain briefly **(a)** liquidation committee; **(b)** provisional liquidator; **(c)** statement of affairs; **(d)** first meetings of creditors and contributories. **(7, 8)**

31
Meetings in a voluntary winding-up

NOTE: Unless otherwise stated, all references in this chapter are to the Insolvency Act 1986.

How a winding-up is effected

1. A voluntary winding-up

This enables a company to wind up without many of the formalities of a winding-up by the court and, in the case of a creditors' voluntary winding-up, the company and its creditors can settle their affairs without any petition to the court.

2. Circumstances in which a company can be wound up voluntarily

A company may be wound up voluntarily in the following circumstances, as provided in s. 84.

(a) When the period (if any) fixed for the duration of the company by the articles expires, or the event (if any) occurs on the occurrence of which the articles provide that the company shall be dissolved; and the company in general meeting has passed a resolution requiring the company be wound up voluntarily, e.g.

Resolved: That the ten-year period fixed for the duration of the Company, in its Articles of Association, having expired, the Company be wound up; and that Mr Albert Blank of 6 West Street, London EC1, be and he is hereby appointed liquidator for the purpose of the winding-up.

NOTE: An *ordinary* resolution is adequate in this case, unless another form of resolution is required by the articles.

(b) If the company resolves by *special resolution to be wound up voluntarily*, e.g.

> *Resolved:* That the Company be wound up voluntarily, and that Mr Albert Blank of 6 West Street, London EC1, be and he is hereby appointed liquidator for the purpose of the winding-up.

> NOTE: In this case, i.e. where the company is wound up voluntarily without assigning any reason for so doing, a *special resolution* is required.

(c) If the company resolves by *extraordinary* resolution that it cannot, by reason of its liabilities, continue its business, and that it is advisable to wind up, e.g.

> *Resolved:* That the Company, being unable by reason of its liabilities to carry on its business, be wound up voluntarily, and that Mr Albert Blank of 6 West Street, London EC1, be and he is hereby appointed liquidator for the purpose of the winding-up.

> NOTE: The liquidator is merely 'nominated' in this case as the creditors at their meeting also have power to nominate a liquidator.

Procedure

3. Notice of the resolution to wind up voluntarily
Notice of such a resolution must be advertised in the *London Gazette* within 14 days after the passing of the resolution (s. 85). Failure to do so renders the company, and every officer in default, liable to fines.

> NOTE: A copy of the resolution must be filed with the Registrar within 15 days after it was passed (s. 84). *See* 19:**5–7**.

4. Commencement of the winding-up (s. 86)
A voluntary winding-up is deemed to commence at the time of the passing of the resolution which authorized it. As from the commencement of the winding-up there are various important consequences:

(a) *Business.* The company ceases to carry on its business, except for the purpose of its beneficial winding-up. Nevertheless, the corporate state and powers of the company continue until it is dissolved (s. 87).

(b) *Transfers of shares* after commencement of the winding-up are *void*, unless to, or with the consent of, the liquidator.

(c) *Status of members.* Any alteration in the status of the members made after commencement of the winding-up shall be *void* (s. 88).

(d) *A statement* that the company is being wound up must be made on every invoice, order for goods or business letter issued by or on behalf of, the company or the liquidator on which the company's name appears (s. 188).

> NOTE: Section 188 applies to *all* forms of winding-up, and the company and any person wilfully authorizing or permitting the default are liable to a fine.

(e) *Company's servants.* The winding-up may operate as a dismissal of the company's servants; if, for example, the company is insolvent. In any case, however, the liquidator may continue to employ the company's servants under a new contract of employment.

> NOTE: The provision in the Act for stay of proceedings does *not* apply in the case of a voluntary winding-up; nevertheless, the court may stay proceedings if the liquidator can show the necessity for it (ss. 112 and 130).

Form and proceedings

5. Forms of voluntary winding-up
There are two forms of voluntary winding-up:

(a) *A members'* voluntary winding-up, i.e. a solvent winding-up; and

(b) *A creditors'* voluntary winding-up, i.e. an insolvent winding-up.

6. The proceedings in a members' voluntary winding-up
These are summarized in Table 31.1, and compared with the relevant proceedings in a *creditors'* voluntary winding-up:

Table 31.1

Members' voluntary winding-up	Creditors' voluntary winding-up
(a) *Statutory Declaration of Solvency.* The directors of the company (or, if there are more than two, a majority of them) may, at a board meeting, make a declaration of solvency (as required by s. 89), which is filed with the Registrar.	**(a)** *Not applicable.* In this case, the form of winding-up is determined by the company's *inability to make a declaration solvency.*
(b) *General meeting of the company* (held not more than 5 weeks after making statutory declaration): (*i*) *to pass a resolution* for winding-up (either ordinary or special according to circumstances); (*ii*) *to appoint* a liquidator (s. 91). However, the statutory declaration is of no effect unless made within 5 weeks immediately preceding the date of passing the winding-up resolution, or on that date, but before the passing of that resolution. It must also embody a statement of the company's assets and liabilities as at the latest practicable date before the making of the declaration. The declaration must be delivered to the Registrar within fifteen days of the date on which the winding-up resolution was passed, otherwise the company and every officer in default will be liable to a fine (s. 89).	**(b)** *Company must summon two meetings:* (*i*) *A general meeting:* to pass a resolution for winding-up, and to *nominate* a liquidator. (*ii*) *A creditors' meeting* (not later than the 14th day after the resolution); to present a statement of the company's affairs, to *nominate* a liquidator, and (if desired) to appoint a liquidation committee. This meeting is called by not less than 7 days' notice by post to the creditors or by advertisement in the *London Gazette* and two newspapers circulating locally (s. 98).

(c) *Notice of liquidator's appointment.* Within 14 days after his appointment, the liquidator gives notice of his appointment:

  (*i*) in the *London Gazette;* and
  (*ii*) to the Registrar of Companies (s. 109)

(d) *Notice of winding-up resolution.* The company must give notice of the resolution within 14 days after it was passed, in the *London Gazette* (s. 85).

(e) *The liquidator's duties.* In general, these are to wind up the company's affairs and to distribute its assets, but, in order to carry out such duties, he seeks and/or exercises powers in the ways set out in Table 31.2.

Table 31.2

Members' voluntary winding-up	Creditors' voluntary winding-up
(a) *Without sanction,* to settle lists of contributories, and to make calls.	**(a)** *Without sanction,* to settle lists of contributories, and to make calls.
(b) *With the sanction of an extraordinary resolution:*	**(b)** *With the sanction of the court* or committee of inspection (or meeting of creditors, if no committee of inspection):
(*i*) to pay any class of creditors in full;	(*i*) to pay any class of creditors in full;
(*ii*) to compromise or make arrangements with creditors (s. 165).	(*ii*) to compromise or make arrangements with creditors (s. 165).
(c) *To summon general meetings* of the company, as he thinks fit, in order to obtain sanction by special or extraordinary resolutions (s. 165).	**(c)** *To summon meetings of creditors,* for the purpose of ascertaining their wishes in all matters relating to the winding up (Rule 4.54).
NOTE: If the liquidator is of the opinion that the company will *not* be able to pay its debts in full within the period stated in the declaration of solvency, he must, within 28 days of forming that opinion, summon a meeting of creditors by giving at least	

7 days' notice by post to the creditors and by advertising in the *London Gazette* and two newspapers circulating locally and lay before the meeting a statement of assets and liabilities (s. 95).

(d) *To summon general meetings of* the company at the end of the first and each succeeding year of the liquidation, and to lay his accounts before the members (s. 93).	**(d)** *To summon general meetings and creditors' meetings* at the end of the first and each succeeding year of the liquidation; and to lay his accounts before the respective meetings (s. 105).

At the conclusion of the winding up:

(e) *To summon a general meeting of the company,* by one month's notice in the *London Gazette* (s. 94).	**(e)** *To summon a general meeting and a creditors' meeting,* by one month's notice in the *London Gazette* (s. 106).
(f) To lay his accounts before the meeting.	**(f)** To lay his accounts before the respective meetings.
(g) *To send a copy of his accounts,* within one week of holding the final meeting, to the Registrar, with a return of the holding of the meeting (s. 94).	**(g)** *To send a copy of his accounts,* within one week of holding the final meetings, to the Registrar, with a return of the holding of the meetings (s. 106).

Three months after registration of the liquidator's return (referred to in Table 13.2 **(g)**), the company is deemed to be *dissolved* (s. 201).

NOTE: The court has power to *defer* the date of dissolution on application of the liquidator or of any other interested person (s. 201).

7. Regulations governing meetings in a members' voluntary winding-up

So long as the winding-up proceeds in the form of a *members'* voluntary winding-up, the meetings, being company meetings, are based almost entirely on the requirements of the Act and/or articles of the company concerned, but the winding-up rules are or may become applicable in certain respects:

(a) *The general meeting* held for the purpose of passing the winding-up resolution will be convened by:

(*i*) *21 days' notice* at least, if a *special* resolution is to be passed (s. 378 Companies Act 1986).

(*ii*) *14 days' notice* at least, if an *ordinary* resolution is to be passed.

(b) *Subsequent general meetings* of the company, including any convened by the liquidator to obtain sanction to pay any class of creditors in full, or to make any compromise or arrangements with creditors, by *extraordinary* resolution under s. 165, will require *14 days' notice* at least.

(c) *The final general meeting* of the company must be summoned by the liquidator in the *London Gazette,* giving *one month's notice,* and specifying time, place and object of the meeting (s. 94).

(d) *Meeting of creditors in case of insolvency* (s. 95). If the liquidator is of the opinion that the company will *not* be able to pay its debts in full within the period stated in the statutory declaration of solvency:

(*i*) He must convene a meeting of creditors within 28 days of forming that opinion, and lay before them a statement of the company's assets and liabilities.

(*ii*) This meeting must be summoned by at least *seven days' notice* of the time and place, such notice to be given once in the *London Gazette,* and once at least in *two local papers,* and to every creditor by *post* (s. 95).

NOTE: Where s. 95 has effect, the winding-up will then proceed as though it were a *creditors'* voluntary winding-up and *not* as a members' voluntary winding-up (s. 96).

8. Regulations governing meetings in a creditors' voluntary winding-up

These may be summarized as in Table 31.3.

Table 31.3

Meetings of the company	Meetings of the creditors
These are governed by the provisions of the Act and/or the company's articles:	These are governed by the Act and/or articles of the company, and subsequently by the Insolvency Rules 4.50–4.71:
(a) *The general meeting* convened by the company for the purpose of passing the *extraordinary* resolution for winding-up requires at least 7 *days' notice* — unless the articles require longer notice (s. 369). Short notice is acceptable when the majority in number of shareholders entitled to attend and vote at the meeting so agree providing the majority together hold 95 per cent or more of the nominal value of shares which give the right to attend and vote at the meeting.	**(a)** The creditors' meeting must be held not later than the 14th day after the day on which the resolution to wind up was passed. It is convened by the company giving not less than 7 days' notice by post to the creditors. The meeting must be advertised once in the *London Gazette* and once at least in *two* newspapers *circulating locally* (s. 98).
(b) *Subsequent general meetings*, i.e. following the liquidator's appointment, will be convened by him and held in accordance with the provisions of the Act and/or the company's articles. This applies, for example, to the meetings he must convene at the end of each year of the winding-up under s. 105, or may call under s. 165.	**(b)** *Subsequent meetings* of creditors are convened and held in accordance with the Insolvency Rules 4.50–4.71. NOTE: These rules are not repeated here, as the most important of them were set out in 30:**8** in relation to meetings of creditors and contributories in a winding-up by the court.
(c) *The final general meeting of the company* is summoned by the liquidator at the conclusion of the winding-up by one month's notice in the *London Gazette* (s. 106).	**(c)** *The final meeting* of creditors is summoned by the liquidator at the conclusion of the winding-up by one month's notice in the *London Gazette* (s. 106).

Progress test 31

1. In what circumstances, and by what forms of resolution respectively, may a company be wound up voluntarily? **(2)**

2. When is a voluntary winding-up deemed to commence? What important consequences follow its commencement? **(4)**

3. List some of the important points of comparison between a members' and a creditors' voluntary winding-up? **(6)**

32
Other insolvency procedures

The Insolvency Act 1986 provides the following procedures for dealing with insolvent companies which in most cases are alternatives to the winding-up of the company.

Appointment of an administrative receiver

1. What is a receiver?

A receiver may be defined as an individual who is appointed to take control of property. Receivers may be appointed, for example, by a court to collect and protect property on a temporary basis until a permanent decision on the future of the property can be made by the court, or by the holder of a charge against property in order to use it to meet the obligation secured by the charge. An administrative receiver takes control of the whole (or substantially the whole) of a company's property, in order to realize it to pay the creditor(s) holding a floating charge. It is possible for a receiver to be in control of all the property of a company and yet not be an administrative receiver. For example, where the company owns one asset such as a block of flats which has been used as security for company borrowing using a fixed charge. Any receiver will be appointed under the fixed charge and, therefore, will not be an administrative receiver.

2. Section 29 defines an administrative receiver as:

(a) *a receiver or manager* of the whole (or substantially the whole) of a company's property appointed by or on behalf of the holders of any debentures of the company secured by a charge which, as created, was a floating charge, or by such charge and one or more other securities; or

(b) *A person who would be such a receiver or manager* but for the appointment of some other person as the receiver of part of the company's property.

3.   Creditors' meeting
An administrative receiver of a company which is not in liquidation must, having prepared a report for the company's creditors, either:

(a) *summon a meeting* of unsecured creditors giving not less than 14 days' notice, before which he will lay a copy of the report; or
(b) *state in the report* that he intends to apply to the court for a direction that no meeting be held (s. 48).

Where a meeting is held it is entitled to establish a committee of creditors which may require the receiver to appear before it at any reasonable time and furnish it with information about the carrying out of his functions, provided he is given not less than 7 days' notice (s. 49). Where the company is in liquidation, no such meeting need be held providing that the receiver has delivered a copy of his report to the liquidator within 3 months of his (the receiver's) appointment (s. 48).

The creditors' meeting and the creditors' committee are subject to procedures laid down in the Insolvency Rules 3.19–3.30. These rules are similar to those relating to first meetings of creditors and contributories and liquidation committees (*see* 30:8–10).

Administration

4.   Nature of administration
The Insolvency Act introduces a procedure whereby a company that is, or is likely to become, unable to pay its debts may obtain a moratorium on actions by creditors while a qualified insolvency practitioner is appointed to formulate a plan for dealing with the company's debts without causing it to go into liquidation. The insolvency practitioner is called the 'administrator' and he is appointed by an administration order

which cannot normally be made without the agreement of all creditors who would be entitled to appoint an administrative receiver.

An administration order is made by the court on the petition of the company or its directors, a creditor or creditors, the supervisor of a voluntary arrangement, or the clerk to a magistrates' court where the company has failed to pay a fine. Where a decision to present a petition has been made by the directors at a properly convened meeting the decision is valid and it becomes the duty of all directors, whether they took part in the decision or voted against it, to implement it: *Re Equiticorp plc* (1989). Such a decision may also be made by all the directors without a meeting: *Re Instrumentation Electrical Services Ltd* (1988). The court may only make an administrative order if it considers that it would achieve one or more of the following purposes:

(a) The survival of the company, and the whole or any part of its undertaking as a going concern.

(b) The approval of a voluntary arrangement.

(c) The sanctioning of a compromise or arrangements between the company and its members or creditors.

The administrator is given three months in which to prepare proposals and to put them to a meeting of the creditors. This time period may be extended by order of the court: *Re N.S. Distribution Ltd* (1989). He must also either send the proposals to the company's members or publish a notice which notifies them of the address where they should write for copies of the proposals to be sent free of charge (s. 23).

5. The creditors' meeting

(a) *Notice.* The administrator must give not less than 14 days' notice of the meeting to the creditors (s. 23).

(b) *Approval of proposals.* The purpose of the creditors' meeting is to approve the administrator's proposals. However, the meeting may modify the proposals but only with the consent of the administrator (s. 24).

(c) *Decision of meeting.* In order for a resolution to be passed at meetings of creditors, a simple majority, in value, of creditors who are present and vote in person or by proxy is required. Only unsecured creditors can vote and, therefore, a secured creditor must be able to show an *excess of debt over security* before being entitled to vote. The administrator must report the result of the meeting to both the registrar and the court and where the meeting decides to reject the proposals the court may discharge the administration order (s. 24). Where the proposals are accepted by the meeting, the administrator is required to manage the affairs, business and property of the company in accordance with the proposals (s. 17). *See: Re Polly Peck International plc* (1991).

(d) *Changes in proposals.* Where the proposals are accepted by the creditors but he subsequently wishes to make amendments which appear to him substantial, then he must circulate the revised proposals to the creditors and summon a fresh meeting. He must not act on the revised proposals until they have been approved by the meeting (s. 25). Although, in exceptional circumstances, the court *have* authorized the implementation of an alternative scheme which needed to be acted on expeditiously and where there was no time to obtain the approval of the creditors: *Re Smallman Construction Ltd* (1989).

(e) *Creditors' committee.* Where the creditors' meeting approves the administrator's proposals, then it is entitled to establish a creditors' committee which may require the administrator to attend before it at any reasonable time and furnish it with information about the carrying out of his functions provided he is given at least 7 days' notice (s. 26).

NOTE: Section 17 provides that the administrator has a general duty to summon a creditors' meeting if he is requested to do so, in accordance with the rules, by one-tenth in value of the company's creditors or if he is directed to do so by the court (e.g. after application by a creditor under s. 27, *see* **6** below).

6. Meeting of members

At any time when an administration order is in force a creditor or member of the company may apply to the court by petition for an order on the ground:

(a) that the company's affairs, business and property are being or have been managed by the administrator in a manner which is unfairly prejudicial to the interests of its creditors or members (including at least himself), or

(b) that any actual or proposed act or omission of the administration is or would be so prejudicial.

The court may make a suitable order giving relief where the petition is justified and one such order is that a meeting of members should be held.

The creditors' meeting and the creditors' committee are subject to procedures laid down in the Insolvency Rules 2.18–2.46. These rules are similar to those relating to first meetings of creditors and contributories and liquidation committees (*see* 30:**8–10**).

Voluntary arrangements

7.   Nature

The purpose of a voluntary arrangement is to provide a suitably simple procedure whereby a company may enter into a legally effective agreement with its creditors for the settlement of its debts. Where the company is not in liquidation or under an administration order, its directors may propose a scheme or composition (s. 1) and nominate a qualified insolvency practitioner to supervise the proposals. This nominee must, within 28 days after he is given notice of the proposals, submit a report to the court stating whether, in his opinion, the proposals should be put to meetings of the creditors and the company. Where he decides that meetings should be held he should also state in the report the date, time and place where the meeting should be held (s. 2).

8.   Creditors' meeting

(a) *Purpose.* The creditors' meeting shall decide whether to approve the proposed voluntary arrangement (with or without modifications).

(b) *Decisions.* In order to pass a resolution adopting any proposals for a scheme or composition or any modification of such proposals there must be a majority of three-quarters in value of the creditors present in person or by proxy and voting on the resolution. All other resolutions require in excess of one-half majority.

(c) *Rights of preferential creditors.* Any modification which is approved must not adversely affect the rights of preferential creditors unless they agree to this.

(d) *Report of the meeting.* After the meeting the chairman must report the result to the court and to such persons as may be prescribed (s. 4).

NOTE: A meeting of the company is held for the same purposes and resolutions require a simple majority.

9. Effect of decisions

Where each of the meetings approves the proposed voluntary arrangement either with the same or without modification, the proposals take effect and are binding on every person who had notice and was entitled to vote at the meeting, whether he was present or not. However, the decision may be challenged by members, creditors, the nominee, the liquidator or the administrator within 28 days of the report being received by the court on the grounds that the arrangement unfairly prejudices a creditor, member or contributory, or that there has been some material irregularity at one of the meetings (s. 6).

10. Effect of a challenge

Where a challenge is successful, the court may give a direction to any person for the summoning of further meetings to consider revised proposals. Where further proposals are not forthcoming the court may suspend or revoke the approval of the original proposals (s. 6).

The meetings of members and creditors are subject to procedures laid down in the Insolvency Rules 1.3–1.21. These rules are similar to those relating to first meetings of creditors and contributories (*see* 30:8).

Progress test 32

1. What are the powers of a committee of creditors in a receivership? **(3)**

2. Under what circumstances would a meeting of members take place in an administration? **(6)**

3. What is the purpose of a creditors' meeting held in connection with voluntary arrangements? **(8)**

33
Directors' report

The essential contents of a directors' report are summarized below.

Statutory requirements

1. State of the company's affairs, required by s. 234(1)
This section requires the directors to prepare for each financial year a report showing:

(a) a fair review of the development of the business of the company and its subsidiaries during the financial year;
(b) the position of the company at the end of that financial year;
(c) dividend (if any) recommended;
(d) amount (if any) to be carried to reserves.

2. Names of directors
Section 234 requires the directors' report to state:

(a) the names of all persons who, at any time during the financial year, were directors of the company;
(b) the principal activities of the company and of its subsidiaries, and any significant changes in those activities during the year.

> NOTE: It is now possible for directors of a company to prepare a revised directors' report, or revised accounts, if it appears to them that the report fails to comply with the requirements of the 1985 Act; s. 245. See also s. 245A for the power of the Secretary of State to question whether accounts comply with those requirements. For the directors' report relating to special category companies (Banking and Insurance) *see* ss. 255–255D, in particular s. 255C.

3. Change in fixed assets
Schedule 7, paragraph 1 requires:

(a) Particulars of any *significant* changes in the fixed assets of the company, or of its subsidiaries, which have occurred in the financial year.

(b) In the case of *interests in land*, if the market value at the end of the year differs substantially from the amount at which it is included in the balance sheet and the difference is, in the opinion of the directors, of such significance as to require that the attention of members or debenture holders should be drawn to it, the difference must be indicated with such degree of precision as is practicable.

4. Directors' interest in shares or debentures

Schedule 7, paragraph 2 requires this information, already shown in the Register of Directors' Interests kept by the company under s. 325, to be shown also in the directors' report. It applies to such interests in the company, its subsidiary or holding company or fellow subsidiary. It is, however, necessary to show only their respective interests at the beginning and end of the year; there is now a need to show whether, according to the register, any right to subscribe for shares in or debentures of the company or another body corporate in the same group was during the financial year granted to, or exercised by, the director or a member of his immediate family, paragraph 2B(1).

Alternatively, this information may be given by way of notes to all accounts, instead of in the directors' report (paragraph 2(3)), except in the case of a special category company (s. 261(5)).

5. Political and charitable contributions

Schedule 7, paragraphs 3 to 5, require:

(a) Where the company has given more than £200 during the financial year for political or charitable purposes, the directors' report must state the amount of each gift.

(b) Where contributions have been given for political purposes, the report must also state the name of each person to whom money has been given for such purposes exceeding £200 in amount, the amount of each contribution and the identity of any political party to which a donation or subscription in excess of £200 was made and the amount given.

NOTE: The above does not apply to a wholly-owned subsidiary incorporated in Great Britain; nor does it apply unless the total given by company and subsidiaries between them exceeds £200. Paragraph 5 defines when a company is to be treated as giving money for political and charitable purposes.

6. Insurance effected for officers or auditors

Where, in the financial year, the company has purchased or maintained any such insurance as is mentioned in s. 310(3)(a) (insurance of officers or auditors against liabilities in relation to the company) that fact shall be stated in the report.

7. Other material facts

Paragragh 6 makes provision for:

(a) Particulars of any important events affecting the company and its subsidiaries which have occurred since the end of the company's financial year.

(b) An indication of likely future developments in the business of the company and its subsidiaries.

(c) An indication of the activities (if any) of the company and its subsidiaries in the field of research and development.

8. Acquisition of company's own shares

Schedule 7, paragraphs 7 and 8 provide that where shares in any company:

(a) are purchased by the company or are acquired by the company by forfeiture or surrender in lieu of forfeiture or in pursuance of s. 143(3));

(b) are acquired by the company's nominee or by any other person with financial assistance from the company in circumstances in which the company has a beneficial interest in the shares subject to s. 146(1)(c) or (d); or

(c) are made subject to a lien or other charge taken by the company and permitted by s. 150(2) or (4), the directors' report shall include:

　　(i) the number and nominal value of shares so purchased, the aggregate amount of the consideration paid and reason for the purchase;

　　(ii) the number and nominal value of the shares so acquired

by the company, acquired by another person in such circumstances and so charged respectively during the financial year;

(*iii*) the maximum number and nominal value of shares which, having been so acquired by the company, acquired by another person in such circumstances or so charged (whether or not during that year) are held at any time by the company or that other person during that year;

(*iv*) the number and nominal value of the shares so acquired by the company, acquired by another person in such circumstances or so charged (whether or not during that year) which are disposed of by the company or that other person or cancelled by the company during that year;

(*v*) where the number and nominal value of the shares of any particular description are stated in pursuance of any of the preceding sub-paragraphs, the percentage of the called-up share capital which shares of that description represent;

(*vi*) where any of the shares have been so charged the amount of the charge in each case; and

(*vii*) where any of the shares have been disposed of by the company or the person who acquired them in such circumstances for money or money's worth, that amount or value of the consideration in each case.

9. Disclosure concerning employment of disabled people

Schedule 7, paragraph 9 requires the directors' report to contain a statement describing such policy as the company has applied during the financial year relating to the employment, training, career development and promotion of disabled persons. This requirement applies where the average number of persons employed by the company in each week during the financial year exceeds 250.

10. Health, safety and welfare

Paragraph 10 requires information about the arrangements in force for securing the health, safety and welfare at work of the employees of the company and of its subsidiaries, and for the protection of other persons against risks to health or safety in respect of the activities at work of employees.

11. Employee consultation arrangements

Paragraph 11 provides that, where a company had an average weekly number of at least 250 employees during the financial year, the report must contain a statement describing the action that has been taken during the financial year to introduce, maintain or develop arrangements aimed at:

(a) providing employees systematically with information on matters of concern to them as employees;

(b) consulting employees or their representatives on a regular basis so that the views of employees can be taken into account in making decisions which are likely to affect their interests;

(c) encouraging the involvement of employees in the company's performance through an employees' share scheme or by some other means;

(d) achieving a common awareness on the part of all employees of the financial and economic factors affecting the performance of the company.

12. Special category accounts

Where accounts are prepared in accordance with special provisions for banking or insurance companies or groups, then the directors' report shall, in addition to complying with Schedule 7, also comply with paragraphs 1–3 of Schedule 10 (recent issues, turnover and profitability; size of labour force and wages paid).

Additionally, information required to be given by paragraphs 6, 8 or 13 of Part I of Schedule 9 may be given in the directors' report instead of in a statement or report annexed to the accounts. Also, if the company takes advantage in relation to its individual or group accounts of certain exemption provided by paragraphs 27 or 28 of Part I of Schedule 9, then paragraph 1 of Schedule 7 (disclosure of asset values) does not apply. The reference in s. 234(1)(b) to the 'amount proposed to be carried to reserves ...' is to be given the meaning within Part I of Schedule 9 (*see* s. 255(c)).

The special provisions are particularly complex and beyond the scope of this book.

13. Auditors' responsibility

Section 237(6) provides that, in preparing their report on the accounts, the auditors are under a duty to consider whether the information given in the directors' report relating to the financial year in question is consistent with their accounts. If they are of the opinion that it is not, they must state that fact in their report.

14. Small companies exemption

Where a company is a small company within the meaning of s. 247, that is within a year it satisfies *two* or more of the following requirements:

(a) *Turnover*: not more that £2 million
(b) *Balance sheet total*: not more than £975,000
(c) *Number of employees*: not more than 50

then by Schedule 8, paragraph 4, a copy of the directors' report need not be delivered.

Stock Exchange requirements

Companies subject to Stock Exchange regulations are required to include in, or to circulate with, each annual directors' report and audited accounts or chairman's statement, the following information. It will be noted that some of the items are additional to, while others are identical with, statutory requirements, though expressed in a different way.

15. General points

(a) A statement by the directors as to the reasons for any significant departure from standard accounting practice.
(b) An explanation when trading results differ materially from any published forecast made by the company.
(c) If the company or, as the case may be, the group, trades outside the UK, a statement showing a geographical analysis of its trading operations.
(d) If the company has subsidiaries, a list giving for each the name of the principal country in which each subsidiary operates.

16. Borrowings of the company or group

A statement at the end of the financial year showing the aggregate amounts repayable:

(a) in one year or less, or on demand;
(b) between one and two years;
(c) between two and five years;
(d) in five years or more.

17. Interests in associated companies

If the company or, as the case may be, the group has interests in associated companies, a list giving for each:

(a) Its *name and country* of operation.
(b) Particulars of its *issued share and loan capital* and the total amount of its reserves.
(c) The *percentage of each class* of share and loan capital attributable to the company's interest (direct and/or indirect).

18. A statement of persons holding or beneficially interested in any *substantial part of the share capital* of the company and the amounts of the holdings in question, together with particulars of the interests of each director ... in the share capital of the company and, otherwise than through the company, any of its subsidiaries, distinguishing between financial and other interests.

19. Taxation

(a) A statement showing whether or not the company is a close company for taxation purposes and any change in that status since the end of the financial year.
(b) A statement of the amount of interest capitalized by the company (or group) during the financial year, with an indication of the amount and treatment of any related tax relief.

20. Particulars of any arrangements whereunder any director has waived or agreed to waive any emoluments

21. Particulars of any contract of significance in which a director of the company is or was, for Stock Exchange purposes, materially interested or, if there has been no such contract, a statement of that fact.

Part four

Local authority meetings

34
The structure of local government

1. Organization

The Local Government Act 1972, s. 1, which came into effect on 1st April, 1974, divided England (apart from Greater London) into administrative counties and then subdivided these counties into districts. The administrative counties were originally of two types: metropolitan and non-metropolitan, but the former were abolished by the Local Government Act 1985 as from April 1986. All references in this chapter relate to the Local Government Act 1972 unless otherwise indicated.

All districts have the same functions but two types have special features:

(a) certain districts may be given the status of 'borough' by Royal Charter under the Act (s. 245);

(b) certain districts may be subdivided into parishes or, in Wales, communities. These are mainly rural areas, although the parish council (community council in Wales) may resolve that they shall have the status of 'town' (s. 245).

The structure in Greater London is regulated by the London Government Act 1963 which is incorporated in Sched. 2 of the Local Government Act. This created a two-tier system consisting of the Greater London Council as the first tier and thirty-two inner and outer boroughs as the other. The GLC was also abolished as from 1 April 1986.

2. Local authorities

Section 270 defines local authorities and these are:

(a) county councils;
(b) district councils;
(c) London borough councils;
(d) joint authorities;
(e) parish councils;
(f) community councils (in Wales).

This section also defines 'principal areas', these being the areas represented by (a)–(c) above and, therefore these are the 'principal councils'.

3. Parish and community meetings
Every parish in England and every community in Wales must call a meeting at least once every year and this may be attended by all local government voters of that parish or community. These meetings are not within the definition of 'local authority'.

4. Functions of local authorities
These are wide, varied and constantly changing, but can be said to be concerned with provision of services for the residents of the authority's area. The provision of these services obviously requires decision-making to take place and, on the face of it, such decisions are made at council meetings of local authorities. However, in practice, much of the decision-making is done in committees, and the advice and reports of such committees are heavily relied on. Nevertheless, the final legal decision which gives authority for the acts of the authority can only be made at a properly convened and constituted meeting of a local authority.

5. Residuary bodies
The Local Government Act 1985 abolished the metropolitan county councils with effect from 1st April, 1986. Part VII of the Act established a residuary body for each of the former counties; these were given the status of a body corporate and responsibilities in respect of such things as the making of compensation and redundancy payments, pensions and custody of certain property.

6. Joint authorities
The Local Government Act, Part VI established the following bodies corporate for each of the former metropolitan counties:

(a) a metropolitan county police authority;
(b) a metropolitan county fire and civil defence authority;
(c) a metropolitan county passenger transport authority.

All the above have responsibility for the former metropolitan county area except the Northumbria Police Authority which includes the metropolitan county of Tyne and Wear and the non-metropolitan county of Northumberland.

7. Joint committees
In preparation for the abolition of the metropolitan counties, the district councils affected were required to establish joint committees for the purpose of arranging the transfer of functions. The functions which were imposed on these committees can be summarized as being to co-operate with each other and with the appropriate bodies to ensure that the provisions of the Act and any necessary transfer of functions, property and staff were properly implemented.

Progress test 34

1. What are local authorities? **(2)**

2. What are the principal authorities? **(2)**

3. How can districts be subdivided? **(1)**

4. Distinguish between joint authorities and joint committees. **(6, 7)**

35
Principal council meetings

NOTE: Unless otherwise stated, all references in this chapter relate to the Local Government Act 1972.

Types of meeting

Part I, Sched. 12 of the Local Government Act 1972 makes the following provisions.

1. Annual meeting
There is a statutory requirement to hold an annual meeting in every year.

(a) In a year where elections of councillors takes place this meeting should be held on the eighth day after the day of retirement or within twenty-one days after the day of retirement.
(b) In any other year the council may fix any day in March, April or May to hold this meeting.
(c) The council may fix the hour of the meeting, but if this is not done the meeting shall take place at 12 noon.

2. Other meetings
In every year the council may hold other meetings as they decide necessary.

3. Extraordinary meetings
These may be called:

(a) at any time by the Chairman himself;

(b) by the Chairman within seven days of the receipt of a requisition signed by five members of the council;

(c) by any five members where the Chairman refuses to call a meeting, or fails to call a meeting after seven days when he has received a requisition signed by five members.

Conduct of meetings

4. Notice of meetings

(a) A council meeting must be duly convened by a summons given or sent at least three clear days before the meeting to every member of the council.

(b) This summons should be left at or sent by post to the place where the member normally resides,or left at or sent by post to any other place upon the direction of the member in writing to the proper officer of the council.

(c) The summons should contain an agenda which should not contain the item 'any other business'. Part 1, Sched. 12(5) states:

> 'Except in the case of business required by or under this or any other Act to be transacted at the annual meeting of a principal council and other business brought before that meeting as a matter of urgency in accordance with the council's standing orders, no business shall be transacted at a meeting of the council other than specified in the summons relating thereto.'

(d) In addition to the summons a notice of the time and place of the meeting must be published at the offices of the council.

(e) If the meeting is called by members (*see* **3(c)** above) it must be signed by those members and specify the business to be transacted.

(f) Failure to serve the summons on a member does not affect the validity of the meeting.

5. The chairman

(a) The chairman of the council shall preside when he is present.

(b) If the chairman is not present the vice-chairman shall preside.

(c) If both the chairman and vice-chairman are absent, a councillor chosen by the members present shall preside.

6. Quorum

(a) No business shall be transacted at a meeting of a principal council unless one quarter of the whole number of members is present, except where

(b) more than one-third of members become disqualified at the same time. Then the quorum should be decided by reference to the number of members qualified rather than the whole number of members. This should continue until the number of members qualified rises to not less than two-thirds of the whole number.

7. Procedure at meetings

(a) The major statutory provision in relation to procedure is that all matters coming before a council meeting are to be decided by a majority of members present and voting. In the case of an equality of votes, the person presiding at the meeting shall have a second casting vote. There has been much discussion on how the chairman should use his casting vote and it has been suggested that, while he has a discretion in how to use his casting vote, he has a duty to maintain the status quo wherever possible. It can also be argued that the chairman has a duty to remain impartial and that the use of his casting vote would interfere with his impartiality. Because of the above arguments a strong tradition has built up that it is proper for a chairman's casting vote, if exercised, to be given against the motion, this will cause the motion to fail and allow its reconsideration at some future date. However, in *R*. v. *Bradford Council ex parte Wilson* (1990) it was held that a chairman who had repeatedly used his second or casting vote in favour of motions had acted lawfully.

(b) The general rules of debate and procedure at council meetings are regulated by standing orders made by that council. Model standing orders for the use of local authorities are available and these may be adopted or amended for use by the council or the council may draft its own original standing orders. In any case the section on meetings would probably include the following rules:

    (*i*)   for order of business;
   (*ii*) for motions (with and without notice);
 (*iii*) restricting length and content of speeches;
 (*iv*) relating to amendments;
  (*v*) relating to suspension of debate;

(*vi*) rescission of resolutions;
(*vii*) appointment of committees and sub-committees;
(*viii*) adjournment of meetings;
(*ix*) suspension of standing orders.

A sample set of standing orders is shown in chapter 39.

(c) As standing orders are subject to the Act any standing order made by a council which is inconsistent with the Act will be *ultra vires* and void. The statutory provision referred to in **7(a)** above means that even if a council has no regulation in its standing orders relating in their suspension, this suspension will be possible at any time by a simple majority vote of the council.

8. Minutes
Minutes must be kept and the rules relating to them in Sched. 12, para. 41 can be summarized as follows:

(a) The minutes must be signed at the same or next meeting by the person presiding.

(b) The minutes must be kept in a minute book or kept on looseleaf paper, in which case each leaf must be numbered consecutively and initialled by the persons presiding at that or the next meeting.

(c) Until the contrary is proved, a meeting for which proper minutes are kept is deemed to have been properly convened and held, and all the members present at the meeting shall be deemed to have been duly qualified.

Progress test 35

1. What are the rules relating to annual meetings? **(1)**

2. What other meetings may be held by principal councils? **(2, 3)**

3. What form must the notice of meetings take? **(4)**

4. How is the procedure at meetings regulated? **(7)**

5. Could a meeting which fails to muster a quorum be presumed to be valid? **(6)**

36
Parish and community council meetings

NOTE: All references in this chapter relate to the Local Government Act 1972 unless otherwise indicated.

Types of meeting

Part II, Sched. 12 of the Local Government Act 1972 makes the following provisions.

1. Annual meeting
There is a statutory requirement to hold an annual meeting in every year.

(a) In a year when elections of councillors takes place this meeting should take place either on or within fourteen days of the date at which the elected councillors take office.

(b) In any other year the meeting must take place in the month of May.

(c) The council may fix the time of the meeting but if this is not done the meeting shall take place at 6.00 pm.

2. Other meetings
Additionally, a parish council must hold at least three other meetings every year, while a community council must hold such meetings as the council deem necessary.

3. Extraordinary meetings
These may be called:

(a) at any time by the chairman himself;

(b) by the chairman within seven days of the receipt of a requisition signed by two members of the council;

(c) by any two members where the chairman refuses to call a meeting or fails to call a meeting when he has received a requisition signed by two members.

Conduct of meetings

4. Place of meeting

The meetings of these councils may be held either within or without the council's area but must not be held in premises licensed for the sale of intoxicating liquor, except in cases when no other suitable room is available for such meetings, either free of charge or at a reasonable cost (Sched. 12, paras. 10 and 26).

5. Notice

The rules relating to notice are as for principal councils (*see* 35:4), except that the notice should be displayed in a conspicuous place in the parish.

6. Quorum

The rules relating to quorum are as for principal councils (*see* 35:6) except that the figure is fixed at one-third of the whole number of members and the quorum cannot be less than three members.

7. Voting

Voting at these meetings is by show of hands unless provided otherwise in the standing orders. Any member of the council may requisition the voting of each member to be recorded. As with principal councils, the person presiding has a second or casting vote if there is an equality of votes.

Progress test 36

1. Where can parish and community meetings be held? **(4)**

2. What differences are there in the rules for principal councils and parish councils with regard to annual and other meetings? **(1, 35:1)**

3. How is the quorum fixed at parish and community meetings? **(6)**

4. What is the procedure for voting at these meetings? **(7)**

The committee system

NOTE: All references in this chapter relate to the Local Government Act 1972 unless otherwise indicated.

Membership and types of committee

1. Appointment

Any local authority may appoint a committee to discharge its functions or to advise them on any matter relating to the discharge of their functions. Section 101 provides that a local authority may arrange for the discharge of their functions by a committee, a sub-committee, an officer of the authority, or by any other local authority. This section also provides that where a function is delegated to a committee then, unless otherwise directed by the local authority, the committee can delegate its functions to a sub-committee or officer of the authority.

Section 102 provides the following for the purposes of discharging any functions in pursuance of arrangements made under s. 101:

1. (a) a local authority may appoint a committee of the authority; or
   (b) two or more local authorities may appoint a joint committee of those authorities; or
   (c) any such committees may appoint one or more sub-committees.
2. subject to the provisions of this section, the number of members of the committee appointed under 1(a) above, their term of office, and the area (if restricted) within which the committee

are to exercise their authority shall be fixed by the appointing authority or authorities or, in the case of a sub-committee, by the appointing committee.

This power to delegate is wide-ranging and includes not only the carrying out of the functions but also the doing of any thing which is calculated to facilitate, or is conducive or incidental to the discharge of those functions (s. 111).

In R. v. *Brent London Borough Council ex parte Gladbaun and Another* (1989) it was held that while a local authority might appoint a committee, it could not appoint a sub-committee, this latter power being reserved by the committee itself. Mr Justice Nolan stated that what was contemplated by the drafting of s. 102 was a rigid and formal hierarchy of committees.

2. Membership

Persons who are not members of the local authority may be co-opted to serve on the committee. The term of office of co-opted members must be fixed by the council, while members of the authority cease to be members of committees when their membership of the authority ends.

NOTE: The finance committee must consist exclusively of members of the appointing authority (s. 102).

3. Voting rights in committees

Section 13 Local Government and Housing Act 1989 deals with co-opted members of committees, joint committees and sub-committees. It introduces a basic division into voting and non-voting members. A person is a non-voting member if he is appointed by a relevant authority under a power to which this section applies, and is not an elected member. This provision also excludes from classification as non-voting status those members of sub-committees who are also members of the parent committee. Therefore a co-opted member of a committee may be a voting member of a sub-committee.

However, the above restrictions are subject to variation by the Secretary of State, and the Local Government (Committees and Political Groups) Regulations 1990 (S.I. 1990 No. 1553) provided certain exceptions which included the following:

(a) Prescribed functions of authorities where all members of committees discharging those function may have voting rights:

    (*i*) management of land;

    (*ii*) functions under ss. 21–26 Housing Act 1985 relating to not more than 1,500 houses or one-quarter of the authority's houses, whichever is less;

    (*iii*) the functions of a harbour authority;

    (*iv*) the promotion of tourism;

    (*v*) the management of a festival;

    (*vi*) for London Borough Councils or the Common Council of the City of London, functions in relations to its capacity as a local authority, police authority or port authority and the training of staff for the purposes of discharging its function under the Social Services Act 1970;

    (*vii*) functions under s. 7 of the Superannuation Act 1972 for metropolitan district councils;

    (*viii*) in the case of a county council, any functions under the Highways Act 1980 of the Local Authority Social Services Act 1970 to the extent that it is discharged by a committee, the members of which consist solely of members of that council and of members of any district council within its area.

(b) Sub-committees where persons may have voting rights.

    (*i*) a person appointed to a sub-committee of a committee which is appointed exclusively to discharge any the functions in **(a)** above;

    (*ii*) a person appointed to a sub-committee of a National Parks Committee;

    (*iii*) persons appointed to certain sub-committees, including:

    (1) a sub-committee appointed by a social services committee under s. 4(2) Local Authority Social Services Act 1970 and a joint committee appointed under s. 4(3) of that Act which is appointed solely to advise that committee of another sub-committee of that committee;

    (2) a sub-committee appointed by an education committee, as defined in paragraph 4(1) of Schedule 1 to the Local Government and Housing Act 1989, where either no non-voting member of the education committee is appointed as a voting member of the sub-committee, or

the sub-committee is appointed solely to advise that committee or another sub-committee of that committee; (3) some specific, locally-established sub-committees.

4.   Political balance on committees

The Local Government and Housing Act 1989 requires 'proportionality' across the formal activities of local authorities, representing the overall political composition of the authority. Sections 15–16 place a duty on local authorities to determine the representation of different political groups on committees and sub-committees when exercising a power to allocate seats. Four overriding principles must be followed. These are:

(a) all the seats are not allocated to the same political group;

(b) the majority of seats go to the political group majority on the full council;

(c) subject to the above two principles, that the number of seats on the total of all the ordinary committees of the authority allocated to each political group bears the same proportion to the proportion on the full council;

(d) subject to the above three principles, that the number of seats on each ordinary committee of the authority allocated to each political group bears the same proportion to the proportion on the full council.

For the purposes of determining these proportions only *voting* members must be taken into account.

Section 17 provides that an authority may make different arrangements for the allocation of seats but only where such arrangements are the result of a vote in which *no member votes against* the decision to adopt alternative arrangements *and* in a manner approved by the Secretary of State.

For the purpose of these provisions a political group is subject to the following definitions:

(1) A political group shall be treated as constituted when there is delivered to the proper officer a notice in writing which —

(a) is signed by two or more members of an authority who wish to be treated as a political group; and

(b) complies with the provisions of paragraph (3).

(2) A political group shall cease to be constituted if the number of persons who are to be treated as members of that group is less than two.

(3) A notice under paragraph (1) shall state —
(a) that the members of the authority who have signed it wish to be treated as a political group;
(b) the name of the group; and
(c) the name of one member of the group who has signed the notice and who is to act as its leader.

(4) A notice under paragraph (1) may specify the name of one other member of the group who has signed the notice and who is authorized to act in the place of the leader when he is unable to act ('the deputy leader').

(5) the name of the group or the name of the person who is the leader or deputy leader may be changed by a further signed notice in writing delivered to the proper officer.

[Local Government (Committees and Political Groups) Regulations 1990].

5. Types of committee

(a) *Standing committees.* These are constituted for the whole of the council's year to administer a particular service such as environmental health and housing.

(b) *Ad hoc committees.* These special committees are appointed to deal with a specific task and the term of office is over when the task is completed.

(c) *Statutory committees.* The authority is required to appoint certain committees and these are listed in s. 101(*a*). An authority must not reach a decision on any business which is the proper concern of a statutory committee until it has received a report or recommendation from that committee. These committees include education, police and social services.

(d) *Sub-committees.* If the volume of work to be carried out by a committee is large, it may decide to delegate some part of its function to a sub-committee. Where standing sub-committees exist the council may delegate duties directly.

Conduct of committee meetings

6.   Standing orders and committees

The practice here is not standardized; some authorities apply the rules for meetings to committees and sub-committees, some choose to adopt them with some relaxation of the procedural requirements. However, in many cases the authority abandons the standing orders completely in order to achieve a less formal and more productive approach.

See chapter 39:8 for example standing orders.

7.   Minutes of committee meetings

The rules relating to the keeping of minutes referred to in 35:8 above apply to committees and sub-committees. Additional rules are:

(a) any minute properly made and signed is presumed to deal with matters within the authority of the committee unless proved otherwise;

(b) minutes of a committee or sub-committee are not open to public inspection unless they have been laid before the council for approval (*Williams* v. *Manchester Corporation* (1897)).

Progress test 37

1.   What are the main kinds of committee and what are their functions?   (5)

2.   How are committees appointed and who can be members?   (1–4)

3.   What rules govern the procedure at committee and sub-committee meetings?   (7)

4.   What records are required for committees and sub-committees?   (7)

38

Access to information and meetings of public bodies

NOTE: All references in this chapter relate to the Local Government Act 1972 unless otherwise indicated.

General

1. The Local Government (Access to Information) Act 1985

The Act inserted Part VA (ss. 100A–100K) in the Local Government Act 1972 . These sections apply to all principal councils, joint authorities, joint boards and joint committees of two or more principal councils and police and fire authorities. The Act also applies with various modifications to committees and sub-committees of these bodies.

NOTE: These provisions do not apply to parish or community councils and parish meetings which are still governed by the provisions of the Public Bodies (Admission to Meetings) Act 1960 (*see* 10).

The main provisions introduced by the Local Government (Access to Information Act are as follows.

Access to meetings

2. Requirement to exclude the public

All meetings which are subject to the provisions of the Act must as a general rule be open to members of the public. However, the public must be excluded from such meetings if it is likely that confidential information would be disclosed to members of the public in breach of an obligation of confidence. Confidential information in these circumstances is:

(a) information furnished to the council by a government department on terms which forbid its disclosure to the public; and
(b) information the disclosure of which to the public is prohibited by or under any enactment or by a court order.

3.   Discretion to exclude the public

In addition, a council may by resolution exclude members of the public from a meeting during an item of business where it is likely that 'exempt information' would otherwise be revealed to them. Exempt information is listed in Schedule 12A of the Act and is as follows:

(a) Information relating to a particular employee, former employee or applicant to become an employee of, or a particular officer, former officeholder or applicant to become an officeholder under the authority.
(b) As above but in respect of a magistrates' court committee or a probation committee.
(c) Information relating to any particular occupier or former occupier of, or applicant for, accommodation provided by or at the expense of the authority.
(d) Information relating to any particular applicant for, or recipient or former recipient of any service provided by the authority.
(e) As above but in respect of financial assistance.
(f) Information relating to the adoption, care, fostering or education of any particular child.
(g) Information relating to the financial or business affairs of any particular person other than the authority.
(h) The amount of any expenditure proposed to be incurred by the authority under any particular contract for the acquisition of property or the supply of goods or services.
(i)   Any terms proposed or to be proposed by or to the authority in the course of negotiations for a contract for the acquisition or disposal of property or the supply of goods or services.
(j)   The identity of the authority as well as any other person, by

virtue of **(g)** above as the person offering any particular tender for a contract for the supply of goods or services.

(k) Information relating to any consultations or negotiations, or contemplated consultations or negotiations, in connection with any labour relations matter arising between the authority or a Minister of the Crown and employees of, or office-holders under the authority.

(l) Any instructions to counsel and any opinion of counsel whether or not in connection with any proceedings and any advice received, information obtained or action to be taken in connection with any legal proceedings by or against the authority or the determination of any matter affecting the authority (whether, in either case, proceedings have been commenced or are in contemplation).

(m) Information which, if disclosed to the public, would reveal that the authority proposes to give under any enactment a notice under or by virtue of which requirements are imposed on a person, or to make an order or direction under any enactment.

(n) Any action taken or to be taken in connection with the prevention, investigation or prosecution of crime.

(o) The identity of a protected informant.

In the above schedule, reference to 'the authority' is to any principal authority or, as the case may be, any committee or sub-committee in relation to whose proceedings or documents the question whether information is exempt or not falls to be determined.

4. General provisions

Whenever the meeting is open to the public there is no other power to exclude members of the public from the meeting except to suppress or prevent *disorderly conduct* or other *misbehaviour*. Duly accredited representatives of the press must be provided with reasonable facilities for taking reports and for telephoning these at their own expense (this provision is not applicable both where the meeting is not held on council premises and where the premises are not on the telephone).

5. Notice of meetings

Public notice of time and place of a meeting of any body subject to the provisions of the Act must be published at the offices of the body three clear days before the meeting or at the time of convening the meeting where it is called at shorter notice.

Access to documents

6. Before the meeting

Copies of the agenda and any reports for a meeting must be open to public inspection at least three clear days before the meeting or when it is convened if called at shorter notice. This provision is subject to the following conditions:

(a) Copies of documents are not required to be open to the public until they are available to council members.

(b) Late items must be open to inspection when they are added to the agenda.

(c) Any report or part of a report which, in the opinion of the proper officer, relates to a part of the meeting likely not to be open to the public may be withheld.

> NOTE: An item of business may not be considered at a meeting unless either the rules of publication of the agenda have been complied with or it is, in the opinion of the chairman, an item of urgency and the reasons for this are entered in the minutes.

7. At the meeting

A reasonable number of copies of the agenda and reports must be available for the use of the public. If the press so request, they must be supplied with a copy of the agenda and reports, such further statements or particulars as are necessary to indicate the nature of the items included in the agenda and, if the proper officer thinks fit in the case of any item, copies of any other documents supplied to members of the council in connection with the item.

8. After the meeting

The following documents must be open to public inspection at the council's offices for *six years*:

(a) The minutes, or a copy of the minutes, of the meeting excluding so much of the minutes of proceedings during which the meeting was not open to the public, as discloses exempt information.

(b) A summary prepared by the proper officer which provides a reasonably fair and coherent record of proceedings without disclosing any exempt information, in circumstances where the exclusion of part of the minutes means the part published does not provide such a record.

(c) A copy of the agenda.

(d) A copy of so much of any report for the meeting as relates to any item during which the meeting was open to the public.

In addition to the above documents, a list and copy of background papers in respect of any report or part of a report which is open to the public must be open to public inspection for a period of *four years*.

Background papers are those documents which disclose any fact or matters on which, in the opinion of the proper officer, the report or an important part of the report is based, and which have been relied on to a material extent in the preparation of the report but do not include any published works.

9. General provisions

(a) All documents must be open to inspection by the public at all reasonable hours and no payment may be required, except in the case of background papers where a reasonable fee may be charged.

(b) Any person entitled to inspect documents may make copies or take extracts from them or require a photocopy to be supplied at a reasonable fee.

(c) The above provision does not allow the infringement of a copyright unless it is held by the principal council.

(d) Where any document in respect of a meeting is open to public inspection, or is supplied for the benefit of a newspaper, the publication thereby of defamatory matter contained in the document is *privileged*, unless the publication is proved to be with malice.

(e) The above rights to inspect, copy and to be supplied with documents are in addition and without prejudice, to any other statutory rights.

Access to other meetings

10. Public Bodies (Admission to Meetings) Act 1960

As from 1 April 1986 this Act applies only to parish or community councils, the Council of the Isles of Scilly and joint boards or joint committees which discharge the functions of such bodies, parish meetings, the Land Authority for Wales, regional, area or district health authorities, community health councils and other specified bodies and committees. The main provisions of the Act are as follows:

(a) *The public has the same right as the press* to attend the meetings of local authorities (s.1 and Sched. para. 1).

(b) *The right of admission* of both press and public applies also to *committee meetings*, although this right applies only to education committees, certain joint committees and to committees composed of the whole of the members of the parent body (s. 2(1)). The Local Government Act 1972, s. 100, requires any meeting of a committee, appointed by a local authority or authorities to discharge functions under arrangements made by the authority or authorities, to be open to the public.

> NOTE: Presumably this section of the 1960 Act was intended to prevent a practice, adopted by certain local authorities, of 'going into committee' when it wished to exclude the press from a council meeting.

(c) The press is given the right, on payment of expenses, to call for a *supply of agenda papers* of meetings which the public are entitled to attend.

> NOTE: In order to safeguard the position as regards defamatory statements, reports, agenda papers and other documents issued to the press are subject to qualified privilege.

(d) A local authority reserves the right to pass a *resolution excluding both press and public* 'wherever publicity would be prejudicial to the public interest by reason of the confidential nature of the business or for other special reasons stated in the resolution and arising from the nature of the business of the proceedings' (s. 1(2)). In *R. v. Liverpool City Council* (1975) the business of a meeting was to consider applications for hackney carriage licences and it was decided to hear each application without competitors being present. This was held to be a valid course of action within 'special reasons' as stated in the Act, but, as the minutes did not refer to this special reason, the Act had not been complied with.

NOTE: The Act imposes no penalty for improper or unnecessary exclusion of press or public from a meeting. This criticism has, in fact, been made of the Act throughout, as it does not anywhere refer to the penalty for any breach of the various sections.

Progress test 38

1. On what grounds may a principal council exclude the public from its meetings? **(2, 3)**

2. Which documents should be open to inspection by the public before and after meetings of principal councils? **(6, 8)**

3. To which meetings does the Public Bodies (Admission to Meetings) Act 1960 apply? **(10)**

39

Rights of members

NOTE: All references in this chapter relate to the Local Government Act 1972 unless otherwise indicated.

1. Access to documents

(a) *Common law.* The common law provides a member with the right to inspect such documents as are necessary to enable him to carry out his duties: *R.* v. *Birmingham City Council, ex parte O* (1983) where it was decided by the House of Lords that a member was entitled to access to all written material in the council's possession providing she had good reason. Membership of a committee is good reason in itself, while in the case of documents relating to other committees the 'need to know' would have to be shown by the councillor. This point is illustrated by the decision in *R.* v. *Sheffield City Council, ex parte Chadwick* (1985) where the leader of the Liberal group on the council applied for a declaration that the council was acting unlawfully by refusing to allow him to attend meetings of the council's budget sub-committee and by refusing to supply him with copies of reports made to that sub-committee. The budget sub-committee was a sub-committee of the policy committee (which was the council's principal committee). Mr Chadwick (the applicant) was a member of the policy committee. *Held*: In order for Mr Chadwick to carry out his duties properly he had the 'need to know' what matters had been considered by the budget sub-committee and therefore his application was granted. These decisions should be contrasted with those in *R.* v. *Barnes Borough Council, ex parte Conlan* (1938) and *R.* v. *Lancashire County Council Police Authority, ex parte Hook* (1980).

(b) *Statute.* In addition to this right, the Local Government (Access to Information) Act 1985 provides a statutory right of access to documents for members of principal councils. It states that any document which is in the possession or under the control of a principal council and contains material relating to any business to be transacted at a meeting of the council or a committee or sub-committee of the council is to be open to inspection by any council member. However, it should be noted that this right is removed where it appears to the proper officer that a document reveals certain classes of exempt information (10 of the 15 classes apply in such cases). The accounts of a local authority or joint authority and of any proper officer may be inspected by any member and he may make a copy of them or take extracts from them.

2. Disqualification from voting

Section 94 states that where a member of a local authority has a pecuniary interest, whether direct or indirect, in any contract, proposed contract or other matter, and is present at a meeting of the authority where the contract or other matter is under consideration, he must, as soon as practicable after the commencement of the meeting, disclose the fact of his interest, and not take part in the consideration or discussion of, or vote on any question with respect to, the contract or other matter.

In *Rands* v. *Olroyd* (1958) a councillor was a director of a concern which had decided not to enter into any contracts with the council while the director was councillor. The councillor voted on council policy regarding tenders for building work and was held to have voted on a matter in which he had an interest.

The receipt of, the right to receive or the possibility of receiving allowances or expenses by members shall not be treated as a pecuniary interest under this section.

3. Pecuniary interest (s. 95)

A person is deemed to have a pecuniary interest if:

(a) he or any nominee of his is a member of a company or other body with which the contract was made or is proposed to be made or which has a direct pecuniary interest in the other matter under consideration, or

(b) he is a partner, or is in the employment, of a person with whom the contract was made, or is proposed to be made or who has a direct pecuniary interest in the other matter under consideration.

The above do not apply to membership of or employment under any public body, and a member of a company or other body shall not by reason only of his membership be treated as having an interest in any contract, proposed contract or other matter if he has no beneficial interest in any securities of that company or other body.

In the case of married persons living together, the interest of one spouse shall, if known to the other, be deemed for these purposes to be also an interest of the other.

4.   Recording of pecuniary interest

Section 96 provides that a general notice given in writing to the proper officer of the authority by a member thereof to the effect that he or his spouse is a member or in the employment of a specified company or other body, or that he or his spouse is a partner or in the employment of a specified person, or that he or his spouse is the tenant of any premises owned by the authority, shall, unless and until the notice is withdrawn, be deemed to be a sufficient notice of his interest for any future occasions.

The proper officer is required to record in a book kept for that purpose particulars of any notices received under this section and any particular notices received under s. 94. This book shall be open at all reasonable hours to the inspection of any member of the local authority.

5.   Exemptions and dispensations

Section 97 states the circumstances where s. 94 will not apply. These include:

(a) where the councillor has an interest in a matter simply as a ratepayer or inhabitant of the area, or only as a consumer of water or passenger on a municipal transport undertaking;

(b) where the councillor has shares in a society or company to an amount not exceeding one thousand pounds or one-hundredth of the total issued share capital of the company (whichever is less);

(c) where the interest is so remote or insignificant that it cannot reasonably be regarded as likely to influence a member;

(d) where the Secretary of State (or the district council in the case of a parish or community council) has given a dispensation for the interested member to vote.

6. Penalty for non-compliance

Section 94 provides that any person who fails to comply with the requirements of disclosure shall, for each offence, be liable to a fine not exceeding level four on the standard scale, unless he proves that he did not know that the matter in which he had an interest was the subject of consideration at that meeting. A prosecution for an offence under this section shall not be instituted except by or on behalf of the Director of Public Prosecutions.

7. Defamatory statements

Statements made at council meetings are subject to the general principles of the law relating to defamation. However, the following defences are available:

(a) *Absolute privilege.* This defence is not generally available to members but it does apply to communications between a local commissioner and local authorities.

(b) *Qualified privilege.* As stated in chapter 14, this defence is available in circumstances where the person making a statement has a legal, social or moral duty to make the statement and the recipient has a right or duty to receive it. Therefore it can be seen that this will apply to many statements made by members in such meetings. However, it should be remembered that proof of malice by the maker of the statement will defeat this defence. As a general rule a person will not be deemed to have been malicious where he honestly believes that his statement is true: *Horrocks* v. *Lowe* (1975).

(c) *Certain other defences,* particularly justification and fair comment on a matter of public interest, may also be available to members (for details *see* chapter 14).

8. Standing orders

The main controls on the rights of members at meetings are to be found in the Council's standing orders which normally contain detailed rules. The following is a sample of the types of rules commonly found in standing orders, set out as a set of specimen standing orders.

(a) *Frequency of meetings*

(1) In addition to the annual meeting of the Council and any meetings convened by the Mayor, or by members of the Council, meetings for the transaction of general business shall be held in each year as follows: On the fourth Tuesday of each month except June and July.

(2) The annual meeting of the Council shall be held on such day as the Council may appoint at 2.00 pm at the Town Hall.

(3) Other meetings of the Council for the transaction of general business shall be held at 7.30 pm at the Town Hall.

(b) *Chairman's powers*

Any power or duty of the Mayor in relation to the conduct of a meeting may be exercised by the person presiding at the meeting.

(c) *Quorum*

If during any meeting of the Council the Mayor, after counting the number of members present, declares that there is not a quorum present the meeting shall stand adjourned. The consideration of any business not transacted shall be adjourned to a time fixed by the Mayor at the time that the meeting is adjourned, or, if he/she does not fix a time, to the next ordinary meeting of the Council.

(d) *Order of business*

(1) Except as otherwise provided by paragraph 2 of this standing order, the order of business shall be:

(*i*) To choose a person to preside if the Mayor and Deputy Mayor be absent.

(*ii*) To deal with any business required by statute to be done before any other business.

(*iii*) To approve as a correct record and sign the minutes of the last meeting of the Council.

(*iv*) To deal with any business expressly required by statute to be done.

(*v*) Mayor's announcements.

(*vi*) To answer questions asked in accordance with the provisions of these standing orders.

(*vii*) To dispose of business (if any) remaining from the last meeting.

(*viii*) To receive and consider reports, minutes and recommendations of committees.

(*ix*) To authorise the sealing of documents, so far as authority is not conferred by other resolution of the Council.

(*x*) To consider motions for which notice has been received.

(*xi*) Other business, if any, specified in the summons.

(2) Items falling under (*i*)–(*iii*) above shall not be displaced, but subject thereto, the foregoing order of business may be varied by the Mayor at his discretion or by resolution.

(e) *Notices of motion*

(1) Notice of every motion other than a motion which under these standing orders may be moved without notice, shall be given in writing, signed by the member or members of the Council giving the notice, and delivered not later than noon on the Thursday next but one before the next meeting of the Council, at the office of the Chief Executive by whom it shall be dated, numbered in the order in which it is received, and entered in a book which shall be open to the inspection of every member of the Council.

(2) The Chief Executive shall set out in the summons for every meeting of the Council all motions of which notice has been duly given, in the order in which they have been received, unless the member giving such a notice intimated in writing when giving it, that he proposed to move it at some later meeting, or has since withdrawn it in writing.

(3) If a motion thus set out on the summons be not moved either by a member on his behalf, it shall, unless postponed by consent of the Council, be treated as withdrawn and shall not be moved without fresh notice.

(4) If the subject matter of any motion of which notice has been duly given is likely to involve the Council in an increase in expenditure it shall be moved and seconded without comment and then stand referred to any Committee within whose Terms of Reference the matter falls and to the Finance Committee for consideration and report.

Provided that the Mayor may, if he/she considers it convenient and conducive to the dispatch of business, allow the motion to be dealt with at the meeting at which it is brought forward.

(5) Every motion shall be relevant to some matter in relation to which the Council have powers or duties, or which affects the District.

(f) *Motions and amendments which may be moved without notice.* The following motions and amendments may be moved without notice:

(1) Appointment of a Chairman of the meeting at which the motion is made.

(2) Motions relating to the accuracy of minutes.

(3) 'That an item of business specified in the summons is given precedence'.

(4) Remission to a Committee.

(5) Appointment of a Committee or members thereof, occasioned by an item mentioned in the summons to the meeting.

(6) Adoption of reports and recommendations of Committees or officers, and any consequent resolutions.

(7) That leave be given to withdraw a motion.

(8) Extending the time limit for speeches.

(9) Amendments to motions.

(10) That the Council proceed to the next business.

(11) That the question be now put.

(13) That the Council do now adjourn.

(14) Authorising the sealing of documents.

(15) Suspending standing orders.

(16) Motions under s. 1(2) Public Bodies (Admission to Meetings) Act 1960 to exclude the public.

(17) That a member named be not further heard or do leave the meeting.

(18) Inviting a member who has a pecuniary interest in a matter under consideration to remain.

(19) Giving consent of the Council where required by the standing orders.

(g) *Questions*

(1) A member of the Council may:

(*i*) if notice in writing has been given to the Chief Executive not less than 48 hours before the time of the meeting, ask the Mayor or the Chairman of any Committee any question on any matter in relation to which the Council have powers or duties or which affects the district.

(*ii*) with the permission of the Mayor, put to him/her or the Chairman of any Committee any question relating to urgent business, of which such notice has not been given; but a copy of any such question shall, if possible, be delivered to the Chief Executive not later than ten o'clock in the morning of the day of the meeting.

(2) Every question shall be put and answered without discussion, but the person to whom a question has been put may decline to answer.

(3) An answer may take the form of:

(*i*) a direct oral answer; or

(*ii*) where the desired information is contained in a publication of the Council, a reference to that publication; or

(*iii*) where the reply to the question cannot conveniently be given orally, a written answer circulated to members of the Council.

(h) *Minutes*

(1) the Mayor shall put the question that the minutes of the preceding meeting of the Council be approved as a correct record.

(2) No discussion shall take place upon the minutes, except upon their accuracy, and any question on their accuracy shall be raised by motion. If no such question is raised, or if it is raised then as soon as it is disposed of, the Mayor shall sign the minutes.

(i) *Confirmation of Committee proceedings*

(1) The confirmation of the proceedings of any Committee shall be moved by the Chairman or some other member of the Committee. The confirmation of the proceedings of the Committee shall then be seconded and thereafter the Chairman, or other member moving the confirmation, shall call over each individual minute and shall, at that time, call the attention of the Council to any resolution or matter of an unusual or special character or one involving considerable expenditure. Each minute

shall be deemed to be the subject of a separate motion for confirmation.

(2) All debate, on a matter the subject of more than one item on the Council minutes, shall take place on the first minute under which it is for consideration.

(j) *Rules for debate for Council meetings*

(1) A motion or amendment shall not be discussed unless it has been proposed and seconded and, unless notice has already been given in accordance with these standing orders, it shall if required by the Mayor, be put into writing and handed to the Mayor before it is further discussed or put to the meeting. The mover of an amendment shall read it before speaking on it.

(2) A member when seconding a motion or amendment may, if he/she then declares his/her intention to do so, reserve his/her right of speech until a later period of the debate.

(3) A member when speaking shall stand and address the Mayor. If two or more members rise the Mayor shall call on one to speak; the others shall then sit. While a member is speaking the other members shall remain seated, unless rising to a point of order or in personal explanation.

(4) A member shall direct his/her speech to the question under discussion or to a personal explanation or to a point of order. No speech shall exceed 5 minutes except by consent of the Council provided that a member may speak for not more than 10 minutes or for such longer period as the Council may allow when:

　(*i*) proposing a motion;

　(*ii*) replying to a debate on a motion he/she has proposed;

　(*iii*) proposing an amendment.

(5) A member who has spoken on any motion shall not speak again while it is the subject of debate, except:

　(*i*) to speak once on an amendment moved by another member;

　(*ii*) if the motion has been amended since he/she last spoke, to move a further amendment;

　(*iii*) if his/her first speech was on an amendment moved by another member, to speak on the main issue, whether or not the amendment on which he/she spoke was carried;

(*iv*) in the exercise of a right of reply given by these standing orders;

(*v*) on a point of order;

(*vi*) by way of personal explanation.

(6) An amendment shall be relevant to the motion and be either:

(*i*) to refer the subject of debate to a Committee for consideration or reconsideration;

(*ii*) to leave out words;

(*iii*) to leave out words and insert or add others;

(*iv*) to insert or add words;

but such omission, insertion or addition of words shall not have the effect of negativing the motion before the Council.

(7) Only one amendment shall be moved and discussed at a time and no further amendment shall be moved until the amendment under discussion has been disposed of. The Mayor may permit two or more amendments to be discussed (but not voted on) together if circumstances suggest that this course would facilitate the proper conduct of the Council's business.

(8) If an amendment be lost, other amendments may be moved on the original motion. If an amendment be carried, the motion as amended shall take the place of the original motion and shall become the motion upon which any further amendment may be moved.

(9) A member may, with the consent of the Council signified, without discussion:

(*i*) alter a motion of which he/she has given notice; or

(*ii*) with the further consent of his/her seconder alter a motion which he/she has moved where the alteration is one which could be made as an amendment.

(10) A motion or amendment may be withdrawn by the mover with the consent of his/her seconder and of the Council, which shall be signified without discussion, and no member may speak upon it after the mover has asked permission for its withdrawal, unless such permission shall have been refused.

(11) The mover of a motion has a right to reply at the close of the debate on the motion, immediately before it is put to

the vote. If an amendment is moved, the mover of the original motion shall also have a right of reply at the close of the debate on the amendment, and shall not otherwise speak on the amendment. The mover of the amendment shall have no right of reply to the debate on his/her amendment.

(12) When a motion is under debate no other motion shall be moved except the following:

(*i*) to amend the motion;

(*ii*) to adjourn the meeting;

(*iii*) to adjourn the debate;

(*iv*) to proceed to the next business;

(*v*) that the question be now put;

(*vi*) that a member be not further heard;

(*vii*) by the Mayor that a member do leave the meeting;

(*viii*) a motion under s. 1(2) of the Public Bodies (Admission to Meetings) Act 1960 to exclude the public.

(13) A member may move without comment at the conclusion of a speech of another member, 'That the Council proceed to the next business', 'That the question be now put', 'That the debate be adjourned', or 'The Council do now adjourn', on the seconding of which the Mayor shall proceed as follows:

(*i*) on a motion to proceed to next business: unless in his/her opinion the matter before the meeting has been insufficiently discussed, he/she shall first give the mover of the original motion a right of reply, and then put to the vote the motion to proceed to the next business;

(*ii*) On a motion that the question be now put: unless in his/her opinion the matter before the meeting has been insufficiently discussed, he/she shall first put to the vote the motion that the question be now put, and if it is passed then give the mover of the original motion his/her right of reply before putting his/her motion to the vote;

(*iii*) on a motion to adjourn the debate or the meeting: if in his/her opinion the matter before the meeting has not been sufficiently discussed and cannot reasonably be sufficiently discussed on that occasion he/she shall put the adjournment motion to the vote without giving the mover of the original motion his/her right of reply on that occasion.

(14) A member may rise on a point of order or in personal explanation, and shall be entitled to be heard forthwith. A point of order shall relate only to an alleged breach of a standing order or statutory provision and the way in which he/she considers it has been broken. A personal explanation shall be confined to some material part of a former speech by him/her which may appear to have been misunderstood in the present debate.

(15) The ruling of the Mayor on a point of order or on the admissibility of a personal application shall not be open to discussion.

(16) Whenever the Mayor rises during a debate a member then standing shall resume his/her seat and the Council shall be silent.

(k) *Disorderly conduct*

(1) If at a meeting any member of the Council, in the opinion of the Mayor notified to the Council, misconduct himself/herself by persistently disregarding the ruling of the Chair, or by behaving irregularly, improperly or offensively, or by wilfully obstructing the business of the Council, the Mayor or any other member may move 'That the member named be not further heard', and the motion if seconded shall be put and determined without discussion.

(2) If the member named continues his/her misconduct after a motion under the foregoing paragraph has been carried the Mayor shall:
either move 'That the member named do leave the meeting' **or** adjourn the meeting of the Council for such a period as he/she in his/her discretion shall consider expedient.

(3) In the event of a general disturbance which, in the opinion of the Mayor renders the due and orderly dispatch of business impossible, the Mayor in addition to any other power vested in him/her may, without question put, adjourn the meeting of the Council for such period as he/she in his/her discretion shall consider expedient.

(l)   *Disturbance by members of the public*
If a member of the public interrupts the proceedings at any meeting the Mayor shall warn him/her. If he/she continues the interruption the Mayor shall order his/her removal from the Council chamber. In case of a general disturbance in any part of the chamber open to the public the Mayor shall order that part to be cleared.

(m)   *Rescission of preceding resolution*
No motion to rescind any resolution passed within the preceding six months, and no motion or amendment to the same effect as one which has been rejected within the preceding six months, shall be proposed unless the notice thereof given in pursuance of these standing orders bears the names of at least 18 members of the Council. When any such motion or amendment has been disposed of by the Council, it shall not be open to any member to propose a similar motion within a further period of six months. Provided that this standing order shall not apply to motions moved in pursuance of a recommendation of a Committee.

(n)   *Voting*
The mode of voting at meetings of the Council shall be show of hands and on the requisition of any member of the Council made before the vote is taken and supported by nine other members who signify their support by rising in their places. The voting on any question shall be recorded so as to show whether each member present gave his/her vote for or against that question or abstained from voting.

(o)   *Voting for appointments*
Where there are more than two persons nominated for any position to be filled by the Council, and of the votes given, there is not a majority in favour of one person, the name of the person having the least number of votes shall be struck off the list and a fresh vote shall be taken, and so on until a majority of votes is given in favour of one person.

(p)   *The common seal*
    (1) The common seal of the Council shall be kept in a safe place in the custody of the Borough Solicitor and shall not be impressed upon any document unless the sealing has been authorized by a resolution of the Council or of a Committee to which the Council has delegated their powers in this behalf, but a resolution of the Council (or

of a Committee where the Committee has the power) authorizing the acceptance of any tender, the purchase, sale, letting or taking of any property, the issue of any stock, the presentation of any petition, memorial, or address, the making of any charge or contract, or the doing of any other thing, shall be a sufficient authority for sealing any document necessary to give effect to the resolution.

(2) The common seal may only be impressed upon a document by an officer duly authorized by the Borough Solicitor.

(3) Every document sealed shall be attested by the Chief Executive or by the Borough Solicitor or an officer nominated by either of them provided that if the Mayor so directs in relation to any document, it shall be attested by the Mayor or a Deputy named by him/her and the Chief Executive or the Borough Solicitor.

(4) An entry of every sealing of a document shall be made and consecutively numbered in a book kept for the purpose and shall be initialled by a person who has certified or attested the seal.

(q) *Appointment of Committees*

The Council shall at the annual meeting appoint such Committees as they are required to appoint by or under any statute and such other standing Committees as they have at that or any earlier meeting resolved to establish, and may at any other time appoint such other Committees as are necessary to carry out the work of the Council but, subject to any statutory provisions in that behalf:

(1) shall not appoint any member of a Committee so as to hold office later than the next annual meeting of the Council;

(2) may at any time dissolve a Committee or alter its membership.

(r) *Proceedings at Committees to be confidential*

All agenda, reports, and other documents and all proceedings of Committees from which the press and public are excluded shall be treated as confidential unless and until they become public in the ordinary course of the Council's business.

(s) *Constitution of Committees*

(1) Except where otherwise provided by statute or a scheme

made under statutory authority, the Mayor, the Deputy Mayor and the Chairman and Vice-Chairman of the Policy and Resources Committee shall be *ex-officio* members of every Standing Committee appointed by the Council.

(2) No member of the Council (except the Mayor, the Deputy Mayor, Chairman or Vice-Chairman of the Policy and Resources Committee) shall serve on more than two Standing Committees (except the Policy and Resources Committee).

(t) *Appointment of Chairmen and Vice-Chairmen of Committees*

The Council shall, at their annual meeting, or whenever there is a vacancy in such office, appoint the Chairman and Vice-Chairman of each Committee from among the members of the Council appointed to serve on that Committee. In the absence from a meeting of the Chairman and Vice-Chairman, the Committee shall appoint a Chairman for that meeting.

(u) *Special meetings of committees*

The Chairman of a Committee or the Mayor may call a special meeting of the Committee at any time. A special meeting shall also be called on the requisition of a quarter of the whole number of the Committee, delivered in writing to the Chief Executive but in no case shall less than three members requisition a special meeting. The summons to the special meeting shall set out the business to be considered thereat, and no business other than that set out in the summons shall be considered at that meeting.

(v) *Sub-committees*

(1) Every Committee appointed by the Council may appoint Sub-committees for purposes to be specified by the Committee.

(2) The Chairman and the Vice-Chairman, if any of the Committees shall be *ex-officio* members of every Sub-committee appointed by that Committee, unless they signify to the Committee that they do not wish to serve.

(w) *Quorum of Committees and Sub-committees*

(1) Except where authorized by statute or ordered by the Council, business shall not be transacted at a meeting of any Committee unless at least one-quarter of the whole number of the Committee is present. Provided that, in no

case shall the quorum of a Committee be less than three members.

(2) Except as aforesaid, or as otherwise ordered by the Committee which has appointed it, business shall not be transacted at a Sub-committee unless at least one-quarter of the whole number of the Sub-committee is present. Provided that, in no case shall the quorum of a Sub-committee be less than two members.

(x) *Voting in Committees and Sub-committees*

Voting at a meeting of a Committee or Sub-committee shall be by show of hands.

(y) *Mover of a motion may attend Committee or Sub-committee*

A member of the Council who has moved a motion which has been referred to any Committee or Sub-committee shall have notice of the meeting of the Committee or Sub-committee at which it is proposed to consider the motion. He/she shall have the right to attend the meeting and if he/she attends shall have an opportunity of explaining the motion.

(z) *Use of standing orders*

(1) The standing orders shall, with any necessary modification, apply to Committee and Sub-committee meetings.

(2) Subject to paragraph (3) of this standing order, any of the preceding standing orders may be suspended so far as regards any business at the meeting where its suspension is moved.

(3) A motion to suspend standing orders shall not be moved without notice unless there shall be present at least one-half of the whole number of members of the Council.

(4) The ruling of the Mayor as to the construction or application of any of these standing orders, or as to any proceedings of the Council, shall not be challenged at any meeting of the Council.

Progress test 39

1. Under what circumstances will a member be disqualified from voting at a council meeting? **(2, 8)**

2. What is a pecuniary interest and how must it be recorded? **(3, 4)**

3. When will the defences of absolute and qualified privilege apply to statements made at council meetings?   **(7)**

Part five

Preparation for meetings

Practical work of the secretary

Although there are certain rules to be followed when preparing for meetings and conferences, obviously the same set of rules cannot be applied in all cases, as the nature, purpose and place of the meeting may entail special treatment. It is, therefore, proposed to deal with a number of separate cases, suggested by, or based upon, questions set by the principal professional secretarial bodies.

1. Timetable of arrangements for a meeting of an association or society, to which a well-known personality is to be invited as *guest speaker*

The Retail Traders' Association

Meeting to held on 30 June, 19.. to consider how the Retail Trade may best comply with recent consumer protection legislation.

Item No.	Date	Item	Remarks and/or action
	19..		
1	May 2	*Accommodation.* Confirm that a suitable hall is available for the meeting, and make a provisional booking.	County Hall, Park Street, EC booked provisionally for 30 June, 19..
2		Make provisional reservation at local hotel for guest speaker.	Provisional booking for 29 June.

3	May 3	*Write guest speaker* (Mr X) or his agent, inviting him to speak at the meeting and informing him of accommodation provisionally arranged.	May 5 Received acceptance from Mr X's agent and agreement to hotel arrangements.
4	May 5	*Confirm hall and hotel bookings* for the dates provisionally agreed.	Acknowledge Mr X's acceptance.
5	May 7	*Prepare agenda* for the meeting (*see* chapter 5) giving some particulars of the guest speaker and topic of his speech.	May 10. Final form of agenda approved by the Management Committee.
6	May 11	*Instruct printers*. Having drafted a form of notice, order supply of notices and agenda forms.	Supply of agenda and notice forms received 25 May.
7	May 27	*Convene meeting*. Post notice and copy of agenda to each member (and any others who are to make up the platform party), so as to comply with standing orders/ rules as regards form, method of service, period of notice, etc, assumed to be 28 days' notice in this case.	Posted 27 May and certificate of posting obtained.
8	June 1	*Arrange for press coverage*. Issue invitation and send particulars of guest speaker to local newspaper(s), also copies of notices and agenda forms.	Arranged with *Daily Sun* and *Weekly News*.
9	June 1/8	*Arrangements at meeting hall*. Make all necessary arrangements for:	Arranged and approved by Management

		(a) seating of platform party; **(b)** appointment of stewards; **(c)** notification to police and arrange parking facilities; **(d)** facilities for press representatives; **(e)** loudspeaker system.	Committee 9 June.
10	June 15	*Confirm travel arrangements with guest speaker.* Ascertain where and at what time he will arrive.	18 June. Confirmed. Mr X to arrive City Airport 3 pm, 29 June.
11	June 22	*Documents for meeting.* Prepare and have ready all documents, records, books, etc, likely to be required at meeting.	List prepared and checked.
12	June 29	*Reception of guest speaker,* by Chairman at airport.	Mr X met with car and conducted to his hotel.
13	June 30	*Attend meeting hall,* and **(a)** take documents, books, etc, **(b)** check all arrangements,	Attended in morning. Checked.
14	June 30	*Transport of guest speaker* to meeting hall.	Mr X fetched by car and met.

Follow-up arrangements

Frequently the convenors of a meeting rely not only upon the meeting but also upon the follow-up arrangements, in order to obtain the maximum benefit from it. It is not suggested that this would necessarily apply in the case of the association referred to in the foregoing example, but it would obviously be important where an association or society is wanting to use, say, a public meeting to spread its doctrine and increase its membership. For this purpose the undermentioned follow-up arrangements are suggested:

(a) *Press notices.* If the press had not been represented at the meeting, supply a copy of any important speech, or other material for publication.

(b) *Circulate copies of any important speech* (or a report of the meeting) to provincial branch secretaries (if any) who were not present at the meeting.

(c) *Any striking phrase or sentence* included in the principal speech may be 'plugged' or adopted as the 'gimmick' of the society or association, in its own quarterly bulletin, and in newspapers, periodicals, TV programmes, etc.

(d) *Provide a full account of the meeting*, including principal speeches, photographs, etc.

(e) *Stewards to make personal contacts* with people present at the meeting, e.g.:

> (*i*) by encouraging them to join the association or society;
> (*ii*) by obtaining names and addresses of people wanting tickets for the next meeting, or literature, etc.

(f) *distribute free literature* concerning the objects of the society or association. Such literature may be distributed by the stewards as people leave the meeting.

2.   Arrangements for the conference of a manufacturing company with overseas sales and service centres

(a) *Prepare a draft* conference plan.

(b) *Submit draft plan to the board* of directors for approval.

(c) *Formal approval given* of the following plan:

Tuesday, 12 October, 19..

Optional arrangements for spouses and other invited guests:

11 am	Reception of conference members and invited guests by Chairman of the company.	
1 pm	Luncheon at Court Hotel.	
2.30 pm	Conference business.	Visit to Harolds for fashion show.

5 pm	Tea provided in annexe to conference hall.
7 pm	Dinner at hotel, for those reserving accommodation at Court Hotel.

Wednesday, 13 October, 19..

10 am	Conference business.	Conducted sightseeing tour of the City.
1 pm	Luncheon provided in annexe to conference hall.	
2.30 pm	Conference business.	Free for shopping, etc.
5 pm	Tea provided in annexe to conference hall.	
7 pm	Dinner at hotel, for those reserving accommodation at Court Hotel.	
8 pm	Theatre (musical show at Empire Theatre); or Dance at Court Hotel available to residents.	

Thursday, 14 October, 19..

10 am	Conference business; last session.	Optional visit to Exhibition of Modern Art.
1 pm	Luncheon for conference members and guests provided at Court Hotel.	

(d) *Draft agenda* for the conference and other documents.
(e) *Submit draft agenda and documents to the board* of directors for approval.
(f) *Formal approval given* of the following conference agenda:

Conference Agenda and summaries of main points to be discussed

Tuesday, 12 October, 19..

2.30 pm	*Opening speech.* Mr A Blank, Chairman of the Company will open the Conference and welcome representatives from provincial and overseas centres.

2.45 pm   *Chairman's Report* on the Company's developments,
               and particularly on the success of the Sales
               Programme originated at the last Conference.

3 pm   *The main purpose of the present Conference.* After
               presenting his report, the Chairman will state the
               terms of reference of the Conference; namely:

               'To look ahead to the day when we shall take a full
               and active part in the European Community, and
               to ensure that all sections of our organisation,
               sales, service and administration alike, will be
               ready to meet the extra demands that will then be
               made of them.'

               He will then call upon Mr I. Hope, the Company's
               Sales Director, to state more fully the various ways
               in which the Conference members may assist, by
               pooling their ideas and making constructive
               suggestions, in achieving the principal purpose of
               the Conference.

4 pm   *Further business of the Conference.* The Chairman will
               call upon Mr E. Cann, the Company's Senior
               Technical Director, to explain the nature of the
               other business which, it is hoped, the Conference will
               be able to transact; in particular:

               (*i*) *Restrictive practices* within the Company's
               manufacturing and transport divisions.

               (*ii*) *Automation* — extension of its use within the
               organization, the problems created, and their
               solutions.

4.20 pm   Question time.

4.50 pm   Close of day's proceedings.

5 pm   Tea will be served in annexe to conference hall.

Wednesday, 13 October, 19..

10 am   *Chairman will open the day's business*, by repeating the
               terms of reference, namely:

               'To look ahead to the day when we shall take a full
               and active part in the European Community ...'
               Discussion.

11 am	Break for coffee, served in the annexe.
11.20 am	*Motions submitted* by Overseas representatives. Questions.
1 pm	Luncheon, served in annexe to conference hall.
2.30 pm	*Motions submitted* by provincial representatives. Questions.
3.30 pm	*Chairman will thank members of the Conference* for the motions submitted and views expressed.
3.40 pm	*Chairman will introduce the next business,* namely:

'Restrictive practices...'

Discussion.

4.20 pm	*Motions submitted* by provincial and overseas representatives. Questions.
4.50 pm	*Close* of day's proceedings.
5 pm	Tea will be served in annexe to conference hall.

Thursday, 14 October, 19..

10 am	*Chairman will open the day's business,* namely:

'Automation — extension of its use . . .'

Discussion.

11 am	Break for coffee, served in the annexe.
11.20 am	*Motions submitted* by provincial and overseas representatives. Questions.
12.30 pm	*Chairman will thank members of the Conference* for the motions submitted and views expressed.
12.40 pm	*The Conference will close with a vote of thanks to be* proposed by the senior Overseas Sales Representative, Mr A.B. Ramsing.
1 pm	Luncheon, for Conference members and guests, at Court Hotel.

(g) *Arrange for printing of documents,* i.e. Conference agenda, invitation and application forms for tickets and accommodation, visits, etc.

(h) *Provisional reservations* for conference hall and hotel accommodation.

(i) *Invitations.* On receipt of documents from printers, issue invitations to provincial and overseas representatives, etc. (To be effective, acceptances must be received by a specified date.)

(j) *Firm reservations.* When acceptances of invitations are received and numbers to be accommodated at conference hall and hotel are known, make firm reservations.

(k) *Arrange visits* to places of interest, etc, and reserve seats where applicable.

(l) *Send conference tickets* to applicants, also (where applicable) receipts for payment in respect of hotel accommodation, etc.

> NOTE: Other documents, such as the detailed agenda, conference handbook, theatre and admission tickets, etc, will be handed out in a cardboard or plastic container to members and guests at the reception.

(m) *Attend conference hall* to make all necessary arrangements re seating, facilities for press (if applicable), stewards, parking, microphones, etc.

> NOTE: These ought to be attended to well in advance of the opening day of the conference.

(n) *Prepare documents.* List all documents required at the conference, arrange in order of use, and check.

(o) *Opening day of conference.*
  (i) *In morning.* Take necessary documents to, and check arrangements at, the conference hall. Attend reception of conference members and guests.
  (ii) *In afternoon.* Attend opening of conference.

3. Arrangements for the annual general meeting of a public company

(a) *Draft the director's report.* As soon as possible after audit of the company's final accounts, the secretary, having been instructed to do so, prepares a draft of the directors' report, the contents of which must follow the requirements of the Companies Act 1985 (s. 235 and Schedule 7). (*See* summaries of statutory and stock exchange requirements in chapter 33, Directors' reports.)

(b) *Prepare a draft notice* of the annual general meeting, bearing in mind that not less than 21 days' notice is required (s. 369).

NOTE: At this stage it is usually advisable to leave blank spaces for date of notice and date of the meeting, as the latter ought to be fixed by and given formal approval of the board.

(c) *Arrange for printing of documents.* Unless it is intended to make use of the company's own form of reproduction, give instructions for the printing of notices, balance sheet, final accounts, and the directors' report.

NOTE: The printers will be required only to set up the type at this stage, and to provide proofs for subsequent board approval.

(d) *Convene a board meeting* to deal with the following business and, where applicable, give formal approval by resolution:

- (*i*) *Directors' report and audited accounts.* Submit a printers' proof of the directors' report and audited accounts for consideration and approval.
- (*ii*) *Authorize the signing of directors' report and accounts* in accordance with requirements of the articles (e.g. two directors may sign the report and the secretary countersign it), and the audited balance sheet in accordance with the requirements of s. 238, i.e. two directors of the company or, if there is only one director, by that one.
- (*iii*) *Approve transfers to various reserves,* where applicable.
- (*iv*) *Recommend the payment of dividend(s),* subject to approval of the company in general meeting.
- (*v*) *Fix a date for the payment of dividend(s),* if applicable.
- (*vi*) *Register of members.* If it is decided to close the register of members, fix the date of closing and the period. Authorize the closing of the register and give instructions to advertise the closing in a newspaper circulating in the district in which the registered office is situated (s. 358).
- (*vii*) *Fix the date, time and place of the annual general meeting,* and give authority for the issue of notices, together with reports and accounts, to those so entitled.
- (*viii*) *Proxies.* Consider whether proxy forms are to be sent along with the report and accounts; if so, authorize their issue.
- (*ix*) *Press notices.* Consider whether to provide a report of the chairman's speech and of the proceedings of the meeting for publication in appropriate newspapers; if so decided, authorize the secretary to that effect.

NOTE: If press representatives are usually present at the company's annual general meetings, the above will not be applicable. Nevertheless, even though press representatives are expected to be present, it is usually advisable to provide them in advance with copies of the chairman's speech, to ensure accuracy.

(e) *Stock Exchange requirements.* On the assumption that the company's shares are 'listed', i.e. that the company has obtained permission to deal on the Stock Exchange:

(i) *Notify the Stock Exchange concerned.* On the day of the board meeting, at which the accounts were approved and dividend recommended, give the Stock Exhange all facts concerning the company's profits and dividends.

NOTE: A specimen form of Preliminary Announcement, drawn up by the London Stock Exchange with the co-operation of various professional bodies, sets out the minimum information that companies should give to their shareholders, the public at large, and the Stock Exchange concerned, in order to ensure uniformity of information.

(ii) *Supply dividend particulars,* on printed form(s) provided by the Stock Exchange, to its Share and Loan Department. This is additional to the information provided in the preliminary announcement, and is required by the Stock Exchange for statistical purposes.

(f) *Press notices.* Supply the various newspapers (either directly or through the company's press agents) with the same information that is given to the Stock Exchange in the preliminary announcement — and at the same time.

(g) *Convene the annual general meeting:*

(i) Give final instructions for the printing of the directors' report and accounts, notices of the meeting — and for any other documents prepared by this time in draft form, e.g. chairman's speech, dividend warrants, proxy forms, etc.

(ii) On receipt of these documents from the printers:

(1) Send notices together with directors' report and accounts to members entitled to attend the meeting.

(2) Send notice also to the company's auditors, as required by s. 387(1) of the Companies Act 1985.

(3) Send copies of the directors' report and accounts *only* to members not entitled to attend the annual general

meeting (e.g. holders of non-voting shares) and debenture holders.

(4) Send *four* copies of the directors' report and accounts to the Share and Loan Department of the Stock Exchange.

NOTE: These must be posted to the Stock Exchange at the same time as the notices and accompanying documents are posted to the members so entitled.

(5) If so decided (*see* (f) above), send, say fifty copies of the report and accounts to the company's press agents for circulation to various newspapers.

(6) Obtain a certificate of posting in all of the above cases.

(h) *Accommodation*. If the meeting is to be held elsewhere than at the company's own premises, reserve a hall or room well in advance.

(i) *Preparation of dividend list*. On the assumption that the members will subsequently approve the board's recommendation at the annual general meeting, the work of preparing the dividend list may be commenced as soon as the closing date for dividends arrives.

(j) *Dividend warrants* may now be prepared from the dividend lists, again on the assumption that the members will approve the board's recommendation. The warrants will not, however, be despatched to members until after the annual general meeting.

(k) *Prepare an agenda*. The notice usually contains a brief agenda which is quite adequate for the main body of members attending, but a more detailed form of agenda may be prepared which will contain the names of proposers and seconders of the various motions to be submitted at the meeting. These will be distributed to the directors and to all proposers and seconders as they arrive at the meeting.

NOTE: Alternatively, the motions to be submitted may be typed on separate slips and handed to the respective proposers before the meeting commences.

(l) *Prepare attendance sheets*. Unless an attendance book is kept for the purpose, prepare attendance sheets. To ensure that a true record is kept, both members (or their proxies) and press representatives should be requested to sign the sheet (or book) on admission.

NOTE: Where it is the practice to send admission tickets along with the notices, arrange for someone to collect them (after signature by the shareholders concerned) and give the same person the additional responsibility of ensuring that all persons attending sign the attendance sheet or book.

(m) *Prepare a list of proxies.* If proxy forms were issued with the notices, carefully examine them and check them with the share register (*see* 22:9). Reject any which do not conform or which are received after the specified time for deposit, then prepare a list of valid proxies.

(n) *Arrangements at the meeting hall.* Make all necessary arrangements at the hall (or other appointed meeting place); for example:

(*i*) Appoint stewards.

(*ii*) Ensure that seating is adequate.

(*iii*) Provide facilities for press representatives.

(*iv*) Check for heating, ventilation, lighting, etc.

(o) *Documents for the meeting.* Prepare and/or have available all records, documents, registers, etc, that are likely to be required at the meeting; in particular:

(*i*) *Agenda,* i.e. spare copies of the brief form of agenda, also copies of the more detailed form of agenda for the chairman, directors, proposers and seconders, referred to in **(k)** above.

(*ii*) *Proxy cards and lists,* i.e. lists of valid proxies.

(*iii*) *Share register.* This may be required for the purpose of checking shareholdings and voting power in the event of a vote by poll. (In the case of a large public company with several thousands of shareholders it would not, of course, be practicable to make the register available at the meeting.)

(*iv*) *Polling lists* may also be made available, if a poll is expected.

(*v*) *Copies of Companies and other relevant Acts.* The secretary may need these for reference purposes.

(*vi*) *Copy of Memorandum of Association* of the company.

(*vii*) *Copy of Articles of Association* of the company.

(*viii*) *Directors' report and accounts.* A few spare copies of these should be available, also a signed copy of the accounts for inspection of the shareholders.

(*ix*) *Register of Directors and Secretaries.* This should be available for reference only, e.g. to ascertain dates of appointment, etc.

(*x*) *Register of Directors' Interests.* Anyone present at the meeting is entitled to inspect this register during the course of the meeting.

(*xi*) *Minute book.* The minute book of general meetings should be available, as *shareholders* are entitled to *inspect* it.

(p) *Attend the meeting hall.* On the day of the meeting, and well in advance of the time it is due to start:

(*i*) Send the above documents to the meeting hall.

(*ii*) Attend the hall, and check all arrangements referred to in **(n)** above.

Progress test 40

1. What arrangements should the secretary make when a visiting speaker is to address a meeting? **(1)**

2. What follow-up arrangements must a secretary undertake after the meeting? **(1)**

3. Draft a timetable of events for a company conference showing the secretary's duties before and after the conference? **(2)**

4. What steps should a secretary take to prepare for a company's annual general meeting? **(3)**

5. List the events for which a secretary should make preparation which may occur during the annual general meeting. **(3)**

Appendix 1
Glossary of terms in relation to meetings

Acclamation. A form of voting, in which those present at a meeting indicate their approval of the motion in no uncertain manner by loud cheering or the clapping of hands, etc. It does not necessarily mean unanimity, but the small minority of dissenting voices (if any) are obviously overwhelmed.

Ad hoc. Literally 'to this' or 'for this'; that is, 'for this purpose', e.g. an *ad hoc* committee is formed for a particular purpose.

Adjournment. The act of extending or continuing a *meeting* for the purpose of dealing with unfinished business, or of deferring the *debate* on a motion which is before a meeting.

Agenda. Literally means 'things to be done', but commonly used to describe the agenda *paper*, which lists the items of business to be dealt with at a meeting.

Agenda paper. A list of items of business to be dealt with at a meeting, indicating the order in which the items will be dealt with — unless the order is altered by the will of the majority.

Amendment. A proposal to alter a motion which has been submitted to a meeting, e.g. by adding, inserting or deleting words of the original motion.

Ballot. A method of voting employed when secrecy is desired, e.g. in Parliamentary and other elections.

Bye-laws. Local laws set up by local authorities; also applied to the internal regulations of a corporate body or of an association.

'Clear days'. Unless otherwise stated in the rules, the number of days specified as the length of time required to convene a meeting must be 'clear days', i.e. they are to be *exclusive* of the day of service of the notice and of the day of the meeting: *Re Railway Sleepers Supply Co.* (1885).

Closure. One of the formal (procedural) motions, which is put in the form 'That the question be now put', with the intention of curtailing discussion on the motion before the meeting and getting a decision upon it (*see also Guillotine* and *Kangaroo* forms of closure).

Committee. A person or body of persons to whom general or specific duties have been delegated by a parent body, e.g. a committee in lunacy may consist of one person appointed by the court.

Debate. Discussion on a motion before a meeting, in which there is argument or reasoning between persons or groups of persons holding differing opinions, prior to putting the motion to the vote of the meeting.

De facto. Actually, in reality.

Defamation. Any statement (written or by word of mouth), picture, effigy or gesture calculated to lower the individual to whom it refers in the estimation of the public or section of the public or to bring him into ridicule or contempt.

Discussion. The general consideration of a subject before a meeting, in which, as far as possible, all persons may be allowed to air their views. Arising out of this discussion, two or more sets of persons holding differing opinions emerge, and this is the stage at which debate commences.

Division. The form of voting more commonly associated with the House of Commons, i.e. the members 'divide', according to whether they are for or against the motion, by proceeding to the respective lobbies. The counting of the votes cast in this way is carried out by tellers.

Dropped motion. A term applied to a motion which, with the consent of the meeting, has been withdrawn, abandoned or allowed to lapse by the original mover. The term is also used to describe a motion which failed to find a seconder, i.e. where the rules require a seconder.

En bloc. When used in connection with meetings, this term usually refers to voting of (say) a committee *en bloc*, i.e. electing or re-electing *all* members of a committee by the passing of *one* resolution. The rules sometimes prohibit this practice.

Ex officio. Literally, by virtue of office or position, as, for example, where a person attends a meeting not in his capacity of member but by virtue of his office; thus, the chairman of the board of a limited company may attend meetings of a committee appointed by the board, not because he is a

member of the committee, but because of his chairmanship of
the board.

Formal motion. A motion intended to alter the procedure of a
meeting, e.g. to curtail discussion, to adjourn the meeting, etc,
and not requiring any previous notice. If misused, it is referred
to as a 'dilatory' motion.

Form of proxy. A document in writing by which one person
authorizes another person to attend a meeting (or meetings)
and vote on his behalf (*see also Proxy*).

Guillotine closure. A form of closure used in the House of Commons,
in which a time limit is fixed for the debate on each section or
stage of a bill. When the time expires, discussion ceases,
whether concluded or not, and the chairman of the committee
concerned has no power to refuse it.

In camera. Held in private, e.g. a meeting or court from which the
public are excluded.

Intra vires. Within the power of the person or body concerned.

Kangaroo closure. A method used in the House of Commons,
whereby the chairman of a committee is empowered to 'jump'
from one amendment to another, omitting those which he
judges to be of minor importance or repetitive. This obviates
much unnecessary discussion, and saves a great deal of time.

Locus standi. Literally, a place of standing, i.e. the lawful or
recognized right of a person to appear and to be heard.

Majority. Unless otherwise indicated, this may be taken to mean a
'simple' majority, i.e. a number which is more than half of the
whole number. Thus, a resolution is passed by a simple
majority where five or more persons vote in its favour out of
a total of nine actually voting.

Minutes. A written record of the business transacted at a meeting.

Month. According to the Interpretation Act 1978, a 'month' means
a *calendar* month, unless otherwise indicated. But a reference
to 'month' in a company's Articles of Association was held to
mean *lunar* month, where the Articles made no provision to
the contrary: *Bruner* v. *Moore* (1904).

Motion. A proposition or proposal put forward for discussion and
decision at a meeting.

Mutatis mutandis. With the necessary alterations.

Nem. con. An abbreviation of *nemine contradicente*, i.e. no one speaking against (a motion or proposal); without contradiction.

Nem. dis. (nemine dissentiente). No one dissenting.

NOTE: *Nem. con.* and *nem. dis.* do not necessarily imply that voting is unanimous.

Omnibus resolution. A resolution containing many parts or items. Unless the parts or items are closely connected, such a resolution is usually considered inadvisable, and may even be forbidden by the rules.

Open voting. Any form of voting 'in public', e.g. on a vote by show of hands, where there is no attempt to preserve secrecy of the voting. It is, therefore, in complete contrast to voting by ballot.

Order of business. The intended order in which the items of business are to be taken at a meeting, as set out in the agenda paper. Nevertheless, it must be borne in mind that the order may be altered by resolution of the meeting.

Order of the Day. An Order of the Day of some business which the House of Commons has ordered to be considered on a particular day, such as the reading of a bill.

Order of speech. The order of speaking during a debate as determined by the chairman. If, however, the order of speaking is disputed, the matter ought to be settled by vote of the meeting.

Ordinary business. What constitutes 'ordinary business' is often defined in the rules, in which case any other business will be regarded as 'special business'.

Plenary power. Full power (for negotiation or decision); e.g. a person or committee may be granted plenary powers.

Point of order. At any meeting, a member may, at any time and without notice, interrupt debate by raising a 'point of order', i.e. by drawing the chairman's attention to some irregularity in the proceedings, such as the use of offensive language, irrelevancy, breach of rules, etc.

Poll. Although the world 'poll' literally means 'a head', i.e. the counting of heads, it is now generally used to describe the method of voting which gives members the right to record their votes proportionately to, say, shares of stock held.

NOTE: There is a common law right to demand a poll unless

excluded by the rules governing the meeting concerned: *R* v. *Wimbledon Local Board* (1882).

Postponement. The action of deferring or delaying a meeting to a later date. The postponement of a meeting which has been properly convened is not permissible at common law: *Smith* v. *Paringa Mines* (1906). The proper course is to hold the meeting and formally adjourn it, without transacting any business.

Previous question. One of the formal (or procedural) motions, which is usually put in the form 'That the question be *not* now put'.

Prima facie. Literally, at the first sight; for example, highly probable *on the face of it.*

Privilege. A peculiar right, advantage, benefit or immunity. As used in relation to the law of defamation, it refers to either of two forms of defence, namely, absolute privilege and qualified privilege.

Procedural motion (*see Formal motion*).

Proxy. Literally, one acting for another, or a document giving authority to one person to act for another. Thus, it may refer to a person appointed to attend a meeting (or meetings) on behalf of the appointor and to vote on his behalf — or to the proxy form on which such authority is given.

Question. A subject for enquiry or discussion. Thus, a motion put to a meeting for its decision is usually referred to as the 'question', e.g. the 'previous question' refers to the original motion.

Quorum. The minimum number of persons entitled to be present at a meeting (or their proxies, if permitted) which the regulations require to be present in order that business of the meeting may be validly transacted.

Requisition. As used in relation to a requisitioned meeting, the action of calling for the convening of a meeting, e.g. a right is sometimes given in the rules entitling a certain specified minority of members to requisition the convening body to call a meeting. The word 'requisition' is also used to describe the document in which the written demand is made.

Rescission. The rescission of a resolution is usually regarded as sufficiently important to merit special treatment; thus, the rules may provide that it cannot be rescinded until a certain time has elapsed and, even then, an extended period of notice may be required for the meeting at which it is proposed to effect the rescission.

Resolution. Although the words 'motion' and 'resolution' are used indiscriminately, a motion is a proposal put to a meeting, whereas a resolution is the *acceptance* of that motion by the meeting.

Rider. An addition of a relative fact or theory to a motion. It is not an amendment, because it does not amend the motion but *adds* to it; and, whereas the addition of words in an amendment usually elucidate and amplify the motion, the addition of a rider *adds a material fact* — usually in the form of a recommendation. Unlike an amendment, a rider can be put either before or after the motion is finally put to the vote.

'Rolled up' plea. The defence of 'fair comment' against an action for defamation is commonly in the form of a 'rolled-up' plea, in the following words: 'In so far as the words consist of allegations of fact, the same are true in substance and in fact; and, in so far as they consist of expressions of opinion, they are fair comment made in good faith and without malice upon the said facts, which are matters of public interest.'

Scrutineer. One who closely examines; for example, the chairman may appoint scrutineers to represent each side at an election, for the purpose of checking the validity of the votes. After the votes have been counted, and checked, the scrutineers complete a report to the chairman in which they state the result of the voting.

Second speech. Usually each member is allowed *one* speech upon each separate motion. As a rule, only the mover of the motion is allowed second speech; that is, he is given the right of reply.

NOTE: The right to second speech is *not* usually given to the mover of an amendment.

Service by post. In some cases, the rules provide a formula for determining when a notice sent through the post is deemed to have been served. If, however, the rules make no such provision, the Interpretation Act 1978 will apply, i.e. unless the contrary is proved service is deemed to have been effected at the time at which a letter would be delivered in the ordinary course of post. *See: Bradman* v. *Trinity Estates plc* (1989)

Sine die. Without an appointed day; indefinitely. Thus, a meeting adjourned *sine die* necessitates fresh notice for the adjourned meeting.

NOTE: This provides an exception to the position at Common Law, namely, that fresh notice of an adjourned meeting need not be given, unless the rules demand it: *Wills* v. *Murray* (1850).

Special business. All business other than that which, according to the rules, constitutes 'ordinary business'. Meetings convened for the purpose of transacting special business often require longer than the usual period of notice. The notice convening the meeting should be explicit, and must draw attention to the fact that special business is to be transacted.

Special proxy. A proxy appointed for one meeting only; the proxy form on which the authority is given requires *no* stamp. On the other hand, a 'general ' proxy covers more than one meeting.

Standing orders. The name given to the rules regulating the conduct and procedure of certain deliberative and legislative bodies, such as the permanent standing orders of local authorities.

Status quo. The existing state of affairs; thus, to 'preserve the *status quo*' is to allow the original state of affairs to remain unchanged.

Sub-committee. A committee appointed by the parent committee for a certain specific purpose, or to relieve the larger committee of some routine work. It usually consists of some of the members of the appointing committee, but specialist non-members may be co-opted to a sub-committee where necessary and where the rules permit.

Substantive motion. Literally, an independent motion. Thus, the term is applied to the motion which replaces the original one after amendments approved by the meeting have been incorporated in it. If the substantive motion is rejected, the original one is not revived.

Suspension of standing orders. Provision is usually made for the suspension of standing orders in cases of urgency or for special purposes. As a rule, a certain specified majority of the members is required to authorize the suspension, e.g. a two-thirds or three-fourths majority may be required.

Teller One who 'tells', e.g. one who counts votes. Two or more tellers may be appointed when a division takes place. In the

House of Commons, for example, there are two tellers appointed for each party, and it is their duty to count the votes 'for' and 'against' as the members proceed to their respective lobbies.

Ultra vires. Beyond the legal power or authority of (say) a company; for example, a company may act *'ultra vires'* if it exceeds the authority it derives from the 'objects' clause of its Memorandum of Association.

Unan. Unanimously, e.g. 'carried unanimously' indicates that a motion or proposal has been agreed to by all present at the meeting.

Una voce. With one voice, i.e. unanimously. Another term used to indicate that all present agree to a motion or proposal put to the meeting.

Unlawful assembly. Although a meeting may be lawful in other respects, it may become an 'unlawful assembly' if the conduct of its members is such as to give rise to fears of a breach of the peace.

Vice versa. The reverse; contrariwise; the terms or the case being reversed.

Waiver of notice. The process of waiving entitlement to notice of a meeting. Such waiver may be expressly given; for example, where *all* entitled to attend agree to excuse lack of notice. In many cases, however, the rules protect the convenors if they inadvertently omit to send notice to a member.

Appendix 2
Examination technique

Preliminaries

1. Preparation

Ample preparation, followed by thorough revision to consolidate the knowledge already gained, is necessary for any examination. Without it, a list of examination hints is virtually useless. Nevertheless, even well-prepared candidates can fail through faulty presentation of work, waste of valuable time, and irrelevancy; it is for such candidates that these hints have been compiled.

2. In the examination room

Even before you come to grips with the actual questions on the examination paper, you can improve upon, or mar, your chances; therefore, at this stage, the following points ought to be borne in mind:

(a) *Read carefully* the instructions on the outside cover of the answer book. This particularly important in sectionalised examination papers.

(b) *Supply the information required* on the outside cover, e.g. date, subject, candidate's letter and number.

(c) *Follow carefully the other instructions* as and when they become applicable, e.g. it is customary to require candidates finally to list their answers in order attempted.

(d) *Write answers legibly* on both sides of the paper provided, but commence each answer on a fresh sheet. An instruction to this effect is usually given on the outside cover.

(e) *Number the answers*. Be careful to number the answers so as to indicate the questions to which they refer and, where applicable, continue the numbering on to any additional sheet or sheets.

(f) *Use the paper provided.* Usually the examining body provides headed paper, with spaces left for subject, and candidate's identification letter and number. This paper only must be used and the spaces properly completed.

3. Planning the approach

Having followed and/or memorized the procedural instructions, the candidate may now turn to the examination paper itself. *This is the crucial stage of the examination*, and the following suggestions for a planned approach are not to be regarded as wasteful of time; just the reverse, in fact, as an answer which has been planned (and is, therefore, logically arranged) saves time in the writing of it and, moreover, avoids much repetition. Another important advantage is that the finished answer will be less haphazard, easier to mark; therefore, the examiner is less likely to miss the points you have attempted to make, and may even be sufficiently appreciative to award bonus marks for a well-planned answer.

(a) *Read carefully through the examination paper.* This enables you to get a general impression of the nature and apparent difficulty (or relative simplicity) of the questions, from which you can plan your approach.

(b) *Read the instructions.* Return to the beginning of the paper to read (or re-read) the instructions, e.g. number of questions to be attempted overall and (where applicable) from each section of the paper; compulsory questions, if any; number of marks allotted to each question, where some questions carry higher marks than others, and any other special instructions.

(c) *Allot the available time* according to the number of questions to be answered, taking into account those cases where some questions earn higher marks than others. An allowance of, say, five or ten minutes ought to be made for the final reading through of the answers.

(d) *Choose the first question* to be attempted. Obviously, it is quite unnecessary to answer the questions in the same order as they appear in the paper, but the candidate must decide at this point whether to deal first with a compulsory question (where applicable), one of the questions earning higher marks, or one of the simpler (or shorter) questions earning lower marks. So long as the compulsory questions are not overlooked, the choice is not vitally important, although it is usually advisable to deal first with a question that you feel is well within your ability to handle. A good start engenders confidence, and may well boost morale.

(e) *Plan the answer* to the first question. Having read the question again in order to understand clearly what is required, it will probably be found that it consists of two, three or more distinct parts. Underline the key word of each part and then make a note of the various key words on a separate rough working sheet. Alongside, or underneath, each key word jot down your ideas at random, leaving space for any after-thoughts. Rearrange the various points you have made and commit them to your examination script in a logical sequence. In this way you will ensure that each part of the question is dealt with; moreover, you are less likely to omit important points which the examiner is looking for in the answer.

Plan the answers to the remaining questions in the same way.

4. Rough notes on working papers

If you use a separate sheet (or sheets) for rough notes, it should be securely attached to the examination script, but you must be careful to cancel the sheet or mark it clearly as 'rough notes'. Failure to do this might cause some confusion for the examiner — and prove disastrous for you.

Answering the questions

The foregoing hints might well be applied to practically any written examination, but it is now necessary to deal specifically with examinations in Meetings — Law and Practice. Questions on this subject are, obviously, capable of classification under these two broad headings.

1. Law of meetings

In answering questions of this type, the following points ought to be borne in mind:

(a) Always be careful to differentiate between the general and the particular; that is, between common law rules and the rules laid down by statute or the articles of a limited company. It is a common fault of examination candidates to give a list of 'rules' taken, perhaps, from Table A, and to give the impression that they are *general* rules.

(b) The examination candidate is required not only to know and understand the law of meetings, but also to be able to *apply* it. Consequently, most examination papers contain one or more questions which introduce a legal problem. Questions of this type are not necessarily capable of a decisive answer; if, however, you give a well-reasoned answer, you will certainly earn good marks. However, many students fail to overcome the first hurdle of problem questions — identifying the issues raised. This may be overcome by the regular practice of answering problem type questions.

(c) It is often advisable to cite cases to support statements or arguments, particularly in dealing with questions of this type. When citing cases, accuracy is, of course, *essential*; nevertheless, it is suggested that you need not refrain from citing a case merely because you are not entirely certain of the full names of the parties to it, or of the date, e.g. *Eley* v. *Positive Government Security Life Assurance Co.* (1876) might reasonably be cited as 'Eley's Case'.

2. Preparation of documents, etc

(a) *Notices.* If a question calls for the preparation of a notice of a *company's* general meeting, the special requirements of the Act in that connection must be taken into consideration. Unless these special requirements are known, the candidate would be well advised (if a choice is given) to prepare a notice for an unincorporated body.

(b) *Minutes.* When drafting minutes of a meeting, care must be taken not to fall into the common fault of report-writing. Arguments for and against a motion are *not* required, nor are the secretary's own comments on the decisions of the meeting. Ideally, minutes ought to be a well-balanced blending of both minutes of resolution and minutes of narration.

(c) *Resolutions.* Considerable care should be exercised in the drafting of specimen resolutions; in particular, it is important to ensure that the resolution becomes effective as and when it is intended to become effective. There is often some criticism of the 'old-fashioned jargon' which is still frequently employed in the drafting of resolutions; nevertheless, the use of the phrase ' ... be and it is hereby ... ' *does* ensure that the resolution concerned becomes immediately effective. On the other hand, candidates are advised *not* to use the phrase merely for the sake of using it; obviously, it must not be used in a resolution which is to have effect as from some future date.

Appendix three
Specimen examination questions

Chapter 1
1. What is a public meeting? How does a public meeting differ from a private meeting? Consider whether there is a right, direct or indirect, to hold a public meeting, making references, as appropriate, to statute and case law. ICSA June 1982

Chapter 2
2. 'A meeting is the coming together of at least two persons for any lawful purpose' (*Sharp* v. *Dawes* (1876)). Explain fully the requisites of a valid meeting and outline any exceptions to the above statement. ICSA June 1980

3. For a meeting to take place there must be a plurality of persons (*Sharp* v. *Dawes* (1876)) and the meeting must have a chairman. Outline the circumstances where one person may constitute a meeting and explain briefly the powers and duties of a chairman. ICSA June 1990.

4. **(a)** Discuss the requisites of a valid meeting, illustrating your answer by reference to decided cases.
(b) Mr Smith wishes to challenge the validity of a meeting of his local workingmen's club at which a resolution expelling him from membership for failure to pay his membership subscription was passed. Mr Smith alleges that the secretary omitted to send him a notice of the meeting and that the notice sent to other members did not contain the resolution proposing his expulsion. In the absence of the chairman, the latter's role was assumed by the secretary who failed to obtain the consent of the meeting to his assumption of this role. When the resolution was passed, only four members including Mr Smith remained present, whereas a quorum for such meetings is six. Mr Smith, who was prevented from speaking in his own defence, has a receipt for his subscription fee, payment of which was not recorded in the club's books owing to a clerical error. Advise Mr Smith. ICSA June 1986.

Chapter 3
5. Consider the value of formal rules of debate to all types of

organizations in which meetings are held, and explain briefly the matters which should be covered by such rules. ICSA June 1982.

6. The Prestown Business Association has been operating for the last 3 years without any rules and a dispute between members has highlighted the need for a written constitution. As secretary of the association you have been requested to draft an outline of the rules required for the conduct of the annual general meeting. ICSA December 1990.

Chapter 4
7. **(a)** Mr Duncan has recently been invited to become the secretary of the 'Law and Order Society'. The Society is currently in the process of formation. You are asked to advise Mr Duncan on the qualities required of the chairman and the duties and privileges which go with such a position.
(b) The Society's constitution is currently being drafted by founding members. Advise them of the rules concerning the appointment and removal of the chairman and any powers which might be given to him in addition to those at common law. ICSA June 1986.

8. You are the Assistant Secretary employed by the Good Deeds Society. The Society has recently appointed a new chairman of its board of management who has sought advice on the duties and privileges attached to this office in order to prepare himself for a forthcoming meeting. The secretary of the Society is currently visiting Africa on a fact-finding mission and you are acting as his deputy. You are required to write a memorandum outlining the powers and duties of a chairman. ICSA December 1990.

9. **(a)** Outline the powers and duties of the chairman of a meeting.
(b) The rules of the Athletes Anonymous Association provide that the chairman may adjourn a meeting when so requested by the majority of members present. At a meeting called to decide on the measures to be taken in respect of urgent repairs to the clubhouse the majority of members present request an adjournment. Mr Pastit, the chairman, believing that it is most important to continue with the meeting, refuses to adjourn it. Advise Mr Pastit whether his decision may be upheld if questioned in a court of law. ICSA December 1991.

Chapter 5
10. **(a)** Discuss the importance of agendas in organizing effective meetings by reference to the form, preparation and contents of agendas and their relationship with minutes.
(b) Draft a short agenda for a committee meeting of an organization of your own choosing amongst the contents of which are some very contentious issues. Give reasons for the order of business which you have chosen. ICSA June 1986.

11. 'It is impossible to lay down a standard method of preparing an agenda paper as so much depends on the nature and importance of the meeting concerned?' Discuss this statement using as many practical examples as possible in your answer. What points ought to be borne in mind in most cases? ICSA June 1988

12. (a) You are the Honorary Secretary of the Talkham Debating Society. Explain the procedure which you would adopt when preparing an agenda paper for the following:
    (i) The monthly meeting of the management committee;
    (ii) the annual general meeting.
(b) Draft the agenda for the annual general meeting. ICSA December 1991.

Chapter 6
13. (a) Explain what forms or methods may be used to give notice of a meeting and the principal contents of such notice.
(b) Draft a simple form of notice embodying a skeleton form agenda.
(c) Explain when such notice is 'served'. ICSA December 1986.

14. (a) Draft the notice of a meeting of an organization of your choice. (7 marks)
(b) Advise the new chairman of your organization on the law relating to entitlement to notice, period of notice and method of service. (13 marks). ICSA December 1988.

15. Mr N. A. Ive has recently been appointed as Chairman of the Greenfingers Gardening Society and has discovered that, although a committee has been appointed at the annual general meeting, it had never met formally. Mr Ive wishes to cultivate a more formal approach to the management of the Society and wishes to convene a committee meeting, but examination of the constitution reveals only one relevant rule which states 'All members of the committee must be given notice of the meetings.' You are required:
(a) to advise Mr Ive on the law relating to entitlement to notice, period of notice and method of service;
(b) to draft an appropriate notice for the above meeting. ICSA June 1990.

Chapter 7
16. 'At common law, apart from any specific provision, the acts of a corporation must be done by a majority of the corporators, corporately assembled.' Discuss and explain this statement with particular emphasis on the common law of, and specific rules relating to, the quorum. ICSA December 1989.

17. Explain the principle of quorum in meetings and consider the effect of the absence of a quorum at a meeting. ICSA December 1982.

Chapter 8
18. A notice convening a meeting states as an item of special business the

appointment of a manager at a salary of £11,500 per annum. A member proposes an amendment to substitute £14,500 for the sum stated in the notice.
(a)   Discuss in the context of the rules on amendments.
(b)   Explain the grounds for the valid rejection of an amendment. ICSA December 1987.

19. (a) Outline the principal rules governing amendments of motions which may be expressly stated in an organization's rules or merely implied, and
(b)   outline one of the procedures for dealing with amendments. ICSA June 1988.

20. (a) Explain the terms 'original motion', 'amendment' and 'substantive motion'.
(b)   Illustrate, by the use of suitable examples, how a motion becomes substantive. ICSA December 1990.

Chapters 9 and 10
21.   Explain the meaning and consequences of adoption and rejection of four formal or dilatory motions.

22. (a) Explain how the procedural motion 'that the question be not now put' should be dealt with by the chairman of a meeting when it is used:
    (i)   as a formal motion, and
    (ii) as a dilatory motion.
(b)   Describe by reference to decided cases when an adjournment motion should be accepted by the chairman. ICSA June 1991.

Chapter 11
23.   'The right is in the assembly itself; for if they be an assembly all consisting of equals, and there is no custom or rule of law to direct the adjournment, the right must be in the persons which constitute the assembly.' (Per Lord Hardwicke in *Staughton* v. *Reynolds* 1737). Discuss this statement by reference to decided cases. ICSA June 1986.

24. (a) 'Adjournment is the act of extending or continuing a meeting for the purpose of dealing with unfinished business.' (*Scadding* v. *Lorant* (1851)). Explain this statement by reference to why and how a meeting may be adjourned.
(b)   the rules of the Globe Trotters Society provide that 'the Chairman may adjourn a meeting when so requested by the majority of members present'. At a meeting called to decide on very urgent matters the majority of members present request an adjournment. Mr Fliehie, the chairman, believing that it is most important to continue with the meeting, refuses to adjourn it. Advise Mr Fliehie whether his decision may be upheld if questioned in a court of law. ICSA June 1988.

25. (a) Explain, by reference to decided cases, the grounds on which a meeting can be adjourned.

(b) Distinguish a postponement from an adjournment, and explain the circumstances under which a postponement is possible. ICSA December 1991.

Chapter 12
26. Explain the functions of minutes and the essentials of good minute writing. Illustrate your answer by drafting the minutes of a meeting of an organization of your choosing which include *inter alia*:
(a) the re-election of the chairman and treasurer;
(b) the appointment of a new secretary;
(c) the appointment of legal and financial advisers on a retainer;
(d) the decision to invite a famous person as a guest speaker at a future event;
(e) the discussion of a contentious issue raised under 'any other business'. ICSA June 1989.

27. (a) Discuss the essentials of good minute writing and explain the circumstances, if any, in which minutes may be altered.
(b) The Kindness and Help Association's Management Committee is holding one of its monthly meetings and the agenda items include a discussion of the Association's financial position, the filling of a casual vacancy caused by the death of a member of the committee and applications by various local charities for grants which are granted periodically by the Association. You are required to draft the minutes of this meeting for the above items. ICSA June 1990.

28. (a) What is the purpose of keeping minutes of a meeting?
(b) Draft appropriate minutes for the following items of business transacted at the annual general meeting of a sports association:
  (i) The raising of registration fees to £50 and annual subscriptions to £100 from £25 and £75 respectively;
  (ii) The removal of Cheetham & Sons as auditors and the appointment of K. Dodds & Co. as replacements. ICSA June 1991.

Chapter 13
29. 'When a meeting is required to carry out a judicial or quasi-judicial function, it is implicit that in the exercise of that function, fairness and honesty of purpose should be shown.' Discuss this statement in the context of the law and procedure of meetings.

30. 'The various committees of a club or society owe a duty to the members to enforce the rules of the organization fairly.' Evaluate this statement by reference to decided cases in the context of the law of meetings. ICSA December 1990.

31. The Association of Childrens' Entertainers' disciplinary committee is meeting to consider the case of Mr Broom, one of its members, who has recently been convicted of a serious public order offence committed at a football match. Mr Broom has received a notice of the meeting which states that he may appear before the committee and make representations. At the meeting Mr Broom's solicitor is prevented from representing him and the committee allow Mr Broom to make a five-minute speech in his own defence. The committee decide to terminate Mr Broom's membership and to withdraw his membership card. This action will seriously restrict the types of engagement which Mr Broom will be able to obtain. The Association's rules state *inter alia* that: 'A member may be expelled from membership where his/her conduct as an entertainer is, in the opinion of the committee, incompatible with the standards of the association' and 'Members are not entitled to legal representation before membership or disciplinary committees.' Advise Mr Broom on the validity of this meeting and whether there is any basis for challenging the decision. ICSA December 1991.

Chapter 14
32. The Society for Bewigged Lawyers is holding a conference on proposed changes to their rules of practice which will have far-reaching effects on the level of competition and earnings of the profession. Lord Slutch gives a passionate speech against the reforms describing them as 'the ill-considered ramblings of an incompetent government department which like its Chief Officer (a public figure) does not have the experience to understand the workings and advantages of the profession'. The next speaker, Sir Blink, responds by describing the current practices of the Bewigged Lawyers as 'the most blatant closed shop in the country which often houses the incompetent and the mediocre sons of the wealthy, who owe their careers more to their background than their talent, the previous speaker not excepted'. These extracts are reported verbatim in the national press, on radio and television. Advise whether any person has been defamed and outline any possible defences to an action of defamation in the circumstances. ICSA December 1989.

33. The Ecclesiastical Guild, a body with about 20,000 members, was granted a Royal Charter in 1983. At the 1990 Annual General Meeting the agenda contained an item which indicated the Committee's recommendation that the sale of one of the Guild properties to the Society for Rural Pastimes should be completed. Representatives of the press and of the local radio were invited to the meeting by the General Secretary of the Guild acting on the instructions of the committee. A small but vociferous section of the meeting was strongly opposed to the sale and during the debate one of these, Mr Bold, stated that the sale was evil and that it was only supported by the Committee for their own financial interests and that the result would be a boost to a Society which encourages killing and generally spoils the countryside. Mr Bold went on to demand the Chairman's resignation. The Chairman stated that Mr Bold was talking nonsense. Mr Bold repeated these remarks on the local radio station later the same evening and the meeting was reported in the *Daily Gossip* the following morning, the Guild's monthly journal and the

Society's journal which is published every two months. Mr Bold's statement and the Chairman's reply were reported verbatim in each of the above publications. Consider whether the Committee, the Chairman or Mr Bold have been defamed and outline any possible defences to any actions for defamation in these circumstances. ICSA December 1990.

34. Explain the principles of the tort of defamation and explain how these relate to:
    (i) the holding of meetings, and;
    (ii) the reporting of meetings. ICSA December 1991.

Chapter 15
35. The Witnesses of Wonder are holding a religious rally in a public park and have engaged the services of Ecclesiastical Brass, a uniformed brass band, to provide appropriate music. As part of the service Sister Angelica, a committed Witness, makes frequent presentations on the need to live a pure life. During one of these presentations Sid Stockbroker and a group of his colleagues, who have just left a nearby public house, enter the park. Sid begins to heckle Angelica with abusive words and gestures and heated exchanges and scuffles break out. At the same time Mr D. Fence, who is instructing a small group of martial arts students, screams whilst demonstrating a flying kick. In the resulting confusion the police arrive and, thinking there is a riot, arrest Sister Angelica, the conductor of the band and Mr Fence. Discuss these events in the context of public meetings and public order, referring to relevant case law and statutory authority wherever possible. ICSA June 1990.

36. Monofulcrum (Wigtown) plc is the major employer in Wigtown and several small businesses in the town are dependent on orders from the company for their economic survival. Recently, there have been rumours that Monofulcrum are to merge with another company and to close down its operations in Wigtown. The Managing Director of Monofulcrum is anxious to dispel the rumours and to assure the local community that any planned mergers will be for the benefit of both the company and the town. He has decided that the best way to do this is to hold a public meeting in the town. There are three possible venues for this meeting:
(a) the civic hall which has a very limited capacity;
(b) the local sports stadium on the outskirts of the town;
(c) the market square in the centre of town.
It is expected that the meeting will arouse considerable local interest and that some local political groups and a national environmental group may organize some form of demonstration to disrupt the meeting. You are Assistant Company Secretary of Monofulcrum (Wigtown) plc and have been requested to write a memorandum to the Managing Director outlining the advantages and disadvantages of each of the possible venues and explaining the relevant provisions of statute and common law in respect of holding public meetings. Write the memorandum. ICSA June 1991.

37. The Society for the Protection of Endangered Species is planning to hold a protest march from The Shay to the Racecourse and there to present a petition concerning the local police authority's poor record on public protection to the Mayor of Oblivion, who will be attending an event, on the same day. The Society also intends to hold a rally at the Racecourse following the march. The march and rally are planned for Wednesday which is the local market day, and it is anticipated that some road congestion may result. Several well-known politicians, notorious for making provocative speeches, have agreed to speak at the rally. There are rumours that radical members of the local farming community may attempt to hold a counter demonstration. Advise the Society of the legal implication of their proposals in the context of the law of meetings. The Society would like to know whether they need to obtain permission from any authority to hold their march and rally. ICSA December 1991.

Chapters 16 and 17
38. Brian is the Managing Director and major shareholder in Plugs Ltd, a family company. After a blazing row with Robert, one of his sons, who is a director and minority shareholder in Plugs Ltd, Brian calls a meeting of the directors at short notice. Robert is deliberately not informed of this. At that meeting, the directors decide that Robert is no longer a director. When Able, the company secretary, points out that this is irregular, Brian calls for an extraordinary general meeting to be held within the week. At this meeting the family shareholders, cajoled by Brian, resolve to dismiss Robert from his directorship. A consent to short notice is prepared by Able two days later and is signed shortly thereafter by the family shareholders who were present at the extraordinary general meeting. Advise on the legality of these events in the context of company meetings and advise Brian on the correct procedures for the removal of a director. Plug Ltd's Articles of Association are in Table A form. ICSA December 1986.

39. Electrobrit plc is a public company which is quoted on the unlisted securities market. The company has recently run into difficulties owing to adverse market conditions and a series of management mistakes. Advise the following persons, who are concerned about the situation and seek to call an extraordinary general meeting, on their rights to do so and the procedures involved:
(a) (i) the auditor who is currently considering resignation;
    (ii) two of the twelve directors who are concerned about the situation;
    (iii) a group of shareholders who collectively hold 11 per cent of the share capital;
    (iv) the recently appointed Director of Finance who has just discovered that the net assets of Electrobrit plc are substantially below its called-up share capital. (15 marks)
(b) How, if at all, would your answer differ if the board of directors decided to convene an extraordinary general meeting in response to the

request of the parties as in **(a)** above but which is to be held on a date in three months' time? (5 marks) ICSA December 1988.

40. Mr N. A. Ive has just been appointed as the Managing Director of Wedoitall plc, a holding company with some 39 subsidiaries which include all possible types of company, some of these have their own specifically designed articles of association, the remainder relying on Table A. Mr Ive has become very confused as to the requirements of the Companies Acts and Table A, in respect of the circumstances in which the various types of meeting should be convened and the periods of notice to be given for meetings and resolutions for these companies. He has asked you, as Secretary, to tabulate these provisions so that he has a quick reference guide to the need to hold meetings and the minimum periods of notice required. Tabulate and advise Mr Ive on these provisions. ICSA June 1991.

Chapters 18 and 28
41. The articles of association of Condor Ltd are in Table A form. The acting directors, Morriss, Herbert and Jake, hold a meeting to discuss potential contracts with third parties. The meeting resolves to purchase coal for the company's boilers from Anthracite Ltd. Herbert does not disclose that he is a shareholder of Anthracite Ltd and is entitled to a shareholder's commission in return for obtaining orders for Anthracite. Herbert voted in favour of the contract. Jake votes in favour of a contract with Delius Ltd, though he does not disclose that he is a director of Delius and has been promised a commission of £500 if Condor Ltd enter into the contract with Delius Ltd. Morriss has never been properly appointed as a director. Discuss the validity of the meeting. ICSA December 1987.

42. Goget Ltd has recently suffered financial loss and damage because of infringement of its trade mark and the passing off of products very similar to its own by a company called Dareget Ltd. Two of Goget directors A and B are major shareholders in Dareget Ltd. At a meeting of Goget's board of directors attended by A and B, who keep their interest in Dareget Ltd secret, the board resolve by a bare majority not to proceed with legal action against Dareget on the basis of costs. A group of dissatisfied shareholders attends the A.G.M. of Goget Ltd which is held six weeks later at which three ordinary resolutions, *inter alia*, are passed. The first resolution removes A and B from their directorships, the second replaces them with C and D who are in favour of legal action and the third resolves that Goget Ltd should commence legal proceedings against Dareget Ltd. Discuss the legal and procedural implications of these events in the context of the law of company meetings. Goget Ltd's articles of association are in Table A Form. ICSA June 1989.

43. Raider plc has a board of directors consisting of 20 executive and 10 non-executive directors. Raider plc launches a takeover bid for Winnow plc on the basis of a decision taken at a meeting of the full board of directors. Simpkin and three other directors form a committee of the board for the purpose of conducting the bid. The full board has delegated its own powers collaterally to the committee. The committee votes to use the services of MEC Ltd in association with the takeover. Simpkin votes in favour of this contract, is counted in the quorum at that meeting but fails to disclose that he is a major shareholder of MEC Ltd as well as an employee of it. Simpkin does most of the work for MEC Ltd which subsequently presents a bill for £2.5 million. Advise Raider plc on the validity of these events on the basis of the relevant law of company meetings and whether any principle of company meetings law has been broken which will enable them to refuse payment to MEC Ltd. Assume that the articles of Raider plc are in Table A form. ICSA December 1989.

Chapter 19

44. (a) Explain the difference between ordinary, extraordinary and special resolutions giving examples of how and when each type is used or required by law, and
(b) the Companies Act 1985 requires the filing of special and extraordinary resolutions with the Registrar of Companies. Give examples of other resolutions which must be similarly filed or registered. ICSA June 1988.

45. (a) The two directors of Ready Ltd, a small private company, have been involved in a serious motorway accident. One has just died as a result. The survivor, Jim, wishes to pass a board resolution very urgently. The company's articles are in Table A form. Advise him of the various ways, if any, in which he can achieve this, and
(b) by reference to appropriate authorities, explain how and to what extent, if any, a valid resolution of the company may be passed without holding a meeting. ICSA December 1991.

Chapter 20

46. Consider fully who has the right to vote at company meetings. ICSA December 1975.

47. Alfred has recently inherited a substantial proportion of the equity shares in Beta Ltd. Alfred is now a full-time manager and a director of Beta Ltd. He seeks your advice on the law concerning his wish:
(a) to use or cast his vote at company meetings as he pleases (5 marks);
(b) to vote in favour of an alteration of articles which proposes to increase his shares voting rights by the creation of a special class of management shares; (7 marks) and
(c) to vote contrary to a proposal for legal action against directors who have taken on work in their private capacities, which was originally intended for Beta Ltd. Alfred is one of the directors involved. (8 marks) ICSA December 1988.

Chapters 21 and 22

48. What are the advantages and drawbacks to the board of directors of a public company of the right of shareholders to demand a poll at the Annual General Meeting? By whom must the demand be made and when must the poll be taken? ICSA December 1980.

49. Electroplasm plc's board of directors resolves to recommend a reduction of share capital by replacing participating preference shares with unsecured loan stock at 6 per cent interest p.a. Gotham Assurance plc is against the proposed reduction. Gotham hold 29 per cent of the affected preference shares and 15 per cent of the ordinary voting shares. Gotham requisition an extraordinary general meeting of Electroplasm plc. The latter's board convene a meeting 12 days after receipt of the requisition. The meeting is to be held in four months' time. At the meeting a poll is demanded on the issue of reduction of capital. The motion for reduction is carried by a majority achieved by the Chairman Basil using a large number of proxy votes. The proxies held by Basil were only deposited with Electroplasm plc six hours before the meeting. Electroplasm's articles of association are in Table A form. Advise Gotham Assurance plc on the regularity of these events and whether they may be able to challenge the reduction of capital at any other meetings required to be held by company law. ICSA June 1989.

50. Derek and Mavis between them hold 26 per cent of the shares in Parsnips plc. On the 1st April, they deposit at the company's registered office a requisition of an extraordinary general meeting, stating as its objective, the removal of all the current board of directors and the approval of a reduction in capital of £200,000. On the 19th April, the directors decided to convene the meeting for the 3rd August. When the meeting is held, an amendment is proposed whereby only the Managing Director, Victor, ought to be removed from his office. This amendment is carried by the Chairman, Mike, purporting to exercise his casting vote. The removal of Mike is subsequently voted on in a poll which has been demanded by Derek and Mavis. Fifty-eight per cent of votes cast are in favour of Mike's removal including 7 per cent of proxy votes which were deposited at the company's registered office, 36 hours before the meeting. On the vote for reduction of capital, only 60 per cent of the votes cast are in favour of the resolution. Discuss the validity of these events in the context of the law and procedure of company meetings. The articles of association of Parsnips plc are in Table A form. ICSA December 1991.

Chapter 23
51. Why is there an obligation to keep minutes of company general meetings? Where should such minutes be kept and who has the right to inspect them? ICSA December 1982.

52. You are required to draft the full minutes of the annual general meeting of a company at which a director was removed from office and the retiring auditors were not reappointed. ICSA June 1976.

Chapters 24–27

53. The Justin Time plc (a recently incorporated company) has just appointed a former politician as Chairman of its board of directors. The Chairman has requested information about the legal position relating to annual general meetings of the company. Specifically he has asked, when must meetings be held, what business must be transacted and what would happen if the company failed to comply with the legal requirements? As assistant secretary of Justin Time plc you have been asked to deal with the Chairman's request for information. You are required to provide the above information in tabular form along with any other related information you consider would be of help to the Chairman. ICSA December 1990.

54. Explain the statutory provisions in respect of the convening of extraordinary general meetings of a company. ICSA June 1990.

55. Brogan is an executive Director of Fleecem Ltd. Graham and Eric, two of the shareholder directors, wish to remove Brogan from office as soon as possible, even though his term of office and current contract of service still have over 12 months to run. Advise Graham and Eric of the procedures, meetings and resolutions necessary to fulfil their objective of removing Brogan from his office of director. ICSA December 1989.

56. Cleo plc has called a class meeting of its preference shareholders for the purpose of altering their class rights. Assume that Cleo plc has articles in Table A form. Advise on the general provisions of the Companies Acts and Articles which apply to such a meeting. ICSA December 1989.

57. Explain what meetings, procedures and resolutions may be needed in any two of the following:
(a)   a reduction of share capital;
(b)   a purchase of a company's own shares;
(c)   an alteration of share class rights contained in the articles which are in Table A form;
(d)   authorizing directors to allot shares. ICSA June 1989.

58. Sylvia has been appointed as first Chairperson of the Board of Directors of Seethrough Ltd, a double-glazing company. You are the company secretary and are required to write a memorandum to Sylvia explaining the business which is normally conducted at the first meeting of the board of directors and at subsequent meetings of the board. ICSA December 1991.

(Chapter 28 *See* Chapter 18)

Chapter 29

59. (a) Explain how the use of committees may enhance the performance of a Board of Directors of a company and give examples of the functions which may be delegated to such committees.
(b)   Describe the principal forms of committee. ICSA June 1991.

60. You are the company secretary of Profitcentre plc whose articles are in Table A form. Mr L. Earner has just been appointed Chairman of the board and needs guidance on his powers and duties. Write a report to Mr Earner explaining the rules relating to the conduct of board meetings and the use of committees. ICSA June 1990.

Chapters 30–33
61. Explain the type and purpose of meetings which may be held when a company is wound up by order of the court. ICSA December 1990.

62. Crazy Care Ltd is a large private company which, because of financial difficulties, has petitioned the court for an order of administration. The petition has been granted and Pluto is appointed administrator in May 1989. Pluto has now prepared a statement of his proposals for achieving the purposes of the administration order. Advise him of the meetings which he must now call including the procedures involved and the purpose and power of such meetings. ICSA June 1989.

63. Outline the nature and sequence of meetings of members which are held in a members' voluntary winding up of a company. Refer to the convention, business and chairmanship of the meetings. ICSA December 1982.

Chapters 34–37
64. (a) Explain how the use of committees may enhance the efficiency of a local authority and give examples of the disposal of local authority business by means of committees and sub-committees.
(b) Describe the principal forms of committee. ICSA June 1991.

65. Explain the rules relating to the calling and conduct of local authority meetings. ICSA June 1991.

66. Explain what meetings may and must be held by:
(a) principal councils;
(b) parish and community councils, and
(c) explain how such meetings are summoned. ICSA June 1990.

67. The notice summoning a meeting of Bedrock City Council states that the business to be transacted is consideration of tenders for construction of the new city hall and any other business. A summons is not sent to Councillor Rubble, who is known to be touring the Amazon on a fact-finding tour in relation to the destruction of the rain forests. At the meeting Councillor Stone, an independent, takes part in considering tenders and votes in favour of the tender supplied by Stone Quarry Ltd which is successful in obtaining the contract. Councillor Stone does not reveal that his father-in-law is a director and substantial shareholder in Stone Quarry Ltd. Under the heading of any other business, Councillor Flintstone, leader of the majority party, puts forward a motion that Councillor Wilma, his wife, be co-opted on to the Policy Committee in place of Councillor Betty who has a long-term illness. After heated exchanges 30 councillors leave the chamber. The remaining 10 councillors unanimously pass the motion. The total number of elected councillors is 100. Advise on the regularity of these events. ICSA December 1991.

Chapters 38–39
69. Explain the right of the public and press to attend the meetings of parish or community councils. ICSA December 1991.

70. Wigshire County Council is about to hold its bi-monthly meeting and it is anticipated that, because some controversial items are on the agenda, there is likely to be some disruption from members of the public. In order that he may be fully prepared to deal with any such interruptions, the Chairman has asked you to clarify the position relating to the exclusion of the public from the meeting. Write a memorandum to the Chairman outlining the appropriate provisions of the law. ICSA December 1990.

71. (a) Mr Jones, an independent member of the Brodfordshire Council, seeks your advice as to whether he has the right to any of the following information:
    (i) The minutes of the Council's Public Footpaths Subcommittee. Mr Jones suspects that preferential treatment is being given to a particular builder.
    (ii) Information on the Council's spending on travel arrangements in respect of visits to its twin-town in France.
    (iii) Information on special grants made by the Education Committee. Mr Jones' nephew has just been refused financial assistance for a course at the local technical college.
Advise Mr Jones on the above. (15 marks)
(b) What documents must be kept for public inspection by a local authority and what are the time periods involved? (5 marks) ICSA December 1990.

72. To what extent is the right of members to participate in debate and to vote at council meetings limited? ICSA December 1990.

73. 'A local authority may make standing orders for the regulation of its proceedings and business.' Discuss this statement explaining the nature and content of standing orders, how they may be varied, revoked or suspended and whether a ratepayer can enforce compliance with them. ICSA June 1990.

Chapter 40
74. Draw up a timetable which shows the preparations which must be made by a secretary of an association for a meeting at which a well-known personality will be attending as guest speaker. ICSA June 1991.

75. You are the secretary of the local chamber of commerce. Explain the steps which you would take in preparing and holding its annual general meeting. ICSA December 1990.

Index